The
NO-STRESS
Bible Guide

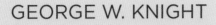

GEORGE W. KNIGHT

The
NO-STRESS
Bible Guide

Learn the Big Picture,
the Key Passages,
and the Divine Plan—
All at Your Own Pace

BARBOUR BOOKS
An Imprint of Barbour Publishing, Inc.

Our mission is to inspire the world with the life-changing message of the Bible.

Member of the
Evangelical Christian
Publishers Association

Printed in China.

CONTENTS

Introduction: Understanding the Bible's "Big Picture"................................. 6

OLD TESTAMENT

1. In the Beginning: Creation and the Fall................................. 9
2. Noah: A Bright Light in a Dark World................................. 19
3. The Patriarchs: Abraham, Isaac, and Jacob................................. 25
4. Moses and the Exodus from Egypt................................. 37
5. Journey through the Wilderness................................. 51
6. Joshua Claims the Promised Land................................. 61
7. Israel under the Judges................................. 71
8. "Give Us a King": The Legacy of Saul................................. 83
9. David Builds a Strong Nation................................. 95
10. Solomon Plants the Seeds of Rebellion................................. 105
11. The Rise and Fall of the Northern Kingdom (Israel)................................. 117
12. The Ups and Downs of the Southern Kingdom (Judah)................................. 135
13. In Exile in Babylon and Persia................................. 153
14. Back Home in Jerusalem................................. 159
15. The Silent Years between the Testaments................................. 169
Job: The Old Testament Book That Doesn't Fit................................. 173

NEW TESTAMENT

16. Jesus the Messiah: Prelude to the Beginning of His Work................................. 175
17. The Early Months of Jesus' Ministry................................. 185
18. Jesus' Ministry in the Region of Galilee................................. 195
19. The Third Year of Jesus' Ministry................................. 213
20. Jesus' Final Days in Jerusalem................................. 233
21. A Gospel for All the World................................. 255
22. Paul's Letters to Young Churches................................. 275
23. Other New Testament Letters................................. 289
24. John's Revelation of the Future................................. 295
A Flexible, No-Stress Plan for Reading the Entire Bible................................. 300
Maps................................. 305
Art Credits................................. 319

INTRODUCTION
Understanding the Bible's "Big Picture"

Perhaps you have heard the story about three blind men and an elephant. None of the men had ever encountered an elephant before. Their friend thought it would be fun to have them feel the animal's body and tell him what it was like.

The first man stroked the elephant's side and concluded, "It's like a wall." The second touched its tusk and said, "It's like a spear." The third put his hand on its leg and declared, "Why, an elephant is like a tree."

All three men were partially correct but profoundly wrong at the same time. They found it impossible to describe an elephant by feeling its individual parts without the ability to see the entire animal. That's exactly the situation with many people when they study the Bible. They dig into its verses or chapters—maybe even its individual books—without having a panoramic view of the Bible as a whole. Isn't it logical that we need to understand the Bible's "big picture" before we can make sense of its individual parts?

That's what this *No-Stress Bible Guide* is all about. It's designed to help you see the "big picture" of God's Word. Throughout the book you will find brief, easy-to-understand summaries of the major biblical sections outlined in the chart on these two pages. Also included within the text of the book are numerous sidebars that encourage you to read selected passages from these segments of the Bible.

MAJOR PERIODS OF THE BIBLE

PERIOD	TIME	SUMMARY
1. Creation and the Fall	Before time began	God creates a perfect world, but rebellion and sin soon mar His creation.
2. Noah and the Flood	Long before Abraham's time	God offers humankind a second chance through a righteous man and his family.
3. Abraham, Isaac, and Jacob	2100–1850 BC	Abraham, Isaac, and Jacob begin to lay the foundation for a nation devoted to God.
4. The Exodus from Egypt	1850–1450 BC	The freed Israelites set out for the Promised Land under the leadership of Moses.
5. Years in the Wilderness	1450–1400 BC	God punishes His people for their disobedience by delaying their entry into Canaan.
6. Claiming the Land of Promise	1400–1350 BC	Joshua leads the Israelites to conquer the land promised centuries before to Abraham.
7. Period of the Judges	1350–1050 BC	Several military heroes take center stage to deliver Israel from its enemies.
8. Saul: Israel's First King	1050–1000 BC	Israel's first king begins well but falls victim to pride and his jealousy of David.
9. David the Warrior King	1000–960 BC	A united Israel expands and prospers under David's capable leadership.
10. Solomon's United Kingdom	960–920 BC	Solomon's lavish lifestyle and harsh policies plant the seeds of rebellion.
11. The Northern Kingdom (Israel)	920–722 BC	Ten northern tribes rebel against Solomon's rule and establish a separate nation.

12. The Southern Kingdom (Judah)	920–587 BC	The two southern tribes continue the dynasty of David and Solomon.
13. Years of Exile	575–540 BC	Citizens of Judah live as captives away from their homeland.
14. Return to Jerusalem after the Exile	540–400 BC	A remnant of Jewish captives return to their homeland and rebuild the temple.
15. The Period between the Testaments	400 BC–5 BC	God uses dramatic world changes to prepare His people for the coming of the Messiah.
16–20. Jesus the Promised Messiah	5 BC–AD 28	Jesus ushers in the kingdom of God with His teachings, miracles, and redemptive death.
21. Growth of the Early Church	AD 28–68	The church spreads from Jews to Gentiles and throughout the Roman world.
22. Letters of the Apostle Paul	AD 49–68	The apostle to the Gentiles encourages new churches and believers with his writings.
23. General New Testament Letters	AD 60–90	Early church leaders instruct a broad audience on the essentials of the Gospel.
24. The Revelation of John	AD 95	The apostle John describes the coming of God's future kingdom and the universal reign of Christ.

For best results, don't rush through this *No-Stress Bible Guide*. Take the time to read thoughtfully and prayerfully from both this book and your Bible. Pay particular attention to the "Think About It" features from the Bible readings. These can offer insights into the scripture that you may have never considered before.

After you come to understand what the Bible is all about, you may have a renewed desire to read more of the Bible. To encourage you in this goal, the book contains "A Flexible, No-Stress Plan for Reading the Entire Bible" (pages 300–304). Use this handy guide to develop a systematic Bible-reading plan that suits your own schedule.

The No-Stress Bible Guide contains several other features that should contribute to your big-picture understanding of the Bible. At the back of the book you will find several maps of important places mentioned in the Bible. These maps are referenced at appropriate places throughout the book. This resource should give you a better understanding of the land of the Bible and how God revealed Himself in a special way to the people who lived in this part of the world.

Scattered throughout the book's chapters on the Old Testament are notations titled "NT Connection." These brief bits of information show how Old Testament themes, concepts, and personalities are cross-referenced and expanded on in the New Testament. This feature should help you understand the close connection between these two major sections of the Bible and how the New Testament fulfills the Old.

My prayer is that this book will give you a better grasp of the Bible as a whole and show how God has worked—and continues to work—through His Word to bless His people.

GEORGE W. KNIGHT
Hartselle, Alabama

God Creates the Sun, the Moon, and the Stars, Jan Brueghel the Younger (1601–1678)

CHAPTER 1
In the Beginning: Creation and the Fall

The grand scheme of the Bible begins with chapters 1–5 of Genesis—the first book of the Bible. Some people have tried to establish an exact time when the events of these chapters took place. But these writings in Genesis were not handed down to us with a precise timetable. We must be satisfied with the knowledge that they happened in the long-ago past with God the Creator, who existed before anything else came to be.

This chapter surveys the Creation, the Fall, the story of Adam and Eve's sons Cain and Abel, and the descendants of Adam and Eve for several generations up to the time of Noah and the great flood.

CREATION (GENESIS 1–2)

We could get caught up in the Bible's creation account and never get to the other periods of Bible history. But since the object of this book is to survey the entire Word of God in rapid fashion, this discussion of creation will be confined to these four topics: (1) the God of creation, (2) the order of creation, (3) the origin of humankind, and (4) the garden of Eden.

THE GOD OF CREATION

"In the beginning God" is how the book of Genesis launches its discussion of the Creation (Genesis 1:1). Here we are brought face-to-face with the wonder-working deity to whom the world and all its inhabitants owe their existence. He is a God of unlimited power who brings the material world into being without having to strain a single muscle. At a simple spoken command from Him—"Let there be. . ."—the entire universe begins to take shape.

The grand message of the Creation account is that God is all-powerful and eternal. He transcends time and the matter that makes up our world. He existed before anything else came into being. Our finite minds have a hard time grasping this truth because our interaction with the world has taught us that everything has a cause. But God is on a different level from our human experience. The psalmist expressed His existence before the beginning of time with these beautiful words: "Before the mountains were brought forth, or ever thou hadst formed the earth and the world, even from everlasting to everlasting, thou art God" (Psalm 90:2).

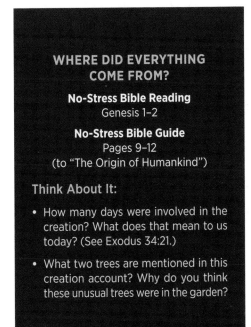

WHERE DID EVERYTHING COME FROM?

No-Stress Bible Reading
Genesis 1–2

No-Stress Bible Guide
Pages 9–12
(to "The Origin of Humankind")

Think About It:

- How many days were involved in the creation? What does that mean to us today? (See Exodus 34:21.)

- What two trees are mentioned in this creation account? Why do you think these unusual trees were in the garden?

Creation of Adam, Michelangelo (1475–1564)

The eternal existence of God sets Him apart from the pagan gods and the creation stories of other ancient civilizations. According to one of these myths, the gods went to war against one another in a cosmic struggle. Several of these gods were killed. The supreme god of this pagan system emerged victorious, and he created the world from the dead bodies of these victims.

By contrast, God created the world not out of strife and struggle but in calm and orderly fashion. With no existing matter to work with, He created the world *ex nihilo*—out of nothing. Not a single bit of matter existed before He began His creative activity. He spun the world into being from an empty vacuum.

from what He has brought into being. He reigns over the universe from a position of ultimate authority. He is not dependent on the world, but the world owes its existence to Him. If the universe should disappear tomorrow, He would continue to exist.

The Genesis Creation account also shows that God has no rivals. The pagan religious systems of Old Testament times featured many gods. Some of these were actually in conflict with one another. But God is the one undisputed Lord and Master of the material world. He is intelligent and wise, undivided in His will and purpose for the physical universe. The purpose of the world He created was to bring glory to Himself and to

NT Connection—CREATION AND FAITH: "By faith we understand that the universe was formed at God's command," the author of Hebrews declared, "so that what is seen was not made out of what was visible" (Hebrews 11:3 NIV).

Another truth about God that emerges from the Bible's Creation account is that He and the material world are not the same. A theory known as pantheism teaches that God does not exist as a separate being from the universe but is actually identical with the physical world. But the biblical account makes it clear that no part of God was used in the world's formation. He is totally separate

serve as a dwelling place for humankind—the crown of His creation.

Just as the Lord brought the material world into being, He is still involved in it. He has placed within the universe certain natural laws that keep it running in orderly fashion. The prophet Jeremiah observed, "When he speaks in the thunder, the heavens roar with rain. He causes the clouds to rise over the earth. He sends the lightning with the rain and releases the wind from his storehouses" (Jeremiah 10:13 NLT).

THE ORDER OF CREATION

The orderly way in which God brought the universe into being is an important element in the Bible's Creation account. A careful study of the text reveals that He performed three different levels of creation in six separate days.

In the very beginning, He created the universe in a primitive state. Then on days one through three, he shaped this formless mass into the orderly universe we know today, also placing plants on the earth on the third day. Finally, on days four through six, he filled the heavens and the earth to complete the creation process. These three levels of creation may be described as originating, shaping, and filling.

Originating. God's first creative act was to bring into being a shapeless mass that was shrouded in darkness (Genesis 1:1–2). Think of this object as a dark blob with land, water, and sky all mixed together. Some people wonder why God chose to begin creating in this fashion. Why not bring everything together in perfect order in one great cosmic act? This is one of those questions that no one can answer. But remember, God had no preexisting matter to work with. Creating a formless mixture of something from nothing is still an achievement that staggers the imagination.

Shaping. In this level of creation, God began working with the formless mass to bring order out of chaos. First He created light and separated the light from the darkness. Then He divided the water in the atmosphere from the water on the earth and placed a firmament or expanse between them. This was the sky that divides the universe into two separate spheres—the heavens and the earth (Genesis 1:3–6). Although the earth was now separated from the heavens, it was covered with water and unfit for habitation. So the Lord gathered the waters into huge basins known as oceans and caused the dry land to appear (Genesis 1:9–10).

The Plains of Heaven, John Martin (1789–1854)

No-Stress Bible Reading
Genesis 3

No-Stress Bible Guide
Pages 12–15
(from "The Origin of Humankind"
to "Cain and Abel")

Think About It:

- What consequences did Adam and Eve suffer for disobeying God by eating from the forbidden tree?

- Why do you think God placed a guard over the tree of life after He banished Adam and Eve from the garden?

Already-dressed Adam and Eve contemplate the forbidden fruit in a stained glass window from Brussels, Belgium.

Filling. Now that God's shaping of the world was complete, He began filling His creation. On day three He filled the earth with trees and other plants. On the fourth day He hung the sun, moon, and stars in space. Day five brought birds and fish to inhabit the sky and the waters. On day six He created land animals of every kind to fill the earth (Genesis 1:11–31).

After every one of these days, the Lord surveyed His world and declared that what He had created was "good." This shows that He took pleasure in His handiwork. The end result was what He had envisioned from the very first. The universe did not come into being through a cosmic accident or by blind chance. God had an orderly plan for creating the physical world, and He executed it with perfection.

Many people wonder about the six days mentioned in the Creation account. Were these literal twenty-four-hour days? Or was the writer of Genesis speaking metaphorically, using "day" in the sense of a long period of time? Bible interpreters have come down on both sides of this issue.

Since God is all-powerful, He could have used either method to bring the world into being. The mention of "evening and morning" in the Genesis account seems to support the literal-day theory. On the other hand, God's way of reckoning time may be different from the measurement we humans use. The apostle Peter declared, "With the Lord a day is like a thousand years, and a thousand years are like a day" (2 Peter 3:8 NIV).

THE ORIGIN OF HUMANKIND

God's final act of creation on day six was His greatest achievement. Now that the physical world was in place and He had filled it with animals and plants, He created Adam, the first human, to serve as its caretaker. The Creation account contains several clues that show Adam's special status.

First, Adam was created not by God's spoken word but by direct action from the Creator Himself. After shaping man from the dust of the earth, the Lord "breathed into his nostrils the breath of life" (Genesis 2:7). Made from common dirt—a preexisting material—Adam clearly was not divine. But he drew his life from God Himself, showing that he had favored status among all the creatures of the earth. (See sidebar, "Go Make Your Own Dirt.")

A second clue about humankind's special standing is the divine conference that God called before creating Adam: "And God said, 'Let *us* make man' " (Genesis 1:26, italics added). This formula does not occur anywhere else in the Creation account. This is probably the Bible's first reference to the triune nature of God. All three persons of the Trinity—Father, Son, and Spirit—participated in the creation of humankind.

The strongest clue about mankind's special status is the declaration that "God created man in his own image" (Genesis 1:27). The most likely meaning of this phrase is that humans alone of all God's creatures have the ability to enjoy a relationship with God. We are able to reason, plan, think, and make moral decisions. These are elements of personhood that set us apart as a unique species.

Along with his favored status, Adam also received a special responsibility. He was to "be fruitful and multiply, and fill the earth and subdue it" (Genesis 1:28 NRSV). The King James Version goes on to add that man was to "have dominion" over the natural world. Taking care of the physical world was Adam's privilege as well as his responsibility. Mankind alone was charged with this job—a duty that involved accountability to the Creator Himself.

Soon after God created Adam, He saw something He didn't like. He issued his first and only "not good" about His creation (Genesis 2:18). He noted that Adam was all alone in the world. His dominion over the physical world was not enough to bring him happiness and fulfillment. He needed a helper and companion. So God created Eve from a rib that He took from Adam's own body (Genesis 2:21–22).

The message of the creation of Eve is that man and woman share the same physical nature. Because of their similarity, they can unite as husband and wife in a union that brings fulfillment to both. To become "one flesh" in the institution of marriage is to be joined together

"GO MAKE YOUR OWN DIRT"

People who believe the Bible's account of Creation enjoy telling the following joke about the scientific explanation for the world's existence.

It seems that a skeptical scientist walked up to God and told Him that He had outlived His usefulness. "We can clone living things now," he declared, "so there's no need for you to keep hanging around."

"Before I go," God replied, "why don't we have a little contest. Let's see who can make a man out of a handful of dirt."

The scientist reached down and scooped up some dirt. But God said, "Hold on. Go make your own dirt."

in a relationship that grows deeper and more meaningful with the passing years (Genesis 2:24–25). Through this one-flesh union, they cooperate with God in His creative actions by bringing children into the world.

THE GARDEN OF EDEN

After God created Adam, He established a beautiful garden known as Eden to serve as his home. On this site He placed many trees and

The Garden of Eden, Thomas Cole (1801–1848)

NT Connection—TREE OF LIFE: This tree probably refers to eternal life. After their sin, Adam and Eve were barred from this tree (Genesis 3:24). But it is now accessible to all people through the atoning death of Jesus Christ (Revelation 22:1–2).

shrubs to provide food for Adam and Eve. Among these plants were the tree of life and the tree of the knowledge of good and evil. God told Adam that he could eat the fruit from all the trees in the garden except one—the tree of the knowledge of good and evil (Genesis 2:8–17).

Adam's job was to take care of this garden (Genesis 2:15). Thus, from the very beginning God's intention was for humans to spend their time in meaningful work. Most people who are truly happy have experienced the thrill of achievement by working hard at their chosen vocations.

The first two chapters of Genesis come to a close with the universe in place and Adam and Eve at home in the garden of Eden with everything they needed for a happy, serene life. But this idyllic existence didn't last long.

THE FALL (GENESIS 3)

Soon after God placed Adam and Eve in the garden, things began to go wrong. Satan appeared to Eve in the form of a serpent, tempting her to disobey God's command not to eat of the fruit from the tree of the knowledge of good and evil.

This tree represented God's sovereignty and His right to place limits on man's behavior. But

Satan planted doubt in Eve's mind that God really meant what He said. Satan also appealed to her pride and sense of fairness. His argument went something like this: "God is not being fair to you. It's true that He has given you lots of good food to eat. But why has He withheld the fruit from this particular tree? Perhaps He realizes that if you eat from it, you will then know as much as He does. He doesn't want that to happen because you would then be equal with Him" (see Genesis 3:1–5).

Eve fell for Satan's trickery and ate some of the fruit from the tree. She also enticed Adam to do the same. They rebelled against God's clear command and, in essence, declared that they had no need for His involvement in their lives. As punishment for their sin and rebellion, God banished them from the garden and the perfect environment they had enjoyed. Another consequence of their sin was the introduction of pain and death into the world (Genesis 3:16–24).

In spite of this stark picture of human sin and its consequences, the account of the Fall also contains an element of hope. God told Satan, the serpent that tricked Eve, "I will put hostility between you and the woman, and between your seed and her seed. He will strike your head, and

CAIN AND ABEL (GENESIS 4)

In the fourth chapter of Genesis, Adam and Eve begin to fulfill God's command to "be fruitful,

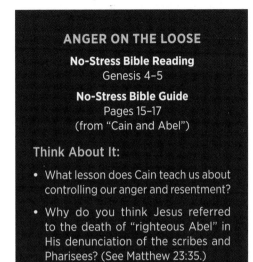

ANGER ON THE LOOSE

No-Stress Bible Reading
Genesis 4–5

No-Stress Bible Guide
Pages 15–17
(from "Cain and Abel")

Think About It:

- What lesson does Cain teach us about controlling our anger and resentment?

- Why do you think Jesus referred to the death of "righteous Abel" in His denunciation of the scribes and Pharisees? (See Matthew 23:35.)

and multiply." Eve gave birth to two sons, Cain and Abel. Both sons must have been reared to honor the Lord, since both brought Him an offering. But God rejected Cain's offering and accepted Abel's.

NT Connection—EVE: The apostle Paul used Eve as an object lesson to show how easily people can be deceived by Satan. He cautioned the believers at Corinth not to let this happen to them (2 Corinthians 11:3).

you will strike his heel" (Genesis 3:15 HCSB).

This verse is known as the *protoevangelium*, or "first good news," because it is the first mention of the Gospel in the Bible. The pronoun "you" refers to Satan, whose attack on Jesus during His earthly ministry would be severe, though not fatal. But Jesus Christ—the "he" of this passage—would eventually overcome death and destroy the forces of Satan (Romans 16:20).

Angry and disappointed, Cain killed his brother, probably because he resented Abel's favored offering. The text hints that he nursed his anger against Abel for some time before taking his life. This first act of murder in the Bible ignited the problem of violence that has plagued the world ever since.

Why did God honor Abel's offering but reject Cain's? The book of Hebrews gives us an answer. It declares that Abel's offering was presented in the spirit of faith (Hebrews 11:4). The implication is that Cain's was not offered in the same spirit. God punished Cain for his crime by sentencing him to wander aimlessly as a fugitive against him. This is a preview of the deplorable conditions in society that led to the flood in Noah's time.

Abel's death is referred to several times in the New Testament as an example of innocence. The

NT Connection—SETH: Adam and Eve's son Seth is listed as an ancestor of Jesus in Luke's genealogy (Luke 3:38).

from his homeland. When Cain protested that this punishment was greater than he could bear, God showed him mercy. He placed a mark on Cain to provide protection against anyone who might try to avenge Abel's death.

Cain eventually settled in a land called Nod, where he married. His descendants developed into a race known for their ability to build cities, shape metal, and play musical instruments. Unfortunately, some of Cain's descendants were also known for their polygamous marriages and their tendency toward violence.

The most violent of Cain's descendants was Lamech, who boasted to his wives that he had killed two men because of their acts of violence

writer of Hebrews compared him to Christ. He called Jesus "the mediator of a new covenant" whose blood, shed for our sins, was "a better word than the blood of Abel" (Hebrews 12:24 NIV).

DESCENDANTS OF SETH AND CAIN (GENESIS 5)

After Cain killed Abel, Adam and Eve had another son whom they named Seth. Genesis 4:17–24 and chapter 5 list the descendants of these two sons of Adam and Eve—Seth and Cain. A careful study of this chapter reveals that the line of Seth was faithful to the Lord, while Cain's offspring were inclined toward violence and rebellion. The chart

COMPARISON OF SETH'S AND CAIN'S DESCENDANTS

SETH: Born after his brother Abel was murdered	CAIN: murdered his brother Abel
Enosh: After his birth, "men began to call on the name of the Lord" (Genesis 4:26 NKJV).	Enoch
Kenan	Irad
Mahalalel	Mehujael
Jared	Methushael
Enoch: "Enoch walked with God" (Genesis 5:24).	Lamech: "I have killed a man for wounding me, a young man for striking me" (Genesis 4:23 NRSV).
Methuselah: lived 969 years	Jabal, Jubal, Tubal-Cain
Lamech	
Noah: the righteous man through whom the world was preserved	

Cain and Abel, Titian (c. 1490–1576)

on page 16 shows the contrast between these two lines of descent.

Note that the birth of Seth's son Enosh ushered in a time of renewed worship and commitment to the Lord. Four generations later, the godly man Enoch was born into Seth's family line. The statement that Enoch "walked with God" implies that he had close fellowship with the Lord and followed His will for his life.

After living for 365 years, Enoch "was no more, because God took him away" (Genesis 5:24 NIV). The book of Hebrews in the New Testament adds this clarifying statement about

beyond the time of his ancestor Cain. This quotation by Lamech is part of an ancient poem known as "Lamech's Song of the Sword." Thus, Cain's act of violence against his brother continued to echo throughout his family line.

Another interesting thing highlighted in this chart is the long life span attributed to Seth's descendant Methuselah—969 years (Genesis 5:27). Many genealogies in Genesis list people who, like Methuselah, lived for several hundred years. How could anyone live that long? Are these ages to be taken literally or figuratively? Several possible explanations have been offered for these long life spans.

One theory is that the names of these long-lived people are not personal names but clan or tribe names. Thus, the entire clan of Methuselah, including people of several generations, lived for 969 years. Another suggestion is that the years cited in these passages refer to cycles of the moon rather than years. Under this theory Methuselah's age of 969 years should be divided by thirteen, or the number of lunar months in a year, to arrive at his real age—seventy-four.

These theories are interesting, but a case can be made for a literal interpretation of these long life spans. Perhaps God allowed people to live longer during these early years of history to speed up the population of the earth. After all, one of God's first commands to Adam and

NT Connection—METHUSALEH and ENOCH: These two ancestors of Noah are included in the family line of Jesus in Luke's genealogy (Luke 3:37; "Mathusala" in the KJV).

what happened to Enoch. He "was taken from this life, so that he did not experience death" (Hebrews 11:5 NIV). This must have been similar to what happened in later years to the prophet Elijah, who was taken into heaven by a whirlwind (2 Kings 2:11).

In contrast to Enoch's godly life in the line of Seth, notice from the chart the violence that characterized Lamech just five generations

Eve was to "be fruitful and multiply, and fill the earth" (Genesis 1:28 NRSV).

The most significant truth revealed by this comparative genealogy is that Seth's line produced a righteous man named Noah (Genesis 5:28–29). The Lord used Noah to save the human race when He unleashed a catastrophic flood on the earth. The next major period of biblical history begins with this righteous man.

Noah's Ark, Edward Hicks (1780–1849)

CHAPTER 2
Noah: A Bright Light in a Dark World

This period of Bible history is recorded in chapters 6–11 of Genesis. Like the Creation narrative in Genesis, the exact time when Noah lived is unknown. All we know for sure is that the flood that he and his family survived occurred sometime before 2100 BC, when Abraham appeared on the scene. Noah and his huge boat, or ark, dominate this period of Bible history. But three other important events of this era are the founding of the nations of the ancient world, the attempt to build the Tower of Babel, and the appearance of Abraham.

NOAH AND THE FLOOD (GENESIS 6–9)

Hebrews 11 is known as the "faith chapter" of the Bible. It contains a list of several heroes of the Old Testament who were known for their great faith. Number three on this list is Noah, who, "being divinely warned of things not yet seen, [and] moved with godly fear, prepared an ark for the saving of his household, by which he condemned the world and became heir of the righteousness which is according to faith" (Hebrews 11:7 NKJV).

There are two good reasons Noah receives such a favorable review. First, he and his family were the only righteous people left in a world filled with violence and corruption. God told Noah that He planned to destroy all living things with a catastrophic flood because of this wickedness. But Noah and his family would be saved so they could repopulate the earth after the flood came to an end.

The Middle East has a notoriously dry climate. Imagine the ridicule that Noah and his sons must have endured as they constructed a boat on dry land in a region where water was in such short supply.

The Lord did not leave a single detail about the ark to chance. He gave Noah its exact dimensions—"450 feet long, 75 feet wide, and 45 feet high" (Genesis 6:15 NLT). Longer than a football field and shaped like a modern barge, the three-story vessel was similar to a huge warehouse. It had to be large enough to hold Noah's family, a pair of animals of every species, and enough food for the ark's occupants for several months.

This mind-numbing blueprint from the Lord would have been enough to cause most contractors to refuse the job. But "Noah did everything exactly as God had commanded him"

> **NT Connection—NOAH:** He is listed as an ancestor of Jesus in Luke's genealogy (Luke 3:36; "Noe" in the KJV).

Second, Noah had great faith in the Lord. He believed that God would do what He promised. In faith, he set about building a massive boat, even though there was not a large body of water anywhere nearby where it could be launched.

(Genesis 6:22 NLT). The Bible doesn't say how long it took Noah and his sons to build the ark. But with the primitive tools available during that era, the project must have continued for many years.

Finally, the Lord directed Noah and his family

to enter the ark. The time for His judgment of the world and its wickedness had arrived. Seven days after they were settled in, torrential rains began to fall. These continued for forty days and forty nights.

receded. When Noah and his family emerged from the ark, he built an altar as a worship site, using some of the clean animals from the ark as a burnt offering to the Lord. Noah made a commitment to continue to serve the Lord as he expressed his thanks for divine deliverance from the perils of the Flood.

God had blessed Noah and his family and kept them alive. But now He charged them with a responsibility: "Be fruitful, and multiply, and replenish the earth" (Genesis 9:1). This is the same command He had given Adam and Eve years before in the garden of Eden.

The Lord also reminded Noah that it was his responsibility to rule over the animal kingdom and take care of the physical world. This is also a repetition of His instructions to Adam. God had not given up on the world, in spite of its wickedness.

Because of the faithfulness of Noah and his family, God made a covenant that prefigured the one He would make with Noah's distant descendant Abraham. This covenant included the Lord's promise that He would never again destroy all living things with a flood. As an everlasting sign of this promise, He placed a rainbow among the clouds. "Whenever the rainbow appears in the clouds," He told Noah, "I will see it and remember the everlasting covenant between

NT Connection—THE FLOOD: The apostle Peter considered Noah's deliverance from the Flood a symbol of God's gift of salvation that cleanses people of their sin (1 Peter 3:20–21).

Adding to this deluge were the "springs of the great deep" (Genesis 7:11 NIV) that gushed from the earth while rain fell from the sky. This burst of underground water contributed to the rapid rise of the floodwaters that eventually covered the earth. All living things were wiped out, but "Noah only remained alive, and they that were with him in the ark" (Genesis 7:23).

After several months the water finally

God and all living creatures of every kind on the earth" (Genesis 9:16 NIV).

Noah and his family represented a new beginning for the human race. This is an early example of God's patience and grace—a theme that runs throughout the Bible. God is patient with our shortcomings, and He always gives us better than we deserve.

Landscape with Noah's Thank Offering, Joseph Anton Koch (1768–1839)

NATIONS OF THE ANCIENT WORLD (GENESIS 10)

Along with Noah, his three sons emerged safely from the floodwaters. Genesis 10 traces the descendants of these sons: Japheth, Ham, and Shem. These genealogies also name the ancient races and nations founded by the descendants of each of these sons. In the widespread settlement of these peoples, we can see the fulfillment of God's command to Noah to repopulate the earth.

Fourteen of Japheth's descendants are listed. The description of these Japhethites as "coastland peoples" (Genesis 10:5 NRSV) suggests that they settled in coastal territories, probably along the shores of the Mediterranean Sea.

Thirty of Ham's offspring are listed in his genealogy. This list of descendants is longer than Japheth's and Shem's. In addition, the region settled by Ham's descendants seems to be larger and more complex than the other two genealogical lines. In general, Ham's offspring settled in the region now occupied by Africa and Egypt. But branches of the Hamites apparently settled as far north as ancient Babylon and Assyria (Genesis 10:10–12 NIV). The Canaanites,

occupants of the land promised to Abraham, were also descended from Ham.

GOD'S STOP ORDER

No-Stress Bible Reading
Genesis 11

No-Stress Bible Guide
Pages 21–23

Think About It:

- Which one of the three sons of Noah is considered the most significant, and why?

- What role did human pride play in the building of the tower of Babel?

- Why do you think God intervened to stop this building project?

The most important of Noah's three sons, from the perspective of biblical history, is Shem. This is because the patriarch Abraham was one of Shem's descendants. The Shemite genealogy lists twenty-six descendants who settled in the desert regions of Mesa and Sephar—a territory now occupied by the modern nations of Jordan, Saudi Arabia, Iran, Iraq, and Syria. Because Abraham is such a key figure in Israel's history, parts of Shem's genealogy are repeated in the next chapter of Genesis (11:10–26).

The Tower of Babel, Pieter Brueghel the Elder (c. 1525–1569)

THE TOWER OF BABEL (GENESIS 11:1–9)

Immediately following the list of the nations after the Flood, an interesting passage about an ancient tower appears in the book of Genesis. A group of people made plans to build a tall tower in a place called Shinar. This was probably the ancient city-state of Babylon. What these people said about this structure shows that its construction was a big ego trip for them. "Let *us* build *ourselves*. . .a tower," they boasted, "so that we may make a name for *ourselves*" (Genesis 11:4 NIV, italics added). It never occurred to them that they should seek the Lord's will in this matter or ask Him to bless their work.

Another problem was that they had lost sight of God's command to populate the entire earth. If they and their children settled in Shinar long enough to build this tower, they would not be "scattered over the face of the whole earth" (Genesis 11:4 NIV), as the Lord had instructed them to do.

But God intervened and stopped the project in its tracks. Then He scattered these tower builders over the entire earth. He also caused races of people in different parts of the world to speak different languages. Perhaps this was a check on the ability of different nations to collaborate on large-scale ventures that defied God and contributed to the spread of evil.

These tower builders lived just a few generations after the time of Noah and the Flood. Their attitude of godless pride shows that the Flood had not solved the problem of sin in the world. Humankind's natural inclination is toward rebellion against God and His authority. This reality is evident through every period of biblical history.

In spite of widespread sin and disobedience, God was working behind the scenes to bring about His purpose for humankind. Through the family line of Shem, a son of Noah, the Lord was preparing to build a nation that would be His special possession.

FROM SHEM TO ABRAHAM (GENESIS 11:10–32)

This section of Genesis repeats part of Shem's genealogy that has already appeared in Genesis 10:21–31. But this second genealogy picks up with Noah's grandson Arphaxad and traces his descendants through several generations to a man named Terah. Although Terah was not a believer in the one true God, he had a son who followed the Lord's will and obeyed His commands. His name was Abram, later called Abraham. With this man of great faith, the next period of Bible history begins.

Abraham's Journey from Ur to Canaan,
József Molnár (1821–1899)

CHAPTER 3
The Patriarchs: Abraham, Isaac, and Jacob

This period of Bible history covers about 250 years, from approximately 2100 BC to about 1850 BC. These were the formative years for the nation of Israel, God's chosen people. The pioneers who laid the foundation for this new nation are known as the patriarchs—a word that means "ruling fathers." The term refers to Abraham, his son Isaac, Isaac's son Jacob, and the sons of Jacob who evolved into the twelve tribes that made up the nation.

Narratives about these patriarchs appear in chapters 12–50 of the book of Genesis. These chapters focus first on Abraham, Isaac, and Jacob in Canaan, the territory that God promised to Abraham and his descendants. Then the focus shifts to Joseph in Egypt. This great-grandson of Abraham was one of the youngest of Jacob's twelve sons. Through a combination of circumstances explained only by God's providence, Joseph became an important Egyptian official who saved Abraham's descendants from starvation.

ABRAHAM: THE JOURNEY BEGINS (GENESIS 12–23)

Abraham comes on the scene at the age of seventy-five (Genesis 12:4). He died as "an old man, and full of years" at the age of 175 (Genesis 25:7–8). He filled the 100 years in between with commitment to the Lord and a genuine concern for the well-being of others.

A MAN ON THE MOVE

From the moment Abraham appears on the pages of biblical history, he is a man on the move. His father, Terah, set out with Abraham and the rest of his family from Ur of the Chaldeans—probably in ancient Babylonia—for a place called Canaan. But for some reason, Terah decided to settle in Haran before moving on to Canaan.

Ur, the place where Abraham grew up, was populated by pagan peoples who worshipped the moon. But in spite of these pagan surroundings, Abraham grasped the truth that the Lord alone was worthy of worship. This one true God of the universe chose Abraham to build a nation of people who would be devoted to Him. Their mission as God's special people would be to bear witness of the one true God to the rest of the world. So while Abraham was living in Haran, he received a life-changing message from the Lord.

"Get out of your country, from your family and from your father's house, to a land that I will show you," God directed Abraham. "I will make you a great nation; I will bless you and make

> **NT Connection—ABRAHAM:** In Matthew's genealogy of Jesus, Christ is referred to as "the son of Abraham" (Matthew 1:1).

Haran was in Mesopotamia, the land between the Tigris and Euphrates Rivers, several hundred miles north of Canaan. Here in Haran Abraham and his family lived until his father died (Genesis 11:31–32).

your name great; and you shall be a blessing. I will bless those who bless you, and I will curse him who curses you; and in you all the families of the earth shall be blessed" (Genesis 12:1–3 NKJV).

Abraham obeyed the Lord and set off with his

family and all his earthly possessions to a place he knew nothing about. For the second time in his life, he was on the move, this time without a road map or a specific destination. All God told him was that He would "show" him this land. This strange statement must have come across to Abraham as something like this: "I'll let you know where you're going as soon as you get there."

Leaving the familiar behind and moving to a new location was a pattern that Abraham followed for the rest of his life. Most people move for economic or social reasons—a higher-paying job, better schools, or closer proximity to family and friends. But Abraham moved in obedience to the call of God.

A careful study of the biblical text reveals several different places where Abraham lived during his years in Canaan: Shechem (Genesis 12:6), Bethel (12:8), the Negev or desert territory around the Dead Sea (12:9), Gerar (20:2), Beersheba (21:27–31), and Hebron (23:19–20).

Soon after he arrived in Canaan, Abraham must have questioned the wisdom of his move from Haran. He discovered that the land was inhabited by the Canaanites, a warlike race made up of several different tribes that worshipped pagan gods (Genesis 12:6). Another problem was the dry climate of the land. The rainfalls of Canaan were few and far between. Since Abraham was a shepherd with large herds of livestock to feed, he had to move his tents and his family from place to place to find pastureland for his flocks.

Sometime after Abraham arrived in Canaan, its sparse rainfall led to famine conditions throughout the land. Crops failed and the grasslands dried up. Abraham was forced to move again, this time to the neighboring land of Egypt and its fertile grazing lands along the Nile River (Genesis 12:10). After the famine ended, he returned to Canaan.

Was Abraham's temporary residence in Egypt an unfortunate circumstance? Or was it a divine preview of another famine that would produce a critical turning point in Israel's history? Many years after Abraham's time, his grandson Jacob also took his family into Egypt to escape a famine. From the hindsight of history, this was one more step in God's plan to produce a nation that belonged to Him. But that famine is part of the Joseph narratives in the final chapters of Genesis. Events of his life will be discussed at the end of this chapter.

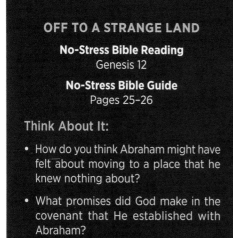

OFF TO A STRANGE LAND

No-Stress Bible Reading
Genesis 12

No-Stress Bible Guide
Pages 25–26

Think About It:

- How do you think Abraham might have felt about moving to a place that he knew nothing about?

- What promises did God make in the covenant that He established with Abraham?

A PROMISE RENEWED

No-Stress Bible Reading
Genesis 15; 17:1–9

No-Stress Bible Guide
Pages 28–29
("A Man Blessed by the Lord")

- Why do you think God needed to reassure Abraham several times that He would keep His promise?

A MAN OF GENEROSITY AND FAIRNESS

Another truth about Abraham that emerges from the biblical record is that he was generous and fair in his treatment of others. The best example of this is his relationship with his nephew Lot. For a time he and Lot shared the same pastureland for their separate flocks. But their herds grew so large they could no longer graze in the same location. Disputes broke out between the shepherds who tended the flocks.

Abraham gave Lot first choice over the disputed territory. Lot decided on the most fertile region in the plain along the Dead Sea near the cities of Sodom and Gomorrah (Genesis 13:3–13). This compromise shows that Abraham was willing to take second best in order to keep peace in the family.

Abraham's generous spirit also came through when he learned about God's plan for Sodom. This city, along with Gomorrah, had become so wicked and corrupt that the Lord planned to destroy it and all its inhabitants. But Abraham stepped forward to play the role of intercessor for Sodom. He appealed to God's sense of fairness: "Suppose there are fifty righteous within the city," he asked God; "will you then sweep away the place and not forgive it for the fifty righteous who are in it?" (Genesis 18:24 NRSV).

God listened to Abraham's reasoning and agreed not to destroy Sodom if it contained fifty righteous people. Abraham continued his pleading with God, persuading Him to postpone Sodom's destruction for the sake of forty-five, then forty, then thirty, then twenty, and finally ten righteous people.

In spite of Abraham's pleading, God eventually destroyed Sodom because He could not find even ten righteous people in the city. But He did warn Abraham's nephew Lot and his family to get out of Sodom before it was destroyed with burning sulfur that fell from the sky. Lot owed his life to his generous and godly uncle because "God had listened to Abraham's request and kept Lot safe, removing him from the disaster that engulfed the cities on the plain" (Genesis 19:29 NLT).

Abraham was also cooperative, fair, and friendly with the original inhabitants of this land to which God had brought him. The Lord had promised this territory to his descendants, but Abraham did not move in and begin making

NT Connection—SODOM: The writer of Jude referred to the evil sister cities of Sodom and Gomorrah as "an example of those who suffer the punishment of eternal fire" (Jude 7 NIV).

outrageous demands. He was content to graze his livestock on the free ranges that were open to everyone. When a dispute arose over rights to a well he had dug, he settled the matter in a friendly manner with the local clan chief (Genesis 21:22–33).

This burial plot purchased by Abraham is known as the cave of Machpelah. After Abraham died, he was buried here (Genesis 25:7–10). In later years four other members of his family also were laid to rest in this cave—Abraham's son Isaac and Isaac's wife, Rebekah, and Abraham's

NT Connection—PROLIFIC ABRAHAM: The writer of Hebrews commended Abraham for continuing to believe God's promise even when he was childless: "From one person, and this one as good as dead, descendants were born, 'as many as the stars of heaven' " (Hebrews 11:12 NRSV).

But the time came when Abraham needed some property of his own. After his wife Sarah died, he approached a local citizen named Ephron about buying a cave from him as a burial site. Negotiating with Ephron in accordance with local tribal customs, he bought the cave at its fair market value. This is the only land in Canaan that he ever owned.

grandson Jacob and Jacob's wife Leah (Genesis 49:29–33).

Today a modern city with the Arabic name el-Khalil has grown up around the cave of Machpelah. The spot above the cave is enshrined by a Muslim mosque. Entrance to the actual burial cave is forbidden, but visitors may enter the mosque compound. Once inside, visitors are shown not only the reputed tombs of these three couples—Abraham and Sarah, Isaac and Rebekah, and Jacob and Leah—but the tomb of Jacob's son Joseph as well.

The Bible says that Joseph was buried at Shechem after he died in Egypt (Joshua 24:32). But according to a Muslim tradition, Joseph's bones were later removed from his original burial site and placed in the cave of Machpelah.

A SOLEMN PLEA FOR A WICKED CITY

No-Stress Bible Reading
Genesis 18:20–33; 19:1–29

No-Stress Bible Guide
Pages 27–28
("A Man of Generosity and Fairness")

Think About It:

- Why do you think Abraham described himself as nothing but "dust and ashes" (Genesis 18:27) when he stood before God to plead for the people of Sodom?

- What happened to Lot's wife as she was leaving the city?

- How did God intervene to save Lot and his family from Sodom's destruction?

A MAN BLESSED BY THE LORD

Before Abraham left Haran and moved to Canaan, God made it clear that his obedience would result in many divine blessings for him and his family. The Lord promised to make Abraham's name great and to make him into a great nation. This is the first mention of the covenant, or agreement, that God made with Abraham. This covenant consisted of God's promise that He would bless the nation that descended from Abraham if they would honor Him and obey His commands.

During the 100 years that Abraham lived

in Canaan, he must have wondered about the validity of God's promise. After all, he remained a foreigner in a land that belonged to the Canaanites during all this time. God assured Abraham on four different occasions that this covenant agreement was still in effect (Genesis 13:14–18; 15:1–21; 17:1–11; 22:15–19).

One of these assurances clarified the original covenant with these words: "Through your *offspring* all nations on earth will be blessed" (Genesis 22:18 NIV, italics added). The Lord wanted Abraham to understand clearly that this promise would not be fulfilled until several generations had passed.

But there was a big problem with the completion of this promise, even on a long-term basis. Abraham and his wife, Sarah, had no children, and there was no prospect of any because of their advanced age. In desperation, the couple took matters into their own hands. Abraham fathered a son through Sarah's servant Hagar. But God declared that this child, Ishmael, would not inherit His covenant promise. This would come to pass through a child fathered by Abraham and conceived by Sarah (Genesis 17:20–21).

The Lord did eventually bless the couple with a son. They called him Isaac, a name meaning "laughter." Abraham was 100 years old when this son was born (Genesis 21:1–5). Finally, everything was in place for the emergence of God's chosen people through the descendants of His servant Abraham.

A MAN OF FAITH

All the characteristics of Abraham highlighted so far would be enough to make him one of the Bible's greatest personalities. But what really sets him apart is the great faith he showed in God at a time when idolatry and paganism flourished. The popular religious systems of his time taught that numerous gods ruled over the

affairs of humankind and the world. Abraham had the spiritual vision to discern that there was only one supreme God of the universe. As the all-powerful, sovereign God, He alone was worthy of worship and the loyalty of humankind.

Abraham's unwavering faith in this great God comes through again and again in the Genesis narratives. The first thing he did when he arrived in Canaan was to build an altar where he "called on the name of the LORD" (Genesis 12:8 NIV). He repeated this pattern of altar building, worship, and prayer several times when he moved his flocks to other grazing spots throughout Canaan.

Would Abraham's faith be strong enough to obey God when doing so required him to harm his precious son Isaac—the one through whom God's covenant promise would be fulfilled? To find out, the Lord issued a puzzling command to Abraham. He told him to take Isaac to a distant mountain and sacrifice him there as a burnt offering. Obeying without question, Abraham traveled to the distant spot, built an altar, put wood on it, placed Isaac on the wood, and raised a knife for the kill before God stopped him.

"Do not lay a hand on the boy or do anything to him," the Lord told him. "For now I know that you fear God, since you have not withheld your only son from Me" (Genesis 22:12 HCSB). Abraham's faith did not falter. He had passed the ultimate test.

This unwavering faith of Abraham is cited often throughout the Bible as a model for other believers. Because of Abraham's close relationship to the Lord and his belief that He would deliver on His promises, he is referred to several times as God's friend (2 Chronicles 20:7; Isaiah 41:8; James 2:23).

Perhaps the greatest tribute paid to Abraham came from the apostle Paul, who considered him the father of all people—Jews and Gentiles alike—who place their faith in God. "Those who have faith are children of Abraham," Paul declared. "Scripture foresaw that God would justify the Gentiles by faith, and announced the gospel in advance to Abraham: 'All nations will be blessed through you.' So those who rely on faith are blessed along with Abraham, the man of faith" (Galatians 3:7–9 NIV).

ISAAC: THE PROMISED SON (GENESIS 24–26)

In contrast to the twelve chapters of Genesis devoted to Abraham, his son Isaac receives little more than a passing glance in only three chapters. Isaac comes across as a man who led a quiet life of little significance after the death of his famous father, Abraham (Genesis 25:5, 9).

But Isaac does fill an important role in God's continuing work of building a nation devoted to Him. Like his father, Isaac worshipped and served the Lord. He also received God's assurance that the divine covenant with Abraham would continue through his family line (Genesis 26:24). And most important of all, Isaac and his wife, Rebekah, had a son named Jacob, whose numerous sons would evolve into the twelve tribes of the nation of Israel. The birth of Jacob—a son who emerged from the womb with a twin brother named Esau—is a milestone in the formative years of Israel's history.

JACOB: FATHER OF MANY TRIBES (GENESIS 27–35)

When the twin boys Jacob and Esau were born, Jacob came out of the womb second, but he was "grasping Esau's heel" (Genesis 25:26 NLT). Jacob's name means "heel grabber" or "supplanter"—one who tries to gain an advantage over others. In his early years, Jacob showed that he intended to live up to his name. One day he offered Esau a bowl of stew in exchange for his birthright. Since Esau was extremely hungry, he accepted the deal (Genesis 25:27–34). By taking advantage of his brother's weakness, Jacob secured Esau's inheritance rights as the firstborn son.

Later, Jacob plotted with his mother, Rebekah, to trick his elderly and blind father, Isaac, into blessing him rather than Esau (Genesis 27:1–38). He dressed in his brother's clothes and brought Isaac a tasty meal so his father would think he was Esau. When Esau discovered what had happened, he vowed to kill Jacob for this act of deception.

Jacob fled from Canaan to live with his mother's brother in Haran (Genesis 27:42–44). This was the ancestral home of Jacob's family— the territory from which his grandfather Abraham had migrated into Canaan many years before.

In Haran, Jacob's cheating of his brother in Canaan came back to haunt him. He met a beautiful woman named Rachel, the daughter of his uncle Laban. To pay the dowry or bride-price that Laban demanded for Rachel's hand, Jacob worked for his uncle for seven years. After the wedding Jacob discovered that Laban had tricked him into marrying his other daughter, Leah, instead. He had to work for seven more years to earn the right to marry Rachel (Genesis 29:16–28).

Finally, after spending twenty years in Haran, Jacob returned to his home in Canaan. The size of his traveling entourage—two wives, numerous sons and daughters, several servants, and large herds of livestock—showed that God had blessed him abundantly while he was away. He and Esau were reconciled after Jacob showered his brother with gifts to make amends for his past misdeeds (Genesis 33:1–11).

Jacob is a case study in a person's ability to change when confronted by the Lord. But

A NEW NAME FOR JACOB

No-Stress Bible Reading
Genesis 25:21–34; 27:1–41; 35:1–12

No-Stress Bible Guide
Pages 31–33
("Jacob: Father of Many Tribes")

Think About It:

- How did Jacob secure the birthright of his brother Esau and the blessing of his father Isaac?

- How did Jacob change over the course of his life?

- Why do you think God changed Jacob's name to Israel?

his change was a slow process. It began when he was on his way out of Canaan to escape his brother's wrath. Camping out under the open sky one night, he had a dream in which he saw angels going up and down a stairway that extended into heaven.

At the top of the stairway stood the Lord, who declared that Jacob and his descendants would inherit the promise that God had made to Abraham many years before: "I will give you and your offspring the land that you are now sleeping on," the Lord promised Jacob. "All the peoples on earth will be blessed through you and your offspring" (Genesis 28:13–14 HCSB).

This dream filled Jacob with awe and fear.

Perhaps this was the first time he had realized that God's covenant promise had been passed on to him. He built an altar to mark this sacred site that he called el-Bethel, a name meaning "house of God." But Jacob's words revealed that his relationship to the Lord was a work in progress.

"If God will. . .watch over me on this journey," he vowed, "and will give me food to eat and clothes to wear so that I return safely to my father's household, then the LORD will be my God" (Genesis 28:20–22 NIV). The Lord had gotten Jacob's attention with this dream. But true to his name, the "supplanter" was trying to make a deal with the supreme ruler of the universe. He still had a way to go in his understanding of God.

But God didn't give up on Jacob. He tried again with a more dramatic encounter soon after Jacob arrived back in Canaan. This time He took on Jacob in a wrestling match. God, of course, could have overcome Jacob at any time. But He allowed the contest to go on for some time, finally dislocating Jacob's hip. Even handicapped in this way, Jacob refused to let the Lord go until

numerous sons who would become the stems from which the tribes of Israel sprang. With twelve sons born to four different wives, he must have taken the idea from this passage of the Psalms literally: "Like arrows in the hand of a warrior, so are the children of one's youth. Happy is the man who has his quiver full of them" (Psalm 127:4–5 NKJV).

NT Connection—JUDAH: Jesus is called the Lion of the tribe of Judah (Revelation 5:5). This title probably refers to Jacob's blessing of his son Judah. He declared that Judah was destined to become a great ruler (Genesis 49:8–12). As a descendant of Judah (Matthew 1:2–3; "Judas" in the KJV), Jesus rules among His people as supreme Savior and Lord.

He had blessed him. During the struggle the Lord did bless him and gave him a new name, *Israel*, meaning "he strives with God" or "God strives" (Genesis 32:24–30).

This account of Jacob's encounter with the Lord is best interpreted as a spiritual struggle. Jacob left Canaan as a proud young man with no purpose and a flawed value system. He was willing to cheat others to get what he wanted. But he returned home with a limp, humbled by his experiences in Haran and now ready to take his place in God's plan to establish the nation of Israel. He was finally a true prince of the Lord who would pursue God's purpose for his life.

One purpose that Jacob served was to father

The twelve sons of Jacob and their respective mothers were (1) Reuben, Simeon, Levi, Judah, Issachar, and Zebulun—sons born to Leah; (2) Joseph and Benjamin—sons born to Rachel; (3) Dan and Naphtali—sons born to Rachel's female servant; and (4) Gad and Asher—sons born to Leah's female servant.

Notice from this list that only two sons, Joseph and Benjamin, were born to Rachel, Jacob's first love and the wife for whom he worked for fourteen years. Joseph and Benjamin were probably Jacob's youngest sons. This detail is an important element in the Joseph narratives that begin with chapter 37 of Genesis.

JOSEPH: THE EGYPTIAN CONNECTION (GENESIS 37–50)

In Old Testament times, a firstborn son was considered a special blessing from the Lord. At his father's death, he inherited a double portion of his property. He also took over his father's role as head of the clan. So Reuben, Jacob's oldest son, would have been the logical one to take center stage in these final chapters of the book of Genesis.

Instead, the spotlight focuses on Joseph, one of Jacob's youngest sons. He was destined to leave his homeland and become the Egyptian

connection that saved the rest of Jacob's family when they fell upon hard times. How all this came about is one of the most amazing stories of God's providence in the entire Bible.

Joseph's story does not begin well. His father, Jacob, spoiled him by treating him as his favorite son, even giving him a beautiful coat or robe (Genesis 37:3). This probably signified his special status among Jacob's twelve sons. Joseph himself made this problem worse by telling his brothers about two dreams he had

GRUMBLING IN THE FAMILY

No-Stress Bible Reading
Genesis 37; 41:1–44

No-Stress Bible Guide
Pages 33–35
("Joseph: The Egyptian Connection")

Think About It:

- What caused the older brothers to grow jealous and resentful toward their young brother Joseph?

- How was God's providence at work in Joseph's life after he arrived in Egypt?

JOY IN EGYPT

No-Stress Bible Reading
Genesis 45

Think About It:

- What lessons in love and forgiveness can we learn from Joseph's reunion with his brothers?

---

that predicted he would rule over them one day (Genesis 37:8–9). These things kindled such strong jealousy among Joseph's brothers that "they hated him and could not speak a kind word to him" (Genesis 37:4 NIV).

This intense hatred finally reached the boiling point when Jacob sent Joseph to check on his brothers, who were tending sheep in a distant location. This was their chance to even the score with their "spoiled brat" brother. They stripped Joseph of his beautiful coat and sold him to a caravan of traders who were passing by on their way to Egypt. They dipped his coat in blood and took it to Jacob to convince him that his favorite son had been killed by a wild animal

(Genesis 37:31–33).

After Joseph arrived in Egypt, he became a slave in the household of an official in the royal court named Potiphar. Joseph refused the sexual advances of Potiphar's wife, only to be thrown into prison on the false charge that he had tried to seduce her. While in prison, Joseph interpreted the dreams of two officials of the Egyptian king, or pharaoh. This brought the young Israelite to the attention of Pharaoh himself when that king had two related dreams that none of his court magicians could interpret (Genesis 41:8–32).

Joseph's response to Pharaoh's request to interpret his dreams shows why he was destined to be blessed by the Lord in this strange country so far from his homeland. "It is beyond my power to do this," he replied. "But God can tell you what it means and set you at ease" (Genesis 41:16 NLT). In spite of all the bad things that had happened to Joseph, he continued to worship and honor the Lord.

Joseph had both good news and bad news for Pharaoh. First the good news: His dreams meant that Egypt would experience seven years of superabundant grain harvests. The bad news was that this period of abundance would be followed by seven years of severe famine. The clear message was that Egypt should get ready for the lean times by storing grain produced during the good years.

Pharaoh rewarded Joseph for his insights and good advice by naming him to a high position in his administration. As a member of Pharaoh's cabinet, Joseph was responsible for storing grain during the plentiful years and distributing it when the famine began. Some translations of the Bible suggest that Joseph was Pharaoh's second-in-command (see, for example, Genesis 41:45 NLT), making him almost equal to the king in power and authority.

Just as Joseph predicted, a series of famines struck Egypt and the surrounding nations after seven years of plenty. Chapters 42–45 of Genesis tell how Joseph and his brothers came face-to-face again when the brothers traveled to Egypt to buy grain for their father's clan back in Canaan. It had been twenty years since they had sold Joseph into slavery, so they did not recognize their brother at first.

Joseph put his brothers through several tests to determine the current state of their character. During these tests he showed a special concern for Benjamin—his only full brother who was also a son of his father's beloved wife, Rachel. The willingness of Joseph's brothers to stand up for one another and to spare their father from further heartbreak convinced him that they had changed for the better. Joseph forgave them for the wrong they had committed against him, and they were gloriously reconciled as brothers of the same clan and sons of their common father, Jacob.

The patriarchal period of Bible history comes to a close with Joseph making plans for the rest of his family to join him in Egypt. He arranged for his father, Jacob, his eleven brothers, and their wives and children—a total of sixty-six people—to settle in the rich Nile delta area of Egypt known as Goshen (Genesis 46:31–34).

Jacob died after several years in Egypt and was carried back to Canaan for burial (Genesis 50:7–14). But at the end of this period of Bible history, his clan of twelve sons and their descendants were still in Egypt. Here they worked, multiplied, and suffered for several centuries until another turning point in their history—their exodus from Egypt.

Joseph's Coat Brought to Jacob, Giovanni Andrea de Ferrari (1598–1669)

CHAPTER 4
Moses and the Exodus from Egypt

This period of biblical history begins with the settlement of the Israelites—Jacob, his twelve sons, and their families—in Egypt. It covers a period of about four centuries, from approximately 1850 BC to about 1450 BC. During part of this time, the descendants of Jacob were enslaved by the Egyptians, but God raised up a man named Moses to help them gain their freedom in an event known as the Exodus. Under his leadership, the Israelites traveled toward Canaan as far as a place called Sinai, where God instructed them in how they should live as a nation devoted to Him.

These events are covered in the books of Exodus and Leviticus; Numbers 1–12; and a few passages from the book of Deuteronomy.

YEARS IN EGYPT (EXODUS 1)

The first chapter of Exodus gives only a few facts about the years the Israelites spent in Egypt. It was clear from what God revealed to Abraham that they were destined to live in this country for several centuries. "Know certainly," the Lord told Abraham, "that your descendants will be strangers in a land that is not theirs, and will serve them, and they will afflict them four hundred years" (Genesis 15:13 NKJV).

As the years passed, the sixty-six members of Jacob's clan who migrated to Egypt grew until the Israelites were very numerous (Exodus 1:7). The Egyptians began to fear that they were a threat to national security. When a new king who did not know about Joseph assumed the throne (Exodus 1:8), he dealt with the problem in two ways. He enslaved the Israelites who were already in the country, and he ordered that all their newborn males be killed to stop their population growth (Exodus 1:11, 22).

But God was working behind the scenes with a plan of His own. He began the process of raising up a leader who would bring His people out of bondage.

PREPARATION OF A LEADER (EXODUS 2–4)

Moses, God's chosen leader for the Exodus, could have been a victim of Pharaoh's death order. But when he was born, his mother placed him in a little basket and hid it among the reeds along the banks of the Nile River. Here he was discovered by Pharaoh's own daughter. She eventually adopted him and brought him up in the royal family (Exodus 2:1–10).

This turn of events meant that Moses was familiar with Egyptian customs and daily life in the royal palace. This equipped him for dealing with Pharaoh in later years when he stood before him as God's spokesman for the enslaved Israelites.

> **NT Connection—MOSES:** Moses is cited for his exemplary leadership in the "faith chapter" of the book of Hebrews. He refused to be intimidated by the pharaoh of Egypt, and he "persevered as one who sees Him who is invisible" (Hebrews 11:27 HCSB).

But familiarity with the Egyptian political system was not enough to make Moses a great leader. He needed to experience the hard side of life in order to identify with his suffering countrymen. This part of his preparation came about when he fled into the wilderness after killing an Egyptian foreman who was beating an Israelite slave.

A BABY IN A BASKET

No-Stress Bible Reading
Exodus 1

No-Stress Bible Guide
Page 37
("Years in Egypt")

Think About It:

- Why did the king of Egypt issue a death order against all Israelite male infants?

- What role did Miriam play in saving her baby brother Moses?

VOICE FROM A BUSH

No-Stress Bible Reading
Exodus 2–4

No-Stress Bible Guide
Pages 37–39
("Preparation of a Leader")

Think About It:

- Why do you think God spoke to Moses through a burning bush?

- What excuses did Moses use to try to avoid God's call?

For about forty years after Moses left Egypt, he served as a shepherd in a territory known as Midian (Exodus 2:15–22; Acts 7:23–34). The Midianites lived as nomadic shepherds in a section of the vast wilderness region between Egypt and Canaan. Thus, Moses learned the skills needed to survive in the very desert the Israelites eventually crossed under his leadership on their way to the land of promise.

Moses was now prepared for the task that God had selected him to do. They only thing missing was his willingness to take on the job. This led to some serious talks between Moses and the Lord.

God began his call of Moses by first getting his undivided attention. He appeared to him in the form of a flame—a bush that burned but was not consumed. "The cry of the Israelites has reached me," he told Moses, "and I have seen the way the Egyptians are oppressing them. So now, go. I am sending you to Pharaoh to bring my people the Israelites out of Egypt" (Exodus 3:9–10 NIV).

Moses was overwhelmed by this divine call. He knew it would not be an easy job, so he gave God several reasons he was not the person who could get it done: He had no self-confidence, the people would not accept his leadership, he was not a good speaker—and to top it all off, he just didn't want to do it (Exodus 3:10–4:13).

But God would not take no for an answer. He gave Moses several miraculous signs to show that he could count on His power to sustain him in his encounters with the Egyptian king. He also promised Moses that his brother, Aaron, would speak for him if he ever felt at a loss for words (Exodus 4:14–16). With these assurances, Moses agreed to take on the leadership role for which he had been prepared through the providence of the Lord.

The Burning Bush,
Sébastien Bourdon
(1616–1671)

MOSES CONFRONTS PHARAOH (EXODUS 5–12)

These chapters are some of the most dramatic in the Bible. They describe a struggle between the purpose of the Lord—the freedom of His people—and the Egyptian pharaoh, who was adamantly opposed to doing the right thing. Like a boxing match, the contest goes through ten rounds, with each round moving a little higher on the drama chart. God sent a series of ten calamities on the land to convince the king to release the Israelites, but he continued to refuse God's demand to release His people (Exodus 8:1).

THE TEN PLAGUES AGAINST EGYPT

1. Water turned to blood (Exodus 7:15–25)
2. Frogs (8:1–15)
3. Gnats or lice (8:16–19)
4. Flies (8:20–32)
5. Death of livestock (9:1–7)
6. Boils or sores (9:8–12)
7. Hail (9:13–35)
8. Locusts (10:1–20)
9. Darkness (10:21–29)
10. Death of Egyptian firstborn (12:29–30)

Death of the Pharaoh's Firstborn Son, Lawrence Alma-Tadema (1836–1912)

These miraculous plagues against Egypt began with the turning of the waters of the Nile River into blood (Exodus 7:20–21). This river was vital to the Egyptian economy. Its annual flooding provided the rich soil that produced the nation's bountiful crops as well as the precious liquid needed for irrigation because of the dry climate. The Egyptians revered the Nile for its life-giving qualities. To have its waters polluted with blood was a blow to their livelihood as well as their religious system.

Several of the other nine calamities were intended to show God's superiority to the pagan gods of Egypt. For example, the death of Egyptian livestock proved that the sacred bull god of Egypt could not withstand the power of the one true God. Likewise, the darkness that covered the land showed that God was more powerful than one of their major deities known as Re, the Egyptian sun god. (See sidebar, "The Ten Plagues against Egypt.")

Pharaoh's stubborn refusal to obey the Lord's command ended badly for him and his people. For the tenth and final plague, God announced that the firstborn sons of Egypt as well as the firstborn of all their cattle would die. During the night when this happened, wailing for the dead filled every Egyptian household, including Pharaoh's palace (Exodus 12:29–30).

Israelite families were not touched by this tragedy. They followed God's orders to mark their houses with the blood of sacrificial lambs (Exodus 12:5–13). This event marked the beginning of an Israelite festival known as Passover. It signified God's provision for His people because He "passed over" their houses while taking the lives of the firstborn sons of the Egyptians (Exodus 12:12–14).

This plague of death finally delivered a message that Pharaoh understood. His words to Moses and Aaron sounded like a desperate command rather than a reluctant grant of permission. "Get out!" he told the two brothers. "Leave my people—and take the rest of the Israelites with you! . . . Take your flocks and herds, as you said, and be gone" (Exodus 12:31–32 NLT).

Getting the Israelites organized and ready to leave on the trek toward Canaan must have taxed Moses' leadership skills. The number of men in the group came to about six hundred thousand (Exodus 12:37)—enough to fill several large football stadiums. When women and children are added in, the total number must have been two million or more.

Some interpreters have questioned these large numbers. But they are not impossible when the rapid rate at which the Israelites multiplied is divided by the four centuries or more that they spent in Egypt.

BREAD AND WATER IN A BARREN LAND

No-Stress Bible Reading
Exodus 16; 17:1–7

No-Stress Bible Guide
Pages 41–43
("Traveling Toward Sinai")

Think About It:

- How long did the Israelites depend on the mysterious bread substitute known as manna that God provided?

- How do you think Moses felt when the people blamed all their problems on him?

TRAVELING TOWARD SINAI (EXODUS 13–18)

After leaving Egypt, Moses led the Israelites toward the edge of the Sinai wilderness to a place called Etham. Here they made camp with the Red Sea in front of them and the border of Egypt to their backs. The Lord guided them with a pillar of cloud during the day and a pillar of fire at night (Exodus 13:20–22). (See map, "The Exodus from Egypt," p. 305.)

Here at the edge of the Red Sea, the Israelites' faith in God was put to a crucial test. Pharaoh's army overtook them at this place, apparently with the intention of making them slaves again and marching them back to Egypt. Why had Pharaoh done such a U-turn in his thinking? Just a few days before, the death of all the Egyptian firstborn had brought the nation to its knees, and he had actually ordered the Israelites to leave the country.

The initial impact of this devastating event had probably worn off, and he and his officials began to have second thoughts about giving up the cheap labor of these Israelite slaves. "What have we done," they asked themselves, "letting Israel leave our service?" (Exodus 14:5 NRSV).

So here at the Red Sea the helpless Israelites hunkered down with an impassable barrier before them and the Egyptian army closing in from behind. But God evened the odds by working through His servant Moses. He instructed him to raise his staff and stretch his hand toward the water.

NT Connection—PASSOVER: Centuries after the first Passover, Jesus was crucified when the Jewish people gathered in Jerusalem to celebrate this festival (Matthew 26:1–5). The apostle Paul declared that Jesus is "our passover," or sacrificial lamb, who gave His life for us (1 Corinthians 5:7).

JOSHUA TO THE RESCUE

The account of Israel's battle with the Amalekites is significant because it introduces a brave warrior named Joshua, who led the Israelites in battle. This young man later succeeded Moses as leader of the Israelites (Deuteronomy 31:7). He led them on their campaign to conquer the Canaanites and take the land that God had promised to Abraham and his descendants.

When Moses did so, God divided the sea, led the Israelites to the other side on dry land, and closed the waters on the Egyptian army when they tried to pursue their former slaves. This great miracle led the Israelites to trust the Lord as never before and to place their confidence in Moses as His leader.

For the next three months, Moses led the Israelites through the wilderness on their way to a mountain known as Sinai, also referred to as Horeb. This is the same high peak where God had appeared to Moses in a burning bush several months before. At that time the Lord had told Moses, "When you bring the people out of Egypt, you will worship me on this mountain" (Exodus 3:12 GNT). This explains why Moses chose Sinai as the first major destination on the journey toward Canaan.

While the Israelites traveled toward Sinai, God performed several miracles to keep them alive in this barren wilderness. He sent manna, a bread substitute, for them to eat (Exodus 16:31–35). At a place called Marah, he turned bad water with a bitter taste into good water that the people could drink (Exodus 15:23–25). He solved another water shortage by providing water from a rock when Moses struck it with his staff (Exodus 17:5–7). When they were attacked by a fierce tribe known

Pharaoh's Army Is Swallowed by the Red Sea, Frederick Arthur Bridgman (1847-1928)

NT Connection—CROSSING THE RED SEA: The writer of the book of Hebrews believed this miracle required the Israelites to have faith that God would save them: "By faith they passed through the Red sea as by dry land" (Hebrews 11:29).

as the Amalekites, God gave them victory, in spite of their limited military experience (Exodus 17:8–13). (See sidebar, "Joshua to the Rescue.")

But even these divine miracles were not enough to keep the people content during their journey. They began to complain about Moses (Exodus 15:24; 16:2; 17:3). Perhaps they were unhappy about other things—scarcity of water, their bland manna diet, and the harsh desert surroundings—and they took their frustrations out on their leader.

Moses himself may have been at least partially responsible for the Israelites' dissatisfaction. His father-in-law arrived on the scene and noticed that Moses was trying to solve every problem that came up all by himself. He advised his son-in-law to appoint capable leaders who would serve as his deputies. They would solve all minor problems in the camp. This would free up Moses' time to concentrate on the most difficult cases.

To Moses' credit, he "listened to his father-in-law and did everything he said" (Exodus 18:24 HCSB). This incident shows that even great leaders should continue to learn and polish their skills at solving problems and working with people.

CAMPED AT MOUNT SINAI (EXODUS 19–40; LEVITICUS; NUMBERS 1–12)

About three months after leaving Egypt, the Israelites arrived at Sinai. Here on the plains around this sacred mountain, they settled down for about a year while they received instructions from the Lord about how He expected them to live as His chosen people. Moses was the mouthpiece through which these divine directives were spoken to the people.

The first message God gave to Moses involved the covenant between Himself and the people. He had established covenants with the Israelites at other periods in their history. But here at Sinai the Lord made it clear that His covenant was conditional. Their status as His chosen people depended on their obedience to His commands. "If you will obey me and keep my covenant," He said through Moses, "you will be my own special treasure from among all the peoples on earth" (Exodus 19:5 NLT).

The Lord also revealed through Moses that He expected His people to live by a high moral standard. They were to be "a holy nation"—pure, righteous, uncontaminated by worldly values, and set apart for His service. The Lord also expected

SMOKE OVER SINAI

No-Stress Bible Reading
Exodus 19

No-Stress Bible Guide
Pages 43–45
(from "Camped at Mount Sinai"
to "Judicial Laws")

Think About It:

- Why do you think everyone but Moses was prevented from getting close to Mount Sinai?

WORDS TO LIVE BY

No-Stress Bible Reading
Exodus 20

Think About It:

- Which one of the Ten Commandments do you think is most important, and why?

Moses on Mount Sinai, Jean-Léon Gérôme (1824–1904)

them to be a "kingdom of priests," or mediators of His blessings to the rest of the world (Exodus 19:6 NIV). This part of the covenant sounded like the promise God had given Abraham several centuries before: "All peoples on earth will be blessed through you" (Genesis 12:3 NIV).

After making these covenant terms clear to His people, God gave them many different laws to guide their behavior. These regulations appear in the last part of Exodus, the book of Leviticus, the first eleven chapters of Numbers, and a few passages from the book of Deuteronomy. Some of these laws appear more than once throughout these books of the Bible. The most important laws from this period of Israel's history fall into three categories: (1) moral laws, (2) judicial laws, and (3) ceremonial laws.

MORAL LAWS

The moral laws that God issued as standards of behavior for His people are summarized in the Ten Commandments. He delivered these laws to Moses while he was in His presence atop Mount Sinai. While Moses was communing with the Lord, the mountain trembled as God descended with fire and smoke (Exodus 19:16–20). This signified His divine power and told the people that His message to Moses held eternal significance. It was clear that God wanted them to take His Ten Commandments very seriously. These moral laws are repeated in the book of Deuteronomy (Deuteronomy 5:7–21).

The first four of these commandments spell out our duties to God, while the last six deal with our obligations to other people. In regard to God, we are to worship Him and Him alone, shun the worship of idols and false gods, honor and revere His name, and observe the Sabbath day by ceasing all work on that day (Exodus 20:1–11). In regard to other people, we are to honor our parents and refrain from committing murder, participating in adultery, stealing the property of others, lying about people, and nursing a greedy desire for material things (Exodus 20:12-17).

One of the ironies of this moral code is that the Israelites were in the process of breaking it while God was delivering it to Moses atop Mount Sinai. With Aaron's help, they cast a statue of a calf and covered it with gold. This probably represented the bull god worshipped by the Egyptians. "This is your god, O Israel," the people declared, "that brought you out of the land of Egypt!" (Exodus 32:4 NKJV). It was clear that they were breaking the first two of the Ten Commandments that prohibited worship of false gods.

Moses was furious when he arrived on the scene. He destroyed the calf idol and reprimanded his brother, Aaron, for taking part in this act of idolatry. Aaron's lame excuse for his behavior is one of the most humorous passages in the Old Testament. "They gave me the gold," he told Moses, "and I threw it into the fire, and out came this calf!" (Exodus 32:24 NIV).

According to an account in the book of Deuteronomy, the Lord delivered the Ten Commandments to Moses a second time. When Moses saw the calf idol the people had made, he was so angry that he broke the stone tablets on which the laws were written by throwing them to the ground. But God inscribed the laws again on new pieces of stone (Deuteronomy 9:17; 10:1-4). The fact that His commands were written in stone shows they were to be a permanent part of the life of His people.

God's moral code as outlined in the Ten Commandments is the basis of several other laws that appear during this period of biblical history. For example, the Israelites were directed to be honest in their business practices. Using one weight for buying and a different one for selling was dishonest and fraudulent, the same as stealing.

God's people were also expected to show kindness and generosity toward the poor

(Leviticus 19:9-10). They were not to take advantage of their helpless condition by withholding their wages (Deuteronomy 24:14-15), charging them interest, or selling them food at

---

JUSTICE IN ACTION

No-Stress Bible Reading
Deuteronomy 19

No-Stress Bible Guide
Pages 45-47
(from "Judicial Laws"
to "Ceremonial Laws")

Think About It:

- How did the ancient laws in this chapter distinguish between an accidental killing and a premeditated murder?

- What was the penalty for presenting false testimony against another person in a judicial proceeding?

---

a profit (Leviticus 25:35-38). These laws reflect the eighth commandment against stealing and, by implication, any form of dishonesty against others, including perverting justice by accepting bribes (Exodus 23:8).

JUDICIAL LAWS

Many judicial laws were handed down during this period of biblical history. These regulations might be compared to the modern civil and criminal laws that guarantee the rights of individuals and preserve order in society. God gave these laws to promote a spirit of fairness, justice, and harmony among His people.

Some of these laws dealt with public safety. For example, a house had to be constructed with a guardrail around the edge of the roof (Deuteronomy 22:8). People of Bible times used the flat spaces on top of their houses much the way outdoor patios are used today for relaxation. These guard rails were needed to prevent accidental falls from the roof.

Other judicial laws specified how slaves and servants were to be treated (Exodus 21:2–11), how people were to be compensated for personal injuries (Exodus 21:12–36) and damaged property (Exodus 22:5–6), and the circumstances that exempted certain people from going to war (Deuteronomy 20:5–9).

Some of the most important of these judicial laws assured fair treatment of people who were accused of various offenses. For example, a person could not be convicted of a crime on the testimony of a single witness. His guilt had to be "established by the testimony of two or three witnesses" (Deuteronomy 19:15 HCSB).

An important judicial safeguard for people accused of murder was guaranteed asylum in a city known as a city of refuge (Deuteronomy 19:1–7). The accused person could stay here in safety until it was determined through due process what punishment, if any, should be levied against him. In Old Testament times, people lived under a "life for a life" rule. Any person who caused the death of another could be sought out and killed by the relatives of the victim. A city of refuge offered asylum for the perpetrator in cases of accidental death.

A few crimes were considered so serious that they could result in the death penalty.

> **NT Connection—TABERNACLE:** The tabernacle symbolizes Christ's continuing presence with His people, beginning with His incarnation when He lived among us in human form: "The Word became flesh and made his dwelling among us" (John 1:14 NIV).

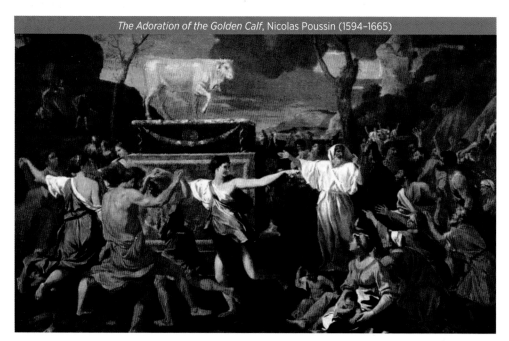

The Adoration of the Golden Calf, Nicolas Poussin (1594–1665)

The Transportation of the Tabernacle of Israel, unknown artist (Saint Paul's Church, Belgium)

These included cursing one's parents (Exodus 21:17), committing adultery (Deuteronomy 22:22), worshipping false gods (Deuteronomy 13:6–11), and leading people astray through black magic and witchcraft (Leviticus 20:27).

These laws seem harsh when compared to the punishments rendered under the criminal justice system of modern times. But at least one judicial regulation in this period of Israel's history has a less severe and more contemporary feel. The Israelites recognized the reality that people could be wiped out economically by hard times. They provided relief for people in these circumstances by designating every fiftieth year as a year of liberty, or a jubilee year.

During this year, any Israelite who had sold himself into slavery to pay off a debt was released from his indebtedness and set free. Land that a family had been forced to sell to pay a debt since the last jubilee year had to be returned to the original owners. This regulation gave the poor and unfortunate a second chance. It might be compared to the bankruptcy laws of our own time.

CEREMONIAL LAWS

Most of the laws in Exodus, Leviticus, Numbers, and Deuteronomy fall into the category known as ceremonial laws. These regulations deal with the distinctive worship rituals of God's chosen people, the Israelites. Many of these instructions are repetitive, appearing in more than one of these books, or in a different form in the same book.

One example of this pattern of repetition is the tabernacle, a movable sanctuary for worship that God directed Moses to build on the plain surrounding Mount Sinai. First, God described the tabernacle and its furnishings to Moses (Exodus 25:1–27:21; 30:1–38). Then Moses passed this description on to the Israelites (Exodus 35:4–19). In the Bible's account of the construction of the tabernacle, its features and furnishings are

NT Connection—HIGH PRIEST: One of the most significant titles of Jesus is Great High Priest (Hebrews 4:14). He stands above even the high priest of Israel because He laid down His own life—not the life of an animal—as the perfect sacrifice for sin.

described yet again (Exodus 36:8–38:20).

Finally, when Moses inspected the finished tabernacle elements and assembled them into the final building, Bible readers are reminded again of what it looked like and what it contained (Exodus 39:32–43; 40:1–33). This emphasis on the tabernacle comes to a climax when we read how God filled it with His glory (Exodus 40:34–35).

Obviously, the tabernacle was a major step in Israel's religious development. To them, it represented God's continuing presence in their midst. In this sacred tent that moved with them on their travels, they worshipped the Lord and presented various types of offerings and sacrifices to the presiding priests.

The priests who conducted these sacrificial ceremonies were descendants of the tribe of Levi, one of Jacob's twelve sons. The formal establishment of the priestly order and its sacrificial rituals occurred while the Israelites were camped at Mount Sinai. In an elaborate ceremony that lasted seven days, Moses consecrated his brother, Aaron, and Aaron's sons as the first priests of Israel (Exodus 28:1; 29:1–45). Aaron was the first high priest, or chief priest, who managed the sacrificial system. This responsibility passed to Aaron's son Eleazar when he died (Deuteronomy 10:6).

The heart of the sacrificial system was a concept known as atonement. The people brought offerings of various types to the priest. He placed these items—usually grain or an animal—on the altar of the tabernacle as sacrificial offerings on their behalf. These offerings were thought to provide atonement, or forgiveness, for the sins of those who had faltered in their commitment to God or committed wrongful acts against others.

One of the most popular offerings was known as the burnt offering. An animal was slaughtered by the priest and placed over a fire on the altar until it was consumed. This type of offering was known as a "whole" burnt offering (Deuteronomy 33:10). But in some offerings of a sacrificial animal, the meat was removed from the fire before it was consumed and eaten by the priests and their families.

One regulation among Israel's ceremonial

NT Connection—FEAST OF WEEKS/FEAST OF HARVEST: This holiday was known as Pentecost in New Testament times. Gathered in Jerusalem to celebrate this festival, early Christian believers experienced a miraculous outpouring of God's Spirit (Acts 2:1–4).

laws addressed the issue of collective sin committed by the entire nation of Israel. This sin was dealt with during an annual holy day known as the Day of Atonement.

On that day the high priest made atonement for his own sins by offering an animal sacrifice (Numbers 29:8). Then he entered the section of the tabernacle known as the Most Holy Place, where he sprinkled the altar with the blood of this sacrifice (Leviticus 16:12–15). Finally, he released into the wilderness a goat designated as the scapegoat to symbolize the pardon of the people (Leviticus 16:22).

Israel's ceremonial laws also specified that the people were to observe three annual feasts or religious festivals. Each of these events lasted several days. In later years, when Jerusalem became the national capital, the people were encouraged to travel to this city to celebrate these major holidays.

The most important of these three feasts was Passover. It commemorated the deliverance of the Israelites from slavery in Egypt, when their homes were "passed over" by the Lord's death sentence against the Egyptian firstborn (Exodus 12:29–30). Passover was also known as the Feast of Unleavened Bread. This referred to the haste with which the Israelites left the country. They left so quickly that they skipped the step of adding yeast to the bread to get it to rise (Exodus 12:34).

The second major festival was the Feast of Harvest. Its purpose was to express thanks to the Lord for the crops He had provided. This holiday was sometimes called the Feast of Weeks because of the "seven weeks" after Passover by which its date was determined (Deuteronomy 16:9–10).

During this harvest celebration, the people brought the first of their crops to be gathered as an offering to the Lord. These were known as "firstfruits" (Deuteronomy 26:1–10). The apostle Paul referred to Jesus as the firstfruits of the resurrection, or the One who had blazed the trail of bodily resurrection and eternal life for all believers (1 Corinthians 15:20–23).

The third annual feast that God commanded the Israelites to observe was the Feast of Tabernacles (Leviticus 23:33–43), also known as the Feast of Ingathering or the Feast of Booths. During the observance of this holiday, the people were to live in huts made from the branches of trees. These crude dwellings would remind them that this was how their ancestors had lived in the wilderness after their deliverance from

AN EVENT TO REMEMBER

No-Stress Bible Reading
Exodus 12:1–14; Deuteronomy 16:1–8

No-Stress Bible Guide
Pages 47–49
("Ceremonial Laws")

Think About It:

- What major event in Israel's history was commemorated by the feast of Passover?

- Why did the people eat unleavened bread during this celebration?

- Why do you think the apostle Paul referred to the sacrifice of Jesus as "our passover" (1 Corinthians 5:7)?

Egypt, and that God had been with them during those years.

God's revelation of His laws to His chosen people brings this period of biblical history to a close. The Israelites were now ready to move on toward Canaan—but not before forty years of aimless wandering in the wilderness.

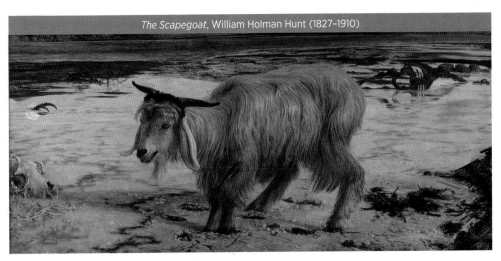

The Scapegoat, William Holman Hunt (1827–1910)

The Gathering of the Manna,
unknown artist (c. 1470)

CHAPTER 5
Journey through the Wilderness

Each period of biblical history reviewed up to now has covered several centuries. But this fifth step in Israel's development involves only about forty or fifty years—from approximately 1450 BC to about 1400 BC. During these crucial years of transition, God's chosen people wandered in the vast wilderness territory between Mount Sinai and the land of Canaan. (See map, "Journey to the Promised Land," p. 306.)

This was a time when the Israelites perfected their tribal organization, dealt with grumbling and rebellion in the ranks, clashed with several enemies who tried to halt their advance, and made final preparations to lay claim to the Promised Land. These events are recorded in Numbers 10–36 and a few passages in Deuteronomy, particularly chapters 27–34.

ORGANIZED BY TRIBES

As early as the time when the Israelites migrated from Canaan into Egypt, the tribal organization of the nation began to take shape. The patriarch Jacob blessed his twelve sons and predicted their future (Genesis 49:1–28). It was clear that these sons would evolve into the tribes that made up the nation of Israel.

But during the years between the times when the people entered and left Egypt, several changes in this twelve-son arrangement occurred. One change involved Joseph, one of Jacob's twelve sons. Joseph is never mentioned as a tribe of Israel. Instead, his two sons who were born in Egypt—Ephraim and Manasseh—represented him in the twelve-tribe hierarchy.

Levi, another son of Jacob, was excluded from the twelve-tribe organization. His descendants evolved into the priests and Levites of Israel. Their task was to minister to all the Israelites. Because of their priestly service, the priests and Levites did not receive an allotment of land in Canaan. They were supported by the other tribes.

When the Israelites camped for a year near Mount Sinai, the tribal organization that would exist for the rest of their history was set in stone. This is clear from the tribal arrangement described in the second chapter of Numbers. The tribes were camped on each side of the tabernacle—east, south, west, and north—in units of three tribes each. The total number of men in each of these units—and even the order in which they would break camp—is cited in this passage. This orderly arrangement is best portrayed in the form of a chart.

ISRAEL'S TRIBES AROUND THE TABERNACLE AND ON THE MARCH

TRIBAL UNIT	SIDE OF TABERNACLE	NUMBER OF MEN IN THESE THREE TRIBES	ORDER OF MARCH
1. Judah-Issachar-Zebulun	East Side	186,400	First
2. Reuben-Simeon-Gad	South Side	151,450	Second
3. Ephraim-Manasseh-Benjamin	West Side	108,100	Third
4. Dan-Asher-Naphtali	North Side	157,600	Fourth

Later, when the Israelites broke camp at Mount Sinai and moved off toward Canaan, they followed the exact details of this tribal organization (Numbers 10:14–28). The Levites who marched with the first group broke down the tabernacle and carried its separate pieces. The furnishings of the tabernacle were transported by Levites in the second unit. The holiest items, including the ark of the covenant, were carried by the Kohathites, a special division of the Levites. The function of the fourth group on the march was to serve as "rear guard for all the camps" (Numbers 10:25 HCSB).

This pattern of tribal divisions reflects the order and precision of a military organization. Counting the number of men in each three-tribe unit may have been a way of reckoning the forces the Israelites could count on in the event of an attack by their enemies.

Before the people entered Canaan, the Lord instructed Moses to take a census of all the people to make sure they were prepared for battle (Numbers 26:1–51). This counting was done tribe by tribe, with special attention to the men "from twenty years old and upward. . .all that are able to go to war in Israel" (Numbers 26:2). The census counted 601,730 men who were available for military duty.

DISCONTENT AND REBELLION

The refinement of Israel's tribal organization was an essential step forward in the nation's development. But it did not solve the problem of grumbling and rebellion in the ranks. Some people had bad-mouthed Moses and his leadership almost from the moment they left Egypt. This negativism got worse with every mile they logged during the wilderness-wandering stage of their journey.

Soon after breaking camp at Mount Sinai, some people began complaining about their bland diet of manna, the bread substitute that God was providing. They longed for the tasty meat and vegetables they had eaten back in

NT Connection—ETERNAL MANNA: Jesus is the bread of life. He declared that His offer of eternal life was superior to the manna provided in the wilderness. "Your ancestors ate manna and died," He said, "but whoever feeds on this bread will live forever" (John 6:58 NIV).

Egypt. In response, God sent flocks of quail into the camp. But before they could eat this miracle meat, He struck them with a plague. The Lord's message was clear: "Be content with the food I am already providing to keep you alive" (see Numbers 11:1–35).

Moses sometimes grew impatient with the constant complaints of the Israelites. Once he

in the crisis. He reacted in dramatic fashion by opening the earth and swallowing Korah and his coconspirators. Then God destroyed the 250 additional leaders of the uprising with fire (Numbers 16:1–35).

When some of the people complained that this punishment was too severe, the Lord sent a plague among them. Several thousand died

NT Connection—JESUS AS THE ROCK: The apostle Paul picked up on this miracle of water from a rock and referred to Jesus as our "spiritual rock" (1 Corinthians 10:1–4). Just as this rock in the desert provided water for the Israelites, Jesus sustains those who place their trust in Him.

asked the Lord, "Why are you displeased with me? Why have you given me the responsibility for all these people?" (Numbers 11:11 GNT). The heavy weight he felt must have really intensified when his own brother and sister, Aaron and Miriam, questioned his authority.

They approached Moses under the pretext that he had compromised his leadership by marrying a Cushite, or Ethiopian, woman. But what they really wanted was a share of his position of authority over the people. "Has the LORD spoken only through Moses?" they asked him. "Hasn't he spoken through us, too?" (Numbers 12:2 NLT).

The Lord answered their questions by assuring them that Moses was the leader whom He had chosen. He was ultimately responsible for leading God's people. As punishment for the audacity of Miriam and Aaron, the Lord struck Miriam with leprosy. But she was restored to health after a few days when Moses and Aaron prayed for her healing (Numbers 12:10–15).

A more serious case of rebellion arose when a man named Korah enlisted two other sympathizers, Dathan and Abiram. These three men convinced a group of 250 Israelite leaders to rise up against Moses and Aaron, whom they accused of exercising high-handed leadership. Moses and Aaron called on the Lord to intervene

before Aaron, as high priest, interceded for them and stopped the plague (Numbers 16:41–50).

After Korah's rebellion was put down, the Lord performed another miracle on behalf

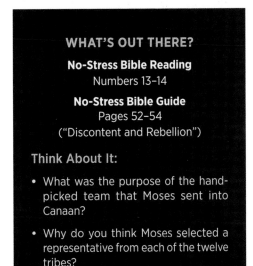

WHAT'S OUT THERE?

No-Stress Bible Reading
Numbers 13–14

No-Stress Bible Guide
Pages 52–54
("Discontent and Rebellion")

Think About It:

- What was the purpose of the hand-picked team that Moses sent into Canaan?

- Why do you think Moses selected a representative from each of the twelve tribes?

- What set Joshua and Caleb apart from the other members of this group?

- How was this team's majority report a reflection of the negative spirit that often plagued the Israelites in the wilderness?

of Aaron and his descendants. Some people apparently questioned Aaron's authority as the high priest. Leaders of the twelve tribes and Aaron—representing the tribe of Levi—placed their staffs in the tabernacle. During the night Aaron's staff budded and bore fruit. This left no doubt that Aaron and his descendants were God's choice to serve as priests among the Israelites (Numbers 17:1–11).

The most serious case of rebellion occurred when the Israelites reached a place known as Kadesh Barnea at the very edge of Canaan. From this site, Moses sent twelve scouts—one from each tribe—into Canaan to determine what the land was like. These men returned forty days later with good news and bad news.

The good news was that the land was fertile and productive. To show its fruitfulness, they brought back figs and pomegranates and a cluster of grapes so heavy that it had to be carried by two men (Numbers 13:21–25). The bad news was that the land was inhabited by several powerful tribes that were entrenched behind their walled cities. "The Amalekites dwell in the land of the south," they told Moses, "and the Hittites, and the Jebusites, and the Amorites, dwell in the mountains: and the Canaanites dwell by the sea, and by the coast of Jordan" (Numbers 13:29).

Paralyzed by fear, ten of the scouts recommended against going into Canaan. But two of their number, Joshua and Caleb, urged bold and courageous action. By trusting the Lord, they declared, the Israelites could even the odds against them and take the land.

But the people lost faith and rebelled against God and His servant Moses. They refused to enter the land and cried out for a new leader to take them back to Egypt (Numbers 14:1–4). As punishment for their lack of faith, God sentenced the people to forty years of aimless wandering in the wilderness. Before these years came to an end, all the adults of this faithless generation, except Joshua and Caleb, would die (Numbers 14:26–38).

When this severe punishment from the Lord was announced, some of the people had a change of heart. Without consulting the Lord, they decided to attack the Canaanites and Amalekites in one section of the land. Moses warned them not to do it because they had rebelled against God and He would not bless their efforts. But they refused to stand down and suffered a humiliating defeat (Numbers 14:39–45). This experience taught the Israelites to seek the Lord's blessings in future battles against their enemies.

During these forty years of wilderness wandering, Moses himself fell victim to the spirit of disobedience that he had observed so many times among the Israelites. The people complained against him at a place called Meribah because they had no water to drink. The Lord instructed Moses and Aaron to gather the people in front of a rock. Then Moses was to speak to this rock, and it would produce water for the people.

Out of patience, Moses told the complainers, "Listen, you rebels, shall we [referring to himself and Aaron] bring water for you out of this rock?" (Numbers 20:10 NRSV). Then he struck the rock twice with his staff, and water poured out.

God was displeased with Moses for this rash act, apparently because he attributed the miracle to himself and Aaron rather than the Lord. He punished them both by forbidding them to enter the land of Canaan (Numbers 20:12).

NT Connection—BALAAM THE GREEDY: The apostle Peter compared the false teachers of his time to Balaam and his love of money: "They have left the straight way and wandered off to follow the way of Balaam. . .who loved the wages of wickedness" (2 Peter 2:15 NIV).

Balaam and the Donkey,
Rembrandt (1606–1669)

DEALING WITH OPPOSITION

Finally, the years of wandering in the wilderness came to an end. The Lord directed Moses to leave the area around Kadesh Barnea and cross the Zered Valley (Deuteronomy 2:13-15). This northerly route would take them into territory where they were sure to meet opposition. This area around the Dead Sea and east of the Jordan River was inhabited by several hostile tribal peoples, including the Edomites, Moabites, Amorites, Midianites, and Ammonites.

The first challenge to Israel came from the Edomites. Their territory south of the Dead Sea had been settled centuries before by the descendants of Esau, the twin brother of Jacob. Moses asked the Edomites for permission to cross their territory, but they refused. The Israelites were forced to detour around Edom by crossing the desert along its eastern border (Numbers 20:14-22).

This detour brought the Israelites into Amorite territory. Here they battled the army of an Amorite king known as Sihon. In the strength of the Lord, Moses and the Israelites defeated Sihon and drove the Amorites out of their walled cities (Numbers 21:21-31).

After the victory over Sihon, the Israelites defeated Og, another Amorite chieftain. He ruled an area known as Gilead, noted for its fertile pasturelands. Two of Israel's tribes, Reuben and Gad, asked Moses for permission to settle this region, although it was across the Jordan River from the land of Canaan. Some clans of the tribe of Manasseh also wanted to settle in the region of Gilead. Moses granted their request on one condition: these three tribes had to agree to accompany the rest of Israel into Canaan and do their part to defeat the Canaanites (Numbers 32:1-33).

Israel's movement toward the border of Canaan along the Jordan River also brought them into conflict with the Moabites. These people inhabited an area of high plateaus on the northwestern edge of the Dead Sea. Here the biblical writer introduced two men who participated in one of the most fascinating dramas in the entire Old Testament. This narrative appears in chapters 22-24 of the book of Numbers.

The first man was Balak, king of Moab. He heard about the victory of the Israelites over the neighboring Amorites. Fearing Moab would fall to the Israelite invaders, he summoned the second man in the drama—a wizard named Balaam—to deal with the problem.

Balaam wanted desperately to collect the fat fee that Balak promised if he would curse the Israelites. But God caused this pagan prophet to pronounce blessings on His people instead. When this happened three times, the king ordered him, "Now get on home! I promised to reward you, but the Lord has kept you from getting the reward" (Numbers 24:11 GNT).

In addition to pronouncing God's blessings

BALAK THE BEWILDERED

No-Stress Bible Reading
Numbers 22-24

No-Stress Bible Guide
Pages 56-57

Think About It:

- Why was Balak, king of Moab, so anxious to have a curse pronounced against the Israelites?

- How many times did Balaam prophesy that God intended to bless the Israelites instead?

- What does this account tell us about God's power and authority?

on the Israelites, Balaam also issued one of the earliest messianic prophecies in the Bible. He predicted that "there shall come a Star out of Jacob, and a Sceptre shall rise out of Israel" (Numbers 24:17). This is a reference to Jesus Christ, the future Messiah, who would rule over His people with supreme power and authority.

One truth that issues from this account of a pagan king and a greedy prophet is that God can use any means necessary to work His will and bless His people.

Camped near Moab and the Jordan River, the Israelites were now closer to the Promised Land than they had been since leaving Egypt. But a few final preparations were needed before they could occupy their new home. These last-minute happenings are recorded in chapters 27–34 of the book of Deuteronomy.

Statue of Moses (San Pietro in Vincoli Church, Rome)

FINAL PREPARATIONS NEAR CANAAN

The most important thing that needed to be done before the people entered the land was a transfer of leadership. Moses was now an old man after leading the Israelites for more than forty years. He called the people together and told them, "I am now 120 years old; I can no longer act as your leader" (Deuteronomy 31:2 HCSB).

Moses also reminded the people that the Lord had prohibited him from entering Canaan because of his sin when he struck the rock at Meribah. It was time for another leader to take over and bring the people into the land they had been promised by the Lord.

The people were not surprised when Moses presented Joshua as his successor. This young warrior had already led the Israelites in at least one battle against their enemies. Moses had probably been training him for some time as his replacement. But most important of all, the Lord had made it clear that Joshua was His choice to lead the people after Moses stepped down (Numbers 27:15–23).

As Joshua stood before the people as their new leader, Moses charged him to be strong, courageous, and faithful to the Lord in carrying out his responsibilities. "The LORD himself goes before you and will be with you," he reminded Joshua; "he will never leave you nor forsake you. Do not be afraid; do not be discouraged" (Deuteronomy 31:8 NIV).

In this time of transition, Moses also had some important instructions for the Israelites. He led them to renew the covenant between themselves and the Lord that they had agreed to at Mount Sinai more than forty years before. He reminded them that they could count on the Lord's blessings if they obeyed His commands. But disobedience would bring death and destruction. He issued a

The breathtaking view from modern Mount Nebo—the place of Moses' grave—looking across the valley to Jordan

strong warning about the dire consequences of slipping into idolatry and worshipping the pagan gods of the Canaanites (Deuteronomy 29:1–29).

These instructions of Moses in the closing chapters of Deuteronomy were actually his farewell speech to the nation of Israel. One of the most interesting parts of this long goodbye is his blessing of the twelve tribes (Deuteronomy 33:1–25). This blessing is similar to Jacob's blessing of his twelve sons in Egypt many years before (Genesis 49:1–28). Those two long speeches are like bookends that mark the Exodus experience—Jacob's blessing just before the Israelites settled in Egypt and Moses' blessing just before they settled in Canaan.

It had been several centuries since the Lord had promised to give Abraham's descendants a land of their own. Moses declared in his blessing of the tribes that this long-awaited promise was about to be fulfilled.

After issuing his blessing, Moses climbed a mountain on the plains of Moab known as Mount Nebo. From this peak that rose about half a mile above the surrounding territory, he could see the entire territory known as Canaan. He had endured forty years of complaints and rebellion to bring his people to this land, only to be denied the pleasure of walking on it. He died later in this region of Moab, just a few miles outside the Promised Land on the eastern side of the Jordan River (Deuteronomy 34:1–5).

The death of Moses is obviously a turning point in the story of Israel's history and development. But his passing from the scene has an aura of mystery. The Bible states that "his vitality had not left him" when he died (Deuteronomy 34:7 HCSB). If he was still in such good health, why did he die? The only explanation seems to be that his task of leading the Israelites was finished. It was time for him to step aside and pass the reins of leadership to Joshua.

GOD'S SUCCESSION PLAN

No-Stress Bible Reading
Exodus 17:8–13; Numbers 27:15–23; Deuteronomy 31

No-Stress Bible Guide
Pages 58–59

Think About It:

- What leadership skills had Joshua demonstrated even before he was selected as Moses' successor?

- How do you think he felt about following such a legendary leader as Moses?

ONLY A GLANCE

No-Stress Bible Reading
Numbers 20:1–12; Deuteronomy 34

Think About It:

- Why did God allow Moses to see the land He had promised His people, but not to set foot on it?

Another strange thing about his death is that the Lord—not the people of Israel—buried him and that "no one knows his burial place to this day" (Deuteronomy 34:6 NRSV). Why was his grave not prominently marked so future generations could pay him honor? Perhaps God knew that such homage by the people of Israel could slip into idolatry.

With the death of Moses this period of biblical history comes to a close. Now it was up to his successor, Joshua, to lead the people into the next chapter of their fascinating story.

Joshua Passing the River Jordan with the Ark of the Covenant, Benjamin West (1738–1820)

CHAPTER 6
Joshua Claims the Promised Land

This period of Bible history focuses on Joshua, the successor of Moses, as leader of the Israelites. Joshua's challenge was to lead the people to claim the land of Canaan that God had promised to His people. This process took about fifty years, from approximately 1400 BC to about 1350 BC.

The events of this crucial half century are recorded in the Old Testament book named for this warrior hero. Joshua's twenty-four action-packed chapters fall neatly into four sections: (1) entering the land, (2) claiming the land, (3) dividing the land, and (4) Joshua's final days.

ENTERING THE LAND (JOSHUA 1–5)

The book of Joshua begins with the Israelites camped on the eastern bank of the Jordan River across from Canaan. The Lord appeared to Joshua and told him to get ready to lead the people to cross over and enter the land. He assured His new leader, "As I was with Moses, so I will be with you" (Joshua 1:5 NIV).

But God's presence did not mean that claiming the land would be an easy task. It would require Joshua to be a model of bravery and discipline as the people went into battle against the Canaanites. So the Lord gave Joshua a pep talk, telling him three times, "Be strong and courageous" (Joshua 1:6, 7, 9 HCSB).

was not intimidated by what had happened in the past, choosing to focus instead on the challenge of the present. He showed in these initial interactions with the Lord and the Israelites that he had the leadership qualities needed for this important time in the nation's history.

As a shrewd leader, Joshua wanted to know what was going on in Canaan before entering the land. So he sent two spies to find out, instructing them to concentrate on the city of Jericho (Joshua 2:1). He probably selected this city because of its strategic location on one of the main trade routes that crossed the land. Capturing Jericho would give his army access

NT Connection—THE NAME JOSHUA: *Joshua* is the Old Testament equivalent of the name *Jesus* in the New Testament. Both names mean "the Lord is salvation." By their names and their lives, Joshua and Jesus demonstrated the salvation or deliverance that comes from God.

Joshua acted immediately on God's orders and got the people ready to enter Canaan within the next three days. He inspired them with his confident attitude and a positive plan of action. Committing themselves to his leadership, the Israelites echoed the words that God had spoken to Joshua: "Be strong and courageous!" (Joshua 1:18 HCSB).

Joshua must have realized more than anyone that Moses was a hard act to follow. But he

to all of Canaan.

When the spies arrived in Jericho, they went to the house of a prostitute named Rahab, probably because their presence there would not arouse suspicion. But the city officials were on high alert. They were alarmed because of the Israelites' recent victory over the Amorite kings Sihon and Og. They knew the Israelites were camped nearby, so any unfamiliar face in town was considered a possible threat. They sent

A MIRACLE REMEMBERED

No-Stress Bible Reading
Joshua 3–4

No-Stress Bible Guide
Pages 61–63
(to "Claiming the Land")

Think About It:

- What sacred object were the priests carrying when their feet touched the waters of the Jordan River?

- Why was it important that future generations remember this miraculous event?

Joshua had one leader from each tribe carry a stone from the river to build a memorial pile.

Israelites victory over their enemies was "the supreme God of the heavens above and the earth below" (Joshua 2:11 NLT). After the coast was clear, she helped the men escape to safety by lowering them over the city wall with a rope.

The two spies returned to Joshua with a positive report. "Truly the LORD has delivered all the land into our hands," they told him, "for indeed all the inhabitants of the country are fainthearted because of us" (Joshua 2:24 NKJV). This was what Joshua wanted to hear. This mood of fear and uncertainty among the Canaanites meant that now was the ideal time to strike.

The first Israelites to move out to cross the Jordan River were the priests carrying the ark of the covenant. The people may have been a little hesitant to approach the river, because it was higher than normal due to recent rains. But as soon as the feet of the priests touched the water, the rushing current stopped, allowing everyone to cross over on dry land (Joshua 3:9–17).

This miracle was God's way of assuring the Israelites of His continuing presence. He had separated the waters of the Red Sea more than forty years before to save His people. They could depend on this wonder-working God to help them as they moved forward to claim the land He had promised.

To commemorate this miraculous crossing, the Lord directed Joshua to select a representative from each of the twelve tribes. These men were to take twelve stones from the middle of the stream and arrange them in the form of a monument on the other side of the river. This would serve as a visible reminder to future generations of God's goodness to His people (Joshua 4:1–7).

After arriving in Canaanite territory, the Israelites camped about two miles from Jericho at a place called Gilgal. This became their base of operations for several years while they battled the Canaanites and settled throughout the land. Also at Gilgal, Joshua circumcised all male

word for Rahab to bring out the two men, whom someone had spotted at her house (Joshua 2:1–3).

Refusing to obey the order, Rahab hid the spies after securing their promise that she and her family would not be harmed when the Israelites attacked the city. She showed her faith by declaring that the Lord who had given the

NT Connection—RAHAB: She is listed as an ancestor of Jesus in Matthew's genealogy (Matthew 1:5; "Rachab" in the KJV). Rahab's faith is also commended by the writer of Hebrews (11:31).

Israelites to signify their covenant with the Lord. Apparently this ritual had not been practiced during their wilderness-wandering years. The first Passover celebration in their new homeland also occurred at Gilgal (Joshua 5:1–12).

CLAIMING THE LAND (JOSHUA 6–12)

Although the Lord had promised to lead the Israelites into battle, Joshua did his part to assure success. A careful study of the book of Joshua shows that he had a three-pronged plan for claiming the land. Some interpreters refer to it as his divide-and-conquer strategy. (See map, "Israel's Battles for the Promised Land," p. 307.)

In the first phase of this plan, Joshua struck quickly into Canaan's heartland, capturing the cities of Jericho and Ai. In phases two and three, he launched campaigns into the southern and northern parts of the territory. Securing a strip of land in central Canaan prevented the local kings or chieftains from forming an imposing alliance

The Victory of Joshua over the Amalekites, Nicolas Poussin (1594–1665)

from north to south against Joshua's army.

The first target in his movement into central Canaan was Jericho, which was "shut up inside and out because of the Israelites" (Joshua 6:1 NRSV). The city leaders were expecting an attack. They knew the Israelites were camped nearby, and they realized that spies from Israel's camp had already gathered information about Jericho's defenses.

AN EASY TARGET

No-Stress Bible Reading
Joshua 6

No-Stress Bible Guide
Pages 63–67
(from "Claiming the Land"
to "Dividing the Land")

Think About it:

• What was to be done with the valuable spoils of war taken from Jericho?

A TOUGH LITTLE CITY

No-Stress Bible Reading
Joshua 7

Think About It:

• Why was Joshua's army so surprised when they failed to capture Ai?

As Joshua prepared his army to attack the city, the Lord gave him a battle plan that must have seemed insane to this veteran commander.

The usual way to capture a walled city was to conduct a siege against it. The invading army would camp outside the walls for months and simply starve the people of the city into submission. But God's plans for Jericho's defeat featured several unusual elements:

• For six consecutive days Joshua's entire army would march around the city.

• Accompanying the army would be seven priests carrying the ark of the covenant and blowing trumpets.

• On day seven this group of warriors and priests would march around the city seven times, with the priests blowing the trumpets as before.

• At a distinctive long blast from the trumpets, apparently on the seventh time around the city, the entire army would give a loud shout.

If the Israelites followed this exact plan, the Lord promised, the walls of the city would fall, and it would be easy prey for the Israelites (Joshua 6:1–5).

Just as the Lord had said, the walls of the city did fall, and the Israelites captured and burned it. They killed all its inhabitants except Rahab and her family. They were spared because she had saved the lives of the two Israelite spies. The account of Jericho's fall is one of the best-known narratives in the Bible. The public's fascination with this event has motivated several different archaeological digs on the site. These studies have shown that the city was one of the oldest settlements in the world, founded by an ancient civilization many centuries before Joshua arrived on the scene. Debris from successive settlements on the site reached a depth of sixty feet.

NT Connection—JERICHO: The writer of Hebrews declared that faith played a role in Jericho's defeat: "By faith the walls of Jericho fell down, after they were compassed about seven days" (Hebrews 11:30).

The Taking of Jericho, James Tissot (1836–1902)

The most impressive feature uncovered by archaeologists was a crude stone wall with a round defensive tower—the oldest city defense system discovered anywhere in the world. This relic from a past civilization never fails to impress modern visitors to the Holy Land.

After Joshua's easy victory over Jericho, he moved his army about ten miles west to the city of Ai. His military scouts expected this battle to be as easy as tossing a log on a campfire. "There's no need for all of us to go up there," they told their commander; "it won't take more than two or three thousand men to attack Ai" (Joshua 7:3 NLT).

GIBEON'S AWESOME WELL

Gibeon, the city that hoodwinked Joshua, has been identified and explored by archaeologists. The most impressive find they uncovered at Gibeon was a huge well or cistern—one of the largest yet discovered in Israel. Measuring thirty-seven feet around, it descended through solid rock to a depth of eighty-two feet. At the bottom of the shaft, a tunnel about 180 feet long was dug to tap into the water from an underground spring. This ingenious water system probably guaranteed a supply of water for the city in the event of a prolonged siege by an enemy army.

This huge well is still visible today. Holy Land visitors marvel at its size and the backbreaking labor required to dig it through solid rock.

But it didn't turn out that way. The defenders of Ai put up a strong resistance, killed some of Israel's warriors, and even chased them from the field of battle. This unexpected defeat humiliated Joshua's troops and paralyzed them with fear (Joshua 7:4–5). Why had the Lord given them victory over Jericho and then turned His back on them when they advanced against this weak little city?

The problem was Israel's disobedience. A man named Achan had confiscated some of the spoils of war from Jericho and hidden them in his tent. His actions were a flagrant violation of God's command that all the booty was to be destroyed. Achan and his family were put to death for their deception. Then God gave the Israelites victory over the city of Ai (Joshua 8:20–28).

After capturing Ai, Joshua prepared to honor a request that Moses had made before he died. Joshua led the people to a site in central Canaan where the twin peaks of Mount Gerizim and Mount Ebal towered above the surrounding territory. Moses had instructed the people to gather here for a public reading of the law after they entered Canaan. Blessings for keeping the law were to be proclaimed to all the people from Mount Gerizim, while curses for disobeying the law were to be announced from Mount Ebal (Deuteronomy 11:29–32).

Joshua gathered the twelve tribes on the plain between these two mountains. He divided them into two groups, one in front of Gerizim and the other in front of Ebal. Then he read to all the people the blessings and curses that Moses had recorded in the book of Deuteronomy (Joshua 8:33–35).

News of Joshua's success in his central campaign against the Canaanites reached the people of Gibeon, a city about eight miles south of Ai. The leaders of Gibeon realized they would be next on Joshua's hit list unless they could fool him into giving them a pass. So they sent a delegation to call on Joshua.

These Gibeonites wore worn-out clothes and carried torn wineskins and stale bread. They pretended they were travelers from a distant country rather than residents of Canaan. Fooled by their trickery, Joshua agreed to grant them asylum and let them live in peace in the land (Joshua 9:3–15).

After he discovered their deception, Joshua honored the covenant he had made with the Gibeonites. But he sentenced them to a life of servitude as woodcutters and water carriers for the Israelites (Joshua 9:21–23). (See sidebar, "Gibeon's Awesome Well.")

Joshua's agreement with the Gibeonites was soon put to the test. The kings of five cities in southern Canaan heard about the treaty between Gibeon and the Israelites. These five kings formed a coalition army to challenge Joshua's forces. Their first move was to attack Gibeon, perhaps as a deliberate strategy to provoke the Israelites into battle.

Joshua rose to the challenge by taking his forces on an all-night march from Gilgal and launching a surprise attack on the Canaanite army. The Lord fought for Israel by sending a severe thunderstorm that pounded the Canaanites with hail. When it seemed that the Canaanites might escape under the cover of darkness, God delayed the setting of the sun to give the Israelites time to finish the fight. The result was a decisive victory for Joshua's forces in southern Canaan (Joshua 10:7–15).

With positions in central and southern Canaan now secured, Joshua turned his attention to the northern part of the land. Here he met another coalition army of several kings at a place called the Waters of Merom. Again, the Israelites were victorious because the Lord promised Joshua, "I will hand all of them, slain, over to Israel" (Joshua 11:6 NIV).

Joshua's campaigns of conquest throughout

Canaan come to a close with a list of thirty-one kings and their cities that the Israelites defeated (Joshua 12:7–24). When Sihon and Og are added (Joshua 12:1–6), this list of defeated kings comes to thirty-three. These victories were not won overnight, although the biblical text makes it seem that Canaan was subdued rather quickly. The reality is that "Joshua made war a long time with all those kings" (Joshua 11:18). Claiming the Promised Land was a process that took years rather than months.

Another fact that is clear from Israel's later history is that the conquest of Canaan was a partial accomplishment rather than a complete success. Pockets of Canaanites with their pagan gods remained after the Israelites settled the land. These caused God's people to stumble into idolatry again and again during later years.

DIVIDING THE LAND (JOSHUA 13–22)

After solving one problem—taking the land from the Canaanites—the Israelites faced another just as difficult: how to divide the land fairly among the twelve tribes. A careful study of the biblical text shows that this was done in several different ways. (See map, "The Tribal Allotments of Israel," p. 308.)

First, Joshua and Caleb as individuals had a

Hula Lake (Israel) in the spring, believed to be the waters of Merom by some scholars

special claim to part of the land. They were the two scouts from forty years before who had recommended immediate invasion of the land. Because of their faith in God's promise, each of them was awarded a captured Canaanite city with adjoining acreage. Caleb received Hebron (Joshua 14:6–15), and Joshua inherited Timnath Serah (Joshua 19:49–51).

Second, the tribes of Reuben and Gad and part of Manasseh had already been promised parcels of land on the eastern side of the Jordan River because of its fertile pasturelands. They had reached this agreement with Moses even before the Israelites entered Canaan (Joshua 13:8–33).

Third, seven of the tribes received their inheritance after the land was divided into seven districts under Joshua's supervision. He appointed a committee to survey the land, to divide it into seven portions, and to write a description of each of these sections. Then he cast lots—a method similar to drawing straws—to determine the inheritance of each tribe (Joshua 18:1–10). The seven tribes that received their inheritance in this fashion were Benjamin, Simeon, Zebulun, Issachar, Asher, Naphtali, and Dan (Joshua 18:5–19:48).

Finally, the remaining two and one-half tribes—Judah, Ephraim, and West Manasseh—were allotted property without going through the procedure of casting lots (Joshua 15; 17:1–18). Does this indicate that they received preferential treatment? Had these tribes already laid claim to their inheritance before the conquest was complete? No one knows. This is one of those puzzles of the Bible that has no neat and easy explanation.

JOSHUA'S FINAL DAYS (JOSHUA 23–24)

God's servant Joshua had now completed the work he had been commissioned to do. He had led the people into Canaan, claimed it, and divided it among the tribes. But like Moses, his predecessor, he had a few additional things to do before he faded from the scene.

Joshua called the leaders of Israel together at Shechem and led them to renew the covenant that God had made with His people. He reminded them of how the Lord had blessed them. He warned them not to associate with the pagan peoples and their false gods over whom the Lord had given them victory (Joshua 24:1–28).

died and was buried at Timnath Serah. This was the city he had been awarded because of his faithfulness to the Lord. The final verses of Joshua also record the death of Eleazar, the son of Aaron who succeeded his father as high priest of Israel. These two personalities had survived the exodus from Egypt and the years of wandering in the wilderness.

The closing verses of Joshua also record the burial of the bones of Joseph at Shechem (Joshua 24:32). When the Israelites left Egypt many years before, they had carried Joseph's

---

NT Connection—JOSEPH'S BONES: "By faith Joseph. . .mentioned the exodus of the Israelites and gave instructions concerning his bones" (Hebrews 11:22 HCSB).

The aging leader ended his speech with an inspiring declaration. "If serving the Lord seems undesirable to you, then choose. . .whom you will serve," he challenged them. "But as for me and my household, we will serve the Lord" (Joshua 24:15 NIV). The people responded, "We too will serve the Lord, because he is our God" (Joshua 24:18 NIV).

Not long after this stirring scene, Joshua

remains with them. His reburial in the Promised Land ties together Jacob's generation that left Canaan to enter Egypt with the generation that left Egypt to claim Canaan as their permanent home.

The burial of these three great leaders—Joshua, Eleazar, and Joseph—brings us to another turning point in biblical history. Next to take center stage as leaders of the Israelites were several forceful personalities known as judges.

Jael, Deborah and Barak,
Salomon de Bray (1597–1664)

CHAPTER 7
Israel under the Judges

Soon after Joshua died, the nation of Israel entered a period of spiritual decline known as the time of the judges. This era of biblical history is recorded in Judges—a book that covers about three hundred years in Israel's history, from about 1350 BC to approximately 1050 BC.

Without a strong authority figure to lead them—someone like Moses or Joshua—the people began to worship the false gods of the Canaanites and other pagan races whom they had not driven from the land. The Bible sums up this period as a time when "everyone did as they saw fit" (Judges 17:6 NIV). As punishment for their idolatry, God allowed His people to be oppressed by their enemies in and around the Promised Land.

After a period of suffering, the Israelites would repent and cry out to God for deliverance. Then the Lord would send a judge to throw off the yoke of oppression. These judges did not render decisions in legal cases, as the name implies. They were actually gifted military leaders who were able to inspire the Israelites to rise up in their own defense.

After God rescued His people through one of these judges, the Israelites would follow Him for a time, only to fall back into the same old pattern of idolatry. Then the cycle of oppression-repentance-deliverance would begin all over again. The onset of this cycle is introduced by the phrase "The children of Israel did evil in the sight of the LORD," which appears seven times throughout the book of Judges (2:11; 3:7, 12; 4:1; 6:1; 10:6; 13:1).

Thirteen judges who came to Israel's rescue are mentioned in the book of Judges. Seven of these are described in some detail, while six receive little more than a passing glance. This chapter will focus on the contribution of the "big seven" among these leaders of Israel—Othniel, Ehud, Deborah and Barak, Gideon, Jephthah, and Samson. (See map, "Israel During the Time of the Judges," p. 309.)

A TASK NOT FINISHED

No-Stress Bible Reading
Judges 1–2

No-Stress Bible Guide
Pages 71–72
(to "Othniel")

Think About It:

- Why do you think the Israelites failed in driving out all the Canaanites who lived in the land?

- Why was God angry with His people in the years soon after Joshua died?

ENEMIES WITHIN AND WITHOUT

No-Stress Bible Reading
Judges 3

No-Stress Bible Guide
Page 72
("Othniel" and "Ehud")

Think About It:

- How did pagan neighbors cause problems for the Israelites?

- How did these problems fulfill the warning of Joshua (see Joshua 23:11–13)?

- What enemies were defeated by the first two judges of Israel?

The closing chapters of the book of Judges describe the moral decay that infected Israel during this period of its history. But these days of sin and rebellion are balanced by the book of Ruth. The events described in this beautiful little book occurred during the time of the judges. So in spite of this dark time in Israel's development, God was still at work in the lives of His people.

OTHNIEL (JUDGES 3:7–11)

The first judge of Israel, Othniel, was Caleb's nephew (Judges 3:9). Perhaps some of the courage and daring of his famous uncle had rubbed off on him. When "the Spirit of the LORD came upon him" (Judges 3:10), Othniel stepped forward to oppose a king named Cushan-Rishathaim. This ruler from a country in Mesopotamia, far to the north of Israel, had oppressed God's people for eight years. With God's help, Othniel delivered Israel from this yoke of oppression.

EHUD (JUDGES 3:12–30)

Ehud, Israel's second judge, used a combination of trickery and careful planning to deliver Israel from its Moabite oppressors. He hid a knife under his clothes when he was sent to deliver tribute money to the king of Moab. He assassinated the king then fled back to Israelite territory, where he mobilized his assembled army into action. By controlling the ford across the Jordan River near Moab, he was able to rout the opposing army and break the stranglehold of Moab on the southern tribes.

DEBORAH AND BARAK (JUDGES 4–5)

Deborah, the only female judge of Israel, was a prophetess who foretold God's will for the people. She was also a clan leader who helped settle disputes among members of the tribe of Ephraim in northern Israel (Judges 4:4–5). The tree under which she sat to hear evidence and render her decisions was a landmark known as the "palm tree of Deborah" (Judges 4:5 HCSB).

a man named Sisera. This Canaanite general boasted a huge army and nine hundred iron chariots.

When no man stepped forward to face the Canaanites, Deborah took matters into her own hands. She sent for Barak, one of Israel's leaders. She used her gift of prophecy to reveal the Lord's will for Israel in this situation. God directed

NT Connection—BARAK: He is listed as one of the great heroes of the faith in the "faith chapter" of the book of Hebrews (11:32).

The threat the Israelites faced during Deborah's time arose from the Canaanites in northern Israel. Behind this oppression was King Jabin of Hazor and the commander of his army, Barak, through Deborah, to raise an army of ten thousand men and march them into battle against Sisera at the Kishon River, where the Lord would hand Sisera over to Barak (Judges 4:7).

Barak refused to lead the Israelite troops into battle unless Deborah went with him (Judges 4:8). This shows the confidence this military commander and all Israel had in this brave and daring woman.

Both Barak and Deborah realized the Israelite army would be no match for the iron chariots of the Canaanites. So they gathered their forces on higher ground near Mount Tabor and waited for the right time to make their move. When the Kishon River overflowed in a sudden rainstorm, they swooped down on the Canaanites in the valley along the riverbanks. The enemy chariots got stuck in the mud, making them easy targets for the Israelite warriors (Judges 4:4–16).

In a hymn known as the Song of Deborah, this courageous leader gave credit to the Lord and the overflowing Kishon River for this decisive victory. "The stars fought from heaven. The stars in their orbits fought against Sisera," she sang. "The Kishon River swept them away—that ancient torrent, the Kishon" (Judges 5:20–21 NLT).

But this was not the end of the story. When Sisera's army was routed by the Israelites, he fled into the territory of the Kenites, a race whom he considered allies of the Canaanites. A Kenite woman provided him sanctuary in her tent. When he fell into a deep sleep because of his exhaustion from the battle, she murdered him by driving a tent peg through his skull (Judges 4:17–21).

So Sisera was doubly humiliated that day, according to the cultural norms of his time—defeated in battle by one woman and then killed by another.

Gideon's Victory, Nicolas Poussin (1594–1665)

GIDEON (JUDGES 6–8)

The account of Gideon and his victory over Israel's enemies is probably the most familiar story in the book of Judges. It begins with a nomadic race known as the Midianites, who created a real problem for God's people. Every year at harvesttime, they rode into Israel "like swarms of locusts" (Judges 6:5 NIV) to steal their crops and livestock. This went on for seven years, and God's

warrior," the angel told Gideon (Judges 6:12 HCSB).

Gideon didn't feel like a mighty warrior, and it seemed to him that God had forgotten His people. So he asked the angel, "Why has all this happened to us if the LORD is with us?" (Judges 6:13 GNT). Through a series of miraculous signs, the angel convinced Gideon that God was still watching over His people. He insisted that

---

NT Connection—GIDEON: He is listed as one of the great heroes of the faith in the "faith chapter" of the book of Hebrews (11:32; "Gedeon" in the KJV).

---

people were reduced to a state of poverty.

When the Israelites cried out in their misery, God sent the angel of the Lord, His own personal messenger, to address this vexing problem. He appeared to Gideon, who was threshing wheat in a winepress to keep it from being confiscated by the Midianite hordes. "The LORD is with you, mighty

Gideon was the right person to lead a military campaign against the Midianite raiders.

Acting on faith, Gideon gathered a huge fighting unit from the northern tribes of Manasseh, Asher, Zebulun, and Naphtali. But the Lord thinned the army down from twenty-two thousand to ten thousand, and then finally to just three hundred warriors (Judges 7:2–7). The Lord apparently wanted to make sure the Israelites attributed their victory to Him rather than to their military might.

Along with trusting the Lord, Gideon realized the value of psychological warfare and the elements of shock and surprise. He and his force of just three hundred warriors advanced on the camp of the Midianites at night while most of them were asleep. Then, at Gideon's signal, his little army blew their trumpets and broke their pitchers with torches inside, flooding the camp in light.

The sudden noise and light convinced the Midianites that they were being attacked by a huge army. In their shock and confusion, they "set every man's sword against his fellow" (Judges 7:22). Their disorganization made them easy prey for the pursuing Israelites.

The Israelites were so impressed with Gideon's leadership that they tried to make

DECISIVE DEBORAH

No-Stress Bible Reading
Judges 4–5

No-Stress Bible Guide
Pages 72–73
("Deborah and Barak")

Think About It:

- How did Deborah's role as a prophetess influence her decision to take a stand against the Canaanites?

- Why do you think Barak refused to lead the battle unless Deborah went with him?

- In her song of victory, which tribes of Israel did Deborah praise for joining the battle?

him a king. After refusing this honor, he went on to ask the people for jewelry that he fashioned into an ephod. This was an apron-like garment similar to the one worn by the high priest of Israel. This ephod eventually became "a snare to Gideon and his family" (Judges 8:27 NIV) because it developed into an object of worship among the Israelites.

One of Gideon's sons, Abimelech, laid claim to the title of king that his father refused. He murdered seventy of his own brothers to eliminate any potential rivals to his authority. Abimelech spent most of his time trying to increase his self-imposed authority as a ruler over his own people. He died when he attacked Thebez, an Israelite city that had rebelled against him (Judges 9:50–55).

JEPHTHAH (JUDGES 11–12)

The next major judge to arrive on the scene after Gideon was Jephthah. The son of a prostitute, he was rejected by his own clan and driven into exile. But his people welcomed him back as their leader when they were threatened by the Ammonites (Judges 11:1–7).

Jephthah was filled with God's Spirit when he agreed to stand against Israel's latest enemy. But he must have felt that His presence was not enough to assure victory. So he made a vow to God. "If you will give the Ammonites into my hand," he promised, "then whoever comes out of the doors of my house to meet me, when I return. . .shall be the Lord's, to be offered up by me as a burnt offering" (Judges 11:30–31 NRSV).

To his dismay, Jephthah was greeted by his own daughter when he approached his house after defeating the Ammonites. "Oh no, my daughter!" he cried. "You have brought me down and I am devastated. I have made a vow to the Lord that I cannot break" (Judges 11:35 NIV). Jephthah apparently did keep the promise he had made in his foolish vow (Judges 11:39). He

AN ARMY OF 300 AND A FOOLISH VOW

No-Stress Bible Reading
Judges 7–8; 11

No-Stress Bible Guide
Pages 74–76
(to "Samson")

Think About It:

- What unusual test did Gideon use to reduce his army to just 300 warriors?

- How did God use an enemy soldier's dream to boost Gideon's courage?

- What demand did the king of Ammon issue to Jephthah and the elders of the tribe of Gilead?

- What does Jephthah's foolish pledge tell us about making thoughtless promises to God?

The Return of Jephthah,
Giovanni Antonio Pellegrini (1675–1741)

serves as a warning to anyone who is tempted to make a thoughtless deal with the Lord.

Another unfortunate result of Jephthah's victory over the Ammonites was that it aroused resentful that they threatened to kill Jephthah. This led to a bloody battle in which thousands of warriors from Ephraim's tribe were wiped out (Judges 12:1–7).

NT Connection—JEPHTHAH: He is listed as one of the great heroes of the faith in the "faith chapter" of the book of Hebrews (11:32; "Jephthae" in the KJV).

---

ill feelings in one of Israel's tribes. His army apparently consisted of warriors from the tribes of Gad and East Manasseh on the eastern side of the Jordan River. The tribe of Ephraim denounced Jephthah because he had not called on them to take part in the battle. The Ephraimites were so

What was Israel coming to that the tribes were warring against one another? The entire country seemed to be coming apart in a spree of violence. The time was right for the emergence of a superhero to restore the nation's confidence.

SAMSON (JUDGES 13–16)

The book of Judges devotes more space to the exploits of Samson than any other judge in the book. Perhaps this is because his is such a tragic story. A man gifted with superhuman strength, he could have become Israel's greatest deliverer.

But he failed to live up to his God-given potential.

Samson's beginning shows that he was destined for greatness. The angel of the Lord appeared to his parents, who had been unable to have a child. The angel promised they would have a son, and he would be devoted to the Lord as a Nazirite. This child's mission in life would be to deliver Israel from oppression by the Philistines (Judges 13:2–5).

A Nazirite was a person who took an oath known as the Nazirite vow. He promised to avoid worldly things and to devote himself totally to the Lord. As evidence of this commitment, a Nazirite was not to drink wine or any intoxicating beverages, and he was not to cut his hair (Numbers 6:5).

The Nazirite vow was voluntary, and it was generally taken for a limited time, perhaps thirty or sixty days. But Samson was designated as a Nazirite for life, even before he was born. This shows that the Lord had some important work for him to do.

Before Samson's judgeship, the leaders

SUPERHERO ON THE SCENE

No-Stress Bible Reading
Judges 13; 16

No-Stress Bible Guide
Pages 76–78
(from "Samson" to
"Days of Darkness in Israel")

Think About It:

• Why do you think Samson was set apart by the Lord as a Nazirite even before he was born?

• How did Samson's final prayer reflect the desire for revenge that motivated his actions?

Samson Battling with the Lion,
Lucas Cranach the Elder (1472–1553)

Statue of Samson

whom the Lord commissioned to rescue His people always rallied other Israelites to face the enemy. But Samson never used his influence to raise an army. Most of his exploits seem to be little more than acts to show off his strength or deeds to repay the Philistines for what they had done to him:

- He killed a young lion with his bare hands (Judges 14:6).

- He murdered thirty Philistines just to take their clothes to pay off a debt (Judges 14:19).

- He wiped out one thousand Philistines with the jawbone of a donkey (Judges 15:14–16).

- He walked away with part of the gate of the city of Gaza to escape a trap the Philistines had set for him (Judges 16:1–3).

In spite of his great physical strength,

Samson had one fatal weakness—sexual passion that degenerated into lust. He married a Philistine woman over the objection of his parents because of her physical attractiveness (Judges 14:1–3). He was almost caught by the Philistines while visiting a prostitute in one of their cities (Judges 16:1–2). And finally, his fatal attraction to the Philistine woman Delilah led to the first haircut of his life, the denial of his Nazirite vow, and imprisonment by his enemies (Judges 16:17–21).

But God did not give up on Samson. He gave him one last chance to accomplish what he had been appointed to do. Through divine providence, the Philistine rulers gathered at Gaza—the very city where Samson was imprisoned—to pay homage to their pagan god Dagon. They called for Samson to appear so they could mock this Israelite champion.

Samson prayed for his strength to return one final time, and God honored his prayer. Then he toppled the pillars of the building where all the Philistines were gathered. He died, along with many leading Philistine officials, in the final demonstration of his superhuman strength (Judges 16:22–30).

This superhero and supersinner of the Bible shows that God can use weak and flawed human beings to accomplish His purpose. Samson is included on the roll call of the faithful in the book of Hebrews in the New Testament (Hebrews 11:32).

DAYS OF DARKNESS IN ISRAEL (JUDGES 17–21)

These final chapters of Judges are an undated appendix to the rest of the book. They record three stories that show the spiritual depths to which Israel sank during this dark period of its history.

MICAH AND HIS IDOLS (JUDGES 17)

The first story is about Micah, a member of the tribe of Ephraim. He stole silver from his mother and used it to make two idols. He placed these in a shrine devoted to worship of these false gods, then hired a Levite to live in his house and officiate at the pagan altar.

Note the irony in Micah's actions—stolen silver fashioned into false gods that were placed in a counterfeit shrine presided over by a false priest! This account shows how the Israelites were falling under the influence of the pagan Canaanites and their depraved religious practices.

DEFECTION BY THE DANITES (JUDGES 18)

Just as Micah was getting settled into his owner-built religious system, a delegation from the Israelite tribe of Dan dropped by. They were looking for territory to add to the allotment they had received when Canaan was divided among the tribes years before. They liked Micah's religious paraphernalia, so they confiscated his idols and his fake priest.

The tribe of Dan installed these idols and the false priest in a city that they renamed Dan, after capturing it sometime later. Although this was an Israelite city, Dan became known for its idolatry. Like Micah, the Danites implemented their own priestly system (Judges 18:29–31). This was a violation of the regulations for the official priesthood of Israel.

WAR AGAINST BENJAMIN (JUDGES 19–21)

These chapters of Judges describe a case of moral depravity that almost led to the annihilation of one of Israel's tribes. When a woman was raped and murdered in a city in Benjamin's territory, the other tribes grew angry that the Benjamites did nothing about the crime. They formed a coalition army and attacked this tribe, killing thousands and burning their cities (Judges 20:46–48).

After the carnage was over, the tribes of Israel realized that the tribe of Benjamin was so devastated it might not recover. They made arrangements for the remaining Benjamite men to marry women from the clan of Jabesh Gilead

in the tribe of East Manasseh (Judges 21:6–14). Males were also given permission to claim wives from among the young women who participated in an annual festival at the city of Shiloh (Judges 21:15–23).

All Israel should have been just as concerned about the state of their nation. Many of its heroic deliverers were flawed, although God managed to use them in spite of their shortcomings. False worship was flourishing among the people. Some tribes were disregarding the clear instructions in God's law. Pettiness and jealousy were causing outbreaks of warfare among the tribes themselves. No wonder the book of Judges concludes with this sobering analysis: "In those days there was no king in Israel; everyone did whatever he wanted" (Judges 21:25 HCSB).

But just when the situation seemed hopeless, a glimmer of light turned back the darkness. God blessed His people through a humble and gracious woman named Ruth "in the days when the judges ruled" (Ruth 1:1).

LIGHT FROM THE BOOK OF RUTH (RUTH 1–4)

The story of Ruth begins with a famine in the land of Israel's tribe of Judah. To escape the famine, a man named Elimelech took his wife, Naomi, and his two sons into the adjoining territory of Moab. While they were there, one of his sons married a Moabite woman named Ruth. Tragedy struck again when all the men of the family died. Destitute and hopeless, Naomi decided to return to her hometown of Bethlehem in Judah.

Ruth insisted on going with her mother-in-law, although she was a non-Israelite who was leaving her own parents and everything that was familiar to her. Her pledge of faithfulness

to Naomi is one of the most inspiring in the Bible.

"Intreat me not to leave thee, or to return from following after thee," Ruth told Naomi, "for whither thou goest, I will go; and where thou lodgest, I will lodge: thy people shall be my people, and thy God my God" (Ruth 1:16). This pledge made it clear that Ruth was swearing her allegiance to the one true God worshipped by the Israelites.

The remainder of the book of Ruth shows how God rewarded this godly woman for her faithfulness. Through divine providence, she

Naomi Entreating Ruth and Orpah to Return to the Land of Moab, William Blake (1757–1827)

met a man named Boaz when she wound up in his field gathering leftover stalks of grain. Ruth's gleaning shows the desperate situation the two women were in; they needed this little bit of grain to keep themselves alive.

But God had something better in mind for Ruth—and through her offspring, a blessing for Israel and the rest of the world. A series of providential events led to the marriage of Ruth and Boaz. They had a son named Obed, who fathered a son named Jesse, who became the father of David, Israel's most famous king (Ruth 4:16–17). Several centuries after Ruth's time, Jesus the Messiah emerged from David's family line (Luke 3:31–32).

One of the ironies of the book of Ruth is that a Gentile woman turned out to be a model of faithfulness to God while His own people, the Israelites, were behaving more like the pagan Canaanites they were meant to dispossess and reject. Ruth also shows that there is no limit on God's love and acceptance. If He can include Gentiles like her in His plan of salvation, there is hope for all people.

Thanks to the book of Ruth, the period of the judges is not a litany of total darkness. But

there had to be a better form of government than deliverance by judges, most of whom

BACK TO BETHLEHEM

No-Stress Bible Reading
Ruth 1

No-Stress Bible Guide
Pages 80–81

Think About It:

- Why did Naomi decide to return to her home city of Bethlehem?

- Why do you think Ruth insisted on going with her mother-in-law?

- Why did Naomi ask her Bethlehem friends to call her Mara?

represented a few tribes rather than the entire nation. Would a central kingship be a better plan? This question brings us to the next stage of biblical history.

Samuel Reads the Judgments of God upon Eli's House to Eli, John Singleton Copley (1738–1815)

CHAPTER 8
"Give Us a King": The Legacy of Saul

After struggling through the dark age of the judges, the nation of Israel was eager to experiment with a new form of government. The eighth period of their history began when they asked for a king to rule over the tribes and become the new authority in the land.

The first king of Israel was a man named Saul from the tribe of Benjamin. The account of his rule appears in the book of 1 Samuel, which covers about fifty years of biblical history—from about 1050 BC to approximately 1000 BC. This book may be divided into five major sections: (1) Saul's predecessor, Samuel, (2) Saul's good beginning, (3) Saul's disobedience, (4) Saul and David, and (5) Saul's tragic end.

SAUL'S PREDECESSOR, SAMUEL (1 SAMUEL 1–7)

The selection of Saul as Israel's first king has a direct connection to the life and ministry of Samuel, one of the nation's greatest leaders. Samuel was born in answer to the prayer of his mother, Hannah, who had been unable to have children (1 Samuel 1:2).

Hannah's prayer for a child included her promise that she would devote him to the Lord's service. When Samuel was about three years old, she made good on her vow. She committed her son to the care of Eli, Israel's high priest. Samuel grew up under his supervision as an assistant at the tabernacle in the city of Shiloh (1 Samuel 1:11–28).

When Samuel was about twelve years old, he had a life-changing experience in the tabernacle as he and Eli were drifting off to sleep. The Lord called to the boy, and he thought it was Eli. But the elderly high priest told Samuel he had not summoned him and he should go back to bed. This happened two more times before Eli realized the Lord was calling the boy. So he told Samuel, "If He calls you, say, 'Speak, LORD, for Your servant is listening' " (1 Samuel 3:9 HCSB).

The message that God delivered to Samuel was a disturbing word of judgment. Eli's own sons, Hophni and Phinehas, were mishandling sacrifices that people brought to the tabernacle (1 Samuel 2:12–17). To make matters worse, Eli had not done anything about the problem. So the Lord revealed to Samuel that He Himself would deal appropriately with the matter. As God put it, "No sacrifice or offering will ever be able to remove the consequences of this terrible sin" (1 Samuel 3:14 GNT).

The next morning, Eli insisted that Samuel tell

A BOY WITH A MESSAGE

No-Stress Bible Reading
1 Samuel 2:12–25; 3

No-Stress Bible Guide
Pages 83–87
(to "Saul's Good Beginning")

Think About It:

- What profane acts were Eli's sons committing at the holy altar?

- How did God's speaking to young Samuel preview his future role as a leader of Israel?

"GIVE US A KING"

No-Stress Bible Reading
1 Samuel 8

No-Stress Bible Guide
Pages 83–87
(to "Saul's Good Beginning")

Think About It:

• What motivated the leaders of Israel to ask Samuel to appoint a king?

A KING IN HIDING

No-Stress Bible Reading
1 Samuel 9–10

Think About It:

• How did Samuel know that Saul was destined to become king of Israel?

• Why was Saul hiding "among the baggage" (1 Samuel 10:22 NLT)?

prophets in Israel's later years, including Isaiah, Jeremiah, Ezekiel, and Daniel.

It was not long before the Lord followed through on His promise of judgment against Eli and his sons. In a battle against the Philistines, Eli allowed the ark of the covenant to be taken from the tabernacle and deployed against the Philistine army. Instead of serving as a good luck charm that brought victory, the ark was captured, and Eli's sons were killed during the battle. When the elderly high priest heard about these setbacks, he fell from his chair and died from a broken neck.

After Eli and his sons died, Samuel led the Israelites to recommit themselves to the Lord in a public ceremony at the city of Mizpah. He sacrificed a lamb as a burnt offering on their behalf. This act shows that Samuel also filled the role of priest among the people.

The Philistines heard that the Israelites were gathered at Mizpah, so they seized this opportunity to launch a large-scale attack. Samuel's sacrifice calmed the people, and they rose up to drive the Philistines from the land. To commemorate the victory, Samuel set up a memorial stone near Mizpah. He named the rock *Ebenezer*, meaning "stone of help," saying, "Thus far the Lord has helped us" (1 Samuel 7:12 NIV).

Because of Samuel's association with some of Israel's battles against the Philistines, he is

him what the Lord had revealed to him during the night. Imagine how difficult it must have been for a twelve-year-old boy to repeat this sobering message of judgment to the high priest of Israel, a man who had been his friend and mentor for

NT Connection—SAMUEL: He is listed as one of the great heroes of the faith in the "faith chapter" of the book of Hebrews (11:32).

many years. But "Samuel told him everything, hiding nothing from him" (1 Samuel 3:18 NIV).

This event shows the prophetic side of Samuel's ministry. A prophet was a person called by the Lord to deliver His message to the people, no matter how unpopular this word from God might be. Samuel paved the way for other great

often referred to as the "last of the judges." This places him alongside Gideon, Samson, and others from the previous era of biblical history. Thus, Samuel combined three significant leadership roles. He was a prophet, a priest, and a judge all rolled into one.

To this impressive list of titles, we can also add another—kingmaker. When the leaders of

Israel decided they wanted to try a different form of government, they approached Samuel with their request to "appoint for us. . .a king to govern us, like other nations" (1 Samuel 8:5 NRSV).

Up to this time, the nation of Israel had not been organized along the lines of a centralized form of government. It existed as a loose tribal society, with each of the twelve tribes living to itself and minding its own affairs. The period of the judges had highlighted the weakness of this type of organization.

With no designated central leader, the individual tribes were often overwhelmed by their enemies. To turn back these threats, the gifted leaders known as judges had to raise an army of volunteers from among all the tribes. After each threat was over, the judge who led the people would fade from the scene. This process had to be repeated all over again with each new threat. The solution to this problem of irregular leadership, the Israelite leaders

told Samuel, was the appointment of a king who would rule over all the tribes.

Like a good leader, Samuel took time to think long and hard about the Israelites' request. He also made the issue a matter of prayer before the Lord. Then he approached the people with some somber warnings about what they could expect from a king. Israel's later history proved that these warnings were actually a prophecy of things to come. According to Samuel and the Lord, an earthly king would do the following:

- "take your sons and make them serve with his chariots and horses";
- "assign [your sons] to be commanders of thousands and commanders of fifties";
- appoint other sons "to plow his ground and reap his harvest, and still others to make weapons of war and equipment for his chariots";

Samuel Meets Saul on the Road,
James Tissot (1836–1902)

- "take your daughters to be perfumers and cooks and bakers";

- "take the best of your fields and vineyards and olive groves and give them to his attendants";

- "take a tenth of your grain and of your vintage and give it to his officials and attendants";

- "take for his own use. . .the best of your cattle and donkeys"; and

- "take a tenth of your flocks, and you yourselves will become his slaves" (1 Samuel 8:11–17 NIV).

In spite of these dire warnings, the people were determined to have a king to serve as Israel's ruler. When Samuel reported this to the Lord, He responded simply, "Listen to them

and give them a king" (1 Samuel 8:22 NIV). This scripture passage contains a great message: sometimes the worst thing God can do for us is give us exactly what we ask for.

Now that the question of a king for Israel had been settled, a person for the job had to be found. Through a providential combination of circumstances, Samuel was led to the man whom the Lord had selected as Israel's first king.

Samuel just happened to be making one of his regular visits to an unnamed city in Israel. The Lord revealed to him that He would send a man from the tribe of Benjamin to that town the very next day. That man was Saul—a tall, impressive young man whom Samuel should anoint as king (1 Samuel 9:2–16).

Saul was searching for his father's lost donkeys when he arrived in the city. Someone had told him there was a prophet in the town who could tell him where to find the lost animals (1 Samuel 9:1–9). Imagine his surprise when Samuel—apparently a stranger to Saul—met him and told him he also had been searching—for Saul. "Who is it that the people of Israel want so much?" Samuel asked him. "It is you—you and your father's family" (1 Samuel 9:20 GNT). In other words, "Saul, you are destined for greatness in all Israel."

Talk about a sudden turn of events. In the blink of an eye, Saul went from looking for lost donkeys to meeting a prophet who had a divine commission for his life. It must have been a little disturbing for a man who had no royal pedigree. "Am I not a Benjaminite from the smallest of Israel's tribes," he asked Samuel, "and isn't my clan the least important of all the clans of the Benjaminite tribe?" (1 Samuel 9:21 HCSB).

After assurances from Samuel that he was God's choice for the kingship, Saul was anointed by Samuel in a private ceremony (1 Samuel 10:1). Later Samuel installed him officially into the royal office in a public ceremony before all the people of Israel. They expressed their pleasure with their new monarch by shouting, "Long live the king!" (1 Samuel 10:24 HCSB).

After Samuel anointed Saul as king, his leadership role in Israel was essentially over. He did anoint David as Saul's successor when Saul turned out to be self-willed and disobedient toward the Lord in later years. Samuel also made one final appearance before the people to encourage them to shun idolatry and remain faithful to the Lord (1 Samuel 12:1–25). But for now, it was up to Israel's first king to carry on as God's chosen leader.

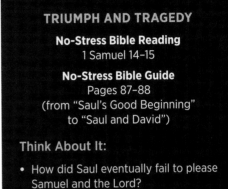

TRIUMPH AND TRAGEDY

No-Stress Bible Reading
1 Samuel 14–15

No-Stress Bible Guide
Pages 87–88
(from "Saul's Good Beginning"
to "Saul and David")

Think About It:

• How did Saul eventually fail to please Samuel and the Lord?

SAUL'S GOOD BEGINNING (1 SAMUEL 8–12; 14)

Israel's first king got off to a good start. He had not sought the office, and he showed genuine surprise and humility that he had been selected (1 Samuel 10:20–22). In addition, his commanding appearance—"head and shoulders above anyone else" (1 Samuel 10:23 NLT)—gave most of the people confidence that he could handle the responsibilities of kingship.

After he was anointed by Samuel, Saul also obeyed the prophet's instructions on how to proceed. He received power when the Spirit of the Lord came upon him. He was even given the gift of prophecy through which he could understand and proclaim God's message to others (1 Samuel 10:9–11).

From the very first, Saul also proved to be a competent military leader. When the Ammonites attacked the city of Jabesh Gilead, he raised an army of more than three hundred thousand warriors from all the tribes. He divided his army into three units and attacked the enemy camp before dawn, killing thousands of Ammonites (1 Samuel 11:1–15). This approach shows that he had the ability to organize an army and to execute an effective battlefield strategy.

Saul's resounding victory in the first battle of his career seemed to remove all doubt about his qualifications as Israel's new leader. In later years he also led successful campaigns against the Moabites, Edomites, Philistines, and Amalekites (1 Samuel 14:47–48).

But a good beginning does not guarantee long-term success. Before long the worst characteristics of Saul's personality began to surface.

SAUL'S DISOBEDIENCE (1 SAMUEL 13; 15)

Saul's biggest problems were his impatience and his disobedience of the clear instructions of the Lord. This character fault became clear during his first campaign against the Philistines. Samuel sent him to Gilgal where the Philistines

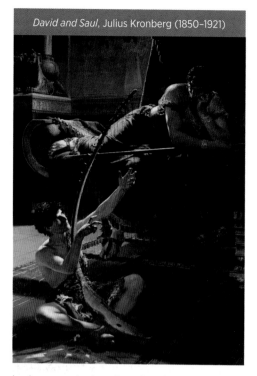
David and Saul, Julius Kronberg (1850–1921)

some of the cattle and sheep of the Amalekites as spoils of war.

To make matters worse, when Samuel confronted the king about his defiance, Saul insisted that he had done exactly as the Lord had directed. "What then is this bleating of sheep in my ears?" Samuel asked him. "What is this lowing of cattle that I hear?" (1 Samuel 15:14 NIV).

Saul claimed that he kept some of the livestock alive in order to offer them as a sacrifice of thanksgiving to God for giving the Israelites victory in the battle. "To obey is better than sacrifice," Samuel told the king, "to pay attention is better than the fat of rams" (1 Samuel 15:22 HCSB). He went on to repeat his declaration that the kingship would be taken from Saul and bestowed on one "who is better than you" (1 Samuel 15:28 HCSB).

SAUL AND DAVID (1 SAMUEL 16–27)

This one better than Saul turned out to be a shepherd boy—one of eight sons of a man named Jesse from the tribe of Judah. God sent Samuel to anoint one of Jesse's sons as the new king when it became clear that Saul could not be trusted to follow the Lord's commands.

Jesse presented each of his sons to Samuel, beginning with the oldest and working on down through the others according to age. But through God's Spirit, Samuel sensed that none of these was God's choice. Finally, Jesse's youngest son, David, was called in from the fields where he was tending sheep. When the boy appeared, the Lord told Samuel, "Arise, anoint him; for this is the one!" (1 Samuel 16:12 NKJV).

David's elevation to the kingly office was a process that took several years. The main reason for the delay was his youth. He needed time to mature before taking on such a heavy responsibility. Besides, Saul did not step aside quietly when Samuel told him his days as Israel's leader were numbered. He continued to serve

had encroached on Israelite territory. But he specifically told the new king to wait here for seven days before going into battle. Samuel promised that he would arrive by then to offer a sacrifice for Saul and his army to seek the Lord's favor in the battle (1 Samuel 10:8).

When Samuel didn't arrive after seven days, Saul decided to offer the sacrifice himself so he could get on with his battle plans. But just as he finished making the offering, Samuel arrived on the scene. He was not pleased with the king's impatience and disobedience of the Lord's directions. He told Saul that God would punish him by appointing another person as king in his place (1 Samuel 13:14).

This was not the only time Saul did as he pleased rather than obey the Lord. A little later on, Samuel directed him to attack the Amalekites and destroy their property, including all their livestock. But Saul allowed his warriors to keep as king for many years after David was set apart as his successor.

But through a series of unusual events, Saul and David got to know each other well while David was waiting in the wings to become the new king.

The first event that brought David to Saul's attention was David's victory over the Philistine giant Goliath (1 Samuel 17:56–58). The king later rewarded him for his bravery as a commander by giving him his daughter Michal in marriage (1 Samuel 18:27). The young David also served for a time as Saul's personal musician and was eventually promoted to a high-ranking officer in the king's army (1 Samuel 18:5–10).

David proved to be such a competent military officer that people began to recognize that his exploits were greater than the deeds of Saul, his commander-in-chief. One day as the king and his army were returning from the battlefield, they were greeted by women celebrating the victory over the Philistines with a song: "Saul hath slain his thousands, and David his ten thousands" (1 Samuel 18:7). This made Saul extremely jealous. From that day on he was plagued by fits of envy and jealousy that drove him to try to kill David.

Fortunately, David had allies within Saul's own family who shielded him from Saul's anger. On one occasion David's wife—the king's own daughter Michal—helped him escape from the king's assassins (1 Samuel 19:11–16).

Jonathan, Saul's oldest son, also looked out for David. He and David became good friends, and Jonathan interceded with his father on David's behalf. On one occasion Jonathan even got Saul to promise that he would not harm David. But the king eventually broke his word and resumed his vicious attacks (1 Samuel 19:4–10).

Jonathan's support of David eventually made Saul so angry that he threw his spear at his own son in a fit of anger (1 Samuel 20:32–33). This frightening incident made both Jonathan and David realize that the young claimant to the

A KING IN WAITING

No-Stress Bible Reading
1 Samuel 16–18

No-Stress Bible Guide
Pages 88–93
(from "Saul and David"
to "Saul's Tragic End")

Think About It:

- How do you see God's hand at work in the circumstances that led to the anointing of David as Saul's replacement?

- Why did David refuse to wear Saul's armor into battle against Goliath?

- Why do you think David and Jonathan, Saul's son, became such close friends?

Young David with the Head of Goliath, Caravaggio (1571–1610)

throne had to go into hiding for his own safety.

So David became a fugitive, hiding out in the wilderness of southern Israel. For many years King Saul wasted his time and the nation's military resources looking for David rather than focusing on Israel's real enemies, the Philistines.

David soon realized just how determined the king was to hunt him down. He and several men who had joined his cause came to a village known as Nob not far from Jerusalem. Ahimelech, a local priest, provided food for David and his hungry men. He also gave David a weapon—the sword he had used to kill the Philistine giant Goliath—to use in his defense.

A man named Doeg, who was loyal to Saul, witnessed Ahimelech's act of kindness to David and reported it to the king. Saul must have thought this was part of a larger conspiracy against him, so he ordered the slaughter of eighty-five priests who lived at Nob.

But the king didn't stop with this senseless slaughter. He wanted to send the message that anyone who assisted David would be dealt with as a traitor. So he sent his assassins to Nob to wipe out the families of these priests, as well as "all the cattle, donkeys, sheep, and goats" (1 Samuel 22:19 NLT).

In later years David wrote a psalm about the betrayal of Doeg that led to the death of these innocent priests. "Your tongue cuts like a sharp razor," he said about Doeg; "you're an expert at telling lies. You love evil more than good" (Psalm 52:2–3 NLT).

In spite of Saul's threats against him, David never tried to harm the king, even though he had opportunities to kill him. Once, when Saul and his soldiers were camped near David's hideout, he crept into the camp at night undetected. He got close enough to the king's sleeping form to steal his spear and his water jug.

The next day David displayed these objects from a distant hill and taunted Saul's general, Abner, about not keeping closer watch over the king. "The LORD delivered you into my hands today," David shouted to Saul, "but I would not lay a hand on the LORD's anointed" (1 Samuel 26:23 NIV). David had great respect for the kingship, in spite of the heinous crimes being committed by the current occupant of the office.

On another occasion, Saul—apparently alone—came into a cave where David and his men were hiding. The deep darkness of the cave allowed David to slip up on the king and clip off a corner of his robe. After Saul left the cave, David showed him the piece of cloth as proof that he could have killed him if he had wanted to. But again David declared, "I won't lift my hand against my lord, since he is the LORD's anointed" (1 Samuel 24:10 HCSB).

After this close call, Saul admitted that David had shown him mercy in spite of his personal vendetta against him. Grudgingly, he admitted, "I know indeed that you shall surely be king, and that the kingdom of Israel shall be established in your hand" (1 Samuel 24:20 NKJV).

MAN ON THE RUN

No-Stress Bible Reading
1 Samuel 21; 22:9–19; 24; Psalm 52

No-Stress Bible Guide
Pages 88–93
(from "Saul and David"
to "Saul's Tragic End")

Think About It:

- What does Saul's slaughter of innocent priests tell us about his character and his hatred of David and his supporters?

- Why did David refuse to kill Saul when he had the chance?

- In Psalm 52, how did David say Doeg would suffer because of his betrayal?

Had Saul really seen the handwriting on the wall? Or was this an admission of a man who stood face-to-face with his number one enemy—a brave warrior and courageous leader who could still kill him if he took the notion? Probably the latter, since the king continued his efforts to kill David after this episode at the cave.

The Bible does not tell us how many years David and Saul played cat and mouse in the wilderness of southern Israel. But it probably went on for several years. During part of this time, David served as commander of several hundred warriors who were loyal to his cause (1 Samuel 22:1–2). Guiding these men in such harsh conditions and avoiding Saul's army helped sharpen his leadership skills. He was ready for the challenge when he moved into the kingship after Saul faded from the scene.

One particular incident from David's fugitive years shows his leadership ability. A party of Amalekites raided his headquarters city of Ziklag and carried away all the women and children. The men in David's army wept for their missing relatives and began to blame him for their loss. But David sought the Lord's counsel and asked Him what to do. The Lord instructed him to begin an immediate pursuit of the Amalekites (1 Samuel 30:1–8).

David set out with six hundred men, but two hundred of this number dropped out from exhaustion. This shows that he was really pushing his men to overtake the Amalekite raiders before they got back to their own territory. Using an informant, he pinpointed the exact location of their camp and then led his men in a surprise attack. In a hard-fought, two-day battle, he defeated the raiders, retrieved the people and property they had stolen, and even confiscated additional spoils of war that

Jonathan Shooting Three Arrows to Warn David,
Frederic Leighton (1830–1896)

Death of King Saul,
Elie Marcuse (1817–1902)

the Amalekites had taken from the Philistines.

On the way back to Ziklag, David and his men picked up the two hundred exhausted warriors they had left behind. Some among his army thought these men who had not participated in the battle did not deserve a share of the booty. But David condemned their selfish attitude as an affront to the Lord, who had given them the victory. "The share of the man who stayed with the supplies is to be the same as that of him who went down to the battle," he declared. "All will share alike" (1 Samuel 30:24 NIV). This spirit of fairness served David well as the leader of God's people.

David even went one step further. When they got back to Ziklag, he sent some of the booty to several other towns throughout southern Israel as an expression of gratitude to "those in all the places where David and his men had roamed" (1 Samuel 30:31 HCSB). David's generosity was exceeded only by his shrewdness. He realized he would need the support of these towns when the time came for him to assume the kingship.

SAUL'S TRAGIC END (1 SAMUEL 28; 31)

As for Saul, his time as king was winding down. A huge Philistine army moved into central Israel, and he realized the odds were stacked against him. He sought direction from the Lord but received no answer. This should not have surprised him, since he had long since turned away from God and pursued his own willful agenda (1 Samuel 28:4–7).

In desperation, the king sought direction from a medium, asking her to call up the spirit of the deceased prophet Samuel. When Samuel's spirit appeared, Saul asked him what he should do in this desperate situation. Samuel did not give him advice, but he did tell him what was about to happen. "The LORD will hand you and the army of Israel over to the Philistines tomorrow," he told the king, "and you and your sons will be here with me" (1 Samuel 28:19 NLT).

To Saul's credit, he did pump up his courage and lead his army against the Philistines in spite of this dire prediction. On one of the peaks of the Gilboa mountain range, he and his three sons were killed, and Israel's army suffered a humiliating defeat (1 Samuel 31:1–6).

With Saul's death, this period of biblical history comes to a close. The barrier that stood between David and the kingship had been removed. Perhaps the new ruler would dodge some of the problems that had afflicted Israel's first king.

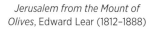
Jerusalem from the Mount of Olives, Edward Lear (1812–1888)

CHAPTER 9
David Builds a Strong Nation

David's rise to power is a rags-to-riches story. He rose from his humble beginnings as a boy tending sheep to the highest position in the land of Israel. But this didn't happen overnight. He spent many years hiding from Saul. He was content to run from the king while waiting for events to run their course before his elevation to the kingship.

The account of David's reign as king appears in the book of 2 Samuel. A second version of some of these events is included in chapters 11–29 of 1 Chronicles, along with a few passages of original material. David's tenure as Israel's ruler covers about forty years of biblical history, from approximately 1000 to 960 BC.

The major elements of David's kingship may be summarized as follows: (1) unification of the nation, (2) victories over his enemies, (3) administration, (4) music and psalms, (5) mistakes and family problems, and (6) preparations for the temple.

DAVID THE UNIFIER

After King Saul was killed by the Philistines, the nation of Israel went through a period of turmoil trying to determine Saul's legitimate successor. David was clearly God's choice for the position. But the tribes of the nation were divided on the question. The southern tribe of Judah—David's own tribe—accepted him as the new king. But the eleven northern tribes recognized Saul's son Ish-Bosheth as the heir to the throne (2 Samuel 2:2–9).

David realized this tense situation called for caution and restraint. So he settled into the kingship over Judah in the city of Hebron, where he reigned and waited patiently for seven years. He was aware that his actions were being watched carefully by the northern tribes.

The first test of David's political skills occurred when an Amalekite warrior showed up to see David after Saul's losing battle with the Philistines. This warrior claimed he had put Saul out of his misery while the king was clinging to life after being seriously wounded. The Amalekite probably expected a reward from David, since he knew about the rivalry between David and Saul.

Instead, David asked the Amalekite, "How was it you were not afraid to put forth your hand to destroy the Lord's anointed?" (2 Samuel 1:14 NKJV). Then he had the warrior executed. After this, David lamented the death of Saul and his son, Jonathan, in a psalm known as the "Song of the Bow" (2 Samuel 1:19–27). These actions sent a message to the northern tribes that he respected the office of the king and that he had nothing to do with the death of Saul.

Events among the northern tribes soon revealed that the real power in the north was not Ish-Bosheth but a man named Abner, the commander of Ish-Bosheth's army. When these two had a disagreement, Abner approached David about bringing the northern tribes under David's rule. But David's general, Joab, was suspicious of Abner's motives. He murdered Abner, thinking he was doing David a favor.

Instead, David issued a curse against Joab. "May Joab's family never be without someone who has a running sore or leprosy," he declared, "or who leans on a crutch or who falls by the sword or who lacks food" (2 Samuel 3:29 NIV).

In spite of this curse, David kept Joab on as his commander. Joab apparently had military skills that David needed during his tenure as king.

After reprimanding Joab for murdering Abner, David ordered that appropriate honor be paid to Abner in a state funeral. David himself assassinated by two of his own officials. Soon thereafter the leaders of the northern tribes met David at Hebron, pledged their loyalty to him, and anointed him king over all the tribes of Israel (2 Samuel 5:3). (See map, "David Secures His Reign Over Israel," p. 310.)

NT Connection—DAVID: He is listed as an ancestor of Jesus in the genealogies of both Matthew and Luke (Matthew 1:6; Luke 3:31). During His earthly ministry, Jesus was often referred to by others as "son of David." David is also listed as one of the great heroes of the faith in the "faith chapter" of the book of Hebrews (11:32).

---

led the funeral procession, and Abner was buried in Hebron. In this way David defused a situation that could have led to further alienation of the northern tribes. Because of his actions, "all the people and all Israel understood that day that the king had no part in the killing of Abner" (2 Samuel 3:37 NRSV).

Finally, David's patient waiting and political sensitivity paid off when Ish-Bosheth was

ONE KING AT LAST

No-Stress Bible Guide
2 Samuel 2:1–10; 5; 8

No-Stress Bible Guide
Pages 95–99
(to "David the Administrator")

Think About It:

- Why do you think David was not immediately accepted as king by all twelve tribes of Israel?

- How did David's early victories over the Philistines show that he sought and followed God's leadership?

- What did David do with the valuables that he took as spoils of war from enemy nations?

With the entire nation now under his rule, David needed a capital city on a neutral site. Hebron was too closely identified with his tenure as king over Judah. So he set his sights on Jebus, a city that belonged to a tribe of Canaanites known as Jebusites. Jebus was ideal as his new capital, since it was centrally located between Judah in the south and the northern tribes.

This ancient city was so well fortified that the Jebusites were confident it could not be captured. "You'll never get in here!" they taunted David. "Even the blind and lame could keep you out!" (2 Samuel 5:6 NLT).

But they had not counted on the tactics of a good military strategist such as David. Rather than mounting a direct attack on the city, he sent a unit of warriors through a tunnel that linked the city with an outside water source (2 Samuel 5:8). Once this party was inside, David's army captured Jebus without tearing down a single stone from its massive defensive walls. From that point on, Jebus—later renamed Jerusalem—was the religious and political capital of the nation of Israel.

One final action was necessary before the unification of Israel was complete. The ark of the covenant, the sacred chest that symbolized God's presence with His people, needed to be brought to the new capital city. For several decades the ark had been housed at the home of a private citizen not far from Jerusalem.

Accompanied by thousands of Israel's leaders, David had the ark placed on a new cart and began the slow trek toward Jerusalem. When the ark shifted on the cart, a man named Uzzah reached out to hold it steady. When he touched the sacred object, he was struck dead instantly by the Lord. Uzzah's sudden death terrified the king, and he canceled his plans to move the ark. David placed it instead in the keeping of another private citizen while he planned his next move (2 Samuel 6:6-10).

To David's credit, he either sought advice or consulted the law of Moses to determine the appropriate way to move the ark. His second attempt to move the sacred object was successful because "the Levites bore the ark of God on their shoulders, by its poles, as Moses had commanded according to the word of the LORD" (1 Chronicles 15:15 NKJV).

This incident shows one of the traits of the

The Triumph of David, Matteo Rosselli (1578-1650)

king that often got him into trouble. David sometimes made rash decisions without considering all the facts or the consequences of his actions. But unlike his predecessor, Saul, he did not persist in doing wrong when his errors were exposed. He really did try to follow the Lord's leadership in his life. His movement of the ark to Jerusalem shows that the spiritual vitality of his people was just as important to him as their political unity.

One final act of the king shows his kindness as well as his political sensitivity. After David was firmly established as ruler over all Israel, he brought a man named Mephibosheth to live under his care at the royal palace in Jerusalem. Mephibosheth, the lame son of David's friend Jonathan, was one of the last survivors of King Saul's family. David's act showed that he had not forgotten the service that Saul had rendered to the nation of Israel.

David's kindness, sensitivity, and devotion to the Lord were amply rewarded when God promised the king, "Your house and your kingdom will endure forever before me; your throne will be established forever" (2 Samuel 7:16 NIV). This was a promise of an unbroken dynasty—that a descendant of David would always reign as king of Israel.

In a physical sense, this promise was fulfilled for more than four hundred years after David's time. One of the last kings of Judah (the southern kingdom) before the nation fell to the Babylonian army was Jehoiachin, a distant descendant of David (2 Kings 24:8–19). This promise was fulfilled more significantly in a spiritual sense through Jesus Christ, the Messiah. He was called the Son of David, and He reigns eternally in the hearts of all believers.

DAVID THE WARRIOR

David's courage as a warrior is legendary. His bravery was evident even during his teenage years when he faced down and defeated the Philistine giant Goliath. But a good military leader needs more than personal courage. Above all, he must be able to recruit, motivate, and deploy an army. King David excelled in these abilities.

No passage in the Bible illustrates this better than chapters 11 and 12 of the book of 1 Chronicles. Chapter 11 gives the names of all the warriors referred to in some translations as David's "mighty men." These troops were apparently an elite unit of fighting men known for their valor in battle.

Another list of soldiers who joined David's army when he was recognized as king of all Israel appears in 1 Chronicles 12:23–37. These warriors, enumerated in round numbers tribe by tribe, brought the king's army to a combined total of more than three hundred thousand.

This huge fighting force served David well during his tenure as Israel's king. Under his leadership, they defeated the nation's major enemies, including the Philistines, the Ammonites

---

AN EYE FOR ORDER

No-Stress Bible Guide
2 Samuel 22; Psalm 18; 1 Chronicles 27

No-Stress Bible Guide
Pages 99–103
(from "David the Administrator" to "David the Temple Planner")

Think About It:

- How do you think David learned the skills he needed to organize his army and appoint his administrative staff?

- Compare 2 Samuel 22 with Psalm 18. Do you see any similarities between these two chapters?

---

and Arameans, the Moabites, the Edomites, and a territory known as Zobah. The king's multiple victories are summed up in one succinct sentence: "The Lord gave victory to David wherever he went" (2 Samuel 8:14 NRSV).

A glance at a map (see "The Extent of David's Kingdom," p. 311) shows how important these victories were to the nation of Israel. The territories of Edom, Moab, and Ammon brought large territories on the eastern side of the Dead Sea and the Jordan River under the control of Israel. The subjugation of Aram and Zobah added to Israel's jurisdiction along its northern boundary. These five acquisitions more than doubled the territory that the nation had controlled during Saul's kingship.

David's success soon attracted the attention of other nations surrounding Israel. Hiram, king of Tyre in Phoenicia, on the Mediterranean coast, provided King David with cedar logs and skilled craftsmen for the construction of David's royal palace (2 Samuel 5:11–12). This relationship paid off in future years when Hiram and Solomon, David's son and successor, worked together on several major projects.

DAVID THE ADMINISTRATOR

In addition to all his other talents, David also showed great skill as an organizer and administrator. He stationed troops in his conquered territories to keep order and suppress rebellion (2 Samuel 8:14). He appointed a cabinet of competent officials to serve as his advisers and help him run the affairs of state. These aides included a commander of the army, a recorder, a secretary, two priests, and his own sons, who served as advisers. (See sidebar, "Did David Have Bodyguards?")

Another list of the king's officials appears in the book of 1 Chronicles. This list includes counselors or advisers and foremen who looked after the royal crops and livestock (1 Chronicles 27:25–34).

Another example of David's administrative ability is his organization of the priests and Levites into units to make their service at the tabernacle more orderly and efficient. This meticulous pattern of organization is recorded in chapters 23–26 of the book of 1 Chronicles.

The king divided the priests of Israel into twenty-four units and directed that these groups preside at the tabernacle on a rotating basis. He also organized the Levites, designating different groups of them to serve as musicians, gatekeepers, treasury supervisors, and assistants to the priests at the altar.

David also came up with a plan for his army that served the nation well in times of peace as well as war. He divided his warriors into twelve units of 24,000 men each. These divisions served for one month on a rotating basis. Going on active duty one month out of the year kept the entire army on the alert and ready for action in the event of a national emergency, when all these divisions could be deployed (1 Chronicles 27:1–15).

DID DAVID HAVE BODYGUARDS?

One of David's officials was Benaiah, who was "over both the Cherethites and the Pelethites" (2 Samuel 8:18). The exact nature of his duties is unknown. But some interpreters suggest that Benaiah supervised the king's personal bodyguards. When David fled Jerusalem to escape Absalom's rebellion, he was accompanied by a large unit of Cherethites and Pelethites, along with other soldiers known as Gittites (2 Samuel 15:18).

DAVID THE MUSICIAN AND PSALMIST

One of David's greatest contributions to the religious life of Israel was as a musician and writer of psalms. He even referred to himself as the "sweet psalmist of Israel" (2 Samuel 23:1). Several of his songs appear in the book of 2 Samuel (1:17–27; 3:33–34; 22:1–51; 23:1–7) as well as the book of 1 Chronicles (29:10–13).

Several songs written by King David also appear in the book of Psalms, a collection containing many hymns sung in worship services of the Israelites. David's creations include Psalm 3, written after the rebellion of his son Absalom, and Psalm 51, his plea for forgiveness and restoration following his sin of adultery with

King David Playing the Harp, Gerard van Honthorst (1590–1656)

Bathsheba. And Psalms 89 and 132, although not written by David, are prayers of thanks for God's promise that David's kingship through his descendants would last forever.

David's most famous psalm is Psalm 23, known as the "Shepherd Psalm." The king compared God to a shepherd who looks out for his sheep. As the ultimate guide and protector, the Lord leads His people to "green pastures" and "quiet waters," where they are fed and renewed by His mercy and love. Generations of believers have found this psalm to be a source of strength during times of sorrow.

Of the 150 psalms in the book of Psalms, a total of seventy-three are attributed to David. But it is unlikely that he wrote all of these. The King James Version phrase "A Psalm of David" in the title of these Davidic psalms is rendered as "To David" or "Of David" in modern translations. The modern phrasing indicates that many of these psalms were written by other psalmists on David's behalf, or were dedicated to him, or were created in his memory. But no matter how the phrase is interpreted, David's close association with the book of Psalms is undeniable.

One of the most interesting of David's psalms appears in 1 Chronicles 16. He wrote it as a psalm of praise and thanksgiving to God after the ark of the covenant was relocated to Jerusalem. Parts of this psalm from 1 Chronicles appear in three different psalms in the book of Psalms: verses 8–22 are in Psalm 105:1–15; verses 23–33 are in Psalm 96:1–3; and verses 34–36 are in Psalm 106:1, 47–48.

This repetition shows that many of David's psalms were probably quoted or sung in worship services in Israel's tabernacle or temple. When the book of Psalms was compiled in its final form, parts of David's psalm from 1 Chronicles 16 were incorporated into three different hymns of praise in the Psalms.

DAVID'S MISTAKES AND FAMILY PROBLEMS

David's commitment to the Lord was unquestionable, but he was far from perfect. Israel's king was subject to temptation and sin just like the rest of the human race. The Bible is honest and realistic in reporting the sins that David committed and the aftermath of his mistakes.

Toward the end of his reign, David's great success became a source of pride. He ordered his commander, Joab, to conduct a census throughout all Israel. The purpose of this project was to count the number of adult Israelite males who could serve in his army. Perhaps the king was getting ready to begin another phase of military conquest to expand Israel's borders.

The Lord was not happy with this unauthorized census, probably because David was trusting in military might rather than God's promise to give Israel victory in battle. To punish the king, He sent a plague among His people, wiping out seventy thousand men who had been counted in the census. To David's credit, he accepted blame for the crisis and prayed for the Lord to show mercy. "LORD my God, let your hand fall on me and my family," the king pleaded, "but do not let this plague remain on your people" (1 Chronicles 21:17 NIV).

Since David's action had caused the plague, the Lord directed him to do something to bring it to an end. He commanded the king to build an altar on a site where a man named Araunah was threshing wheat. David bought the site and erected an altar on which he presented burnt offerings and fellowship offerings to the Lord. God honored David's prayer, accepted his offerings on behalf of the nation, and stopped

A REQUEST DENIED

No-Stress Bible Reading
1 Chronicles 22; 28

No-Stress Bible Guide
Page 103
("David the Temple Planner")

Think About It:

- Why do you think David was so eager to have the temple built during his reign?

- How do you think David might have felt when God denied his request?

A JOB FOR SOLOMON

No-Stress Bible Reading
1 Chronicles 29

Think About It:

- Do you think David was confident that his son Solomon could complete the task?

the plague (2 Samuel 24:25).

David had another moral lapse that is one of the most infamous in the Bible. The aftereffects of this sin could not be cured by the simple act of offering sacrifices on an altar on a site where grain was being threshed.

The account of David's most serious sin appears in 2 Samuel 11. It began with the king taking a relaxing stroll on the roof of his palace in Jerusalem. On the roof of a house below he spotted a beautiful woman taking a bath. His leisurely glance soon turned into unbridled lust, and he had the woman brought to his palace, where they committed adultery together.

As it turned out, this woman was Bathsheba, the wife of Uriah the Hittite—one of David's "mighty men" or brave warriors—who was away from Jerusalem on a military campaign against the Ammonites.

Bathsheba soon discovered that she was pregnant from her illicit affair with the king. In desperation, David had Uriah brought home to Jerusalem, hoping his reunion with his wife would convince him that he had fathered the child. But this scheme backfired when the loyal soldier refused to sleep with Bathsheba. Uriah's comrades-in-arms were "camping in the open fields," he told David. "How could I go home to wine and dine and sleep with my wife?" (2 Samuel 11:11 NLT).

Now the king was really desperate. The quickest way out of his tangled web of deceit was to dispense with Uriah. So he ordered his general, Joab, to place Uriah on the front lines of the battle against the Ammonites. The brave warrior was killed, and the king brought Bathsheba to the palace as one of his wives.

A sin this heinous could not go unchallenged, so the Lord sent a prophet named Nathan to confront the king. Through a parable about a poor man and his pet lamb, Nathan pointed out the seriousness of David's crime and led him to confess, "I have sinned against the LORD" (2 Samuel 12:13).

Nathan assured David that the Lord had forgiven his sin because of his repentance and confession. But the prophet made it clear that the king would not escape the consequences of his sin. His wrongdoing would sow the seed of calamity in his own household and among the members of his family.

It was not long before Nathan's prediction began to be fulfilled. The baby conceived through David and Bathsheba's adulterous relationship died (2 Samuel 12:14–19). One of David's sons, Amnon, raped his half sister Tamar (2 Samuel 13:1–4). Tamar's brother Absalom avenged her assault by murdering

Amnon (2 Samuel 13:23–38).

Most troubling of all, David's son Absalom incited a revolt among the Israelites and tried to topple his father from the throne. The king and his top officials were forced to flee Jerusalem to escape Absalom's army. They settled in the northern part of Israel, where David rallied his supporters and prepared for a final showdown with his son.

When Absalom was killed in the ensuing battle, David mourned for his son in some of the saddest words in the Bible: "O my son Absalom! My son, my son Absalom! If only I had died instead of you—O Absalom, my son, my son!" (2 Samuel 18:33 NIV).

After putting down Abaslom's rebellion, David returned to Jerusalem as king. But he never seemed to garner the widespread support he had enjoyed before his own son challenged his authority. The old animosity between Judah in the south and the northern tribes seemed to be simmering just beneath the surface (2 Samuel 19:43).

Before long another troublemaker named Sheba rallied enough support among the northern tribes to lead a revolt against the king. But Joab, David's general, managed to snuff it out before it grew into a full-fledged war (2 Samuel 20:1–22).

DAVID THE TEMPLE PLANNER

One of King David's final contributions occurred toward the end of his reign. Apparently one of his long-range goals had been to build an ornate temple to replace the tentlike tabernacle as a place of worship and sacrifice. But the Lord revealed to the king that he would not be allowed to build this structure because he had "shed much blood and waged great wars" (1 Chronicles 22:8 HCSB). This task would be accomplished by David's son and successor, Solomon.

David did not question the Lord's decision regarding who would build the temple. But he did give the project a head start by making extensive preparations for it. He knew the project would be an expensive undertaking, so he made the first large gift toward the temple's construction (1 Chronicles 29:3). This personal gift was over and above what he had already provided for the project from the nation's resources, including gold and silver from the spoils of war, iron, bronze, cedar logs, and the dedicated skills of craftsmen who could do the work.

Motivated by the king's example, the leaders of Israel also stepped forward to make generous gifts for the temple project. Then David offered a beautiful prayer of thanks to the Lord for the people's response, acknowledging that "we have only given back what is yours already" (1 Chronicles 29:14 GNT).

Before he died, King David had some words of encouragement for his son Solomon. His message to his successor shows that the building of the temple was one of the goals he was not able to reach during his forty-year reign as king. But he hoped this ambition would catch on with his son. "The LORD God. . .will be with thee," he told Solomon; "he will not fail thee, nor forsake thee, until thou hast finished all the work for the service of the house of the LORD" (1 Chronicles 28:20).

This period of Bible history comes to a close with David's passing from the scene. Solomon inherited a land of peace and prosperity, thanks to his father's competent leadership as the warrior king. Would this new ruler handle the responsibility of the kingship as well as the beloved King David? The answer to this question will emerge during our review of the next period of biblical history.

King Solomon,
Simeon Solomon (1840–1905)

CHAPTER 10
Solomon Plants the Seeds of Rebellion

When Solomon succeeded his father, David, as king of Israel, he had everything going for him. Growing up in the royal family, he must have gained some experience in how to run a country. The nation was at peace, and David's organizational skills had brought stability and prosperity to God's people. The new king had been given every advantage by his famous father.

Like David before him, Solomon served as king for forty years—from about 960 to 920 BC. The account of his reign appears in chapters 1–11 of the book of 1 Kings. Some events of his administration are also reported in chapters 1–9 of the book of 2 Chronicles.

The highlights of Solomon's tenure may be summarized as follows: (1) his beginning, (2) the building of the temple, (3) other building projects, (4) commercial enterprises, (5) his wisdom and wisdom writings, and (6) his shortcomings.

SOLOMON'S BEGINNING

Like David, Solomon did not become king without some controversy and bloodshed. David had clearly designated Solomon as his successor (1 Kings 1:28–35), although he was not his oldest son. So when it became evident that David was on his deathbed, his oldest son, Adonijah, tried to lay claim to the throne.

Solomon's mother, Bathsheba, and Nathan the prophet told the king what was going on. David promptly made it clear that Solomon was his choice as his successor. After Solomon was anointed in a public ceremony, all Israel recognized him as the new king (1 Kings 1:32–40).

But Solomon still faced a dilemma—what to do about Adonijah and his supporters. One by one, over a period of several months, he eliminated the major conspirators who had challenged his right to the throne. The first to go was Adonijah himself, who foolishly sought to marry Abishag, the woman who had been David's nurse in his old age. This gave the king the excuse he needed to have Adonijah executed (1 Kings 2:22–25).

Next on Solomon's hit list were Joab, David's former general, who had supported Adonijah's bid for the kingship; and Shimei, a relative of King Saul, who had cursed David when he was fleeing from his son Absalom's rebellion (1 Kings 2:28–46). With these troublemakers out of the way, "the kingdom was established in the hand of Solomon" (verse 46).

After this less-than-ideal beginning, King Solomon showed a better side of his nature by traveling to Gibeon to offer sacrifices to the Lord. This city, about six miles northwest of Jerusalem, may have been a major place of worship in the days before the temple was built at Israel's capital city.

While the king was at Gibeon, the Lord appeared to him in a dream. He told Solomon to ask for whatever he wanted. To the king's credit, he did not request wealth, long life, or

NT Connection—SOLOMON: He is listed as an ancestor of Jesus in Matthew's genealogy (Matthew 1:6).

victory over his enemies. He asked for godly wisdom and insight—"an understanding heart to judge Your people, that I may discern between good and evil" (1 Kings 3:9 NKJV).

The king was beginning to feel the weight of his new responsibilities. He described himself as a child or youth, although he was probably about twenty years old at the time. Still, he was green and inexperienced in comparison to his father, David. The Lord honored Solomon's request and promised to give him "a wise and an understanding heart" (1 Kings 3:12).

It was not long before Solomon's wisdom was put to the test. Two prostitutes who lived in the same house presented a child custody case before the king. Each of the two women had given birth to a child about the same time. When one of the babies died, the mother of the dead child swapped her baby for the living infant while the mother was asleep. Now both were claiming that the baby was theirs. Solomon had to decide which woman was the child's actual mother.

The king ordered an aide to bring him a sword. He directed that the baby be cut in two and half given to one woman and half to the other. This caused the child's real mother to plead for his life and to ask that he be given to the other woman, while the second woman agreed with the king's decision.

The love and compassion of the real mother told Solomon what he needed to know. He ordered that the child be given to her. This incident from early in his reign convinced all Israel that their new king had godly wisdom that would make him a good ruler (1 Kings 3:28).

THE BUILDING OF THE TEMPLE

Before he died, David had charged his son Solomon to complete the task of building the temple of the Lord in Jerusalem. David had even stockpiled some materials for the project and raised funds to support the ambitious undertaking. Four years into his reign, Solomon decided it was time to begin to fulfill his father's dream (1 Kings 6:1).

Solomon realized that Israel alone did not have the raw materials and skilled craftsmen needed to build the temple, so he entered an agreement with Hiram king of Tyre in the territory of Phoenicia. This territory was north of Israel along the Mediterranean Sea. The king of Tyre and David had worked together several years before to build David's royal palace in Jerusalem.

Hiram agreed to provide cedar logs for the temple project from the forests of Lebanon in exchange for food for his royal household. In an ingenious delivery system, Hiram floated timber down the Mediterranean Sea to a pickup point on Israel's coast. From there it was hauled overland to the construction site in Jerusalem (1 Kings 5:8–9).

The temple would also need stone for its foundation and walls. Solomon and Hiram also worked together to quarry and prepare the stones needed for this part of the project. Hiram's skilled stonecutters served as supervisors, and Solomon provided the manpower needed for this labor-intensive process.

A total of thirty thousand laborers from Israel worked at the quarries. These workmen were divided into three groups of ten thousand each, with each group working for one month every three months. Some of these workers were probably "conscripted laborers"—non-Israelites living in the land who were drafted into service by the king (1 Kings 5:13–14).

With all these workmen at his disposal, Solomon's plan was apparently to use a whirlwind approach in building the temple. The construction was completed in seven years (1 Kings 6:38). The temple itself was not that large—ninety feet long by thirty feet wide by forty-five feet high (1 Kings 6:2)—about twice the size of a typical house with a taller-than-normal profile. This modest size, when placed alongside the thousands of man hours required for its construction, shows that the king spared no expense in the building of this magnificent structure. Gold and bronze were used extensively in its construction.

Descriptions of the temple appear in 1 Kings 6–7 and 2 Chronicles 3:1–17. It is difficult to get an exact picture of the building from these two descriptions, but the text is clear about several of its distinctive features.

The entire temple complex covered an area much larger than the temple itself. The complex had a large outer court where animals were prepared and offered by the priests as burnt offerings on an ornate altar. Also in the outer courtyard was a huge basin known as the

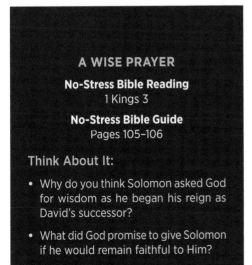

A WISE PRAYER

No-Stress Bible Reading
1 Kings 3

No-Stress Bible Guide
Pages 105–106

Think About It:

- Why do you think Solomon asked God for wisdom as he began his reign as David's successor?

- What did God promise to give Solomon if he would remain faithful to Him?

molten sea, or simply "the sea." This basin held water used by the priests for ritual washings. It rested on the backs of statues of twelve bulls. These bulls, cast from bronze, were arranged in groups of three. They faced north, south, east, and west—probably to symbolize the eternity and perfection of the Lord (1 Kings 7:23–27).

Several steps led from the outer courtyard up to a porch that stood just outside the inner part of the temple. On this porch stood two massive bronze pillars, each seventy feet high. These pillars bore the names Jakin ("He establishes") and Boaz ("in Him is strength"), symbolizing the

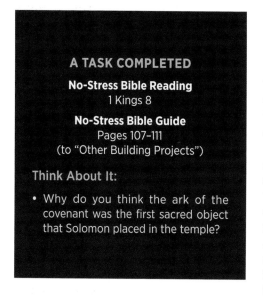

A TASK COMPLETED

No-Stress Bible Reading
1 Kings 8

No-Stress Bible Guide
Pages 107–111
(to "Other Building Projects")

Think About It:

- Why do you think the ark of the covenant was the first sacred object that Solomon placed in the temple?

true source of strength for the nation of Israel (see 1 Kings 7:15–22).

The interior of the temple was divided into two separate areas. The larger section was known as the Holy Place, a large room where only priests were permitted. Here is where ordinary sacrificial rituals occurred. The Holy Place contained a table for the bread of the presence, an altar where incense was burned, and five ornate lampstands with burning lamps.

The smaller of the two rooms in the interior

of the temple was known as the Most Holy Place, or the Holy of Holies. It was configured in the shape of a cube—forty feet long by forty feet wide by forty feet high. These dimensions were probably intended to symbolize God in all His power and holiness. This room contained the ark of the covenant, the sacred chest that represented God's presence among His people (1 Kings 6:16–28).

Another fixture in the Most Holy Place was a pair of cherubim with outstretched wings that spanned the width of the room (1 Kings 6:23–28). These angelic beings probably represented worship of the Lord and the praise that belongs exclusively to Him.

A massive curtain or veil separated the Holy Place from the Most Holy Place. This most sacred part of the temple was strictly off-limits to everyone except the high priest. And he could enter the Most Holy Place only once per year when he went in to make atonement for himself and the entire nation (Leviticus 16:1–6).

After the temple was completed, Solomon planned an elaborate ceremony to celebrate this significant event in the life of his nation. He timed the festivities to begin a week before the Feast of Tabernacles was scheduled (1 Kings 8:2). Many people from throughout the nation traveled to Jerusalem every year for this annual festival, which celebrated God's provision for His people during the wilderness-wandering years. Scheduling the temple dedication ceremony during that festival assured good attendance.

The first event on the agenda was the placement of the ark of the covenant in the Holy of Holies or Most Holy Place in the temple. Levites carried the ark to its new home, accompanied by the king, Israel's leaders, and a crowd of the nation's citizens. The priests did their part to celebrate the ark's relocation by offering sacrifices—"so many sheep and cattle that they could not be recorded or counted" (1 Kings 8:5 NIV).

When the ark was placed in the Most Holy Place, the Lord showed His presence by filling the entire temple with a cloud. This was a repetition of how He had affirmed His presence among His people when the temple's predecessor, the tabernacle, was completed several centuries before (Exodus 40:34–35).

King Solomon then led the Israelites in a prayer of dedication for the temple. This is one of the longest and most remarkable prayers in the entire Bible. The king admitted that this beautiful temple, as opulent as it was with its eye-popping gold furnishings, was nothing in comparison with the glory and eternity of the Lord. "Even heaven, the highest heaven, cannot contain You," he declared, "much less this temple I have built" (1 Kings 8:27 HCSB).

Although the king realized that no earthly building could contain the Lord, he asked God to honor the temple by blessing those who worshipped here. He mentioned several specific cases in which the Lord's blessings would be especially beneficial to His people (1 Kings 8:31–45):

- In cases before the courts of the land, God was asked to vindicate the innocent and punish the guilty.

- When the nation's army suffered defeat because of Israel's sins, God was asked to hear the people's prayers for His forgiveness.

- When the crops failed because of drought caused by sin, the Lord was requested to send rain when the people repented of their wrongdoing.

- When the land was plagued by disease, famine, or other disasters, God was asked to hear the people's prayers for His forgiveness and to intervene on their behalf.

- When a foreigner or Gentile turned to the true God, the Lord was asked to hear and answer the prayer of such a proselyte.

- When Israel went to war, God was requested to hear the Israelites' prayers and give them victory over their enemies.

Solomon's prayer also included an element of prophecy. He foresaw a time when the Lord would punish the sin of His people in a humiliating way by allowing them to be captured by a foreign enemy. When the people repented and turned to God, the king asked the Lord to "uphold their cause" and "make their captors merciful to them" (1 Kings 8:49–50 NLT).

This prophecy was fulfilled nearly four hundred years after Solomon's time when God's people were captured by the nation of Babylon. The Babylonians were eventually overrun by the Persians, who showed mercy to the Israelites by allowing them to return to their homeland.

Soon after the temple dedication was over and all the people had returned to their homes, the Lord appeared to Solomon in a dream. This dream was similar to the one in which God had appeared to the king at the beginning of his reign. God renewed the promise He had made to Solomon's father, David, that one of David's descendants would always rule over

Dream of Solomon, Luca Giordano (1634–1705)

Israel. The Lord made it clear that this promise also applied to Solomon and his descendants (2 Chronicles 7:17–18).

But God made it equally clear that this promise to Solomon and all Israel depended on the faithfulness and obedience of the nation. If the people turned away from the Lord and worshipped false gods, He would bring disaster on the land as punishment for their sins (2 Chronicles 7:19–22).

OTHER BUILDING PROJECTS

With the temple completed, King Solomon turned his attention to other building projects. The first phase of this building frenzy included the construction of his royal palace and a public building for the administration of his kingdom. These structures were probably erected in the same general area as the temple.

Solomon's father and predecessor, King

NT Connection—THE TEMPLE: Jesus showed His regard for the temple as a place of worship by driving out merchants and money changers who had turned it into a marketplace (Mark 11:15–17).

David, had also built a royal palace (2 Samuel 5:11–12). But Solomon apparently thought a more ornate structure was needed to reflect the glory of his kingdom. Thirteen years were devoted to the construction of his personal residence—six years more than was required to build the temple (1 Kings 6:38; 7:1).

Solomon's public administration building was apparently the structure referred to as the "house of the forest of Lebanon" (1 Kings 7:2). This name may refer to the cedar wood from Lebanon that was used in its construction. This building contained the Hall of Justice, where the king rendered decisions in judicial cases that were brought to his attention (1 Kings 7:7 NIV).

The furnishings of the house of the forest of Lebanon show that Solomon spared no expense in the construction of this building. It contained two hundred large ornamental shields and three hundred small decorative shields, all overlaid with gold.

This building also contained the king's ornate throne that was inlaid with ivory and overlaid with gold (1 Kings 10:18). Ivory, made from the tusks of elephants, was a rare and expensive item generally found only in royal palaces and homes of the very wealthy. Solomon's throne was reached by climbing six steps. Statues of twelve lions, representing royalty and majesty, stood on both sides of these six steps (1 Kings 10:19–20).

The king also built a residence for his Egyptian wife in the same general area where his palace and administration building were located. He had married this daughter of the Egyptian pharaoh early in his reign to seal an alliance with Egypt (1 Kings 3:1). This house built especially for her—his most prestigious political wife—gave her living quarters that were worthy of her prestige.

Solomon was fortunate that he served as king during a time of peace in Israel. But this did not prevent him from building up his military defenses. He focused his defense-oriented construction in several key cities throughout the nation to provide protection from Israel's enemies.

The king built one city from the ground up. Known as Tadmor, it was located along the extreme northern border of Israel. Tadmor sat on the main east-west trade route that ran from Mesopotamia into Israel. This city grew into an important commercial and military outpost. Solomon may have collected taxes from

BOUNTIFUL BUILDER

No-Stress Bible Reading
1 Kings 7:1–12; 10:18–19;
2 Chronicles 8:1–6

No-Stress Bible Guide
Pages 111–112
("Other Building Projects")

Think About It:

- Do you think Solomon's lavish lifestyle is a reflection of his true character? Why or why not?

- Why did Solomon need "store cities" as well as "chariot cities?"

trading caravans that passed through Tadmor (2 Chronicles 8:4).

About twenty miles northwest of Jerusalem, Solomon fortified twin cities known as Upper Beth Horon and Lower Beth Horon (2 Chronicles 8:5). These cities, just a few miles apart, sat at the upper and lower ends of a steep descent through the mountains about halfway between Jerusalem and the Mediterranean Sea. These walled cities were a strategic defense against an attack on Jerusalem from the west.

The king also strengthened the walls of three other key cities throughout the nation. These were Hazor, in Israel's far north; Megiddo, in Israel's northwest corner; and Gezer, west of Jerusalem (1 Kings 9:15). Solomon wanted to make sure Jerusalem was well protected, particularly from the north—the capital city's most vulnerable side.

In addition to strengthening these walled cities for Israel's defense, Solomon also built up and designated certain cities throughout the land as "store cities" (2 Chronicles 8:6). These cities may have held military supplies. Or they could have been used as storehouses for goods to support the king's lavish lifestyle and ambitious building projects.

Other passages in 1 Kings and 2 Chronicles show clearly that Solomon made heavy demands on his people to support his administration. He divided the nation into twelve administrative districts. The citizens of each of these districts were required to supply the king with what he needed to run the central government for one month out of the year (1 Kings 4:7-28).

Each of these twelve districts had a governor or administrator appointed by the king. This organization did an end run around tribal loyalties, thus assuring Solomon that the officials in charge of collecting supplies were always loyal to him. It's possible that these goods were gathered into the king's store cities before being forwarded on to his headquarters in Jerusalem.

LIFE AT THE TOP

No-Stress Bible Reading
1 Kings 10:1-15; 2 Chronicles 9:21-28

No-Stress Bible Guide
Pages 113-115
(to "Solomon's Shortcomings")

Think About It:

- In Solomon's trading ventures, what did he bring into Israel?

- Do you think the queen of Sheba was more impressed with Solomon or the nation he'd built?

A KING GONE WRONG

No-Stress Bible Reading
1 Kings 11

No-Stress Bible Guide
Page 115
("Solomon's Shortcomings")

Think About It:

- What was the main problem that grew out of Solomon's marriages with women from several pagan nations?

- Why do you think Solomon eventually turned away from the Lord and began to worship false gods?

COMMERCIAL ENTERPRISES

King Solomon made a major contribution to his nation by developing trade relationships with surrounding nations. Some of this trade was conducted by land through camel caravans. But the most important commercial enterprise was carried out by water via the Mediterranean Sea. This enterprise came about through an alliance with Hiram, the same king of Tyre who had supplied cedar lumber for the temple. Hiram apparently provided the ships that Solomon used for his international trading ventures (1 Kings 10:22).

Solomon eventually ruled over a vast commercial empire. His ships apparently went as far west as Spain to bring back gold, silver, and ivory (2 Chronicles 9:21). Archaeologists have uncovered an old mine in ancient Ethiopia that may have been one of the king's sources of silver.

The point of embarkation for Solomon's ships was Ezion Geber in southern Israel, along with a neighboring city known as Elath on the modern Gulf of Aqaba (1 Kings 9:26 NIV). Archaeologists believe the area near Ezion Geber eventually developed into a center for the mining and smelting of copper. Excavations at the site have yielded evidence of smelting furnaces dating back to King Solomon's time.

The success of Solomon's trading ventures may have been the reason the queen of Sheba paid him a visit. Perhaps she wanted to enter a trade agreement with Israel. She had heard amazing stories about Solomon's empire, but she told the king, "Your wisdom and prosperity far surpass the report that I had heard" (1 Kings 10:7 NRSV).

Solomon and the Queen of Sheba, Giovanni De Min (1786–1859)

SOLOMON'S WISDOM WRITINGS

King Solomon developed quite a reputation as a writer of proverbs and other wise sayings. The writer of 1 Kings declared, "The whole world wanted an audience with Solomon to hear the wisdom that God had put in his heart" (1 Kings 10:24 HCSB). This may be a bit overstated, but there is little doubt that he was a prolific writer of a distinctive type of literature known as wisdom writings. He is credited with composing 3,000 proverbs and 1,005 songs (1 Kings 4:32).

Solomon either wrote or contributed to three wisdom books in the Bible: Proverbs, Ecclesiastes, and the Song of Solomon. These are classified as wisdom writings because they deal with important issues such as the meaning of life and behavior that leads to happiness and contentment in daily living.

THE BOOK OF PROVERBS

The very first verse of this book identifies the author as "Solomon the son of David, king of Israel" (Proverbs 1:1). But some chapters within the book are attributed to other writers, including Agur (Proverbs 30:1) and King Lemuel (Proverbs 31:1). King Solomon probably wrote the basic core of Proverbs but added some writings from other sources and gave proper credit to their writers.

This book is the most practical, down-to-earth book in the Old Testament. It contains wise sayings on how to live in harmony with God as well as other people. The underlying theme of Proverbs is that true wisdom consists in showing respect for God and living in harmony with His commands. It reads like a manual of instruction for daily life, even using occasional humor to make an important point: "A person who. . .meddles in a quarrel that's not his is like one who grabs a dog by the ears" (Proverbs 26:17 HCSB).

THE BOOK OF ECCLESIASTES

The author of Ecclesiastes identifies himself in its first verse as "the Preacher, the son of David, king in Jerusalem" (1:1). The theme of Ecclesiastes appears in the very next verse: "Meaningless! Meaningless! . . . Utterly meaningless! Everything is meaningless" (1:2 NIV). Solomon wanted his readers to understand what he had learned

The Shulamite, Albert Joseph Moore (1848–1893)

through his own personal experience—that all human achievements are empty and unfulfilling when pursued as ends in themselves.

Solomon probably wrote Ecclesiastes as his life drew to a close—perhaps as a disillusioned old man—and he looked back and measured the meaning of all his achievements. The book shows that earthly possessions, popularity, and great accomplishments do not bring lasting happiness. True joy is a result of serving God and following His will for our lives. As the king put it in the book's final verse, "Fear God and obey his commands, for this is everyone's duty" (12:13 NLT).

THE SONG OF SOLOMON

This book is also referred to as "Solomon's Song of Songs," perhaps because it was his favorite or the most important among all the songs he wrote. This is significant because he is credited with writing more than a thousand songs.

Perhaps this was the king's favorite song because it describes his love for a young woman whom he refers to as the "Shulammite" (6:13 NIV). Solomon had hundreds of wives and concubines in his harem. But many of these were political marriages to seal treaties with other nations.

This book leads Bible students to ponder an interesting question: Is it possible that Solomon's relationship with the Shulammite—a peasant vineyard keeper whose skin had been darkened by long exposure to the sun (1:5–6)—was the only meaningful and intimate marriage he ever had? No one knows, of course. But his love for this woman from a humble background is undeniable.

SOLOMON'S SHORTCOMINGS

Although King Solomon was noted for his wisdom, he made some very foolish decisions. Some of his lapses in judgment would even have to be categorized as dumb mistakes and fatal sins.

One of his worst mistakes was building a harem of seven hundred wives and three hundred concubines (1 Kings 11:3). His foreign wives, most of whom he married for political reasons, made many demands on the king. He allowed them to worship their pagan gods to the point where his faith in the one true God began to weaken.

Finally, he himself succumbed to worship of some of these gods (1 Kings 11:5). Because of his lapse into idolatry, the Lord told the king He would tear his kingdom from him and give it to one of Solomon's subordinates (1 Kings 11:11). This would happen after Solomon died. God also promised that part of the nation would remain faithful to David's line because of the promise of an eternal kingship that He had made to David.

Solomon's lavish lifestyle and his expensive government bureaucracy were other serious problems. To support these, he placed a heavy burden of taxation on his people. In the last years of his reign, the nation began to come apart as a spirit of rebellion spread throughout his kingdom (1 Kings 11:14–25).

Solomon's reign came to an end with his death and the elevation of his son Rehoboam to the throne (1 Kings 11:41–43). Would Rehoboam be able to calm the stormy waters and continue to rule over a united Israel? We will discover the answer to this question as we examine the next period of biblical history.

CHAPTER 11
The Rise and Fall of the Northern Kingdom (Israel)

Soon after Solomon's death, the ten northern tribes of his kingdom rebelled and formed their own nation known as Israel. The two southern tribes, Judah and Benjamin, remained loyal to Solomon's son and successor, Rehoboam. This nation, the Southern Kingdom, became known as Judah. (See map, "The Kingdom Divides," p. 312.)

The history of these two separate kingdoms appears in chapters 12–22 of 1 Kings, the book of 2 Kings, and chapters 10–36 of 2 Chronicles. This history is hard to follow because the biblical narrative often switches back and forth between Israel and Judah. This intermingling of events, without any warning about which kingdom is being discussed, causes confusion for many Bible students.

The names of the kings of these two nations present another dilemma. Both Israel and Judah had three kings with the same name (Ahaziah, Jehoahaz, and Joash). And even within the same nation, some kings had dual names. For example, Israel's king Joram was also known as Jehoram, and Judah's king Uzziah is also referred to as Azariah.

To bring order out of this confusion, the interwoven biblical history of these two nations has been separated into two chapters, one focusing on Israel (this chapter) and the other following the ups and downs of Judah (chapter 12).

As you work your way through these two chapters, use the separate charts of the kings of Israel (see below) and Judah (see chapter 12, p. 135–36) to follow the interesting history of these two nations. This chapter discusses the high points of Israel's two-hundred-year existence, from about 920 to 722 BC. Chapter 12 will focus on the major events in the parallel history of Judah.

KINGS OF THE NORTHERN KINGDOM (ISRAEL)

KING	LENGTH OF REIGN	SCRIPTURE
1. Jeroboam I	22 years	1 Kings 12:20–14:20; 2 Chronicles 10:2–15; 13:1–20
2. Nadab	2 years	1 Kings 14:19–20; 15:25–31
3. Baasha	24 years	1 Kings 15:16–17, 32–34; 16:1–7; 2 Chronicles 16:1–6
4. Elah	2 years	1 Kings 16:8–14
5. Zimri	7 days	1 Kings 16:15–20
6. Omri	12 years	1 Kings 16:21–28; Micah 6:16
7. Ahab	22 years	1 Kings 16:29–22:40; 2 Chronicles 18:1–34
8. Ahaziah	2 years	1 Kings 22:51–53; 2 Kings 1:1–18
9. Jehoram/Joram	12 years	2 Kings 1:17; 3:1–27; 9:14–26

10. Jehu	28 years	2 Kings 9:13–10:36; Hosea 1:4
11. Jehoahaz	17 years	2 Kings 13:1–9
12. Joash/Jehoash	16 years	2 Kings 13:10–13; 14:8–15; 2 Chronicles 25:17–24
13. Jeroboam II	41 years	2 Kings 14:23–29; Hosea 1:1; Amos 1:1; 7:9–11
14. Zechariah	6 months	2 Kings 15:8–11
15. Shallum	1 month	2 Kings 15:13–15
16. Menahem	10 years	2 Kings 15:16–22
17. Pekahiah	2 years	2 Kings 15:23–26
18. Pekah	20 years	2 Kings 15:27–31; Isaiah 7:1
19. Hoshea	9 years	2 Kings 15:30; 17:1–6

The major events of Israel's existence as a separate nation may be outlined as follows: (1) the northern rebellion, (2) Israel's early years, (3) Israel's middle years, (4) Israel's final years, and (5) writing prophets of the Northern Kingdom.

REBELLION OF THE NORTHERN TRIBES

One cause for the separation of Solomon's kingdom into two factions was the long-simmering animosity between the north and the south. This was evident as far back as King David's time. He ruled for seven years in the south before being accepted by the northern tribes as king over the entire nation (1 Kings 2:10–11).

This north-south distrust reached its peak during Solomon's administration. He placed a heavy taxation burden on all his constituents to support his lavish lifestyle in the nation's capital city. When Solomon died, the northern tribes sent a delegation to Jerusalem to confer with the king's son and successor, Rehoboam. They made it clear that their continuing support depended on Rehoboam's relaxation of these burdensome policies.

"Your father put a heavy yoke on us," they told the new king, "but now lighten the harsh labor and the heavy yoke he put on us, and we will serve you" (1 Kings 12:4 NIV).

Rehoboam consulted with his advisers, listening to the young members of his staff who advised him to continue Solomon's policies. The king told the northern tribes he had no intention of making a change—indeed, that things would only get worse. "My father scourged you with whips," he told them; "I will scourge you with scorpions" (1 Kings 12:14 NIV).

The young king's foolish response drove the northern tribes to rebel against his authority and to form their own separate nation. Their leader and Israel's first king was a man named Jeroboam. A former official in Solomon's administration, he had fled to Egypt when it became clear that the northern tribes were forming a coalition around him to oppose Solomon. When he returned from Egypt after Solomon died, he became king of this breakaway nation in the north (1 Kings 11:27–40; 12:1–3, 22–24).

The land area of this new nation was larger than Judah's, and its population was more numerous than the Southern Kingdom's. Israel was also better situated for trade with other nations, and its soil yielded more abundant crops.

But these advantages were offset by some distinct problems. Israel had no capital city, no standing army, and little organization. The priesthood and the people's center for worship, the temple, were located in Jerusalem, in the Southern Kingdom.

A comparison of the charts of the kings of these two nations also reveals that the Northern Kingdom suffered from instability, in comparison to the Southern Kingdom. Seven of the nineteen northern kings ruled for less than four years. Several of these short-term kings were assassinated by claimants to the throne. None of the northern kings were lineal descendants of David. By contrast, all twenty rulers of Judah descended through David's family line. In general, these southern kings ruled over a stabler government than that of their sister kingdom to the north.

So Israel got off to a shaky start with a rebellious king. The Northern Kingdom's destiny depended on how Jeroboam and his successors handled the challenges of building a new nation in the north.

ISRAEL'S EARLY YEARS

During the first five decades or so of Israel's history, five different kings ruled over the nation. These were crucial years that set the stage for the type of nation the Northern Kingdom would become.

KING JEROBOAM I

The first king of Israel is referred to as Jeroboam I to set him apart from another Jeroboam who ruled in the nation's later history. Jeroboam I got off to a strong start by selecting Shechem as his capital city. This walled city occupied the site where Jacob had erected an altar devoted to worship of the Lord many centuries before Jeroboam's time (Genesis 33:18–20). But Shechem was too close to Jerusalem, Judah's capital, to become Israel's permanent chief city. In later years Shechem was replaced by Tirzah, and then finally by Samaria—a city farther to the west.

Early in his reign Jeroboam spent too much time and effort in a fruitless conflict with Judah, the Southern Kingdom. Rehoboam, Judah's king, apparently went to war with Israel to try to force the breakaway nation back into union with Judah. The Bible describes these conflicts as "war between Rehoboam and Jeroboam all their days" (1 Kings 14:30). But Rehoboam's efforts failed, and Israel continued to exist as a separate nation.

The thing for which Jeroboam is most remembered is a mistake that haunted Israel for the rest of its days. He grew concerned that his subjects would continue to travel to Jerusalem, Judah's capital, to worship the Lord at the temple. So he set up two competing sanctuaries for worship in his own territory—one at Bethel in southern Israel and the other at Dan in the northern section of the country (1 Kings 12:28–30).

At these sanctuaries he set up two gold-plated calves, probably intended to replace the ark of the covenant in Jerusalem, which was associated with God's presence in the minds of the people. This act by the king was purely political; he wanted to direct the people's religious commitment away from Jerusalem to these worship centers in the north. But they proved to be the crack in the dike that led to outright idol worship in the Northern Kingdom in its later years.

The Coronation of Zimri, from *Chronicle of the World* by Rudolf von Ems (c. 1200–1254)

The Lord was not pleased with these counterfeit worship centers. Through a prophet named Ahijah, He informed Jeroboam that his dynasty would not last because the king had rejected the Lord and led his people to worship false gods (1 Kings 14:7–13).

KING NADAB

After his death, Jeroboam was succeeded by his son Nadab. During his reign of only two years, Nadab went to battle against the Philistines. These ancient enemies of God's people had been subdued by David about seventy years before, but they apparently regained strength when the nation split into two competing factions. Jeroboam's short dynasty came to an end when a man named Baasha assassinated Nadab and the rest of Jeroboam's descendants and occupied the throne (1 Kings 15:27–31).

KING BAASHA

Baasha ruled over Israel for twenty-four years. Most of what is known about him is intertwined with the reign of his contemporary in the south, King Asa of Judah. Baasha and Asa went to war in a battle for supremacy over the territory covered by the two separate nations. Asa even enlisted the help of Ben-hadad of Syria in his battles with Baasha, but he was not able to conquer Israel (2 Chronicles 16:1–6). When Baasha died, his son Elah succeeded him as king of Israel.

KING ELAH AND KING ZIMRI

The combined reign of these two kings lasted only two years and seven days. About two years after Elah became king, one of his own officials—a man named Zimri—plotted against him. Zimri assassinated the king while he was in a drunken stupor and assumed the throne, only to be attacked a few days later by the army of Israel under the command of a man named Omri.

While under attack in the royal palace, Zimri burned the house down around him and committed suicide, thus ending his reign of only seven days. His was the shortest reign of any king of either Israel or Judah (1 Kings 16:18).

Upon Zimri's death, Omri and a man named Tibni struggled with each other to lay claim to the kingship. Omri's forces eventually prevailed, and he became the sixth king of Israel (1 Kings 16:21–22).

KING OMRI

Omri's greatest contribution to Israel during his twelve-year-reign was the building of a new capital city. He decided to build his headquarters city from the ground up on a high hill in the central part of the nation. This site became known as Samaria. It was named for Shemer, the man from whom the king bought the hill on which the city was built.

Some time before Omri became king, the nation's capital had been moved from Shechem to Tirzah. After reigning at Tirzah for six years, Omri decided to relocate to Samaria's more defensible position just a few miles away. Excavations at Tirzah's ruins have uncovered buildings that were started but never finished. Archaeologists speculate that these were abandoned in mid-construction when the king decided to move to a new location.

Samaria sat on a three-hundred-foot-high hill that gave it good protection on all sides from an enemy attack. The city resisted a three-year siege before finally falling to the Assyrian army about 150 years after Omri's time. So King Omri chose wisely when he selected this location for his new capital city.

But Omri's contribution to the security of his nation was offset by his spiritual mistakes. He continued the practices of his predecessors that led the people of Israel away from God and plunged them into worship of false gods. The writer of 1 Kings gives this sad summary of the king's reign: "Omri wrought evil in the eyes of the LORD, and did worse than all that were before him" (1 Kings 16:25).

BAD LEADERS IN ISRAEL, ONE AFTER ANOTHER

No-Stress Bible Reading
1 Kings 13:33–34; 14:25–26, 33–34; 16:12–13, 18–19, 25–26

No-Stress Bible Guide
Pages 117–121

Think About It:

- What sin of Jeroboam set the tone for all the kings of Israel who followed him?

- Why was God so angry with this particular sin?

Just when it seemed that things couldn't get any worse in Israel, they did. Omri passed his legacy of wrongdoing on to his son and successor, Ahab—a king whose very name conjures up images of wickedness, idolatry, and injustice.

ISRAEL'S MIDDLE YEARS

The middle years of Israel's history cover about one century. These years began with the twenty-two-year reign of Ahab. The Bible devotes more space to his reign than any other king of Israel either before or after his time (1 Kings 16:29–22:40), perhaps because of his outright promotion of idol worship. Six other kings also ruled over Israel during this period. These middle years, while spiritually corrupt, were a time of political stability and material prosperity in the nation.

KING AHAB

Ahab's biggest mistake was his marriage to Jezebel, the daughter of a king of Sidon, a country that lay along Israel's northern border. This was probably a political marriage to seal an alliance with this pagan king.

Jezebel, a worshipper of the pagan gods Baal and Ashtoreth, led Ahab to establish a temple devoted to Baal worship in Israel's capital city, Samaria (1 Kings 16:32). She also openly promoted Baal worship throughout the land, apparently with the king's blessing. (See sidebar, "Baal and Ashtoreth.")

BAAL AND ASHTORETH

Baal, the chief pagan god of the Sidonians and Phoenicians, was thought to provide fertility for crops and livestock. As a symbol of the productive forces of nature, he was often worshipped through immoral sexual practices with temple prostitutes.

Ashtoreth, a pagan goddess of sensual love and fertility, was often considered Baal's companion or partner. An "Asherah pole" (1 Kings 16:33 NIV) was probably a wooden image of this pagan goddess.

The Lord could not allow Ahab's wicked acts to go unchallenged, so He raised up a messenger to confront the king. Ahab must have been shocked when a courageous prophet named Elijah appeared out of nowhere and declared, "There will be no dew or rain for the next two or three years until I say so" (1 Kings 17:1 GNT).

After delivering this message of judgment, Elijah was ordered by the Lord to hide in the wilderness area along the Jordan River, apparently to escape the king's wrath. While the land suffered from famine, Elijah was miraculously kept alive by ravens that brought him food. The Lord also sustained His prophet through a miraculous preservation of the meager food supply of a kind widow in the territory of Sidon (1 Kings 17:2–16).

After the famine had lasted for three years, God told Elijah to appear before Ahab with the news that rain would soon descend on the land. But first Elijah would challenge the system of false worship that Ahab and Jezebel had promoted throughout Israel. The king agreed to summon the prophets of Baal from throughout the land and have them face off against the Lord's prophet in a contest at a place known as Mount Carmel.

Elijah and the prophets of Baal placed a sacrificial animal on a pile of wood. Each side took turns calling on their god to consume the sacrifice. First up were the Baal competitors, who danced around the altar for several hours, shouting, "Baal, answer us!" (1 Kings 18:26 NIV).

When Baal did not respond, Elijah taunted them about their god's lack of action. Perhaps he was silent, the prophet suggested, because he was preoccupied with other matters, was away on a journey, or was taking a nap (1 Kings 18:27). Elijah's comments sent the false prophets into a frenzy, and they began to cut themselves with knives. But still their god Baal did not make a move toward the altar.

Elijah called on the Lord not with pleas and shouts but with a quiet prayer for His intervention. Fire fell immediately from heaven and consumed the sacrificial animal on the altar (1 Kings 18:38), proving that God heard the prayers of His people and was superior to the false god Baal. (See sidebar, "Elijah on Mount Carmel.")

Elijah followed up this dramatic victory by having these false prophets executed in the valley below Mount Carmel (1 Kings 18:40). This kindled the wrath of Jezebel, and the prophet had to flee for his life. God assured him that he was not alone in his opposition to Israel's idolatry, that he could count on the Lord's presence, and that God still had work for him to do. Then the Lord sent Elijah to anoint a person to replace Ahab as king and to appoint the prophet Elisha as his successor (1 Kings 19:15–21).

Meanwhile, King Ahab was showing that false worship was not the only defect in his character. His greed, along with Jezebel's treachery, led him

ELIJAH ON MOUNT CARMEL

The place where Elijah's epic contest with the prophets of Baal took place is believed to be a high point near the Mediterranean Sea known as Keren Carmel ("Horn of Carmel"), so named because this peak stands out like an animal's horn from the surrounding territory. Here a Catholic order known as the Carmelite monks have built a monastery and a little church to commemorate Elijah's victory at this site.

In the church courtyard stands a statue of Elijah with upraised sword. The statue symbolizes the mass execution of the false prophets at Elijah's command.

to have an innocent man—a landowner named Naboth—put to death. It was all part of their plot to confiscate Naboth's prized vineyard near Ahab's summer palace in the city of Jezreel (1 Kings 21:1–16).

The Prophet Elijah, Daniele da Volterra (1509–1566)

Such an injustice did not escape the Lord's attention. He sent Elijah to confront the king and announce his punishment for such a heinous crime. "In the place where dogs licked up the blood of Naboth," the prophet told Ahab, "dogs will also lick up your blood" (1 Kings 21:19 NRSV).

several years later when King Ahab was seriously wounded in a battle against an enemy nation known as Aram, or Syria. The king died in his chariot after bleeding profusely for several hours. After the battle his chariot was returned to Samaria for cleanup. As his blood was flushed

NT Connection—ELIJAH: When Jesus was transfigured before His disciples, Elijah—along with Moses—appeared on the scene (Mark 9:2–4; "Elias" in the KJV). Elijah showed that Jesus was the last in a long line of prophets whom God had sent to His people. Moses' appearance signified that Jesus was the fulfillment of the Old Testament law.

The Lord also made it clear that Jezebel would pay for her part in the crime as well as her other wicked deeds in Israel. The day would come when dogs would eat her body in the city of Jezreel (1 Kings 21:23).

These gruesome predictions were fulfilled

away, "the dogs licked up his blood, as the word of the LORD had declared" (1 Kings 22:38 NIV).

Jezebel's death was even more gruesome. She was tossed from the window of Ahab's summer palace in Jezreel when Ahab's dynasty came to an end with the accession of Jehu to the throne. Her body was trampled by the horses of Jehu's army. Most of her body apparently was eaten by dogs, since "they went to bury her, but they found no more of her than the skull and the feet and the palms of her hands" (2 Kings 9:35 NKJV).

Contrast these grisly death scenes with the passing of God's prophet Elijah. After a ministry devoted to the Lord's service, Elijah appointed another prophet, Elisha, as his successor. Then Elijah was taken into heaven in the midst of a whirlwind (2 Kings 2:11).

Elisha picked up where Elijah left off. His prophetic ministry occurred during the final years of King Ahab's reign as well as the administrations of several succeeding kings of Israel. He was not as forceful in his opposition to the actions of the kings as Elijah was. He is best known as a worker of miracles, with more than a dozen attributed to him in the book of 2 Kings. Here is a list of his most spectacular miracles.

TWO PROPHETS AT WORK

No-Stress Bible Reading
2 Kings 2:1–15

No-Stress Bible Guide
Pages 122–125 (through "Miracles of the Prophet Elisha")

Think About It:

- How do you think Elijah knew it was time to turn his prophetic ministry over to Elisha?

- Why do you think Elisha asked Elijah for a double portion of his spirit?

- How did Elisha continue the work of his predecessor?

- Why do you think miracles were so prominent in Elisha's work as a prophet?

MIRACLES OF THE PROPHET ELISHA

MIRACLE	SCRIPTURE
1. Purified the bad waters of a spring	2 Kings 2:19–22
2. Caused punishment of boys for their mockery	2 Kings 2:23–25
3. Provided water for the combined armies of Israel and Judah	2 Kings 3:14–20
4. Replenished a widow's cooking oil	2 Kings 4:1–7
5. Brought a widow's dead son back to life	2 Kings 4:8–37
6. Purged a meal of poison	2 Kings 4:38–41
7. Fed prophets by multiplying food	2 Kings 4:42–44
8. Healed a Syrian military officer of leprosy	2 Kings 5:1–27
9. Recovered a lost ax head	2 Kings 6:1–7
10. Was miraculously delivered from enemy soldiers	2 Kings 6:8–23
11. Dead man revived when his body touched Elisha's bones	2 Kings 13:20–21

KING AHAZIAH

After Ahab was killed in a battle against the Arameans, he was succeeded as king by his son Ahaziah. Ahaziah reigned only two years before dying from an injury he suffered in a fall at the royal palace in Samaria (2 Kings 1:2, 17). Ahaziah continued the policies of Ahab, worshipping the pagan god Baal (1 Kings 22:53).

KING JEHORAM/JORAM

Since Ahaziah had no sons, his brother Jehoram—another son of Ahab—succeeded Ahaziah as king. Jehoram is also referred to in some translations of the Bible as Joram. His major contribution was putting down a rebellion among the Moabites, who seized the opportunity after Ahab died to declare their independence. Jehoram enlisted the help of Jehoshaphat king of Judah to defeat the Moabites (2 Kings 3:1–27).

King Jehoram was not so successful in his war against the Arameans—a struggle that had been going on since Ahab's time. Wounded in a battle against Aramean forces, Jehoram withdrew to his summer palace at Jezreel. Here he was assassinated by Jehu, commander of his army, who became the tenth king of Israel (2 Kings 8:28–29; 9:14–26).

Jehu's murder of Jehoram brought the dynasty of Ahab to an end. Several years before, the Lord had commanded the prophet Elijah to anoint Jehu as the person who would eventually replace Ahab and his sons as Israel's king (1 Kings 19:15–16).

KING JEHU

Jehu reigned over Israel for twenty-eight years—longer than any other king of the Northern Kingdom up to that time. His reign was a mixed bag of good and bad.

The greatest good that Jehu achieved was his campaign against Baal worship in the nation. Worship of this pagan god had become so entrenched through Ahab and Jezebel's influence that a temple devoted to Baal had been erected in Samaria, Israel's capital city. Jehu pretended that he wanted to honor this pagan god by assembling all the priests of Baal at this temple for worship. Then the king sprang his trap and had all these pagan priests executed.

So thorough was this destruction that Baal worship was wiped out in Israel. The pagan temple was destroyed, and the ground on which it stood was turned into a public toilet (2 Kings 10:20–28).

Jehu was also faithful to his commission to bring the dynasty of the wicked Ahab to an end. He had Jezebel killed, and he murdered Ahab's son and successor Jehoram to become king himself. But once the killing started, it accelerated out of control, far beyond what God commanded and what was necessary to establish Jehu's authority as the new king. His litany of violence established his reputation as Israel's most bloodthirsty king:

- He had seventy male descendants of Ahab killed to eliminate all claimants to the throne (2 Kings 10:6–8).

- He killed all officials who had served in the administrations of Ahab and his sons, including "his great men, close friends, and priests" (2 Kings 10:11 HCSB).

- He assassinated King Ahaziah of Judah, apparently because he was an ally of Ahab's son Jehoram, king of Israel (2 Kings 9:27).

- He killed forty-two members of King Ahaziah's royal family (2 Kings 10:12–14).

The biblical writer's evaluation of Jehu's leadership reflects the mixture of good and bad that characterized his administration. He was commended for ending Ahab's dynasty. But at the same time, he did not follow all the commands of the Lord (2 Kings 10:30–31). Specifically, he failed to put a stop to worship of the golden calves that Israel's first king, Jeroboam I, had erected at Bethel and Dan (2 Kings 10:29).

During Jehu's long reign, the nation of Aram, along Israel's northern border, continued to harass and intimidate the Northern Kingdom. The Arameans were able to conquer most of Israel's territory east of the Jordan River (2 Kings 10:32–33).

KING JEHOAHAZ

This king—son and successor of Jehu—had the misfortune of ruling over Israel when the nation of Aram, or Syria, was a powerful force. The power struggle that had given the Arameans a slight edge over Israel in previous years gave way to outright dominance during the reign of Jehoahaz.

The biblical writer gives this bleak picture of Jehoahaz's problems during his reign: "Jehoahaz's army was reduced to 50 charioteers, 10 chariots, and 10,000 foot soldiers. The king of Aram had killed the others, trampling them like dust under his feet" (2 Kings 13:7 NLT). Jehoahaz may have been happy to relinquish the throne when his seventeen-year reign came to an end.

KING JOASH/JEHOASH

Joash, also known as Jehoash, succeeded his unlucky father, Jehoahaz, as king. The major event of Joash's sixteen-year reign was victory over Amaziah, king of the sister southern kingdom of Judah.

Riding a wave of euphoria after a victory over Edom, Amaziah thought he could extend his winning streak into Israel. Instead, Joash defeated and captured Amaziah, tore down a section of Jerusalem's wall, and carried some of the valuable articles in the temple back to Samaria (2 Kings 14:11–14). Amaziah must have regretted the day he picked a fight with this strong-willed king of the Northern Kingdom.

KING JEROBOAM II

The thirteenth king of Israel was Jeroboam, son of Joash. He is referred to as Jeroboam II to distinguish him from the Jeroboam who served as the first king of Israel (1 Kings 12:20). The second Jeroboam brought stability and prosperity to Israel during his tenure of forty-one years—the longest tenure of any king of the Northern Kingdom.

In spite of his long, stable administration, the Bible has little to say about Jeroboam II. He was apparently successful in his military exploits, since he recaptured some of the territory that had been taken from Israel and Judah by enemy nations (2 Kings 14:25, 28). His reign serves as a bridge between the middle and final years of the Northern Kingdom's history.

ISRAEL'S FINAL YEARS

Jeroboam's extended reign was like the quiet before the storm. After his death, Israel went through a period of chaos and instability that lasted about forty years. These were the final years of the nation's existence under a succession of six different kings.

KING ZECHARIAH AND KING SHALLUM

Zechariah became king after the death of his father, Jeroboam II. Zechariah was the last king of Jehu's dynasty. He ruled for only six months before being assassinated by a man named Shallum. This chain of violence and treachery continued with the assassination of Shallum only one month into his kingship (2 Kings 15:8–15).

KING MENAHEM

Shallum's assassin and the new man on the throne was Menahem, who reigned over the Northern Kingdom for ten years. According to the biblical

Tiglath-Pileser III, alabaster bas-relief in the British Museum, London. Originally from the king's central palace in Nimrud (modern-day Ninawa Governorate, Iraq), Mesopotamia (c. 730–727 BC).

account, the only thing he accomplished was reaching an agreement with the king of Assyria not to overrun his nation. This arrangement required Israel to pay a heavy tribute to Pul (also known as Tiglath-Pileser III), the king of Assyria (2 Kings 15:16-22). (See sidebar, "The Assyrian Threat.")

Menahem soon discovered he had paid a heavy price to keep the peace: "Every wealthy person had to contribute fifty shekels of silver to be given to the king of Assyria" (2 Kings 15:20 NIV). This protection money had the potential to bleed the country dry. And even more disturbing, this turn of events showed that Israel was no match for the power-hungry Assyrians.

KING PEKAHIAH AND KING PEKAH

Pekahiah assumed the throne after the death of his father, Menahem. But the new king's hold on power lasted only two years. His army commander, a man named Pekah, conspired against Pekahiah, assassinated him, and became the eighteenth king of Israel. In contrast to Pekahiah's brief reign, Pekah ruled Israel for twenty years. But on the matter of their commitment to God, these two kings with similar names were like two branches on the same tree. Both Pekahiah and Pekah "did that which was evil in the sight of the LORD" (2 Kings 15:24, 28).

The Northern Kingdom seemed to be defenseless against the Assyrian threat, and events were spiraling out of control. Too many kings of the nation had failed to obey the one true God and had led the people to worship the false gods of their neighbors. A time of reckoning was just around the corner.

KING HOSHEA

Hoshea became the nineteenth and final king of Israel by assassinating Pekah (2 Kings 15:30). For a while he continued to pay tribute to Assyria under an agreement reached by one of his predecessors, King Menahem, several years before. Finally, he rebelled against Assyria's oppression, stopped paying the protection money, and appealed to Egypt to form an alliance against the Assyrians (2 Kings 17:3-4).

These actions were guaranteed to bring a quick response from the brutal Assyrians. King Shalmaneser V marched his army to Israel, captured the capital city of Samaria after a prolonged siege, took Hoshea prisoner, and carried away many inhabitants of the Northern Kingdom to the Assyrian Empire (2 Kings 17:5-6).

Thus, Israel came to an end in 722 BC after existing as a separate nation for about two hundred years. The biblical writer makes it clear that Israel fell because of its persistent disobedience of the Lord and its worship of pagan gods.

Although Israel failed to follow the Lord during its history, God was not silent during these turbulent years. He raised up several prophets to try to turn Israel from its stubborn march toward destruction. In addition to the prophets Elijah and Elisha, He worked through messengers known as the writing prophets to address the problems of the Northern Kingdom.

WRITING PROPHETS OF THE NORTHERN KINGDOM

Four prophets whose books appear in the Old Testament—Isaiah, Hosea, Amos, and Micah—directed at least part of their writings to the kings and people of Israel.

THE PROPHET ISAIAH

Isaiah, the best known prophet of the Old Testament, was called by the Lord to the prophetic ministry in approximately 740 BC—about twenty years before Israel fell to the Assyrian army. His ministry was directed mostly to the Southern Kingdom, but a few passages

---

ISRAEL ON THE DOWNGRADE

No-Stress Bible Reading
2 Kings 15:14-22

No-Stress Bible Guide
Pages 126-129 (from "King Ahaziah" to "Writing Prophets of the Northern Kingdom")

Think About It:

- How did King Menahem's actions reflect the disorder that gripped the Northern Kingdom during its final years?

JUDGMENT BY FIRE

No-Stress Bible Reading
2 Kings 17

Think About It:

- Why did the Assyrians attack Israel's capital city of Samaria?

- What happened to the people of the Northern Kingdom after the city fell?

- What serious sins caused the downfall of the nation of Israel?

---

in his book deal with the shortcomings of the Northern Kingdom. He condemned the kings and people of Israel for their wayward ways: "Those who guide this people mislead them," he declared, "and those who are guided are led astray" (Isaiah 9:16 NIV).

Isaiah also predicted that Israel would be punished by the Lord for its rebellion and idolatry. This punishment would consist of a total destruction of the nation: "The LORD will cut off from Israel both head and tail, both palm branch and reed in a single day" (Isaiah 9:14 NIV).

Isaiah the prophet as depicted by Michelangelo (1475–1564) on the ceiling of the Sistine Chapel in the Vatican

THE PROPHET HOSEA

Hosea ministered in the Northern Kingdom during the last thirty years of its existence. He declared to the people that they were marked for destruction unless they turned from their sinful ways, especially their worship of false gods.

But the message for which Hosea is most remembered is his declaration that God had not given up on His people. Even though they were sinful and rebellious, the Lord still loved them and worked patiently to restore them to their favored status as His special people.

This truth about God was demonstrated in Hosea's own life. At the Lord's direction, the prophet married a prostitute. Several children were born into this marriage. But just as it appeared that his wife had given up her sinful ways, she left Hosea and returned to her life of prostitution.

Hosea searched for his wayward spouse and discovered that she had been sold into slavery. He bought her from her master and restored her as his wife. This object lesson showed that God had not rejected the Northern Kingdom, although the people had turned their backs on Him by worshipping false gods (Hosea 3:1–5). But they would have to pay the consequences of their rejection of Him. They had sown the wind, and they would "reap the whirlwind" of God's judgment (Hosea 8:7).

THE PROPHET AMOS

Amos was a native of the Southern Kingdom, but the Lord sent him into Israel to denounce the sin and corruption of the wealthy class of the north. His ministry probably occurred during the reign of King Jeroboam II and several other kings who ruled during Israel's final years.

Amos is known as the great prophet of righteousness and social justice of the Old Testament. He condemned the wealthy people of Israel who were cheating the poor (Amos 2:6–7). He criticized the wives of the rich leaders of the nation for their selfishness and greed (Amos 4:1–3). The prophet also declared that the religion of the people was shallow and meaningless. Their worship had degenerated into empty rituals and ceremonies that had no relationship to daily life (Amos 5:18–27).

THE PROPHET MICAH

The prophet Micah delivered God's message to the citizens of both Israel and Judah, probably during the final years of the Northern Kingdom's

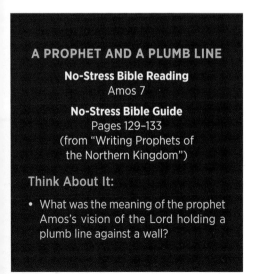

A PROPHET AND A PLUMB LINE

No-Stress Bible Reading
Amos 7

No-Stress Bible Guide
Pages 129–133
(from "Writing Prophets of
the Northern Kingdom")

Think About It:

- What was the meaning of the prophet Amos's vision of the Lord holding a plumb line against a wall?

The Prophet Amos, Gustave Doré (1832–1883)

existence. His book included prophecies of both judgment and promise. God would send His punishment upon His people because of their sin. But He was just as determined to bless them to fulfill the promise of the covenant that He had made with Abraham many centuries before (Micah 7:18–20).

Micah made it clear that the people of both Judah and Israel would be punished by the Lord for their sin and rebellion. But in the future, God would restore His people through a remnant of those who would remain faithful to Him (Micah 2:12–13).

In spite of these warnings from the prophets, Israel refused to turn from its sinful ways. God's punishment fell when the Assyrians ransacked the nation and carried its most influential citizens away as captives. The nation of Israel was never restored.

But some former citizens of the Northern

Kingdom may have been among those Jews who repopulated the territory of Judah more than two centuries later. This happened after the people of Judah—also defeated and exiled by a foreign power—were allowed to return to their homeland by a benevolent Persian king known as Cyrus.

But that is a story for the next chapter and the next stage of biblical history. Chapter 12 focuses on the ups and downs of the Southern Kingdom and its succession of kings through the line of David.

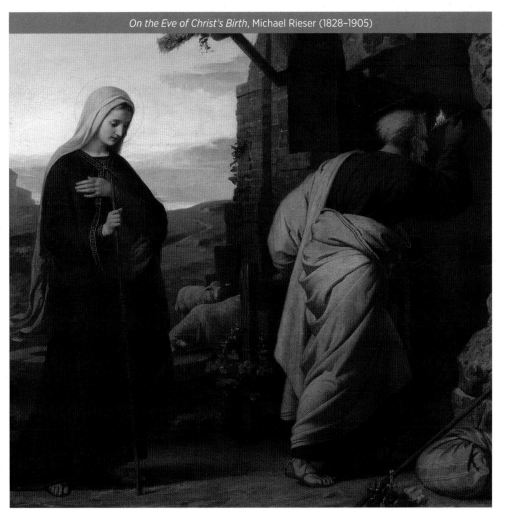

On the Eve of Christ's Birth, Michael Rieser (1828–1905)

King Asa of Judah Destroying the Idols,
François de Nomé (1593–1620)

CHAPTER 12
The Ups and Downs of the Southern Kingdom (Judah)

When Solomon's united kingdom split in about 920 BC, the territory that remained—the Southern Kingdom known as Judah—was reduced to about one-half of its previous size. Only the two southern tribes, Judah and Benjamin, remained loyal to Solomon's successor, Rehoboam. The other ten tribes revolted against Rehoboam's authority and formed their own independent nation known as Israel, or the Northern Kingdom.

Reduced in land area and population, the Southern Kingdom went through a succession of twenty different kings over a period of approximately 335 years—from about 920 to 587 BC. All these rulers—with one exception, Queen Athaliah—were descendants from David's royal line. A thumbnail summary of these kings and their reigns appears in the chart below.

KINGS OF THE SOUTHERN KINGDOM (JUDAH)

KING	LENGTH OF REIGN	SCRIPTURE
1. Rehoboam	17 years	1 Kings 14:21-31; 2 Chronicles 11:1-22; 12:1-16
2. Abijah/Abijam	3 years	1 Kings 15:1-8; 2 Chronicles 13:1-22
3. Asa	41 years	1 Kings 15:9-24; 2 Chronicles 14:1-16:14
4. Jehoshaphat	25 years	1 Kings 22:41-50; 2 Chronicles 17:1-21:1
5. Jehoram/Joram	8 years	2 Kings 8:16-24; 2 Chronicles 21:1-20
6. Ahaziah	1 year	2 Kings 8:25-29; 9:27-29; 2 Chronicles 22:1-9
7. (Queen) Athaliah	6 years	2 Kings 11:1-16; 2 Chronicles 22:10-12; 23:1-21
8. Joash/Jehoash	40 years	2 Kings 11:4-21; 12:1-21; 2 Chronicles 23:1-21; 24:1-27
9. Amaziah	29 years	2 Kings 14:1-21; 2 Chronicles 25:1-28
10. Uzziah/Azariah	52 years	2 Kings 15:1-7; 2 Chronicles 26:1-23
11. Jotham	16 years	2 Kings 15:32-38; 2 Chronicles 27:1-9
12. Ahaz/Jehoahaz I	16 years	2 Kings 16:1-20; 2 Chronicles 28:1-29
13. Hezekiah	29 years	2 Kings 18:1-20:21; 2 Chronicles 29:1-32:33; Isaiah 36:1-39:8
14. Manasseh	55 years	2 Kings 21:1-18; 2 Chronicles 33:1-20
15. Amon	2 years	2 Kings 21:19-26; 2 Chronicles 33:20-25
16. Josiah	31 years	2 Kings 22:1-23:30; 2 Chronicles 34:1-35:27

17. Jehoahaz II/Shallum	3 months	2 Kings 23:31–34; 2 Chronicles 36:1–4
18. Jehoiakim/Eliakim	11 years	2 Kings 23:34–24:6; 2 Chronicles 36:4–8
19. Jehoiachin/Coniah	3 months	2 Kings 24:8–15; 25:27–30; 2 Chronicles 36:9–10
20. Zedekiah/Mattaniah	11 years	2 Kings 24:17–25:7; 2 Chronicles 36:10–19

Narratives of the major events from Judah's history under these kings appear in chapters 14, 15, and 22 of 1 Kings; chapters 8–25 of 2 Kings; and chapters 11–36 of 2 Chronicles. These events may be grouped into four major divisions: (1) Judah's early years, (2) Judah's middle years, (3) Judah's final years, and (4) writing prophets of the Southern Kingdom.

JUDAH'S EARLY YEARS

After Judah's rocky start—the northern rebellion caused by King Solomon's excesses—the nation of Judah settled into the first ninety or so years of its existence. Unlike the Northern Kingdom, Judah had a long tradition of stable government and loyalty to the Lord through worship at the temple in Jerusalem. The first five kings of Judah inherited these distinct advantages.

KING REHOBOAM

This headstrong king, son and successor of Solomon, caused the northern tribes to revolt when he promised to continue the oppressive policies of his father (1 Kings 12:1–11). For the first few years and ended these foolish and fruitless military campaigns.

Perhaps Rehoboam's greatest contribution was the building up of Judah's defenses. He fortified several key cities throughout the territories of Judah and Benjamin to protect the nation from attack along its southern and northern borders (2 Chronicles 11:5–12).

But Rehoboam failed to learn from the mistakes of his father. Like Solomon, he built a harem of many wives and concubines (2 Chronicles 11:21). Some of these must have been foreign wives whom he catered to by setting up altars to their pagan gods, even

NT Connection—REHOBOAM: He is listed as an ancestor of Jesus in Matthew's genealogy (Matthew 1:7; "Roboam" in the KJV).

of his reign, Rehoboam tried to make amends for this mistake by forcing the Northern Kingdom to reunite with Judah through military action.

Finally, the Lord sent a prophet named Shemaiah to confront the king about these actions. "This is what the LORD says," he declared to Rehoboam. "You are not to march up and fight against your brothers" (2 Chronicles 11:4 HCSB). To the king's credit, he obeyed the Lord including "male shrine prostitutes in the land" (1 Kings 14:24 NIV).

God was not pleased with these detestable religious practices. He punished and humiliated the king by sending Shishak, pharaoh of Egypt, to ransack Judah. The Egyptian army captured several fortified cities of Judah and carried away many treasures from the temple and the royal palace in Jerusalem (2 Chronicles 12:4, 9).

Rehoboam died after reigning over Judah for seventeen years. He was succeeded by his son Abijah (1 Kings 14:31).

KING ABIJAH/ABIJAM

This king, also known as Abijam, reigned only three years in Judah. His only accomplishment was a decisive victory over the superior forces of King Jeroboam of the Northern Kingdom (2 Chronicles 13:1–18). The Bible gives no explanation for the renewal of hostilities between the two kingdoms, since the Lord had specifically instructed Abijah's father not to go to war against Israel.

The writer of 1 Kings declared, "But the high places were not removed" (1 Kings 15:14).

Asa followed up his cleansing operation by pushing for genuine moral and religious reform throughout Judah. He called an assembly of all citizens in Jerusalem, where he led them to renew the covenant with the Lord and to declare anew their commitment to Him as the one true God.

Joining in this great recommitment were many people from the Northern Kingdom. They had left Israel and settled in Judah because of Asa's reform campaign when they saw that Asa was committed to following the Lord

---

NT Connection—ABIJAH: He is listed as an ancestor of Jesus in Matthew's genealogy (Matthew 1:7; "Abia" in the KJV).

Abijah received a failing mark from the writer of 1 Kings: "He committed all the sins that his father did before him; his heart was not true to the LORD his God, like the heart of his father David" (1 Kings 15:3 NRSV). This verse shows clearly that all future kings of Judah were measured by the standard of the nation's greatest ruler—the godly King David.

KING ASA

When Abijah died, his son Asa succeeded him as king. Asa got off to a good start by attacking pagan worship throughout the land. He removed altars devoted to pagan gods and expelled pagan male prostitutes from the land. He even removed his own grandmother, Maacah, from her position as queen mother because she had set up an Asherah pole in honor of the pagan goddess Ashtoreth (1 Kings 15:11–15; 2 Chronicles 14:2–5). But there is some question whether the king purged all forms of false worship from the land.

(2 Chronicles 15:9).

During his reign Asa also achieved success as a military leader. When a huge army from Cush, or Ethiopia, attacked Judah, he prayed fervently for the Lord's intervention. God honored the king's request by giving him a resounding victory over the Cushites (2 Chronicles 14:9–15).

Toward the end of his reign, Asa made some mistakes that marred his otherwise perfect record as king. When the security of the Southern Kingdom was threatened by King Baasha of Israel, he made a deal with the king of Aram, or Syria, to drive the Israelite army away from Judah's northern border. This arrangement was successful, but it came at a price. Asa had to rob the temple and his palace of gold and silver to pay the king of Aram for his military intervention (2 Chronicles 16:1–3).

The Lord sent a prophet named Hanani to reprimand the king for his actions. God was not pleased that Asa had relied on gold and silver

---

NT Connection—ASA: He is listed as an ancestor of Jesus in Matthew's genealogy (Matthew 1:7).

---

and the king of Aram for deliverance rather than trusting in the power of the Lord. Then, instead of asking God's forgiveness for his error, the king grew angry at the prophet and had him thrown in prison (2 Chronicles 16:10).

In spite of this high-handed action, Asa is commended as a good king who "did that which was good and right in the eyes of the LORD" (2 Chronicles 14:2). He contracted a mysterious disease of the feet in his old age and died after a long and fruitful reign of forty-one years (1 Kings 15:10, 23–24).

KING JEHOSHAPHAT

Asa set a good example for his son and successor, Jehoshaphat. As the fourth king of Judah, Jehoshaphat continued to suppress pagan worship and to encourage worship of the one true God as his father had done. He implemented a nationwide program of teaching his officials and the people of the land to practice justice and follow the Lord's commands (2 Chronicles 17:7–9).

The king himself practiced what he preached. When confronted by a huge army composed of Edomites, Moabites, and Ammonites, he prayed to the Lord for divine assistance. "We do not know what to do," he admitted, "but we are looking to you for help" (2 Chronicles 20:12 NLT).

His army marched off to battle with the words of a psalm on their lips. When Judah's army arrived at the battle site, there was no battle to fight. The allied enemy army had been mysteriously ambushed by an unknown foe. This created confusion among the soldiers of the allied enemy army, and they began to slaughter one another. The only thing Jehoshaphat's troops had to do was pick up the spoils the confused army had abandoned (2 Chronicles 20:22–25).

During Jehoshaphat's reign the bitter feelings between Judah and Israel grew more cordial. He and Ahab, king of the Northern Kingdom, formed an alliance against their common enemy—the nation of Aram, or Syria. They attempted to recapture the city of Ramoth Gilead from the Syrians, but their campaign was not successful. As it turned out, the wicked king Ahab was killed in this battle (1 Kings 22:29–38).

Jehoshaphat died after reigning over Judah for twenty-five years. He was commended for his leadership because "he walked in the way of his father Asa" and did "what was right in the sight of the LORD" (2 Chronicles 20:32 NKJV).

KING JEHORAM/JORAM

After Jehoshaphat's long and positive reign, his oldest son, Jehoram—also known as Joram—became the fifth king of Judah. One of his

---

REHOBOAM THE FOOLISH

No-Stress Bible Reading
2 Chronicles 10; 12

No-Stress Bible Guide
Pages 135–139
(to "Judah's Middle Years")

Think About It:

- Why do you think Rehoboam rejected the counsel of his senior advisors and listened to the advice of his young associates?

- How do you think Solomon might have felt if he had lived to see the kingdom come apart because of his son's actions?

first acts was a preview of things to come: he murdered all of his father's other sons—his own brothers—to eliminate all claimants to the throne (2 Chronicles 21:4).

Jehoram followed up this heinous crime by setting up high places devoted to idols and leading the people to worship false gods. To seal an alliance with the Northern Kingdom, he married a woman named Athaliah, who was a daughter of Ahab of Israel. This planted the seed for Baal worship among the people and led to later trouble for the nation (2 Kings 8:18).

The king's sins resulted in God's punishment in the form of rebellion by the Edomites, who had previously been under Judah's control. The Philistines and several Arabian tribes also invaded the nation and carried off the king's treasures as well as members of the royal family (2 Chronicles 21:8–17).

But the Lord's severest punishment for Jehoram was a mysterious and incurable intestinal disease. After reigning for only eight years, he died in great pain. The biblical writer summarizes his evil reign with this brief epitaph: "He died to no one's regret" (2 Chronicles 21:20 HCSB).

KING AHAZIAH AND QUEEN ATHALIAH

At Jehoram's death, his son Ahaziah succeeded him as king. Ahaziah's mother was Athaliah, a daughter of Ahab of the Northern Kingdom whom his father had married to seal an alliance with Israel. Because of this connection to Ahab, Ahaziah came under the influence of the advisers of King Jehoram of Israel, Ahab's successor (2 Chronicles 22:3–4).

These advisers convinced Ahaziah to join forces with the army of the Northern Kingdom in a campaign against the Arameans, or Syrians, at Ramoth Gilead. During the battle Jehoram was wounded, and a new king named Jehu murdered the wounded king to assume Israel's throne. Jehu then murdered Jehoram's royal family. Jehu

> **NT Connection—JEHORAM:** He is listed as an ancestor of Jesus in Matthew's genealogy (Matthew 1:8; "Joram" in the KJV).

considered Judah's king an ally of the king of Israel, so he continued his mop-up campaign by murdering Ahaziah (2 Kings 9:27).

Into this violent and confusing situation stepped the opportunist Athaliah, mother of Judah's murdered king. After seizing power when her son was killed by Jehu, she murdered all her own grandsons to make sure no one could challenge her power grab. But unknown to her, one young prince named Joash escaped her evil scheme. Joash's sister hid him in the temple during the six years of Athaliah's tumultuous reign (2 Chronicles 22:10–12). With these chaotic events, the first years of Judah's existence came to an end, and the nation entered its relatively calm middle years.

JUDAH'S MIDDLE YEARS

The middle period of Judah's existence lasted for about two hundred years. Seven different kings enjoyed long and stable reigns during this time of prosperity, although not all of them were faithful to the Lord.

KING JOASH/JEHOASH

Joash, also known as Jehoash, was the son of King Ahaziah and thus the legitimate claimant to the throne (2 Kings 11:2). He was only one

Ruins of ancient Lachish, where Amaziah was assassinated after a twenty-nine-year reign

year old when Queen Athaliah seized power and murdered Ahaziah's other sons. Only the infant Joash escaped her spree of violence. For six years he was hidden by his aunt and tutored by a priest named Jehoaida. Finally, Jehoiada plotted against Athaliah, had the young Joash acclaimed as king, and ordered the assassination of Athaliah (2 Kings 11:4–16).

Joash was only seven years old when he became king. It is likely that he reigned at this early age under the oversight of advisers, including the priest Jehoiada. Soon after Joash was installed as king, this zealous priest led the people to renew the covenant with the Lord. Jehoiada also led a campaign to tear down the altars devoted to pagan worship. These had probably been erected during Athaliah's reign (2 Kings 11:17–18).

King Joash is most remembered for his campaign to renovate the temple in Jerusalem. It had fallen into disrepair since its construction by his distant ancestor Solomon more than a century before. Joash raised money for the project by diverting fees collected at the temple into a special building fund. With this money, skilled workmen purchased "timber and hewed stone to repair the breaches of the house of the LORD" (2 Kings 12:12).

AMAZIAH'S STRANGE DESCENT INTO IDOLATRY

No-Stress Bible Reading
2 Chronicles 25

No-Stress Bible Guide
Pages 139–141
(from "Judah's Middle Years to "King Uzziah/Azariah")

Think About It:

- Why do you think King Amaziah began to worship the false gods of the Ammonites?

- According to a prophet sent by the Lord, how would God punish the king for this blatant sin?

In spite of this positive contribution to the religious life of his people, Joash faltered in his commitment to the Lord toward the end of his reign. He led the people to abandon the Lord and return to false worship (2 Chronicles 24:17–19). A prophet named Zechariah condemned the king for his sin, and Joash had him stoned to death. Ironically, this prophet was the son of Jehoiada the priest—the very person who had placed the young king on the throne and mentored him during the early years of his reign.

The Lord punished King Joash by sending the army of Aram, or Syria, to invade Judah. Joash was forced to pay tribute to the Arameans by stripping the temple and his royal palace of their treasures (2 Kings 12:17–18). His forty-year reign came to an end when his own officials conspired against him. They murdered him in his own bed while he was recovering from a wound inflicted by the Arameans (2 Chronicles 24:25).

KING AMAZIAH

Amaziah became the ninth king of the Southern Kingdom upon the death of his father, Joash. Amaziah is known as a warrior king who raised a huge army and defeated the Edomites in a major battle (2 Kings 14:7).

For some unexplainable reason, Amaziah adopted the pagan gods of the Edomites as his own and bowed down to worship them in the land of Judah. This blatant sin angered the Lord. God sent a prophet to ask the king, "Why do you turn to gods who could not even save their own people from you?" (2 Chronicles 25:15 NLT).

After Amaziah tasted success against the Edomites, he rekindled the rivalry between Judah and the northern kingdom that had been dormant for several years. But he should have quit while he was ahead. He suffered a humiliating defeat, and Jerusalem was plundered by the army of Israel (2 Chronicles 25:18–24).

Amaziah's twenty-nine-year reign ended when he fled Jerusalem to escape a rebellion among his own people, apparently brought on by his rejection of the Lord. The rebels chased him as far as the city of Lachish, where he was assassinated (2 Chronicles 25:27).

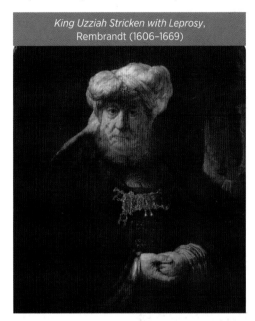

King Uzziah Stricken with Leprosy, Rembrandt (1606–1669)

KING UZZIAH/AZARIAH

When Amaziah was assassinated, his son Uzziah—also known as Azariah—became king in his place. Uzziah was only sixteen years old when he took the throne. His reign lasted fifty-two years—the second-longest tenure of any king of Judah (2 Chronicles 26:1–3).

Uzziah was a powerful king who brought great prosperity to the southern kingdom. He defeated the Philistines and occupied their territory. He also conquered the Ammonites

NT Connection—UZZIAH: He is listed as an ancestor of Jesus in Matthew's genealogy (Matthew 1:8; "Ozias" in the KJV).

and forced them to pay tribute to Judah. He strengthened the defenses of Jerusalem and dug wells and cisterns to water the crops and livestock of the nation (2 Chronicles 26:6–10). The king's fame "spread far abroad" (2 Chronicles 26:15) because of his administrative skills and progressive policies.

But excessive pride was Uzziah's undoing. He thought his position of unchallenged power gave him the authority to take over the role of the priests in Judah's religious life. When he attempted to burn incense on the altar in the temple, the priests on duty stopped him. The king lashed out at them in anger and was stricken with leprosy, a dreaded skin disease.

Uzziah was forced to spend the rest of his days in isolation while his son, Jotham, carried out his orders as a regent (2 Chronicles 26:16–21).

AHAZ THE UNFORTUNATE

No-Stress Bible Reading:
2 Chronicles 28

No-Stress Bible Guide
Pages 141–143 (from "King Uzziah/ Azariah" to "King Hezekiah")

Think About It:

- What was the root cause of the problems that plagued Ahaz during his reign?

KING JOTHAM

When his father, Uzziah, died, Jotham was finally recognized officially as king—a responsibility he had performed for his ailing father for several years. Jotham continued the policies of his father by strengthening the walls of Jerusalem, building towns throughout Judah, and receiving tribute from the conquered Ammonites (2 Chronicles 27:1–5).

Jotham is one of the few kings of Judah of whom the biblical writer declared—without exception: "[He] grew powerful because he walked steadfastly before the Lord his God" (2 Chronicles 27:6 NIV). He ruled over the southern kingdom for sixteen years (2 Chronicles 27:8).

KING AHAZ/JEHOAHAZ I

Jotham was succeeded as king by his son, Ahaz, also known as Jehoahaz. Ahaz is referred to as Jehoahaz I to distinguish him from another king of the same name (Jehoahaz II) in Judah's later history.

Ahaz's reign is significant because it occurred during the time when the Assyrians were developing into the dominant power in the ancient world. Ahaz formed an alliance with this pagan nation by appealing to its king, Tiglath Pileser, to help him turn back an attack on Judah by the Northern Kingdom and the Arameans. The Assyrians came to Judah's rescue after Ahaz paid the king off with treasures from the temple and his royal palace (2 Kings 16:5–9).

Judah's sister kingdom to the north was not so fortunate. A few years after Ahaz died, the northern kingdom came to an end when the Assyrians overran Israel and carried its leading citizens into exile.

One unfortunate result of Ahaz's entanglement with Assyria was the king's slide into idolatry. To show his solidarity with Assyria, Ahaz had an altar to one of the Assyrian gods built in Jerusalem. He presented sacrifices on this altar and encouraged the people of the land to do the same. Ahaz even had some sacred objects

---

NT Connection—JOTHAM: He is listed as an ancestor of Jesus in Matthew's genealogy (Matthew 1:9; "Joatham" in the KJV).

moved from the courtyard of the temple "to satisfy the king of Assyria" (2 Kings 16:18 HCSB).

The king's compromise with the Assyrian religious system is just one example of Ahaz's descent into false worship. Several other acts of idolatry by Ahaz are mentioned in the biblical text:

- He "made high places to burn incense unto other gods" (2 Chronicles 28:25).

- He "shut up the doors of the house of the LORD" (2 Chronicles 28:24).

- He "burnt his children in the fire" (2 Chronicles 28:3).

KING HEZEKIAH

After Ahaz's disastrous reign, the nation of Judah desperately needed a king who would do the right thing and follow the Lord's leadership. That's exactly what happened when Ahaz's son, Hezekiah, succeeded him on the throne. The biblical writer summarized Hezekiah's reign with these complimentary words: "He trusted in the LORD the God of Israel; so that there was no one like him among all the kings of Judah after him, or among those who were before him" (2 Kings 18:5 NRSV).

King Hezekiah got off to a good start by stamping out the idol worship that had been promoted by his father, Ahaz. He tore down all the altars to pagan gods that had been erected throughout the land (2 Kings 18:4).

His next step was to restore worship of the one true God among the people. He instructed the priests and Levites to purify the temple of any defilement that had occurred from pagan objects. He also ordered the return of any sacred objects that had been removed from the temple in recent years (2 Chronicles 29:3–16).

HEZEKIAH THE FAITHFUL

No-Stress Bible Reading
2 Kings 18–19

No-Stress Bible Guide
Pages 143–145 (from "King Hezekiah" to "Judah's Final Years")

Think About It:

- How did King Hezekiah show that he was totally committed to following the Lord?

- Why do you think he sought the advice of the prophet Isaiah?

- How did Isaiah's response reassure the king about the threat from Assyria?

Hezekiah also led the people to celebrate important religious festivals, including Passover and the Feast of Unleavened Bread, which had been neglected in recent years. He turned these events into commitment ceremonies, leading the people to renew their determination to serve the Lord. This return to their religious roots brought "great joy in Jerusalem, for since the time of Solomon the son of David. . .there had been nothing like this in Jerusalem" (2 Chronicles 30:26 NKJV).

In matters of national security, King Hezekiah showed good judgment, balancing careful preparation with trust in the Lord for deliverance from the nation's enemies. His faith in God was put to the test in his interaction with the nation of Assyria.

Hezekiah's father, Ahaz, had turned back the

Inside Hezekiah's tunnel, built to bring water into Jerusalem when Judah was being attacked by Assyria

HEZEKIAH'S AMAZING TUNNEL

The water tunnel that Hezekiah's laborers dug is considered one of the most remarkable engineering achievements of Bible times. It runs for more than seventeen hundred feet through solid rock to a spring outside the Old City of Jerusalem known as the Gihon Spring.

An inscription describing the project was chiseled into the wall of the tunnel. It reveals how one group of workers began digging at the spring and another group started work at the opposite end. After what was probably months of backbreaking labor, they met in the middle more than one hundred feet beneath the city. This inscription was discovered several years after the tunnel itself was uncovered by archaeologists.

Modern visitors to the Holy Land may walk through this amazing tunnel. But the trip is not for the claustrophobic. It is only five feet high by two feet wide.

Assyrian threat by paying tribute to this pagan nation. Hezekiah apparently continued this policy for a while but then stopped paying the protection money (2 Kings 18:7). This brought the Assyrian king, Sennacherib, to his front door with the threat to wipe out Judah unless the king bowed to his authority (2 Chronicles 32:9–15).

Hezekiah had expected this to happen, so he prepared Jerusalem for an Assyrian onslaught. He reinforced the city's defensive wall, added a second wall, built defense towers atop the double walls, and stockpiled weapons (2 Chronicles 32:5).

But the king's greatest and most permanent accomplishment was a tunnel that ran from inside these walls to a spring outside the city—a channel to provide water for Jerusalem's citizens in the event of a prolonged Assyrian siege (see 2 Chronicles 32:30). (See sidebar, "Hezekiah's Amazing Tunnel.")

As it turned out, the king didn't need any of these defensive measures. The Lord answered his fervent prayer for protection by sending the prophet Isaiah to assure him that He would deliver His people (see 2 Kings 19:14–34). While the Assyrian army was camped outside Jerusalem, it was struck by a mysterious illness that wiped out 185,000 soldiers. Sennacherib was forced to retreat without laying siege to the city.

One final episode in the life of this good and godly king shows how the Lord honored him for his faithfulness. After he had reigned for about fourteen years, Hezekiah fell ill and was not expected to survive. Even the prophet Isaiah told him that his days were numbered (2 Kings 20:1–2).

But Hezekiah prayed to the Lord, and God prolonged his life so his positive influence would continue in the nation of Judah for fifteen more years. He died after reigning for twenty-nine years and was succeeded by his son, Manasseh (2 Kings 18:2; 20:21).

KING MANASSEH

Whoever said "like father, like son" didn't know about good king Hezekiah and his evil son Manasseh. He was the exact opposite of his father. Manasseh seemed determined to wipe out all the good his father had done and to plunge the nation of Judah into the depths of idolatry and godlessness.

King Manasseh rebuilt many of the pagan shrines that Hezekiah had destroyed. He practiced worship of the stars and other heavenly bodies, even promoting this practice at an altar that he erected in the temple. He reintroduced worship of the pagan gods Baal and Ashtoreth. He dabbled in the occult, practicing sorcery and witchcraft and consulting fortune-tellers and spiritists who claimed to be able to communicate with the dead (2 Chronicles 33:3–6).

To top off this list of wrongdoing, the king "sacrificed his children in the fire" (2 Chronicles 33:6 NIV), offering his own flesh and blood as a burnt offering to the pagan god Molech. This was the same heinous sin that his grandfather, King Ahaz, had practiced years before.

The Lord punished Manasseh for these wrongdoings by allowing the Assyrians to invade and humiliate the nation of Judah. The king himself was carried away to Assyria, where he was imprisoned for a time. This experience humbled Manasseh and caused him to turn to the Lord. Finally, he was allowed to return to Judah, probably on his pledge of loyalty to the Assyrian king (2 Chronicles 33:10–13).

Back in Jerusalem, Manasseh tried to make up for the evil he had brought on Judah by getting rid of the foreign gods he had introduced and restoring worship of the one true God. But his change of heart seemed to have little effect on the religious sentiments of the people. His long reign of fifty-five years—longer than any other king of either Judah or Israel—had planted seeds of weakness and evil that led to a downward spiral of the nation. Manasseh's death marked the beginning of the end for Judah as it limped through its final years.

JUDAH'S FINAL YEARS

Six different kings ruled over Judah during the final fifty-five years of its existence. These kings, with the exception of Josiah, reigned for brief periods, reflecting the chaotic nature of these final years as the nation struggled with the threat of takeover by powerful nations that were beginning to dominate the ancient world.

KING AMON

Manasseh's son and successor, Amon, continued the evil practices of his father. But he was not as fortunate as Manasseh in the length of his reign. He ruled over Judah only two years before being assassinated by his own officials (2 Kings 21:19–23).

KING JOSIAH

After Amon was murdered, his son Josiah became the new king. Josiah was a godly ruler who did his best to stamp out idolatry and turn the southern kingdom back to God. He tore down pagan altars, purified the temple from defilement by idols, and implemented a fund drive to repair the temple (2 Chronicles 34:1–9). This must have been the most ambitious temple improvement project since the time of King Joash, more than 150 years before.

While the temple repairs were going on, a priest discovered a copy of "a book of the law of the Lord given by Moses" (2 Chronicles 34:14). This was probably a scroll that contained the Pentateuch, or the first five books of the Old Testament.

The Death of King Josiah, Antonio Zanchi (1631–1722)

When the contents of the book were revealed to the king, he tore his robe in despair because he realized how far the nation had strayed from God's original instructions to His people. Josiah used this book as a guide for a religious reform movement that swept the nation under his direction. He led the people to renew their covenant with the Lord (2 Chronicles 34:18–32).

To seal their pledge of faithfulness to God, the king led the citizens of Judah in a massive celebration of the Passover to express their thanks to God for His deliverance and protection. This celebration must have followed every detail of God's commands as recorded in the law of Moses. "No Passover had been observed like it in Israel since the days of Samuel the prophet," the biblical writer declared. "None of the kings of Israel ever observed a Passover like the one that Josiah observed" (2 Chronicles 35:18 HCSB).

One disturbing result of the discovery of this book of the law was a clear warning about Judah's future. The king sent several of his advisers to ask a prophetess named Huldah about the message of the book. She revealed that the Lord would bring disaster on the Southern Kingdom because of its sin of idolatry. But this would not happen until some years after the death of King Josiah (2 Chronicles 34:19–28).

Josiah's long and fruitful reign of thirty-one years came to an end about 609 BC, when a shift among two strong world powers was taking place. Assyria was in decline, and Babylon was stepping into the spotlight as the dominant nation of the ancient world. Egypt formed an alliance with Assyria to try to stop the Babylonian advance. As the Egyptian army marched northward, Josiah interpreted this movement as a threat to Judah's national security. He led an attack against the

Egyptians, suffering a mortal wound during the ensuing battle (2 Chronicles 35:20–24).

KING JEHOAHAZ II/SHALLUM

As the prophetess Huldah had predicted, Judah was on a roller coaster headed for destruction after Josiah passed from the scene. His son and successor, Jehoahaz, had the misfortune of serving as king during this time of rapid change in Judah's fortunes.

The Egyptians followed up their victory over Josiah by turning their attention to Jehoahaz. After he had occupied the throne for only three months, he was deposed and carried away as a prisoner to Egypt, where he died (2 Kings 23:31–34).

Jehoahaz is referred to as Jehoahaz II to set him apart from another king of the same name (Jehoahaz I), who reigned during the middle years of Judah's history. Jehoahaz II was also called Shallum by the prophet Jeremiah (Jeremiah 22:11).

KING JEHOIAKIM/ELIAKIM

When the Egyptians deposed Jehoahaz II, they placed Eliakim—a brother of the previous king, Josiah—on the throne. They changed his name to Jehoiakim, probably to show their control over the king and the nation of Judah. Jehoiakim was forced to tax the citizens of the land in order to pay the heavy tribute demanded by the Egyptian king (2 Kings 23:34–35).

During Jehoiakim's reign, the Babylonians grew powerful enough to invade Judah. They forced Jehoiakim to switch his loyalty from Egypt to Babylon and to pay tribute to the Babylonian king. After three years under this oppression, Jehoiakim rebelled (2 Kings 24:1–2). The Babylonians retaliated by overrunning Judah and taking the king to Babylon as a prisoner (2 Chronicles 36:6).

Jehoiakim was succeeded as king by his son Jehoiachin (2 Chronicles 36:8). This change of kings may have happened during the chaotic days when Judah was making preparations for a siege of Jerusalem by the Babylonian army.

KING JEHOIACHIN/CONIAH

Jehoiachin faced a dire situation when he succeeded his father, Jehoiakim, as the nineteenth king of Judah. After the Babylonian army laid siege to Jerusalem, Jehoiachin realized the situation was hopeless, so he surrendered the city to the inevitable. He and the rest of the royal family, along with his administration officials, were carried away to Babylon as captives.

Nebuchadnezzar, Babylon's king, also seized the treasures of the temple and the royal palace.

JUDAH'S FINAL KING

No-Stress Bible Reading
2 Kings 25:1–8; 2 Chronicles 36:11–21

No-Stress Bible Guide
Pages 145–151 (from "Judah's Final Years")

Think About It:

- Why do you think the king of Babylon was so severe in his punishment of King Zedekiah and his sons?

- What happened to the people of Judah after Jerusalem fell?

A PROPHET'S DIRE WARNING

No-Stress Bible Reading
Jeremiah 37

Think About It:

- Why do you think King Zedekiah sought the opinion and advice of the prophet Jeremiah?

He carried many of the leading citizens of Judah into exile, leaving only the peasants and the poor to work the land (2 Kings 24:8–15).

Jehoiachin, also known as Coniah (see Jeremiah 37:1), apparently remained in Babylon for the rest of his life. After thirty-five years as a prisoner, he was released by a new king and given a place of honor in the royal Babylonian palace (2 Kings 25:27–30). Perhaps he was treated kindly because he had not resisted the Babylonian takeover of Judah.

KING ZEDEKIAH/MATTANIAH

With Jehoiachin off the scene, the Babylonians needed someone in charge in Jerusalem to look after their interests in the nation of Judah. So they placed Mattaniah, an uncle of Jehoiachin, on the throne as a puppet king. They changed his name to Zedekiah (2 Kings 24:15–17).

Only twenty-one years old, Zedekiah faced the difficult task of governing a nation with dwindling resources. Many of Judah's leaders had been taken into exile. It must have been close to impossible to wring enough taxes out of the poor people left behind to pay the tribute demanded by the Babylonian king.

After struggling under these tough circumstances for nine years, Zedekiah rebelled and stopped paying off the Babylonians. This brought on the wrath of King Nebuchadnezzar, who marched his army to Jerusalem to settle matters with Judah once and for all.

Jerusalem withstood a siege from the Babylonian army for more than a year. But finally the walls were breached and the city fell to the enemy. King Zedekiah and his sons fled, only to be captured a short distance away. The king was forced to watch while his sons were murdered. Then he was blinded and carried away to Babylon as a prisoner (2 Kings 25:1–7).

Nebuchadnezzar had lost patience with Jerusalem and its rebel kings, so he showed no mercy to the city. He tore down its walls and burned the temple, the royal palace, and the houses of its citizens. He carried away anything of value, including the furnishings of the temple (see 2 Kings 25:9–17).

Thus, the nation of Judah that began with Solomon's successor more than three centuries before came to a disastrous end in 587 BC. The prophecy spoken by the prophetess Huldah in King Josiah's time had been fulfilled: "This is what the LORD says: I am going to bring disaster on this place and its people. . .because they have forsaken me and burned incense to other gods and aroused my anger by all that their hands have made" (2 Chronicles 34:24–25 NIV).

WRITING PROPHETS OF THE SOUTHERN KINGDOM

Huldah was not the only messenger of God who warned the people of Judah that God's punishment was inevitable unless they turned from their idolatry. Several writing prophets of the Old Testament were called by the Lord to hold the nation accountable for its sin and rebellion. These prophets are Isaiah, Jeremiah (and his book Lamentations), Joel, Micah, Nahum, Habakkuk, and Zephaniah.

THE PROPHET ISAIAH

Isaiah probably came from a family that was related to Judah's royal line. He apparently served as a recorder in King Uzziah's administration (2 Chronicles 26:22). Uzziah's death was a troubling event that brought about his dramatic vision of the Lord and his call to the prophetic ministry. "In the year that King Uzziah died," Isaiah later recalled, "I saw also the LORD sitting upon a throne, high and lifted up" (Isaiah 6:1).

Isaiah preached for forty years among the people of both Judah and Israel, but he is best known as a prophet to the Southern Kingdom. He witnessed the conquest of the Northern Kingdom by Assyria. He declared that the same thing would happen to Judah unless the people stopped worshipping false gods and turned back to the one true God.

One major theme of the book of Isaiah is the foolishness of worshipping idols. The prophet described the deluded thinking of a person who thought nothing of cutting down a tree and using part to burn for fuel and another part to fashion into an idol. He found it hard to believe that a person would worship something that was nothing but a lifeless block of wood (Isaiah 44:19).

Two kings of Judah are mentioned by name in Isaiah's prophecies. He advised King Ahaz to avoid entangling alliances with Syria (Isaiah 7:1–9). His discussion with Ahaz is the context for Isaiah's famous declaration about the birth of the Messiah to a virgin—an event that happened about seven hundred years later when Jesus was born (Isaiah 7:14).

The other king of Judah mentioned by Isaiah was Hezekiah. The prophet assured Hezekiah that Jerusalem would not be overrun by the Assyrians (2 Kings 19:32–34). This encounter with Judah's king also appears in the book of Isaiah (Isaiah 37:33–35). Likewise, the miraculous extension of Hezekiah's life is repeated in Isaiah's book (Isaiah 38:1–8).

Isaiah usually approved of the actions of Hezekiah. But one exception occurred when the king gave in to pride and showed off his valuable possessions to a friendly delegation from the king of Babylon. The prophet predicted correctly that these royal treasures would one day be carried away by the very people who had come to pay their respects to Judah's king (2 Kings 20:16–18; Isaiah 39:1–7).

THE PROPHET JEREMIAH AND LAMENTATIONS

About seventy-five years after Isaiah passed from the scene, God raised up the prophet Jeremiah to continue delivering His message to the southern kingdom. Like Isaiah, Jeremiah ministered for a period of about forty years. He

Jeremiah Lamenting the Destruction of Jerusalem, Rembrandt (1606–1669)

witnessed the chaotic final years of Judah. Three of its last kings are mentioned at the beginning of his book—Josiah, Jehoiakim, and Zedekiah (Jeremiah 1:2–3).

In addition, two other kings of Judah during its final years—Jehoahaz II and Jehoiachin—are mentioned in specific prophecies in the book of Jeremiah. He predicted that Shallum, also known as Jehoahaz II, would never return to Jerusalem after he was carried away by the Egyptians (Jeremiah 22:11). The prophet also described King Jehoiachin as "a despised, broken pot, an object no one wants" (Jeremiah 22:28 NIV) when the king and the rest of the royal family were taken into exile by the Babylonians.

One of the most famous passages in Jeremiah's book describes his encounter with King Jehoiakim about four years after he became the new king of Judah. The Lord told Jeremiah to dictate a message of God's impending judgment to his

Jeremiah's blunt reply was not what the king wanted to hear. "Thou shalt be delivered into the hand of the king of Babylon," he told Zedekiah (Jeremiah 37:17). This is exactly what happened when Jerusalem was overrun by the enemy.

Although Jeremiah predicted the fall of Jerusalem, he was not happy when it happened. He wrote a series of laments, or cries of despair, over the sad state of Judah's capital city and the nation of Judah. These writings appear in the book of Lamentations.

Lamentations shows the sensitive side of Jeremiah's personality. He had been compelled by the Lord to deliver a harsh message of judgment against his fellow citizens. But this did not lessen his love for Jerusalem and his native land. He found it depressing to see the city in ruins, sacked and burned by the Babylonian army. He actually wept over the devastated city (Lamentations 1:16).

NT Connection—GOD'S SPIRIT: Joel's prophecy about the outpouring of God's Spirit was fulfilled during the days of the early church. The Holy Spirit fell upon the followers of Jesus while they were praying for God's guidance on the day of Pentecost (Acts 2:1–4, 16–21).

scribe, Baruch, who wrote it on a scroll. When this scroll was read to the king, he cut it up and burned it, showing his contempt for the prophet and his message of doom (Jeremiah 36:20–23).

But God's message could not be snuffed out so easily. Jeremiah dictated God's message to Baruch a second time, "and many other words like them were added" (Jeremiah 36:32 HCSB).

For Judah's final king, Zedekiah, Jeremiah also had a message from the Lord. Zedekiah had the prophet thrown into prison on the false charge that he was deserting his own people to seek refuge among the Babylonian army while they were besieging Jerusalem. The king sent for the prophet and asked him if there was any word from the Lord on what to do in this situation.

THE PROPHET JOEL

The book of Joel paints a disturbing picture of the coming judgment of God against the people of Judah because of their sin. The prophet describes the devastation of the Southern Kingdom by a swarm of locusts. These destructive insects, similar to grasshoppers, destroyed all the crops and stripped the leaves from shrubs and trees. This was a foretaste of the judgment of God that would fall on the nation unless the people repented and turned from their wicked ways (Joel 1:2–4).

Along with this message of judgment, Joel also had words of hope for Judah. God promised to bless His people if they would turn to Him and obey His commands. He would renew their zeal and commitment through a great outpouring of His Spirit (Joel 2:28–29). The entire world would take notice when He gathered His people in Jerusalem to serve as their sovereign ruler (Joel 3:2).

THE PROPHET MICAH

Micah delivered his prophecies to the citizens of both Judah and Israel. He mentioned three kings of Judah—Jotham, Ahaz, and Hezekiah (Micah 1:1). Like most of the prophets of the Old Testament, Micah's book includes prophecies of both judgment and promise. God would punish His people because of their sin. But He was just as determined to bless them to fulfill the promises He had made to Abraham many centuries before (Micah 4:10–13).

The book of Micah is best known for its promise of the coming Messiah. Micah even foretold the place where He would be born: the village of Bethlehem (Micah 5:2). This is one of the most remarkable messianic prophecies in the entire Old Testament.

THE PROPHET NAHUM

The book of Nahum is a prophecy written by the prophet Nahum during the final years of the nation of Judah. He predicted that Nineveh, capital city of the Assyrian Empire, would fall as a result of God's judgment against its rebellion and cruelty. By this time, the Assyrian threat to Judah was declining, and Babylon was growing into the superpower of the ancient world.

Nahum declared that God would destroy the idols and images of the pagan Assyrian religious system. But He would eventually restore the nation of Judah and its commitment to the worship of the one true God (Nahum 1:9–15).

THE PROPHET HABAKKUK

Habakkuk was a prophet to the Southern Kingdom who had the audacity to question the ways of God.

First, Habakkuk declared that God was being lenient for not punishing the people of Judah for their sin. The Lord assured him that punishment was forthcoming in the form of the Babylonian army from the north (Habakkuk 1:1–11).

Then Habakkuk questioned whether it was just and fair for the Lord to use a pagan nation as an instrument of His judgment. Weren't the Babylonians more sinful than those against whom God was sending them? (Habakkuk 1:12–17).

The Lord reminded Habakkuk that He was the sovereign ruler of the universe who could do as He pleased. He did not owe the prophet an explanation for His actions (Habakkuk 2:2–20). Habakkuk finally accepted this truth about the Lord and His ways in submissive faith (Habakkuk 3:1–19).

THE PROPHET ZEPHANIAH

Zephaniah ministered in the Southern Kingdom during the reign of King Josiah (Zephaniah 1:1). This prophet was probably a contemporary of Jeremiah. Like Jeremiah, he predicted that the kingdom of Judah was marked for destruction by the Lord as punishment for its sin (Zephaniah 1:4–6).

But even as the Lord was punishing His people and sending them into exile, the prophet declared, He was not giving up on His people. He would preserve a faithful remnant who would remain loyal to Him. God would use them to resettle the land and bear witness of Him to others when they returned from their time of captivity in a foreign land (Zephaniah 3:20).

Zephaniah's prophecy was eventually fulfilled. But not before the nation of Judah had suffered under the thumb of its enemies for several decades. This brings us to the next chapter in the history of God's chosen people—their sad existence in exile in a foreign land.

The Mourning Jews in Exile,
Eduard Bendemann (1811–1889)

CHAPTER 13

Judah's devastation by a foreign power was not a surprise to the prophets who lived during the nation's final years. They had been predicting for years that the idolatry of the Southern Kingdom would result in God's punishment. This is exactly what happened when the Babylonians overran the Southern Kingdom and carried its leading citizens into exile.

The prophet Jeremiah even predicted how long this exile would last. "After seventy years are completed at Babylon," the Lord revealed to the prophet, "I will. . .perform My good word toward you, and cause you [the exiles] to return to this place" (Jeremiah 29:10 NKJV). Some scholars believe that Jeremiah's "seventy years" refers to the length of Babylon's reign rather than the length of the exile. At any rate, the exile lasted from about 575 BC to approximately 540 BC. This period is not described in detail by any specific book of the Bible. But glimpses of this crucial period of Bible history appear in the books of Ezekiel, Daniel, and Esther. Major events of these years may be organized as follows: (1) the number of exiles, (2) life in exile, (3) Ezekiel among the exiles, and (4) the ministry of the prophet Daniel.

THE NUMBER OF EXILES

The deportation of citizens of Judah to Babylon actually happened on three separate occasions. The first occurred when King Jehoiachin of Judah surrendered to Nebuchadnezzar of Babylon without a fight. A total of ten thousand people were carried to Babylon at this time (2 Kings 24:12-14). This happened about 575 BC, several years before the city of Jerusalem fell to the Babylonian army.

About ten years later, after King Zedekiah's rebellion, the Babylonians destroyed the city of Jerusalem. An unknown number of Jews who had been left behind after the first deportation were taken away to Babylon on this occasion (2 Kings 25:8-12).

Finally, about five years later, Nebuchadnezzar sent his army back to Jerusalem. This time he intended to punish the people who had assassinated the governor, Gedaliah, whom he had placed in authority over the city. Most of the residents of Jerusalem had fled to Egypt. But the Babylonians did find 745 people whom they transported back to Babylon (Jeremiah 52:30).

HOW MANY PEOPLE WENT INTO EXILE?

The books of 2 Kings and Jeremiah do not agree on the total number of Jewish exiles who were deported to Babylon (2 Kings 24:12-14; Jeremiah 52:28-30). All we know for sure is that it was not all the people of Judah—probably no more than 20 to 25 percent of the total population. The Babylonians deported only the leading citizens, including skilled craftsmen, artisans, government officials, those with a good education, and members of the upper class. They left behind the poor to work the land (Jeremiah 52:16).

LIFE IN EXILE

Life for the exiles in Babylon was nothing like the drudgery their distant ancestors had experienced as slaves in Egypt many centuries before. The Babylonian captives were settled in a rich plain on a river known as Chebar, or Kebar (Ezekiel 1:1–3). This channel was actually an irrigation canal near Babylon. It probably carried water from the Tigris and the Euphrates Rivers to the fertile agricultural lands outside the capital city.

In this fertile region the exiles from Judah were given the freedom to grow their own crops, buy and sell their goods, trade among themselves and the Babylonian population, and govern their own affairs. Archaeological evidence at ancient Babylon reveals that some of the Jewish exiles became so prosperous that they chose to remain here rather than return to Judah after the exile came to an end.

In spite of being treated like colonists rather than slaves, most of the exiles missed their homeland and longed to return. They were particularly homesick for their capital city, Jerusalem, and its temple. To them, this place of worship represented the presence of God. It was difficult for them to sing praises to the Lord when separated from the holy city and its central place of worship. Their sadness and despair come through in the words of a psalm written during these years of absence from their beloved country.

"Beside the rivers of Babylon, we sat and wept as we thought of Jerusalem," the psalmist lamented. "We put away our harps, hanging them on the branches of poplar trees. For our captors demanded a song from us. Our tormentors insisted on a joyful hymn: 'Sing us one of those songs of Jerusalem!' But how can we sing the songs of the LORD while in a pagan land?

"If I forget you, O Jerusalem, let my right hand forget how to play the harp," the psalmist continued. "May my tongue stick to the roof of my mouth if I fail to remember you, if I don't make Jerusalem my greatest joy" (Psalm 137:1–6 NLT).

In spite of the despair of these years, living apart from Jerusalem and the temple for six or seven decades brought about some positive changes for God's people. The most beneficial change was their rejection of idolatry and all forms of religious compromise. Worship of false gods was common among the people of both Judah and Israel before they were taken into exile. Their years of domination by a foreign power turned them back to God, who assured them through the prophets that He had not turned His back on His chosen people.

During the exile the people were forced to develop different worship customs, since they

THE ULTIMATE REJECTION

No-Stress Bible Reading
Psalm 74

No-Stress Bible Guide
Pages 153–155
(to "Ezekiel Among the Exiles")

Think About It:

- Why did the writer of Psalm 74 feel that the Lord had rejected His people during the years of the exile?

IN NEED OF HOPE

No-Stress Bible Reading
Psalm 102

Think About It:

- What metaphors or figures of speech did this psalmist use to express his feelings of despair while in exile in Babylon?

had no temple to attend. This void led them to establish local synagogues. These community-based centers focused on the teaching of the law rather than on rituals of animal sacrifice. After the exile and the people's return to Judah, synagogues were established throughout their homeland. These local worship centers played a prominent role in the spread of the Gospel during the early years of the New Testament church.

Another positive result of the exile was that it fashioned the Jewish people into a unified nation with a distinct purpose and mission. God's purpose for His people from the very beginning was that they would serve as a light to the nations by influencing the rest of the world to worship and obey the one true God (Genesis 12:2–3).

This understanding of God's plan was rekindled during the exile by the prophet Ezekiel. From the restored and unified nation of Judah, He declared, a future Messiah would come. This descendant of David would serve as a blessing to the entire world (Ezekiel 37:24–28).

EZEKIEL AMONG THE EXILES

The prophets Ezekiel and Daniel are the best-known personalities of the exile. Both were taken into captivity during one of the early invasions of Judah by King Nebuchadnezzar of Babylon. Ezekiel came from a priestly family (Ezekiel 1:3). He was probably about twenty-five years old when he went into exile. He addressed his prophecies to the Jewish exiles across a period of twenty years, from about 593 to 573 BC. The site of his ministry was a place not far from the city of Babylon.

In the early prophecies of the book of Ezekiel, he wrote as a captive who expected the city of Jerusalem to be destroyed. This happened in 587 BC, after he had been in Babylon for about five years. He must have drawn from eyewitness accounts of this tragedy to describe the beginning of the siege of the city that appears in chapter 24 of his book.

The day the siege began was such a sad occasion that the Lord instructed Ezekiel to write it down as a memorial of this tragedy (Ezekiel 24:2). Another tragic happening on this day was the death of the prophet's wife. Ezekiel was forbidden to mourn her death, to symbolize God's judgment on the sinful nation of Judah (Ezekiel 24:15–24).

Ezekiel is known for his strange visions, as

> ### STRENGTH FOR A PROPHET
>
> **No-Stress Bible Reading**
> Ezekiel 2–3
>
> **No-Stress Bible Guide**
> Pages 155–156 (from "Ezekiel Among the Exiles" to "The Ministry of Daniel")
>
> **Think About It:**
>
> - Why do you think God commanded Ezekiel to eat a scroll that contained sad and gloomy words?

well as his use of symbolic behavior and object lessons to drive home his messages. He portrayed the people of Judah as a helpless newborn baby (Ezekiel 16:4–5) and as a useless vine (Ezekiel 15). He also drank water "with trembling" and ate bread "with quaking" (Ezekiel 12:17) to symbolize God's wrath against His wayward people.

In the first part of his book, Ezekiel reminded the people of Judah of their sins and the losses they had suffered and predicted other disasters. But beginning with chapter 36, he began to give them assurance that better days were ahead. The exile would eventually come to an end.

After their years of domination by a foreign power, God would lead His people back to their homeland and establish His universal rule among the nations.

The most famous passage in Ezekiel's prophecies that represents this hope for the future is his vision of a valley of dry bones. As the prophet stood in the middle of this valley, surrounded by dead skeletal remains, God told him to speak to the dry bones. When he did so, the bones sprang to life as they were energized by God's Spirit. This represented the future restoration of God's people. The Lord Himself declared to the prophet, "These bones are the people of Israel. . . . I will bring [them] back to the land of Israel" (Ezekiel 37:11–12 NIV).

THE MINISTRY OF DANIEL

Like his contemporary Ezekiel, the prophet Daniel was also taken into captivity during one of the invasions of Judah by the Babylonians. This probably happened when Daniel was a young man, perhaps a teenager (Daniel 1:3–7). The events recorded in the book of Daniel show that the prophet remained in exile for at least sixty years. He rose to a high position as an adviser to several different Babylonian kings, and he continued his prophecies even after Babylon was defeated by the Persian army.

One of the problems that confronted the Jewish captives in Babylon and Persia was how to remain faithful to God in the midst of pagan surroundings. Was it even possible? Several episodes recorded by Daniel gave a bold yes to this question.

The first episode involved the food the king of Babylon provided for Daniel and his three Jewish friends—Shadrach, Meshach, and Abednego—to acclimate them to Babylonian customs. They refused to eat the rich food that was part of the royal diet, probably because of their strict observance of Jewish food laws. They asked to be tested instead on a diet of vegetables and water for ten days to determine which foods were superior.

At the end of this period, "they looked better and healthier than all the young men who were eating the king's food" (Daniel 1:15 HCSB). Daniel and his friends had passed the first test of their faith in convincing fashion.

A little later, Daniel's three friends were thrown into a hot furnace because they refused to bow down and worship an image of King Nebuchadnezzar. This incident implies that the king was claiming to be a god whom the

A SUCCESSFUL TEST

No-Stress Bible Reading
Daniel 1

No-Stress Bible Guide
Pages 156–157
(from "The Ministry of Daniel")

Think About It:

- How do you see God's hand at work in the selection of Daniel and his three friends as trainees to serve the Babylonian king?

DANIEL'S DELIVERANCE

No-Stress Bible Reading
Daniel 6

Think About It:

- What motivated Daniel's accusers to plot his arrest?

- Why do you think the king himself went to the lion's den to check on Daniel?

Daniel's Answer to the King, Briton Rivière (1840–1920)

entire nation was expected to worship. When Shadrach, Meshach, and Abednego emerged from the furnace unharmed because of God's miraculous intervention, the Babylonians developed a reverent respect for this awesome God who was served by Daniel and his friends (Daniel 3:8–29).

This respect for God grew even stronger when Daniel refused to cave in to his enemies. They convinced the king to pass a law requiring the people to worship no god but the king of the land. When Daniel continued to worship the one true God, he was thrown into a den of lions. The ruler of Babylon was amazed when the prophet emerged unharmed after spending a night among these beasts. The king issued a royal decree encouraging the people of his empire to "tremble and fear before the God of Daniel" (Daniel 6:26).

Daniel is best known for his prophecies about world-changing events that have taken place since his time. His vision of four beasts has been interpreted to refer to four different empires that successively dominated the ancient world: Babylon (lion), Persia (bear), Greece (leopard), and Rome (beast with ten horns) (Daniel 7:4–7).

Daniel's most famous prophecy was revealed to him by the angel Gabriel. Known as his "seventy weeks" prophecy, it has been interpreted as a period of 490 years, or seventy times seven (Daniel 9:20–27). These 490 years, according to some interpreters, refer to the coming of the Messiah, Jesus Christ, about 490 years after the Jews were allowed to return to Jerusalem when the exile came to an end.

The prophet Daniel also had the ability to interpret dreams. He was summoned for this purpose by King Nebuchadnezzar (Daniel 2:1–16; 4:1–37) and by Belshazzar, the last king of Babylon. Daniel revealed the meaning of the strange writing that appeared on the wall of the royal palace. It meant that the days of Belshazzar's reign were numbered; his kingdom would be defeated by the Medes and Persians (Daniel 5:25–30).

Exactly as Daniel predicted, the Babylonian Empire was defeated about 540 BC by an allied army of the Medes and Persians. Under the Persians, the Jewish exiles were allowed to return to their homeland, and thus a new chapter in the history of God's people was opened.

Queen Esther, Edwin Long (1829–1891)

CHAPTER 14
Back Home in Jerusalem

Unlike the Babylonians who forced their captives into exile, the Persian policy toward a vassal state was to allow its citizens to remain where they lived. A Persian-appointed governor ruled these captive territories, collecting taxes for the empire's royal treasury. This more benevolent policy toward subject nations set the stage for the return of the citizens of Judah to their homeland. (See sidebar, "What Joy!")

The return of the Israelites to Judah began about 540 BC, soon after Persia became the undisputed power of the ancient world. The return and the years soon after this event bring us to the end of the Old Testament in about 400 BC. Six different books of the Old Testament—Ezra, Nehemiah, Esther, Haggai, Zechariah, and Malachi—shed light on this period of Bible history and the unique problems it presented for God's people. The major players in these books may be summarized in this order: (1) Ezra and Nehemiah, (2) Haggai and Zechariah, (3) Esther, and (4) Malachi.

"WHAT JOY!"

Psalm 126 records the joy that filled the hearts of those exiles who returned to Judah. The psalmist praised God for bringing His people back to their homeland: "When the Lord brought back his exiles to Jerusalem, it was like a dream! We were filled with laughter, and we sang for joy. And the other nations said, 'What amazing things the Lord has done for them.' Yes, the Lord has done amazing things for us! What joy!" (Psalm 126:1-3 NLT).

THE BOOKS OF EZRA AND NEHEMIAH

A careful study of these two books reveals that three different groups of exiles returned to their homeland during this period of biblical history. These separate treks back to Judah were led by Zerubbabel, Ezra, and Nehemiah.

FIRST RETURN UNDER ZERUBBABEL

Soon after King Cyrus of Persia defeated the Babylonians, he issued a decree authorizing the exiles from Judah to return to their homeland (Ezra 1:2-4). This decree was much broader than his permission for this event to take place.

The king specifically wanted the exiles to rebuild the temple in Jerusalem that had been destroyed by the Babylonian army about sixty years before. He even directed that all the furnishings of the temple taken by the Babylonians be returned. He also instructed his own people, the Persians, to provide the exiles with silver, gold, livestock, and supplies, probably to finance the expedition back to Judah (see Ezra 1:4).

NT Connection—ZERUBBABEL: He is listed as an ancestor of Jesus in the genealogies of both Matthew (1:12) and Luke (3:27). His name is "Zorobabel" in the KJV.

HOMEWARD BOUND

No-Stress Bible Reading
Ezra 1; 4

No-Stress Bible Guide
Pages 159–161 (to "Second Return under Ezra")

Think About It:

- Why do you think Cyrus allowed the Jewish exiles to return to their homeland?

A SHOCK FOR EZRA

No-Stress Bible Reading
Ezra 7; 9

No-Stress Bible Guide
Pages 161–163 (from "Second Return Under Ezra" to "Third Return Under Nehemiah")

Think About It:

- Why was Ezra so upset when he arrived in Jerusalem?

The person chosen to lead the first group of exiles to return to Jerusalem was a man named Zerubbabel, also referred to as "Sheshbazzar" (see Ezra 1:11). His name means "begotten in Babylon," so it is likely he was born during the Babylonian exile. Zerubbabel may have been a member of the family of King Jehoiachin, the king of Judah who was taken into exile during the chaotic years before Judah fell to the Babylonians. Zerubbabel's royal lineage may explain why he was selected as the leader of the first return. (See map, "Exiles Return to Judea," p. 313.)

Accompanying Zerubbabel on this first return to Judah were 42,360 citizens of Judah, along with numerous servants and large herds of livestock (Ezra 2:64–67). As soon as they arrived in Jerusalem, they took an offering to be used in the temple-rebuilding project. But they soon realized they faced a daunting task.

One problem was the impoverished condition of the nation of Judah. The returnees found a land that had suffered under near-starvation conditions for more than fifty years. The poor class that had been left in Judah during the exile had taken over the land and claimed it as their own. They resented the exiles who returned and wanted to assume their ancestral property rights. Surrounding tribal groups such as the Ammonites, Moabites, and Edomites harassed the returnees. These ancient enemies had gotten a foothold in Judah and intended to continue their influence in the land.

Among all these opposing groups, the most troublesome were the Samaritans. These half-breed Jews had intermarried with foreigners after the Northern Kingdom fell to the Assyrians many years before Judah went into exile. The Samaritans apparently felt they were entitled to a stake in Judah's future, so they offered to help Zerubbabel rebuild the temple.

When Zerubbabel refused their offer, they used their influence with Persian officials to get the work stopped (Ezra 4:11–24). More than a decade went by before the stop order was lifted and the people could resume construction (Ezra 6:1–12). By this time Zerubbabel and the people were so discouraged about the prospects of a new temple that they stopped working on the house of the Lord. They turned instead to building their own permanent houses. The temple foundation had been laid, but it served as a silent witness to their neglect and lack of commitment. (See sidebar, "Zerubbabel as a Signet Ring.")

This was the situation that the prophets Haggai and Zechariah found when they arrived on the scene in about 520 BC. They urged the

Cyrus's Defeat of the Babylonians, John Martin (1789–1854).
This defeat led to Cyrus's decree allowing the exiles to return to Israel.

people to get their priorities straight and resume construction on the Lord's house (Haggai 1:7–15; Ezra 5:1–2). The people obeyed the Lord's prophets and got back to work, finishing the project within about five years (Ezra 6:13–15). Although this temple was not as ornate as Solomon's original structure, the people celebrated the dedication of the house of the Lord with great joy (Ezra 6:16). It was a visible reminder of God's presence among His people.

SECOND RETURN UNDER EZRA

About fifty years after the completion of the temple under Zerubbabel, a second group of exiles returned to Jerusalem. This expedition was led by Ezra, a priest and scribe who was a careful student of the law of the Lord (Ezra 7:10).

ZERUBBABEL AS A SIGNET RING

The prophet Haggai compared Zerubbabel to a signet ring on the hand of the Lord (Haggai 2:23). In ancient times a signet ring functioned much like a personal signature does today. A king or other high official would stamp an official document with the symbol on his ring to establish its legality and show that it was issued under his authority.

This comparison showed that God had invested his servant Zerubbabel with the highest honor. He would use him as His representative to bring about His purposes in the city of Jerusalem and the restored nation of Judah.

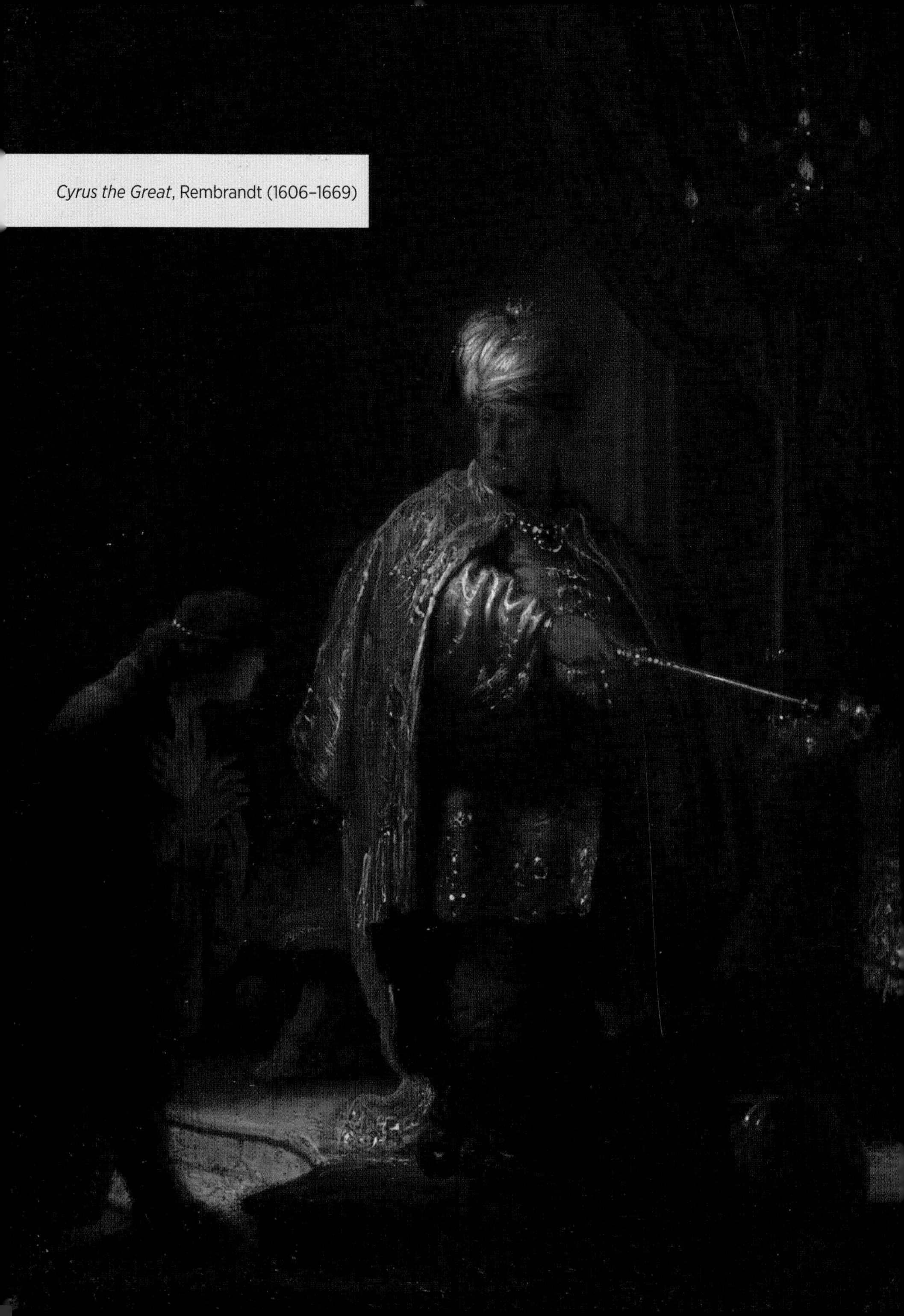

Cyrus the Great, Rembrandt (1606–1669)

His mission was spiritual in nature—to reestablish the law of the Lord in Judah—in contrast to Zerubbabel's work, which involved the physical restoration of the temple.

Like Zerubbabel's homecoming, Ezra's return had the blessing and support of the Persian king. In Ezra's time Artaxerxes reigned over the Persian Empire. He issued a decree authorizing Ezra's return, directing his officials to provide the supplies Ezra needed to make the trip (Ezra 7:21–22).

The exact number of exiles who returned with Ezra is unknown, although some statistics are cited in chapter 8 of his book. Accompanying him were heads of families and their descendants, priests, Levites, and temple servants (Ezra 8:15–20).

When he arrived in Jerusalem, Ezra discovered that many of the people were neglecting God's law and had grown lax in their religious commitment. He was particularly concerned that many of the Israelite men had taken wives from among the foreigners in the land who worshipped pagan gods.

Burdened by this clear violation of God's command, Ezra offered a fervent prayer of confession to the Lord. This prayer is one of the longest and most remarkable in the Old Testament. He admitted that the sins of God's people were "higher than our heads" (Ezra 9:6 NIV) and that "not one of us can stand in your presence" (Ezra 9:15 NIV). At the same time, he acknowledged that the Lord had punished His people "less than our sins deserved" (Ezra 9:13 NIV).

Ezra's sincere prayer moved the people to confess their sins and plead for God's forgiveness. Many men of Judah also took an oath to divorce their foreign wives. The book of Ezra records the names of all the men who made this promise and followed through on their commitment (Ezra 10:18–44).

In addition to these marriage reforms, Ezra also led the people of Judah to focus

REBUILD THIS WALL!

No-Stress Bible Reading
Nehemiah 2; 4

No-Stress Bible Guide
Pages 163–165 (from "Third Return Under Nehemiah" to "The Books of Haggai and Zechariah")

Think About It:

- How did Nehemiah prepare for this project, even while he was still in Persia?

- What leadership abilities did Nehemiah demonstrate before the Jewish leaders in Jerusalem after inspecting the wall?

- Why do you think Nehemiah's enemies were so determined to keep the wall from being built?

on the teachings of the law of the Lord. He called an assembly of the people, mounted a platform, and read portions of the law from a scroll—loudly and distinctly so everyone could understand. This reading went on for several hours, with the Levites explaining the meaning of these divine commands. The people pledged their assent to God's instructions by declaring, "Amen" (Nehemiah 8:1–8).

During this time of commitment to God's law, the people also celebrated the Feast of Tabernacles, one of their major religious festivals. This event commemorated God's provision in the wilderness during their exodus from Egyptian slavery. This concentration on their spiritual heritage brought on a spiritual revival. The people confessed their sins and renewed their covenant with the Lord (Nehemiah 9–10).

THIRD RETURN UNDER NEHEMIAH

About a dozen years after Ezra arrived in

Jerusalem, the Lord stirred the spirit of a layman known as Nehemiah to undertake a third return of exiles to Judah. Nehemiah's brother, Hanani, who had gone back to Judah, happened to be visiting Persia. Nehemiah asked him how things were going back in their homeland.

"The remnant in the province, who survived the exile, are in great trouble and disgrace," Hanani told him. "Jerusalem's wall has been broken down, and its gates have been burned down" (Nehemiah 1:3 HCSB).

Nehemiah was shocked at the news. It had been a century since the first group of exiles had gone back to Jerusalem under Zerubbabel. It was hard to believe that nothing had been done during all these years to rebuild the city's defensive wall. Without it, Judah's capital city was flirting with catastrophe, open and exposed to its enemies.

Nehemiah was so upset that he wept and mourned for several days (Nehemiah 1:4). Then he prayed about the situation and discovered that he was the answer to his own prayer. He determined that he would ask the Persian king, Artaxerxes, for permission to go to Jerusalem and rebuild the city walls.

Nehemiah needed the king's blessing because he was one of his court officials. His boss not only granted his request for a leave of absence; he also sent some of his own military officers along as an escort and authorized Nehemiah to cut timber from the royal forest for use in the building project (Nehemiah 2:8–9).

After reaching Jerusalem, Nehemiah surveyed the walls at night to keep from rousing suspicion among Judah's enemies. Then he reported the city's perilous situation to local officials and recruited laborers to begin the work (Nehemiah 2:15–18).

Nehemiah and his construction crew were threatened by three enemies: a Samaritan known as Sanballat the Horonite; Tobiah, an Ammonite official; and an Arab man named Geshem. But Nehemiah refused to be intimidated by their threats and harassment. He directed the laborers to work on the wall with tools in one hand and weapons in the other (Nehemiah 4:17). Thanks to his courageous leadership, the project was completed in fifty-two days (Nehemiah 6:15).

Nehemiah's work did not stop with the completion of Jerusalem's defensive wall. He also put a stop to the exploitation of the poor by Judah's upper class (Nehemiah 5:1–13), prohibited buying and selling on the Sabbath, and implemented reforms that assured adequate financial support for priests, Levites, and other officials who took care of the temple in Jerusalem (Nehemiah 13:10–22).

THE BOOKS OF HAGGAI AND ZECHARIAH

The prophets Haggai and Zechariah arrived on the scene in the early years after the Jewish exiles returned to Judah. Both prophets encouraged those who had returned with Zerubbabel to get on with the business of rebuilding the temple (Haggai 1:1–11). Zechariah is known for his eight visions. One of these, a lampstand with olive branches on each side (Zechariah 4:1–14), is interpreted as a promise that the Lord would provide the resources needed by Zerubbabel to complete the temple-building project.

The greatest contribution of Zechariah's book is his description of the coming Messiah. He depicted a coronation scene (Zechariah 6:9–15) in which a priest named Joshua, symbolizing the Messiah, was crowned as king as well as priest. He declared that the Messiah would reign in justice from the city of Jerusalem (Zechariah 8:3–16).

Zechariah even described the manner in which the Messiah would enter the city: "See, your king comes to you, righteous and victorious, lowly and riding on a donkey, on a colt, the foal of a donkey" (Zechariah 9:9 NIV). This prophecy was fulfilled when Jesus rode into Jerusalem on a young donkey just a few days before His crucifixion (Matthew 21:5).

THE BOOK OF ESTHER

The book of Esther shows clearly that not all the Jewish exiles in Persia took advantage of the opportunity to return to Judah. Many chose to remain in Persia, probably because they had built a comfortable and successful life in this pagan nation during their long separation from their native land.

Esther, the young Jewish woman for whom the book is named, rose to the position of queen under the Persian king, Ahasuerus, who reigned from about 485 to 465 BC, so the book of Esther can be dated to the time after the exile. His reign occurred about fifty to sixty years after the Persians allowed the first group of exiles to return to their homeland.

The main people in the book of Esther are King Ahasuerus; his wife, Queen Esther; his top official, an evil man named Haman; and Mordecai, Esther's relative, who was also a palace official and a leader among the Jewish people who were living throughout Persia.

Haman developed a hatred for the Jewish people because he felt they did not pay him the respect he deserved as a high official of the Persian government. He tricked the king into issuing an order for their wholesale execution. But Queen Esther, at Mordecai's encouragement, used her influence with the king to expose Haman's plot. Haman was hanged on the gallows that he had built for Mordecai's execution, and Mordecai was promoted by the king to a higher position.

The Jewish people were allowed to resist their enemies, and they were granted victory by the Lord. The book ends with their celebration of this miraculous deliverance through a special holiday known as the Feast of Purim (Esther 9:27–28).

Zechariah the prophet as depicted by Michelangelo (1475–1564) on the ceiling of the Sistine Chapel in the Vatican

THE BOOK OF MALACHI

As a prophet after the exile, Malachi faced the same situation as Haggai and Zechariah, although he ministered several decades after these two earlier prophets. Malachi's name means "messenger of the Lord," and he was bold and forthright as God's appointed spokesman to the people during these crucial years.

Malachi ministered in Judah about one hundred years after the first group of exiles returned from captivity. This was a time of great moral laxity and indifference in the nation of Judah. A general air of worldliness pervaded the land. Many people had grown cold in spiritual matters and in their commitment to the Lord.

This tone of indifference was evident when worshippers stopped bringing tithes and offerings to the temple. Others offered defective animals as sacrifices rather than the finest from their flocks, as the Lord demanded. Intermarriage with pagan peoples was commonplace. Even the priests grew careless and negligent in presiding over the ceremonies at the temple.

Malachi declared that these lax practices were unacceptable to the Lord. Unless the people and the leaders changed their ways, they would face His punishment. He urged the people to be faithful to God's law and to await the coming of the Messiah's forerunner, who would come in the spirit and power of the prophet Elijah (Malachi 4:5). This referred to John the Baptist, who announced the coming of Jesus into the world.

With Malachi's prophecy, the Old Testament comes to an end in about 400 BC. It would be four centuries before God's promise of a coming Messiah would be realized with the birth of Jesus. These years between the testaments were a dark time when no prophets arose to deliver God's message to His people. But after the long darkness, a glorious new age would dawn upon the world. The intertestamental period of biblical history is explored in the next chapter.

PRIESTLY PROBLEMS

No-Stress Bible Reading
Malachi 1

No-Stress Bible Guide
Page 167

Think About It:

- How were the priests of Judah failing to please the Lord in the sacrifices they offered at the altar?

A SERIOUS ACCUSATION

No-Stress Bible Guide
Malachi 3

Think About It:

- What do you think Malachi meant by his accusation that the people were "robbing" God?

Statue of Alexander the Great, who attempted to capture the known world of his time

CHAPTER 15
The Silent Years between the Testaments

A four-hundred-year gap—from about 400 BC to about 5 BC—separates the final events of the Old Testament from the greatest event of all time—the birth of Jesus into the world. This period is often referred to as the intertestamental period or the silent years between the Old Testament and the New.

Not a single prophet stepped forward throughout this period to encourage the Jewish people to remain faithful to the Lord. But God was not on an extended leave of absence during these years. He was working behind the scenes through the turmoil of earthly events to prepare the world for the coming of the Messiah.

The turbulent years between the testaments may be divided into five distinct periods: (1) dominance by the Persians, (2) life under the Greeks, (3) the Maccabean Revolt, (4) Jewish independence, and (5) the rise of Rome.

PERSIAN PERIOD

While Persia allowed the Jewish exiles to return to their homeland, it still retained control over the nation of Judah. As the dominant world power of the time, the Persians ruled over the Jewish people by appointing local officials who were loyal to the Persian king. These officials collected taxes from the people and otherwise looked after Persian interests in the area. This dominance of Persia continued for about the first sixty years of the intertestamental period.

GREEK PERIOD

Persia's hold on the ancient world began to unravel when Alexander the Great became king over the Greek city-states that his father had gathered into one united kingdom. Beginning in about 330 BC, Alexander launched a campaign of world conquest. Within a decade, this brilliant young commander (he was only twenty-two years old at the time) succeeded in conquering Persia, Babylon, Palestine, Syria, Egypt, and western India. Greece was firmly entrenched as the dominant power of the ancient world when he died unexpectedly at the age of thirty-two. (See sidebar, "Alexander in the Bible?")

Alexander's burning ambition was to establish an empire united under the umbrella of Greek culture, customs, religion, and traditions. This was a system that came to be known as Hellenism. The term comes from *Hellas*, the Greek word for Greece. Even after the physical nation of Greece

ALEXANDER IN THE BIBLE?

Alexander is not mentioned by name in the Bible. But some scholars think he is mentioned in code fashion in the book of Daniel. The "mighty king" in Daniel's vision (Daniel 11:3–4) may refer to him (see also Daniel 8:21).

waned, the influence of Greek thought continued throughout the ancient world, persisting into

New Testament times, even after the Roman Empire became the number one power on the world stage.

Perhaps the greatest contribution of Hellenism was the adoption of the Greek language as the universal language of the time. In New Testament times, most well-educated people spoke Greek. Even the New Testament was written originally in Greek. The language's universality was an important factor in the rapid spread of the Gospel throughout the Roman world during the time of the apostle Paul and the early years of the church.

When Alexander died, a struggle for control over the territory he had conquered broke out among several of his generals. Eventually one of these, Antiochus IV, gained the upper hand in Syria and the neighboring region of Palestine. Antiochus was also known as "Epiphanes," an egotistical name he had given himself. It meant "God manifest," and it spelled trouble for the Jewish people.

Up until the reign of Antiochus, the Jews of Palestine had been able to maintain their traditional forms of worship. They had not been forced to bow down to the pagan Greek gods. But Antiochus was determined to force Hellenism in the extreme upon his Jewish subjects. He outlawed the rite of circumcision, forbade observance of the Sabbath and major Jewish festivals, and made it illegal to offer sacrifices to God in the temple. He topped off these oppressive acts by marching into the most sacred place in the temple and sacrificing a pig on the altar to the false Greek god known as Zeus.

This heinous act was guaranteed to outrage the Jews. They responded by taking up arms against Antiochus and his successors—a struggle that lasted about twenty-five years. This rebellion came to be known as the Maccabean Revolt.

REBELLION UNDER THE MACCABEES

The spark that ignited the Jewish revolt against their oppressors was struck in the village of Modein just outside Jerusalem in 167 BC. An army officer under orders from Antiochus attempted to force an aged priest named Mattathias to offer a sacrifice of swine flesh. Mattathias refused, and another man of the community stepped forward to commit the blasphemous act. Overcome by anger, Mattathias attacked the man and the army officer, killing them both. Then the old priest and his five sons fled into the wilderness.

This family gathered around them an army of Jewish zealots who battled their oppressors for the next twenty-five years. They led many successful guerilla attacks against the forces of Antiochus throughout the countryside. After Mattathias died, he was succeeded by his son Judas.

Judas became known for his surprising attacks and solid blows against the enemy. His supporters referred to him as "the hammerer." In the Aramaic language, this term was *makkaba*. Its Greek equivalent was *Maccabee*. Thus, the entire rebellion came to be known as the Maccabean Revolt.

Most of what we know about this Jewish rebellion comes from two apocryphal books—1 and 2 Maccabees—that were written during this time. These two books were excluded from early editions of the Old Testament but included in others. This explains why Bibles favored by Roman Catholics contain the Old Testament Apocrypha—which includes the two books of the Maccabees—while these books do not appear in most Protestant editions of the Bible, which tend to use earlier editions as their guide.

The first book of Maccabees contains a history of the Maccabean Revolt. It describes how the Jewish forces under Judas eventually recaptured the temple, cleansed it of its defilement by Antiochus, and instituted a celebration of this event. This festival, known as the Feast of Lights or the Feast of Dedication, is still celebrated by Jews today. Known as Hanukkah, it occurs at about the same time as the Christian celebration of Christmas.

The second book of Maccabees contains speeches, laments, prayers, and songs of victory. These are woven into a history of the Jewish people of that period.

Herod the Great, James Tissot (1836–1902)

JEWISH INDEPENDENCE

After the cleansing of the temple, the Jews continued the struggle against their oppressors for several more years. When Judas was killed in battle, his brother Simon, who was high priest, succeeded him as leader of the Maccabean Revolt. Simon was able to negotiate a treaty with Seleucid ruler Demitrius II that granted independent status to the Jewish state of Palestine. This occurred in 142 BC. For the first time in many centuries, the Jewish people controlled their own destiny.

The Jews existed as an independent nation for about eighty years—from 142 BC to 63 BC. During this time they were able to expand their territory northward to take in the territories of Samaria and Galilee. But widespread corruption, political infighting, and struggle among competing rulers eventually doomed the nation.

By 63 BC, Rome had become the new superpower of the ancient world. In that year a Roman general named Pompey marched on

NT CONNECTION—HEROD: After Herod the Great died, his territory was divided among three of his sons. All three are mentioned in the Gospels: Herod Archelaus, who ruled Judea (Matthew 2:22); Herod Antipas, tetrarch of Galilee and Perea (Mark 6:17–18); and Herod Philip, tetrarch of Galilee (Luke 3:1). Antipas was the Herod who had John the Baptist beheaded (Matthew 14:3–10).

Jerusalem and designated one of the Jewish officials as its puppet ruler, thus placing the Jewish people under foreign domination again.

ROMAN PERIOD

Soon after Rome gained control over Jewish territory, the emperor appointed a man named Antipater as the governor of Judea (this was the name assigned by the Romans to the province of southern Israel). When Antipater was murdered, his son Herod the Great succeeded him as ruler over this province.

Herod the Great ruled over the Jews for almost forty years—from 40 BC until his death in 4 BC. He was on the throne when Jesus was born in Bethlehem. (See sidebar, "Herod and the Birth of Jesus.")

JOB: THE OLD TESTAMENT BOOK THAT DOESN'T FIT

The twenty-four chapters in this book touch on every book of the Bible but one—the book of Job in the Old Testament. Job is such a unique book that it doesn't fit into any of the periods of Bible history that are explored in these pages.

Although the setting of Job is probably the period of the patriarchs, the themes explored in the book have nothing to do with Abraham, Isaac, or Jacob. And while Job belongs with the poetic and wisdom literature of the Old Testament, it is not associated with David or Solomon, the authors of other Old Testament books of poetry and wisdom such as Psalms and Proverbs.

But Job's resistance to neat and easy classification does not mean that the book is unimportant. Indeed, it struggles with the question that humankind has been asking since the dawn of history: Why do the righteous suffer? Although Job was a righteous man who worshipped God and shunned evil (1:1), God allowed Satan to take away everything Job owned, as well as his children.

As Job cried out to God in his misery, three of his friends arrived to offer comfort. But they actually drove Job into deeper despair because of their outspoken conviction that Job was being punished by the Lord because of his sins. In Job's time, people believed that human suffering was a direct result of sin in one's life. Throughout the book, Job protested to these three spokesmen that he was a righteous man and that God was treating him unjustly.

After Job and his friends had argued back and forth on this issue for a long time, God Himself finally spoke from a whirlwind. He made it clear that He was the all-powerful, all-knowing Lord of all creation. He assured Job that He could be trusted to do what was right, although His ways might seem strange and puzzling to human minds.

Job was humbled by this statement from the Lord. He finally learned to trust God, in spite of his imperfect understanding. He stopped questioning God and declared, "I take back my words and repent in dust and ashes" (42:6 HCSB). The Lord was pleased with this profession of faith and trust. He restored Job's fortunes and gave him additional children.

The book of Job teaches us that it is futile to try to understand the reason behind our suffering. It is enough to know that God is in control and that He is our refuge and strength in times of trouble. Like Job, we also need to learn that God is not bound by our understanding or by our lack of it. He is free and subject to no will but His own. He does not owe us an explanation for His actions.

Jesus' Incarnation, Piero di Cosimo (1462–1521)

CHAPTER 16
Jesus the Messiah: Prelude to the Beginning of His Work

Jesus launched His public ministry when He was about thirty years old (Luke 3:23). Since He was born about 5 BC, the year when He began His work was about AD 25. (See sidebar, "Herod and the Birth of Jesus," chapter 15, p. 172.) His work on the earth lasted about three years, so the dates of His life and ministry can be estimated at about 5 BC through AD 28.

But long before Jesus was born into the world, preparations were being made for the coming of the Messiah. This chapter focuses on several important biblical insights that help Bible students understand His life and the divine mission He was sent to accomplish.

JESUS, THE ETERNAL ONE, IN HUMAN FORM

The first dramatic truth about Jesus is that He existed with God the Father long before He was born into the world as a man. This insight comes from the Gospel of John. "In the beginning was the Word, and the Word was with God, and the Word was God," John declared. "He was with God in the beginning. All things were created through Him" (John 1:1–3 HCSB).

This verse is an obvious reference to the first three words of the first book of the Bible—Genesis 1:1. Just as God was "in the beginning," so Jesus existed "in the beginning" as the eternal Word. This Word is comparable to the words that God used to speak the universe into being (Genesis 1:3).

Jesus is the eternal Word who has always been. But God the Father sent Him to earth at a specific point in time to redeem fallen humankind from the bondage of sin. He came to us in a physical body in order to identify with the weaknesses and problems that afflict human beings. John the Gospel writer expressed it this way: "The Word became flesh and took up residence among us" (John 1:14 HCSB).

These words from the Gospel of John are the strongest affirmation of the doctrine of the incarnation in the entire New Testament. The adjective *incarnate* means "embodied in flesh." Jesus, the Eternal One, took on a human body as a necessary step in carrying out God's plan of redemption in a sinful world.

JESUS THE MESSIAH

Jesus was born into a Jewish world that had been looking forward for many centuries to the coming of the Messiah. The word *messiah* is a transliteration of a Hebrew word that means "anointed one." The kings from Israel's past had been anointed by having oil poured over their heads. So it was natural for the Jewish people to assume that their long-expected Messiah would be an earthly king.

Since David had been a popular king who represented the glory days of their past, they expected this Messiah to come from David's royal line. This expectation is echoed in the prophet Isaiah's famous messianic prediction that "there shall come forth a rod out of the stem of Jesse, and a Branch shall grow out of his roots" (Isaiah 11:1). Jesse was the father of King David (Matthew 1:5–6).

Jesus was, indeed, the Messiah whom God had promised to send to His people. But He was not the type of messiah they expected. He came as a spiritual leader who delivered people from their bondage to sin rather than as an earthly king who would lead the Jews to victory over their political enemies.

This role for the Messiah was not totally foreign to the Jewish mind. Isaiah the prophet had spoken of a coming leader who would deliver His people through redemptive suffering on their behalf. In one of his famous Servant Songs, the prophet declared that this servant "was pierced for our transgressions, he was crushed for our iniquities; the punishment that brought us peace was on him, and by his wounds we are healed" (Isaiah 53:5 NIV).

Jesus identified Himself specifically as the Suffering Servant from God the Father, whom Isaiah had predicted. At the beginning of His public ministry, He quoted Isaiah's first Servant Song (Isaiah 42:1–3; Matthew 12:18–21). His words made it clear that the mission of God's Suffering Servant was being fulfilled through His teaching and healing ministry.

While Jesus was clearly God's long-awaited Messiah and Savior of His people, He downplayed his identity as the Messiah during most of His public ministry. He realized He could not fulfill the people's expectations for a military messiah. So He avoided the title and even asked others not to call Him by that name (Mark 8:30).

The name Jesus preferred for Himself was "Son of man" (John 3:14). This title was probably inspired by a prophecy from the book of Daniel in the Old Testament. Many centuries before Christ was born into the world, the prophet spoke of a special messenger known as the son of man who would come on a mission of redemption (Daniel 7:13–14).

THE FAMILY HISTORY OF JESUS

Since Jesus is the Son of God who has existed before time began, some people assume He has no family history. But this assumption is wrong. Two Gospels of the New Testament—Matthew and Luke—contain family histories of Jesus. And these genealogies give us valuable information about Him and His revolutionary ministry that changed the world.

Matthew begins his Gospel with a family history of Jesus (Matthew 1:1–17). He declares that Jesus was "the son of David, the son of Abraham" (Matthew 1:1). Then he traces Jesus' family line through three units of fourteen generations each—from Abraham to David, from David to the Babylonian captivity; from the Babylonian captivity to Jesus Christ.

Matthew wrote his Gospel to show that Jesus was the fulfillment of Jewish hopes for the messianic king who would be born through David's royal line. The Jews emphasized the importance of family genealogies. They would be more likely to accept Jesus' claim to be God's promised deliverer if He had the appropriate family credentials to prove it.

This genealogy in Matthew is important for another reason. In the Old Testament, God promised David an everlasting kingdom (2 Samuel 7:16). This promise seemed to disappear when Judah was taken into exile by the Babylonians and the nation never recovered from this tragedy. But Matthew's family history declares that this promise will be fulfilled—although in a spiritual sense—through "Jesus Christ, the son of David."

The genealogy in Matthew, thoroughly Jewish in some ways, is surprisingly non-Jewish at certain points. For example, Matthew included two Gentiles—Rahab and Ruth—and four women—Tamar, Rahab, Ruth, and Bathsheba. Two of these women—Rahab and Bathsheba—committed the sin of adultery. Jewish genealogies normally did not include women—certainly not women who had committed such a serious sin.

Jesus' family history in Matthew declares that He came into the world for all people, not just Jewish males. The apostle Paul expressed this revolutionary truth like this: "There is neither Jew nor Greek, there is neither bond nor free, there is neither male nor female: for ye are all one in Christ Jesus" (Galatians 3:28).

Like Matthew, the Gospel of Luke also includes a family history of Jesus. But Luke does not insert his genealogy until the point where Jesus began His public ministry (Luke 3:23-38). Luke apparently traced Jesus' lineage through His mother, Mary's, family line. Many scholars believe the "Heli" mentioned here as Joseph's father (Luke 3:23) was actually the father of Mary.

Luke's genealogy goes all the way back to Adam, the first man, emphasizing the universality of the Messiah. He is identified not with the Jewish people alone but with the entire human race.

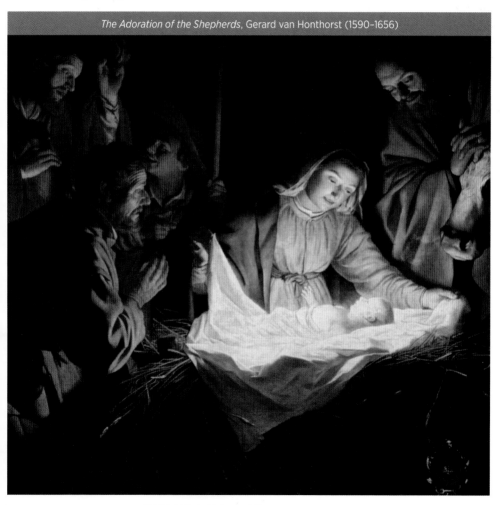

The Adoration of the Shepherds, Gerard van Honthorst (1590-1656)

THE BIRTH OF JESUS

The only two New Testament books that tell us anything about the birth and early life of Jesus are the Gospels of Matthew and Luke. But before Jesus was born, another important birth had to take place. The angel Gabriel announced to a godly couple, Zechariah and Elizabeth, that they would be blessed with the birth of a baby boy. This child would grow up to become John the Baptist. His role in life would be to pave the way for the coming of the Messiah (Luke 1:11–17).

While Zechariah and Elizabeth were pondering this profound news, the same angel announced to a peasant girl named Mary that she would give birth to the long-awaited Messiah. Mary was puzzled and disturbed by the news because she had not had sexual relationships with a man. And to complicate matters even more, she was betrothed, or promised in marriage, to a man named Joseph. Both of them lived in the village of Nazareth in the northern section of Palestine (Luke 1:26–38).

In New Testament times, a marriage was arranged through an agreement between the parents of the groom and the bride. The groom's parents selected a woman for their son to marry, then paid the bride's parents a dowry, or bride-price, to compensate them for the loss of her services as a daughter.

The period between the time of this agreement and the actual marriage of the couple was known as the betrothal. It was a binding contract that could be broken only by a legal proceeding similar to a divorce. Mary's out-of-wedlock pregnancy was certainly legal grounds for Joseph and his family to dissolve their marriage agreement with Mary and her parents.

But Joseph was informed by an angel that Mary's pregnancy was due to the miraculous action of the Holy Spirit. This child from her womb would be the Messiah, the Son of God, who would "save his people from their sins" (Matthew 1:21). This story about Mary's miraculous conception must have been hard for Joseph to believe. But he accepted this message from the Lord as the truth, and he proceeded to take Mary as his wife.

The events that led to the actual birth of Jesus were no less miraculous than His conception without a human father. God worked through a decree from the Roman emperor to send Mary and Joseph to the village of Bethlehem, about six miles south of Jerusalem. The purpose of this visit was to register for a taxation census that was required periodically of all citizens of the countries under Rome's control. Here Jesus was born in fulfillment of the Old Testament prophecy that the Messiah would be born in Bethlehem (Micah 5:2; Luke 2:1–7).

The place where Jesus was born was probably a stable where livestock were kept.

A KING IN A STABLE

No-Stress Bible Reading
Matthew 2; Luke 2:1–40

No-Stress Bible Guide
Pages 175–180
(to "The Childhood of Jesus")

Think About It:

- Why do you think the virgin Mary was chosen to give birth to the Messiah?

- How do you see God at work in the events that led to Jesus' birth in Bethlehem?

- Why was Herod troubled when he learned that the wise men were looking for a "newborn king of the Jews" (Matthew 2:1 NLT)?

According to Luke's account of His birth, Mary "wrapped him in swaddling clothes, and laid him in a manger; because there was no room for them in the inn" (Luke 2:7). The inns or public lodging places of New Testament times were nothing like our modern motels. They were little more than primitive shelters or camping sites near a well where people and their animals could bed down for the night.

Since all these shelters were taken, Mary and Joseph were allowed to camp in the adjoining stables. According to an ancient Christian tradition, the stable in which Jesus was born was located inside a cave. Holy Land visitors to modern Bethlehem are ushered into a cave beneath an ancient landmark known as the Church of the Nativity. Here they are shown a star on the cave floor that marks the reputed place where Jesus was born.

Mary and Joseph had traveled alone to Bethlehem. None of their relatives were by their side to help welcome their baby into the world. But news of the Messiah's birth was too marvelous not to be celebrated with someone. So God spoke through angels to announce the birth of Jesus to the closest audience He could find—a group of shepherds who were watching their flocks in the pasturelands outside Bethlehem.

The angels told the shepherds that a world-changing birth had just happened in the town of David. This was a reference to Bethlehem, the village where David had grown up. They described this child by giving Him three names: Savior, Christ, and Lord. These titles referred to His threefold relationship: with sinners, with the Jewish people, and with God Himself. Yet such an important baby would be found not in a palace but among the animals in a stable. The shepherds hurried off to Bethlehem to see for themselves. Convinced that this baby was everything the angels had claimed, they left to tell others the good news (Luke 2:8–20).

In New Testament times, shepherds were considered lowlifes by the religious elite of Jewish society. This attitude reflected their belief that the occupation of tending sheep kept shepherds from observing the requirements and rituals of the Jewish faith. But by sending news about Jesus' birth first to these humble shepherds, God declared that no one is excluded from His love.

About a month after Jesus was born, Mary and Joseph took Him to the temple in Jerusalem to present Him before the Lord. Here they presented an offering required of all Jewish parents of firstborn sons. A righteous man named Simeon happened to be in the temple that day. As soon as he saw the baby, he recognized Him as the Lord's Messiah. Quoting one of Isaiah's prophecies about the Messiah, he declared that Jesus would be a light to all people—Gentiles as well as Jews (Luke 2:21–32).

An aged prophetess named Anna overheard Simeon's comments. She agreed with His pronouncements, then offered her own thanks to God for sending a Savior. Immediately she began to tell others this good news about Jesus (Luke 2:36–38).

After looking at several events connected with Jesus' birth from the Gospel of Luke, we must switch over to Matthew's Gospel to get a complete picture of His years as a small child. Matthew is the only Gospel that tells us about the visit of the wise men and Herod's death threat soon after He was born. These events from Matthew probably happened when Jesus was a young child—perhaps one to two years old.

The key event from Matthew is the visit of the wise men from the east, who arrived in Jerusalem seeking "he that is born King of the Jews" (Matthew 2:2). These wise men were members of a priestly caste from Babylon known as magi, who practiced the art of astrology. They believed the sun, moon, and stars gave off periodic signs that foretold future events and the destiny of individuals and nations. They saw a mysterious star that they associated with the birth of a future king, and they traveled to Jerusalem to pay homage to him.

After they arrived in Bethlehem, the wise men presented gifts of gold, frankincense, and myrrh to the young Jesus. Each of these gifts symbolized important elements in His future life and ministry. The gold represented His royalty and kingship. The frankincense suggested the worship that God alone deserved. Myrrh, a spice used in burial of the dead, symbolized Jesus' future sacrificial death.

The appearance of the magi and their search for a newborn king posed a threat to Herod the Great, Roman ruler in that part of Palestine. He feared that a future rival to his throne had been born. So he ordered the slaughter of all male infants in the vicinity of Bethlehem who were two years old and under.

But God's purpose was not thwarted by Herod's murderous plot. He warned Joseph, through an angel, to take his family and flee into Egypt. Here they waited in safety until Herod died. Then they returned to Palestine and settled in Nazareth, a village in the region of Galilee where Jesus spent His growing-up years (Matthew 2:13–23).

THE CHILDHOOD OF JESUS

The Gospels record very little about Jesus' growing-up years. Only one incident from his childhood is recorded. And for that event, we have to jump from Matthew back to the Gospel of Luke (Luke 2:41–52).

According to Luke, Mary and Joseph took Jesus with them to Jerusalem when He was twelve years old. They went for the Passover Festival, a Jewish holiday that commemorated God's deliverance of the Jewish people from Egyptian slavery many centuries before.

On their way back to Nazareth after the festival had ended, Jesus' parents discovered that He was missing. They traced their steps back to Jerusalem, where they found Him in the temple among the learned Jewish teachers.

These teachers were experts in the Old Testament law. After expounding on the law in a temple service, they invited any interested person to meet with them for further discussion and learning. Jesus was eager to learn, and He impressed them with His probing questions (Luke 2:47).

Mary was upset that her son had lagged behind in Jerusalem. "Child, why have you treated us like this?" she asked. "Look, your

---

LOST AND FOUND

No-Stress Bible Reading
Luke 2:41–50

No-Stress Bible Guide
Pages 180–181
("The Childhood of Jesus")

Think About It:

- How do you think Mary and Joseph felt when they discovered their son Jesus was missing?

- Why were the people amazed at Jesus' discussion with the religious teachers?

DISCOVERING A DESTINY

No-Stress Bible Reading
Luke 2:51–52

Think About It:

- Do you think Jesus as a boy understood the mission for which He had been sent into the world? Or did He sense it gradually as He grew into manhood?

father and I have been searching for you in great anxiety" (Luke 2:48 NRSV).

Jesus' answer to His mother—"Why were you searching for me?"—are His first recorded words in the Gospels. He went on to ask her, "Did you not know that I must be in my Father's house?" (Luke 2:49 NRSV). This response shows that He was aware of His mission as God's Son, even at the age of twelve. Learning about God in the temple was just what you would expect of a boy who was destined to become the Savior of the world.

But it was not yet time for Jesus to begin His ministry as God's Messiah. First He had to grow up "in wisdom and stature, and in favour with God and man" (Luke 2:52). This He did when He returned with His parents to Nazareth, where He learned a trade, worked with His father Joseph, and grew up like any other Jewish boy.

A WORD ABOUT THE GOSPELS

The most trustworthy accounts we have of Jesus' life and ministry appear in the four Gospels of the New Testament—Matthew, Mark, Luke, and John. These Gospels are not formal biographies because they do not give a complete account of His life and work. The Gospels are made up of selective narratives; they tell us about the events from His ministry that the Gospel writers considered significant.

The purpose of the Gospel writers was to show how God revealed Himself uniquely in the life and ministry of His Son. They wanted to show their readers that Jesus was One in whom they could place their faith and trust. They wrote to encourage people to pledge their commitment to Him as Savior and Lord (John 20:31).

The Gospel of Mark was probably the first one to be written. This was followed within a few years by Luke and Matthew. Finally, the Gospel of John appeared toward the end of the first Christian century, probably about AD 85 to 90.

Matthew, Mark, and Luke are known as the synoptic Gospels because they follow basically the same pattern in reporting on the events in Jesus' life. The word *synoptic* is derived from the Greek word *synopsis*, meaning "a seeing together." The synoptic Gospels are a lot alike in the words they use to describe Jesus' work and in the arrangement of their narratives.

Since Mark was the first Gospel to be written, many scholars believe Matthew and Luke followed his lead in the materials they included. As the shortest Gospel (only sixteen chapters), Mark contains only a few verses that are not paralleled by accounts in Matthew

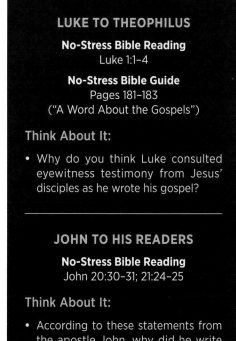

LUKE TO THEOPHILUS

No-Stress Bible Reading
Luke 1:1–4

No-Stress Bible Guide
Pages 181–183
("A Word About the Gospels")

Think About It:

- Why do you think Luke consulted eyewitness testimony from Jesus' disciples as he wrote his gospel?

JOHN TO HIS READERS

No-Stress Bible Reading
John 20:30–31; 21:24–25

Think About It:

- According to these statements from the apostle John, why did he write his gospel?

The Finding of the Savior in the Temple, William Holman Hunt (1827–1910)

or Luke. Scholars believe Matthew and Luke used some of Mark's narratives as a baseline, supplementing these with material contributed by other eyewitnesses.

The apostle John, author of the Gospel of John, probably had access to the three synoptic Gospels when he took his pen in hand to write his own account of Jesus' life. He chose to use a different approach in his account. He was not satisfied just to report the facts about Jesus' ministry. He went beyond the obvious to reveal the meaning and significance of Jesus' teachings and miracles.

For example, not a single parable of Jesus appears in John's Gospel. And only a few of the short sayings of Jesus in Matthew, Mark, and Luke appear in the Gospel of John. His approach was to expand on an incident from Jesus' ministry and give its deeper meaning. A good example of this technique is Jesus' long discussion with Nicodemus about the new birth (John 3:1–21).

John's Gospel is also unique because it gives us a more accurate estimate of the length and order of Jesus' public ministry. The three synoptic Gospels report extensively on His ministry in the region of Galilee. But they record only one journey that Jesus made to Jerusalem to celebrate the annual Passover festival. This might lead us to believe that Jesus' public ministry lasted only about one year.

But John's Gospel corrects this misconception by reporting that Jesus made at least three trips to Jerusalem to celebrate the Passover (John 2:13, 23; 6:4; 12:1). John's Gospel reveals that Jesus did indeed have a short public ministry, but it lasted at least about three years.

To get a complete picture of Jesus and His ministry, we have to read and compare all four Gospels. They were written by four different people, each of whom gives a little different perspective on His life. Matthew was written primarily to the Jewish people to show that Jesus was the fulfillment of Old Testament prophecy. Mark describes Jesus as a man of action who identified with sinful humanity through the human side of His nature. Luke, a Gentile physician, portrayed Jesus as the Savior of all people, Gentiles as well as Jews. John wrote his Gospel for the widest possible audience, using concepts from both Greek and Jewish culture. All four Gospels contribute to our understanding of Jesus and His mission of redemption for a sinful world.

The following chapters take a detailed look at the four different stages of Jesus' three-year public ministry: (1) the early months, (2) the Galilean ministry, (3) the third year, and (4) the final days in Jerusalem.

*St. John the Baptist
Preaching in the Wilderness,*
Anton Raphael Mengs (1728–1779)

Jesus launched His public ministry when He was about thirty years old (Luke 3:23). He sensed through God's Spirit that the time was right for Him to begin the work that God His Father had commissioned Him to do. Leaving His hometown of Nazareth, He traveled to the lower regions of the Jordan River where His forerunner, John the Baptist, was preaching and calling people to repentance. The initial phase of His ministry, lasting about six months, took place mostly in the southern region of Palestine known as Judea.

JOHN PREACHES IN THE WILDERNESS

Even before Jesus arrived on the scene, John the Baptist had been in the wilderness area of Judea near the Dead Sea for a while. Here he lived like a hermit, foraging for locusts—flying insects of the grasshopper family—and honey from the nests of bees. His clothes were made from animal skins (Mark 1:6).

John probably lived like this to identify with the prophets of Israel's past—particularly the great prophet Elijah (2 Kings 1:8). The prophet Malachi had predicted that God would send Elijah the prophet back to earth before the future day of the Lord (Malachi 4:5-6). Some people thought John was the fulfillment of this promise.

It had been more than four hundred years since a prophet had walked among the Jewish people. The major purpose of John's ministry was to show that the ultimate Prophet—the Messiah who had been promised for centuries—was about to burst upon the scene.

John thought of his ministry as a fulfillment of Isaiah's prophecy: "Prepare the way for the Lord" (Isaiah 40:3 NIV). In Old Testament times, primitive roads had to be smoothed and straightened to provide more comfortable travel for a king or other dignitary. John called for such work to be done—in a spiritual sense—not for a king but for God's Savior, Jesus Christ.

John's preaching was basically a call for

people to repent to get ready for the arrival of the Messiah. He would come in judgment to separate the righteous from the sinful. So John called on people to repent of their sins. He baptized those who did so as an outward symbol of their turning from sin and turning to

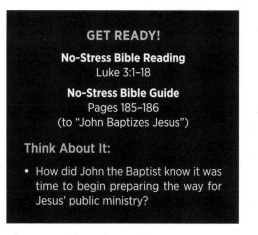

GET READY!

No-Stress Bible Reading
Luke 3:1–18

No-Stress Bible Guide
Pages 185–186
(to "John Baptizes Jesus")

Think About It:

- How did John the Baptist know it was time to begin preparing the way for Jesus' public ministry?

God for forgiveness.

News about John's preaching and baptizing soon reached the religious authorities in nearby Jerusalem. They sent a delegation to find out what he was up to. These officials were probably concerned because John was not a part of their group yet was attracting large crowds and a lot of excitement about the message he was preaching.

They asked John to identify himself, implying that he seemed to be claiming to be the Messiah about whom he was preaching. John denied emphatically that he was the Messiah. Neither was he the prophet Elijah or any other prophet who had been foretold in the Old Testament.

When these religious leaders persisted in their questions, John told them he was setting the stage for the arrival of "the One coming after me, whose sandal strap I'm not worthy to untie" (John 1:27 HCSB). When Jesus arrived on the scene the next day, John pointed Him out to them and the rest of the crowd by declaring Him to be "the Lamb of God, who takes away the sin of the world!" (John 1:29 HCSB). (See sidebar, "Jesus as the Lamb of God.")

JESUS AS THE LAMB OF GOD

Of all the names John could have used for Jesus—King, Messiah, Prophet—he chose to identify Jesus as a symbolic sacrificial animal. These lambs were choice young sheep used as sacrificial offerings in Jewish worship rituals. Thus, at the very beginning of Jesus' ministry, John realized the role He was destined to fill as the suffering Savior who offered Himself as a sacrificial Lamb for sinners.

JOHN BAPTIZES JESUS

Jesus approached John and asked to be baptized. But John protested. He recognized Jesus as the Sinless One and the Messiah about whom he had been preaching. "I am the one who needs to be baptized by you," he declared, "so why are you coming to me?" (Matthew 3:14 NLT).

When Jesus insisted, John agreed to baptize Him. Immediately the Spirit of God descended on Jesus, and God the Father declared that He was pleased with His Son. This ritual performed by John might be compared to the swearing-in ceremony or inauguration of a public official. It marked the official beginning of Jesus' public ministry.

By submitting to baptism by John, Jesus announced that He identified with—and planned to continue—the work that John had started. In later Christian thought, baptism became a symbol of death to sin and rebirth as a new person committed to Christ and His lordship. In His baptism, Jesus proclaimed that He was the Savior who had come to offer hope to a sinful world.

This account of Jesus' baptism gives us the first glimpse of the doctrine of the Trinity in the New Testament. All three Persons of the Trinity are mentioned: God the Father spoke, God the Spirit descended, and God the Son was baptized. The depiction of God in three different persons appears often throughout the rest of the New Testament.

AN APPROVING VOICE

No-Stress Bible Reading
Matthew 3:13–17

No-Stress Bible Guide
Pages 186–188
("John Baptizes Jesus")

Think About It:

- Why did Jesus insist on being baptized by John?

- Why do you think God expressed His approval of Jesus in an audible voice that everyone could hear?

John Baptizing Jesus,
Juan Fernández Navarrete
(1526–1579)

How can God be one but three at the same time? This is a difficult concept for our human minds to grasp. But God as a triune being does match the experience of all true Christian believers. We know God as the Creator and Father to whom we pray, as the Son who died for our salvation, and as the Spirit who gives us strength for living the life of faith.

SATAN'S TEMPTATIONS

Soon after Jesus was baptized by John, He withdrew into the desert region near the Dead Sea where He fasted and prayed for forty days. During this time He must have thought long and hard about the work He was beginning and the commitment it would require. The Gospels make it clear that this was a time when He struggled with the burden of His calling. Although He was led into the desert by God's Spirit, His series of three temptations came from none other than Satan himself (Luke 4:1–13).

The first temptation was to use His power to meet His own physical needs. After about six weeks of eating very little, Jesus was hungry. So Satan attacked Him at His point of greatest need. He directed Him to turn stones into bread to satisfy his gnawing hunger. This temptation also implied that Jesus would be welcomed by the crowds if He became a "bread Messiah"—one who used His divine power to feed the hungry.

Another temptation was to jump from the highest point of the Jewish temple in Jerusalem into the deep valley below. Such a stunt would electrify the crowds and assure Him an immediate following of curiosity seekers.

The most serious temptation was Satan's promise to give Jesus "all the kingdoms of the world" if He would devote Himself to serving Satan rather than God (Luke 4:5 HCSB). With this temptation, Satan offered Jesus a way out of

Temptations of Christ, a mosaic in the Basilica di San Marco, artist unknown

the divine mission on which He had been sent. He wouldn't have to suffer and die if He would just pursue the "good life" and use His powers to become rich and famous.

Jesus was able to resist all of Satan's temptations because of His close relationship with God. His knowledge of the scriptures kept Him focused on the task He had been sent to do. He quoted the Word of God to counter each of Satan's claims.

WATER INTO WINE

The first recorded miracle of Jesus in the Gospels occurred at a wedding in Cana, a village not far from Nazareth, His hometown. According to the Gospel of John, Jesus' mother, Mary, attended this wedding. Jesus and His disciples were invited as well (John 2:1–11).

No sooner had Jesus arrived on the scene than His mother pointed out a problem that threatened to turn the joyful occasion into a disaster. She told Jesus that the wine had run out. The host had miscalculated and failed to provide enough for all the guests in attendance. And wedding celebrations in New Testament times sometimes went on for days.

At first it seemed as if Jesus wouldn't do anything about the shortage. "Dear woman, that's not our problem," He told her. "My time has not yet come" (John 2:4 NLT). He must have thought this was not the right time or place to reveal His supernatural powers. But then He decided to act by performing a miracle to produce wine from common water. His intervention saved the host from embarrassment and allowed the joyful celebration to continue.

The site of ancient Cana is now occupied by an Arab village. In the village stands a church known as the Wedding Church, said to be built on the very spot where the water-into-wine miracle took place. This church is a popular wedding site as well as a place where many married couples renew their wedding vows.

Jesus' first miracle at Cana is cited by the Gospel of John as the first of seven signs that Jesus performed to show His messiahship and His unique mission as God's Son. These signs increase in power and intensity throughout John's Gospel, concluding with Jesus' raising of Lazarus from the dead. (See sidebar, "The Seven Miraculous Signs in John's Gospel.")

THE SEVEN MIRACULOUS SIGNS IN JOHN'S GOSPEL

1. Turning water into wine (2:1–11)
2. Healing an official's son (4:46–54)
3. Healing a paralyzed man (5:1–9)
4. Feeding the five thousand (6:5–14)
5. Walking on water (6:15–21)
6. Healing a man born blind (9:1–7)
7. Raising Lazarus from the dead (11:38–54)

JESUS' VISIT TO CAPERNAUM

One little verse from John's Gospel yields an important insight into Jesus' activities in the early months of His ministry. Even after He performed His first miracle, He and His disciples were found in the company of His mother and His earthly brothers. "He went down to Capernaum with his mother, his brothers, and his disciples," John recorded, "and they remained there a few days" (John 2:12 NRSV).

At this point in His ministry, Jesus may have still been living with His mother and brothers in Nazareth. Capernaum was about twenty miles northeast of Nazareth on the shore of the Sea of Galilee. Perhaps this visit to Capernaum was just a trip to buy food or other provisions for Jesus' family. Or He could have been checking out the city to determine if it was a place that would be responsive to His message. What is known for sure is that He later made Capernaum the headquarters for His extended ministry in the surrounding region of Galilee.

JESUS' CLEANSING OF THE TEMPLE

After this short visit to Capernaum, Jesus apparently traveled to Jerusalem to observe the Passover festival. Here He found the outer courts of the temple cluttered with merchants who were selling sacrificial animals to pilgrims who had come to the Holy City for the annual Jewish holiday. Other agents were busy exchanging foreign currency for the Jewish coins needed to pay the annual temple tax (John 2:13–25).

Jesus drove these merchants out of the temple courts. "Get these things out of here!" He demanded. "Stop turning My Father's house into a marketplace!" (verse 16 HCSB). He addressed His rebuke to the temple priests, since the selling of animals was being done with their permission and the money changers were their agents.

The religious officials demanded that Jesus give them some evidence or sign of His authority to interfere with their operation of the temple. He replied, "Destroy this temple, and in three days I will raise it up" (John 2:19). These words were not a sign but a prediction. Just as the religious leaders were desecrating the physical temple, so they would eventually destroy His body, but He would rise from the grave after three days.

TURMOIL IN THE TEMPLE

No-Stress Bible Reading
John 2:13–25

No-Stress Bible Guide
Pages 188–190
(from "Satan's Temptations"
to "Jesus and Nicodemus")

Think About It:

- Why do you think Jesus used this event to predict His future death and resurrection?

- Why did the religious leaders ask Jesus to show them a sign?

A MAN IN THE DARK

No-Stress Bible Reading
John 3:1–21

No-Stress Bible Guide
Pages 190–191 ("Jesus and Nicodemus")

Think About It:

- Why do you think Nicodemus came to talk with Jesus at night?

- Why do you think Nicodemus had difficulty understanding Jesus' teaching about a spiritual rebirth?

JESUS AND NICODEMUS

While Jesus was in Jerusalem for the Passover celebration, He met a Pharisee named Nicodemus. Although Nicodemus was a Pharisee and a respected Jewish teacher, he was curious about Jesus and His message. He sought Him out at night to learn more about this young teacher who had burst upon the scene seemingly from out of nowhere. Within a few weeks, He was stirring the crowds with His miracles and teachings (John 3:1–20).

Jesus puzzled Nicodemus with a strange

Jesus Cleanses the Temple, artist unknown (17th century; on display at the church Chiesa di San Gaetano and the chapel of the Crucifixion)

new teaching about the kingdom of God and what a person had to do in order to enter it. By God's kingdom or the kingdom of heaven, He referred to God's rule of grace in the world. To enter this kingdom, a person must experience a spiritual transformation that Jesus referred to as the "new birth" or being "born again."

Nicodemus struggled to understand what Jesus meant by these concepts. To the Pharisees, a person was made righteous by keeping the law. But Jesus seemed to be saying that righteousness is not something that can be earned. It comes about by placing one's faith in God's Son as the basis of human salvation—or the new birth. To help Nicodemus understand this, Jesus told him, "For God so loved the world, that he gave his only begotten Son, that whosoever believeth in him should not perish, but have everlasting life" (John 3:16).

With the phrase "everlasting life," Jesus referred not just to what happens to a person at death. It also describes the new life—or the new birth—into which people enter when they place their faith in Jesus Christ as Savior and Lord.

Did Nicodemus respond in faith to what Jesus told him? This question is not immediately answered. But later events in John's Gospel show that he probably did. He stood up for Jesus when other religious leaders condemned Him (John 7:50-52). And he and Joseph of Arimathea gave Jesus a dignified burial, when even His disciples failed to claim His body (John 19:38-40).

Nicodemus Coming to Christ, Henry Ossawa Tanner (1859–1937)

JOHN CONTINUES TO HONOR JESUS

After Jesus launched His public ministry, He began to preach and baptize in the same area where John the Baptist was working. Jesus invited at least two of John's disciples to join His ministry team. One of these was Andrew, the fisherman and brother of Peter. The other is unknown, but many people think he was the apostle John, the son of Zebedee. If John the Baptist objected to these disciples leaving him to follow Jesus, we see no hint of such an objection in the biblical account (John 1:35–39).

Another development that could have caused friction between the two was the decline of John's influence and the increasing popularity of Jesus.

Some of John's disciples saw this happening. They reported that Jesus was attracting more people and baptizing more people than John was. "Everyone is flocking to Him," they told him (John 3:26 HCSB). John replied with no trace of ill will, "He must increase, but I must decrease" (John 3:30 HCSB).

John compared his relationship to Jesus with that of the groom's friend to the groom in a Jewish wedding. The groom's friend was responsible for getting everything ready for the appearance of the bride and groom after the ceremony was over (John 3:27–29). This analogy means that John was more than a passive observer of the coming of the Messiah. He was an essential part of God's plan for sending His Son into the world.

THE WOMAN OF SAMARIA

Sometime after Jesus' conversation with Nicodemus, He decided to leave Judea, or the southern part of the country. He traveled through the territory of Samaria on His way to the region of Galilee in the north. While resting beside Jacob's Well, a well-known landmark in Samaria, He met a woman who came to draw water from the well (John 4:1–42).

Jesus was thirsty, and He had nothing to use to collect water. So He asked the woman for a drink from her water jug. His request surprised her because she knew that Jews and Samaritans generally had nothing to do with each other. The Jews looked down on the Samaritans as half-breeds because their bloodline had been corrupted by intermarriage with foreigners. Most Jews were so hostile toward the Samaritans that they would not even travel through Samaritan territory, let alone stop there, talk with a woman, and ask her for drink of water.

When the woman expressed her surprise that He, a Jew, was asking her for a drink of water, He told her that He could give her living water. This water would quench her spiritual thirst, filling her heart with the life-giving presence of God's Spirit. This spiritual water was another way of describing the new life that Jesus had offered to Nicodemus when He spoke of being born of the Spirit.

Jesus revealed to this woman that He knew all about her troubled past. She had been married several times and even then was living with a man who was not her husband. But He didn't condemn her. He kept encouraging her to drink of the living water that could transform her life.

Finally, the excited woman hurried off to her village. She invited her fellow citizens to follow her back to the well and meet this stranger who "told me everything I ever did" (John 4:29 NIV). After meeting Jesus, the Samaritans were convinced that He was who He claimed to be—God's promised Messiah. At their request, Jesus stayed with them for two days, teaching them about the kingdom of God. Many of them became believers after they were convinced that he was indeed "the Christ, the Saviour of the world" (John 4:42).

After this brief visit to Samaria, Jesus continued His northward journey. In the territory just north of Samaria, he entered the next stage of His work—His ministry in the region of Galilee.

ENCOUNTER AT THE WELL

No-Stress Bible Reading
John 4:1–30

No-Stress Bible Guide
Pages 192–193

Think About It:

- Why was the woman at the well surprised when Jesus asked her for a drink of water?

- What do you think Jesus meant by His statement that "God is a spirit: and they that worship him must worship him in spirit and in truth" (John 4:24)?

- Why were Jesus' disciples amazed when they saw him talking to a woman?

The miraculous Draught of Fishes,
Raphael (1483–1520)

CHAPTER 18
Jesus' Ministry in the Region of Galilee

The territory of Galilee in northern Palestine is where Jesus spent about half of His entire three-year ministry. Perhaps He chose to spend extended time here because He knew it better than any other region of the country. The town of Nazareth, where He grew up, was located in Galilee. He also recruited most of His disciples from this area. (See map, "Jesus' Ministry in Galilee and Beyond," p. 314).

Another possible reason for Jesus' long ministry in Galilee was the diverse population of the region. Many people of Gentile, or non-Jewish, background lived here. It was often referred to as "Galilee of the Gentiles" (Matthew 4:15). The Galileans had been influenced by both Jewish and Gentile culture. They may have been more open to Jesus' message of God's love for all people than the citizens in the vicinity of Jerusalem; in this region, known as Judea, the tradition-bound Pharisees and scribes exerted a powerful influence on the people's thinking.

Soon after arriving in Galilee, Jesus called on the people to "repent and believe the good news" (Mark 1:15 NIV). This reference to repentance made it clear that Jesus would continue the work of John the Baptist. But the Messiah would add a new dimension to John's message. Now people would need to place their faith and trust in Jesus, who embodied this good news.

In Galilee this good news from God the Father would be revealed through the teachings and miracles of Jesus and His up-close-and-personal interaction with the people.

A HEALING FROM A DISTANCE

One day Jesus was in Cana, the same village where He had turned water into wine a few months before. He was approached by a man who was probably an official in the administration of Herod Antipas, the Roman ruler in the area. This government aide asked Jesus to come to Capernaum, a city about twenty miles away, and heal his son, who was critically ill (John 4:46–54).

Jesus did not leave Cana, but He assured this father that his son would not die. Soon after leaving Jesus, the man was met by his servants with good news—his son's fever had broken at the exact time the day before when Jesus had declared him healed.

This miracle shows that Jesus is master over space and time. He restored this boy to health even though He was miles away from the place where the miracle occurred. This remarkable ability is one of the reasons John's Gospel cites this miracle as the second of the seven miraculous signs that demonstrated God's awesome power in the person of Jesus Christ (John 4:54).

REJECTION AT NAZARETH

While visiting His hometown of Nazareth, Jesus was invited to read the Old Testament scripture in a service at the local synagogue. He chose two passages from the Servant Songs in the book of Isaiah. After the reading, He identified Himself as the servant of the Lord whom the prophet had written about. "This passage of scripture has come true today," He declared, "as you heard it being read" (Luke 4:21 GNT; see 4:21–30).

The people in the synagogue had known Jesus since He was a boy. They refused to believe that He was the special messenger whom God had promised to send to His people. When Jesus suggested that God loved all people, not just the Jews, they turned violent and tried to throw Him off a cliff at the edge of town. But Jesus slipped away from them and returned to Capernaum in Galilee.

Toward the end of His ministry in Galilee, Jesus visited His hometown a second time. But the attitude of the people had not changed. They still considered Him nothing but "the carpenter" who had grown up among them.

Jesus described Himself as a prophet who received no respect among the people who knew Him best. Their lack of faith kept them from receiving the blessings He had to offer (Mark 6:1–6).

FOLLOW ME

No-Stress Bible Reading
Matthew 4:18–22; Luke 5:1–11

No-Stress Bible Guide
Pages 195–197
(to "An Encounter with a Demon")

Think About It:

- Why do you think these four fishermen left their nets so quickly and followed Jesus without hesitation?

The Calling of Saint Peter and Saint Andrew, James Tissot (1836–1902)

THE CALLING OF FOUR FISHERMEN

According to the Gospel of Matthew, Jesus was walking beside a lake known as the Sea of Galilee when He saw two pairs of fishermen brothers working at their nets. They were Peter and Andrew and James and John. He challenged them to leave their nets and follow Him as His disciples, and they immediately obeyed (Matthew 4:18–22).

This probably was not Jesus' first encounter with these four fishermen. According to the Gospel of John, Andrew was a disciple of John the Baptist when Jesus first met him and invited Him to His home for a long talk (John 1:35–42). The other of the "two disciples" mentioned in this account (verse 37) may have been John, the brother of James.

So it's possible that all four of these men had met Jesus before. But perhaps they did not commit to become His disciples until Jesus arrived in their territory, looked them up, and enlisted them to follow Him. Luke's account of the calling of Peter and Andrew adds the interesting detail that Jesus produced a miraculous catch of fish for the two brothers (Luke 5:4–7). If they had any doubt about Jesus and His credentials, this miracle should have convinced them that He was everything He claimed to be.

AN ENCOUNTER WITH A DEMON

On one occasion Jesus was teaching in the synagogue at Capernaum when He was interrupted by a miserable cry. It came from a man who was possessed by a demon, or an evil spirit. This demon recognized Jesus and called His name—Jesus of Nazareth—in an apparent attempt to convince Him to leave him alone (Mark 1:21–26).

Jesus told the demon to quiet down. Then He commanded, "Come out of him!" (verse 25 NIV). With a frightening shriek, the evil spirit obeyed and left the man.

Some interpreters claim that this man's problem was nothing more than a severe form of mental illness. But demons and demonic possession cannot be explained away so easily. In New Testament times, demons often caused physical problems, including blindness and deafness (Matthew 12:22; Mark 9:25). Not all the illnesses and ailments healed by Jesus were caused by demons. The Gospels seem to draw a clear distinction between possession by demons and normal illness (Matthew 4:24).

This encounter between Jesus and a demon is only one of several such healing events recorded in the Gospels. These miracles show clearly that Jesus is superior to all forms of evil, including Satan and his demons.

This miracle created great excitement among the people in the synagogue. They probably knew this man whom Jesus had delivered from such a miserable existence. News of this event spread quickly throughout the entire region of Galilee.

PETER'S MOTHER-IN-LAW HEALED

In His healing ministry, Jesus did not overlook the needs among His closest circle of followers. While in Peter's house with His other disciples, He learned that Peter's mother-in-law was sick with a fever. He helped her up from the bed, and she was restored to health. Her recovery was so quick and complete that she immediately began to wait on the guests in the house (Mark 1:29–31).

A FATAL RECOGNITION

No-Stress Bible Reading
Mark 1:21–28

No-Stress Bible Guide
Pages 197–201
(from "An Encounter with a Demon"
to "The Sermon on the Mount")

Think About It:

- Why was this demon able to call Jesus by name?

ABOVE THE SABBATH

No-Stress Bible Reading
Matthew 12:1–18; John 5:1–18

Think About It:

- How did Jesus justify to the Pharisees His healing of a man on the Sabbath day?

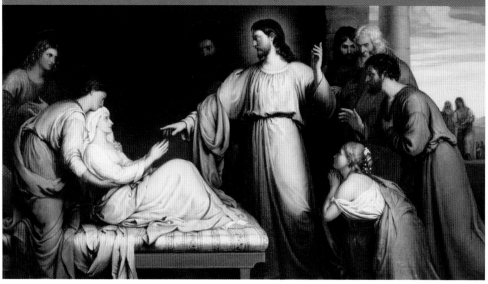
Christ Healing the Mother of Simon Peter's Wife, John Bridges (1818–1854)

A MAN WITH LEPROSY HEALED

Jesus and His disciples were walking through Galilee on a teaching and healing tour when a man with leprosy sought Him out (Mark 1:40–45). Leprosy was a dreaded skin disease that required people who suffered from it to be quarantined from the rest of the community. According to the Old Testament law, lepers were considered unclean and therefore untouchable. They were required to warn people to keep their distance to avoid contamination.

This particular leper broke the law by approaching Jesus. He must have heard about His miraculous healings, so he took the chance that He might also ignore the law and allow him to get close. He got down on his knees in front of Jesus and pleaded, "If You are willing, You can make me clean" (verse 40 HCSB).

In an act of compassion, Jesus reached out and touched the man, and he was restored to health. He could have healed him without a physical touch. But this leper had not been near another person for a long time. Jesus' compassionate touch reassured him that he could now rejoin the human community and enjoy close association with his family and friends.

THE HEALING OF A PARALYZED MAN

One day Jesus was teaching and healing in a house in Capernaum. When the people who lived nearby heard what was going on, they crowded into the house and overflowed around the doorway, preventing anyone else from getting inside.

A paralyzed man was desperate to enter the house so he could be healed. Several of his friends took him to the roof, removed several roof tiles, let him down through the ceiling, and placed him right in front of Jesus (Luke 5:17–26).

Jesus was impressed with this show of faith, and He declared that this man's sins were forgiven. Several scribes and Pharisees in the crowd thought Jesus was guilty of the sin of blasphemy. They thought, "Who can forgive sins but God alone?" (verse 21 NRSV).

Jesus knew what these religious authorities were thinking. He told them that His claim to forgive sins was something that no one could prove. But to show them that He had the ability to do so, He would perform a miracle that would leave no doubt about His divine power and authority. Then He ordered the paralyzed man to stand. When he did so, the people were astonished at this healing miracle.

JESUS CALLS MATTHEW

Jesus shocked the religious leaders by enlisting the tax collector Matthew, also known as Levi, as one of His disciples. From a tax booth, probably at Capernaum, Matthew collected taxes from the citizens of Galilee, which were then forwarded to the government treasury at Rome (Luke 5:27–32).

The citizens of Palestine were heavily taxed by their Roman overlords. This heavy burden caused the people to hate anyone who participated with Rome in collecting taxes. Tax collectors were grouped with "sinners" as people who were degenerate and corrupt.

After Matthew left his tax booth to follow Jesus, he hosted a big meal at his house for Jesus and his tax collector friends. The scribes and Pharisees criticized Jesus for associating with such blatant sinners. But Jesus replied that these were the type of people He came to save—not self-righteous people like the Pharisees who thought they had a monopoly on God's love and thus saw no need to repent.

The Calling of St. Matthew, Hendrick ter Brugghen (1588–1629)

FASTING AND THE NEW WORLD ORDER

One day some people came to Jesus with a concern. They had noticed that the disciples of the Pharisees and John the Baptist observed the ritual of fasting. They wanted to know why Jesus and His disciples did not follow this practice (Mark 2:18–22).

In His reply Jesus compared Himself to the groom at a wedding. As long as the groom was present, there was no need for the wedding guests to fast. But if the groom were taken away, then the guests should fast. With these words Jesus foretold the future time when He would no longer be physically present with His followers.

He went on to tell the inquirers that no one poured new wine into old wineskins. The new wine would ferment and cause the old wineskins to burst. This was a parable of the new order that He was bringing into being. The Old Testament law was being replaced with God's love and grace in a new world order known as the kingdom of God.

SABBATH CONTROVERSIES

During His Galilean ministry, Jesus clashed with the scribes and Pharisees over appropriate observance of the Sabbath on three different occasions. The first conflict appears only in the Gospel of John.

According to John's account, Jesus made a trip from Galilee to Jerusalem, probably to observe the Passover festival. While in Jerusalem, He healed a lame man at the Pool of Bethesda. The Pharisees criticized Jesus for this healing miracle because it occurred on the Sabbath. They believed any work done on the Sabbath—even an act of mercy—was a violation of the Old Testament law (John 5:1–18).

Jesus responded to their criticism with a long speech about His relationship to God the Father (John 5:19–47). He claimed that His act of restoring the lame man to wholeness was part of God's continuing work in the world that He had created. Jesus had the authority to do God's work—even on the Sabbath—because of His credentials as God's Son. He declared, "The works which the Father has given Me to finish—the very works that I do—bear witness of Me, that the Father has sent Me" (verse 36 NKJV).

But the Pharisees were not convinced. They continued to watch Jesus closely to try to catch Him in the act of violating the Sabbath law. One Sabbath Jesus and His disciples passed through a field of grain and picked a little to satisfy their hunger. Before eating it, they rubbed the grain between their palms to remove the husks. To the Pharisees, this action was a violation of the Sabbath law because they were harvesting and threshing grain (Matthew 12:1–8).

Jesus defended their conduct by citing the example of David from the Old Testament. In an emergency, David and his men ate the sacred bread in the tabernacle that was supposed to be consumed only by the priests (1 Samuel 21:1–6). Jesus interpreted this to mean that human need is more important to God than keeping laws and observing ceremonial rituals. In the parallel passage in Mark's Gospel, Jesus stated the principle like this: "The Sabbath was made for man, not man for the Sabbath" (Mark 2:27 NIV).

Jesus' third clash with the Pharisees on the question of Sabbath observance is reported in Matthew's Gospel (12:9–14). One Sabbath day Jesus went into a synagogue, where he saw a man with a withered hand. The Pharisees were waiting for Him. They asked Jesus directly if it was lawful to heal this man on the Sabbath. Jesus pointed out that a sheep that had fallen into a pit should certainly be rescued immediately, even on the Sabbath. Then He declared, as He restored the crippled hand, "How much more valuable is a human being than a sheep!" (verse 12 NRSV).

This action upset the Pharisees. Perhaps they were humiliated by His response or angry because their attempt to trap Him had failed. For whatever reason, they began to plot His death.

THE SELECTION OF THE TWELVE

All three of the synoptic Gospels give an account of Jesus' selection of His disciples. But only Luke reveals that He spent an entire night in prayer before making His choice (Luke 6:12–16). These were the men who would continue His ministry after His death, resurrection, and ascension. So He sought God's will in this decision through fervent prayer.

By this time in His Galilean ministry, Jesus had probably attracted several followers, or disciples, who supported Him. He selected the Twelve from among this larger group and designated them as "apostles" (Luke 6:13). An apostle was a person who knew Jesus in the flesh and who was commissioned by Him to bear His message of redemption to all the world.

A comparison of the lists of the Twelve in the Gospels, along with Acts 1:13, yields some puzzling results. The names in these lists are not the same. This problem occurs because some of Jesus' apostles were known by more than one name. Below is a list of the Twelve, with their variant names noted and a brief description of each.

1. Simon or Peter: a fisherman, brother of Andrew

2. Andrew: a fisherman, brother of Peter

3. James: a fisherman, brother of John and son of Zebedee

4. John: a fisherman, brother of James and son of Zebedee

5. Philip: from Bethsaida

6. Bartholomew or Nathanael: from Cana

7. Thomas or Didymus the twin: perhaps a fisherman

8. Matthew or Levi: a tax collector from Capernaum

9. James: not the same as James son of Zebedee, this James was the son of Alphaeus

10. Lebbaeus Thaddaeus or Judas, called Judas son of James to distinguish him from Judas Iscariot

11. Simon or the Zealot: from Cana, associated with the Zealots, revolutionaries opposed to Rome

12. Judas Iscariot: betrayer of Jesus, from Kerioth in Judea, perhaps the only disciple who was not a Galilean

THE SERMON ON THE MOUNT

Jesus' most famous teachings are found in a long speech known as the Sermon on the Mount. In these teachings He instructed His disciples and other followers how to live as citizens of the kingdom of God. It is called the Sermon on the Mount because He taught these principles from a mountainside (Matthew 5:1–7:29). The Gospel of Luke contains a shorter version of the same sermon (Luke 6:17–49).

Jesus began His teachings in Matthew's Gospel with a section known as the Beatitudes (5:3–12). In a series of "blesseds," He described those people who know the blessedness of God's favor because of their commitment to His way of life.

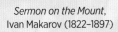
Sermon on the Mount,
Ivan Makarov (1822–1897)

The people who are blessed by God include the poor in spirit who realize their need for Him; those who mourn over their sins; the meek and humble; those who thirst for God's righteousness; those who show mercy to others just as God has shown mercy to them; the pure in heart who have a single-minded devotion to God; those known as peacemakers because they reconcile people to one another and to God; and those who suffer ridicule and persecution from others because of their commitment to the Lord.

Here's a thumbnail summary of other major principles in Jesus' Sermon on the Mount.

Salt and light. Jesus declared that Christian influence matters in a wicked world. Just as salt was used as a meat preservative in Jesus' time, so believers are called to be a preserving element in society, bearing witness of God's love to others. As light, followers of Jesus are to shine for God so He will be glorified (Matthew 5:13–16).

Genuine righteousness. Jesus' followers are called to live by the deeper meaning of God's law. This involves guarding the heart against anger, revenge, and sexual lust; refraining from adultery and divorce; avoiding any form of swearing or oath taking in ordinary conversations; refusing to retaliate against others for their hateful acts; and loving one's enemies (Matthew 5:17–48).

Shun hypocrisy. Jesus taught that good deeds performed by His followers should issue from the right motives. They should not make a big show of their giving, praying, or fasting so people will be sure to notice. Such acts done for earthly glory will not be honored and rewarded by the Lord (Matthew 6:1–18).

First things first. Those who follow Jesus should put God's kingdom ahead of everything else. Doing so will free citizens of God's kingdom from anxiety over lesser matters. If our main goal in life is to bring glory to God, He will take care of our physical needs (Matthew 6:19–34).

Leave judging to God. Jesus used the comical picture of a person with a plank in his eye trying to remove a speck of sawdust from the eye of another person to show that believers should avoid judging people in a harsh and thoughtless manner. Only God knows all the facts in a given situation, and only He has the wisdom to be the final judge (Matthew 7:1–6).

Genuine prayer. Jesus told His followers how to claim the privileges and blessings of prayer. With His words *ask*, *seek*, and *knock*, He emphasized the need for persistence in prayer. Our constant and consistent prayer shows that we are serious about what we pray for and that we have faith in the Father who answers prayer. He may not always give us what we want, but we can trust Him to give us what we need (Matthew 7:7–12).

Choosing wisely. Jesus cautioned us to take the narrow road that leads to life rather than the broad road that leads to destruction. The narrow road is the self-disciplined path that requires submission to God and service to Him and others (Matthew 7:13–14).

Bearing good fruit. Members of God's

LIFE BEYOND THE LAW

No-Stress Bible Reading
Matthew 5–7

No-Stress Bible Guide
Pages 201–204
(from "The Sermon on the Mount"
to "A Gentile's Servant Healed")

Think About It:

- What do you think Jesus meant by His statement that He came to fulfill the law?

- How did Jesus go beyond the Old Testament law in His teachings about treatment of one's enemies?

kingdom will be known and judged by their fruits, or deeds. Just as a tree in an orchard is known by the fruit it bears, so genuine followers of Jesus can be identified by their godly actions and deeds of righteousness performed in His name (Matthew 7:15–20).

Action, not talk. Jesus made it clear that some people who claim to be His followers are talking a good game but failing to do what He requires of kingdom citizens. The acid test of discipleship is obedience to God and His will (Matthew 7:21–27).

A GENTILE'S SERVANT HEALED

A centurion whose beloved servant was gravely ill had heard about Jesus' healing miracles. He sent a party of Jewish officials to ask Jesus to come to his house and heal the man. A Roman centurion was a military officer who commanded a unit of one hundred foot soldiers (Luke 7:1–10).

As Jesus approached the house, the centurion sent several of his friends to tell Jesus not to come inside. Perhaps he knew that most Jews would not enter the house of a Gentile because they considered Gentiles unclean. But he knew about Jesus' ability to heal at a distance. "Say the word," he directed Jesus, "and my servant will be healed" (verse 7 NIV).

Such faith expressed by a Gentile amazed Jesus, perhaps because so many of His own Jewish countrymen refused to place their faith in Him. He honored the centurion's request and restored his servant to health.

AN AMAZING HAPPENING AT NAIN

One day Jesus and His disciples were visiting the village of Nain, about twenty-five miles from Capernaum. As they entered the town, they were met by a funeral procession bearing the body of a young man. Jesus learned that the man was the only son of a widow. He may have been his mother's only means of support. Jesus must have sensed the desperate situation immediately, and His heart went out to this distraught woman (Luke 7:11–17).

Jesus touched the stretcher the body lay on and directed the young man to get up. Immediately he sat up and began to talk, and Jesus presented him to his mother. This spectacular miracle increased Jesus' fame as word about the young man's resurrection spread throughout the province of Judea to the south as well as the province of Galilee where He was working. (See sidebar, "Nain and Shunem.")

NAIN AND SHUNEM

One of the most interesting things about this miracle at Nain is how the people of the town reacted to it. They declared, "A mighty prophet has risen among us" (Luke 7:16 NLT). Perhaps they were comparing Jesus to the prophet Elisha, who had brought another widow's son back to life several centuries before. Elisha's miracle had occurred at Shunem, a town only about three miles north of Nain (2 Kings 4:8–37).

A TRIBUTE TO JOHN THE BAPTIST

One day several disciples of John the Baptist approached Jesus with a question from John. He wanted to know, "Are You the Coming One, or do we look for another?" (Matthew 11:3 NKJV; see 11:1–19). John had been imprisoned by Herod Antipas, the Roman ruler in the area. Perhaps John sensed that his death was near. In his loneliness and isolation, he may have wanted reassurance that his life had not been in vain—that Jesus was, without a doubt, the Messiah whom John had identified to the crowds during his ministry along the Jordan River.

Jesus sent these men back to tell John that the work He was doing—performing miracles and preaching the good news—was certain proof of His messiahship. Then He delivered a moving tribute to John for paving the way for the Messiah's ministry.

Jesus declared that John was linked with the great prophets of Israel's past, but he was much more than a prophet. He bridged the gap between God's spokesmen from the past and the future messengers of the Gospel—including Jesus and all who came after Him to continue the work of the church that Jesus came to establish.

ANOINTED BY A SINNER

Jesus was a guest in the home of a Pharisee named Simon when a woman with a bad reputation sought Him out. She paid Him honor by pouring a jar of precious perfume on His feet

The Feast of Simon the Pharisee, Peter Paul Rubens (1577–1640)

Jesus read Simon's thoughts. He told the Pharisee a short parable about two debtors. One debtor owed five hundred denarii—more than a year's pay for a common laborer. The other debtor owed only fifty denarii. The generous person to whom both owed money forgave both debts.

Jesus asked Simon which of these debtors would be most grateful for such forgiveness. Simon replied that the greater the debt forgiven, the more gratitude a person should have.

Jesus pointed out the difference between Simon's thoughtless attitude and the generous actions of this woman. Simon had not extended to Jesus any of the common courtesies usually expressed by a host to a guest—particularly the washing of a guest's dusty feet. But this woman had compensated for his lack of hospitality with her extravagant actions.

Then Jesus declared to the woman that her sins were forgiven. The self-righteous Simon remained in his sins because he saw no need for forgiveness, but she was delivered from her sin because of her faith in the Savior.

and wiping them with her hair (Luke 7:36–50).

Simon must have known this woman and her reputation. He wondered why Jesus would allow a sinner like her to touch Him. He thought to himself that Jesus must not be the prophet people were making Him out to be.

THE PHARISEES' ACCUSATION

Jesus' healing of a man who was blind, deaf, and possessed by demons set off a long dispute with the Pharisees. They could not deny the fact that the man had been healed, so they attacked Jesus on another front. They accused Him of healing by the power of Beelzebub, an agent of Satan (Matthew 12:22–30).

Jesus answered their charge with a statement of the obvious. He pointed out that a nation cannot survive if its citizens war against one another. In the same way, Satan cannot survive if he wages war against himself by casting out his own evil forces. Thus, the charge that Jesus used Satan to cast his own demons out of a man did not make sense.

Then Jesus turned the accusation of the Pharisees back on themselves by charging them with blasphemy (Matthew 12:31–32). To declare that the unmistakable work of God's Spirit through Jesus Christ is actually the work of Satan is a serious sin that God will not forgive. The Pharisees had become so hardened and stubborn in their opposition to Jesus that they attributed the work of God to evil forces.

The Pharisees continued their assault on Jesus by asking Him to show them a miraculous sign to verify His authority. But He refused to do so. They had already witnessed several of His miracles. If these had not convinced them that He was a messenger from God, nothing would (verses 38–42).

Jesus told them that the only sign they would

be given was the sign of the prophet Jonah (verse 39). This was a reference to His future death, burial, and resurrection. Just as Jonah was in the stomach of a great fish for three days, so Jesus would arise from the grave after three days.

Parable of the Hidden Treasure by either Rembrandt (1606–1669) or Gerrit Dou (1613–1675)

PARABLES ABOUT THE KINGDOM OF GOD

Jesus got into a boat and taught the people who stood along the shore of the Sea of Galilee. He told them several parables to help them grasp the meaning of the kingdom of God (Matthew 13:1–52). The concept of God's kingdom—also referred to as the kingdom of heaven—was one of the most important themes of His ministry. The phrase refers to God's rule of grace in the world, a period that had been foretold by the Old Testament prophets. The dawning of this kingdom occurred when Jesus was born into the world.

The first kingdom parable was about a farmer who sowed seed on three different types of soil. The seed failed to sprout and take root in rocky and hardened soil, but it flourished in good soil and produced a bountiful harvest. This parable symbolized the proclamation of the Gospel, or the good news about God's love and grace. Some people would reject this message, but others would accept it and receive the blessings that God promises to all true believers. (See sidebar, "Why Jesus Used Parables.")

WHY JESUS USED PARABLES

Jesus' stories or parables were one of His most effective teaching methods. The word comes from a term that means "comparison" or "a casting alongside." He compared familiar activities such as sowing seed with the spiritual truths He was trying to get across to His audience. The common people could understand such simple analogies.

Another parable described wheat and weeds that were growing together in the same field. In this life, citizens of God's kingdom as well as citizens who live by worldly values will exist together. But in the final judgment, God will separate believers from unbelievers and send them to their appropriate rewards. The parable of the net hauling in both edible and worthless fish conveys the same message.

Two other parables of the kingdom declared its great value. A man discovered a treasure buried in a field, so he bought the property to claim the precious item as his own. Likewise, a merchant looking for fine pearls sold everything he had in order to buy one of exceedingly great value. The message of these parables is that people should be willing to pay any price and make any sacrifice in order to claim the riches of the kingdom of God.

Finally, two additional parables emphasized the potential of God's kingdom. Jesus compared His kingdom to a tiny mustard seed that grew into a huge plant, and a little bit of leaven that spread throughout a lump of dough and caused it to rise. In the beginning, God's kingdom in the person of Jesus was tiny, and its truths were revealed to people in a seemingly insignificant part of the world. But Jesus foresaw that this kingdom would grow into a mighty force and eventually influence the entire world.

MASTER OVER THE STORM

Jesus and His disciples were crossing Lake Galilee when a sudden storm came up and threatened to capsize the boat. But He ordered the storm to stop. The disciples were amazed when the wind quit blowing and the water grew calm (Mark 4:35–41).

The disciples had witnessed many of Jesus' miracles. But the fishermen in this boat knew firsthand about the fury of a storm on the lake. To them this was the greatest demonstration of His power they had seen. All the disciples were terrified, perhaps because they realized they were in a boat with the One who ruled over nature itself. "What manner of man is this," they asked, "that even the wind and the sea obey him?" (verse 41).

AN ENCOUNTER WITH A WILD MAN

When Jesus and His disciples reached the other side of Lake Galilee, they found a scene almost as frightening as the furious storm they had just escaped. In this Gentile region, they were met by a demon-possessed man who lived among the tombs in a cemetery (Mark 5:1–20).

This poor man was possessed not by one demon but by many—an entire legion, he admitted, when Jesus asked him his name. Most people would have fled when approached by this violent and uncontrollable man, but Jesus stood His ground and talked with him face-to-face.

The demons in the man sensed that Jesus was about to cast them out. They begged Him not to send them away but to let them enter a nearby herd of pigs. Jesus did as they asked, and the pigs rushed into nearby Lake Galilee and drowned.

Now healed and in his right mind, the man asked permission to accompany Jesus and His disciples on their travels. But Jesus asked him to stay in this Gentile region and tell others about how he had been restored to his right mind. People were amazed when they heard the story of his miraculous healing.

A MIRACLE AMONG THE TOMBS

No-Stress Bible Reading
Mark 5:1–20

No-Stress Bible Guide
Pages 206–211
(from "The Pharisees' Accusation")

Think About It:

- Why do you think the townspeople were frightened when they saw this wild man sitting quietly in the presence of Jesus?

- Why did the people want Jesus to leave their territory?

BACK-TO-BACK HEALINGS

Leaving Gentile territory, Jesus and His disciples crossed Lake Galilee back to the area near Capernaum. Here they were met by a man named Jairus, a leader in the local synagogue. He asked Jesus to come to his house and heal his twelve-year-old daughter, who was at the point of death (Mark 5:21–43).

As Jesus was following Jairus through the crowd, a woman slipped up next to Him and touched His robe. She had suffered from a hemorrhage for many years. Immediately her flow of blood stopped. Although Jesus was on His way to another emergency situation, He paused to talk with her and offered assurance that her faith had made her well.

While Jesus was talking with this woman, several people informed Jairus that his daughter had just died. But Jesus ignored their words and resumed His journey to the little girl's bedside. Here He performed a greater miracle than anyone hoped for by raising her from the dead.

Jesus cautioned the people in the house not to tell anyone what had happened. Perhaps He did not want the crowd outside to know what He had done, lest their excitement get out of hand. He was not interested in popular acclaim. He resisted the efforts of the crowd to turn Him into nothing but a wonder-worker.

The Raising of Jairus's Daughter, Gabriel Max (1840–1915)

A MISSION FOR THE TWELVE

Near the end of His Galilean ministry, Jesus divided His disciples into teams of two and sent them out on a teaching and healing mission. This would be a good hands-on test of what they had been learning from Him. He did not go with them Himself, but He sent them out in His name and under His authority (Matthew 10:1–42).

The disciples were to travel light and depend on those to whom they ministered for their meals and lodging. If they were rejected, they were to "shake the dust off [their] feet" (verse 14 NIV) and move on to the homes of others who would be more receptive to their message.

Jesus warned His disciples that they might be ridiculed and persecuted, just as He was being condemned by His enemies, the Pharisees. They should respond with good judgment, common sense, and a gentle spirit—not retaliating against those who opposed their work.

This special mission of the Twelve was a valuable training exercise for Jesus' disciples as well as an extension of His ministry. Their teaching and healing in His name announced the good news about God's kingdom, establishing a pattern that is still followed by modern proclaimers of the Gospel.

THE EXECUTION OF JOHN THE BAPTIST

Just as Jesus stirred the opposition of the Pharisees in the north, John the Baptist made enemies in the region near Jerusalem in the south. John was imprisoned by Herod Antipas because he condemned the Roman ruler's adulterous marriage with a woman named Herodias. She got even with John by persuading Herod to have the prophet executed (Mark 6:17–29).

John's execution marked a turning point in Jesus' public ministry. Perhaps this tragedy made Him realize with new urgency that His work would be brief like John's and would end with His own violent death. He began to prepare His disciples for this future event by withdrawing for times of instruction and reflection in regions beyond Galilee. This shift in focus marks the beginning of the third year of Jesus' ministry.

The Beheading of St John the Baptist, Pierre Puvis de Chavannes (1824–1898)

The Transfiguration, Carl Heinrich Bloch (1834–1890)

CHAPTER 19
The Third Year of Jesus' Ministry

After working for about eighteen months in Galilee, Jesus expanded His reach. During the next year, He traveled over a broader territory—in and out of Galilee, retreating north of Galilee to the region of Tyre and Sidon, teaching and healing in the area east of the Jordan River, and heading to Jerusalem, where He was eventually arrested and executed by His enemies. Jesus' wide-ranging travels in this third year were some of the most fruitful of His public ministry. (See map, "Jesus' Ministry in Galilee and Beyond," p. 314.)

THE FEEDING OF THE FIVE THOUSAND

With His disciples, Jesus sought refuge from the crowds at a secluded place near the Sea of Galilee. But the people followed them there, bringing the sick for healing. Toward the end of the day, Jesus noticed that the people were hungry but had brought nothing to eat in this out-of-the-way place. So He miraculously multiplied five loaves of bread and two small fish to feed the huge crowd. He produced so much food from this meager supply that His disciples gathered several baskets of leftovers (John 6:1–15).

This spectacular miracle had one unfortunate result. The people were so pleased with it that they tried to force Jesus to rule over them as a king. They wanted to make Him into a "bread Messiah"—a miracle worker who would provide for their physical needs. But Jesus rejected their advances and retreated to a solitary place not far away.

JESUS AS THE BREAD OF LIFE

Not long after the miraculous feeding of these people, Jesus criticized them for following Him because of the food He had produced. He declared that He was the living bread, or the spiritual sustenance that God offered to all who would place their faith in Him (John 6:25–70). He offered inner nourishment that satisfied forever—in contrast to physical bread that lasted only from one meal to the next.

These concepts were difficult for some of Jesus' followers to understand. So they "turned back and no longer followed him" (verse 66 NIV). But Jesus' disciples declared that they believed His words and would remain loyal to Him.

A GHOST ON THE WATER

The disciples were caught by rough water while crossing the Sea of Galilee in a small fishing boat. Jesus set out to join them by walking on the water toward the vessel. At first the disciples thought Jesus was a ghost. But He set their minds at ease by assuring them that it was Him (Mathew 14:22–36).

When Jesus climbed into the boat, the churning waves immediately calmed down, causing His disciples to declare, "Truly you are the Son of God" (verse 33 NRSV).

Jesus Walks on Water, Amédée Varin (1818–1883)

TWO MIRACULOUS MULTIPLICATIONS

No-Stress Bible Reading
Matthew 15:29–39; John 6:1–15

No-Stress Bible Guide
Pages 213–215

Think About It:

- In Matthew's account of the feeding of the four thousand, why do you think the disciples doubted Jesus' ability to feed the crowd?

- What differences do you see in the details of these two feeding accounts?

- Why do you think the crowds followed Jesus to the places where these two miracles occurred?

A CLASH OVER UNCLEAN HANDS

Several scribes and Pharisees came to Jesus with a complaint that His disciples were eating with unwashed hands. They were ignoring the ceremonial law that required an elaborate ritual of hand washing to avoid uncleanness and defilement (Mark 7:1–23).

Jesus made it clear in His response that He had no patience with the scribes and Pharisees and this meaningless ritual. It was nothing but a human tradition that had grown up around the original written law. Jesus accused them of substituting these traditions for the authentic teachings of God in His written word, the Old Testament scriptures.

After this confrontation with the scribes and Pharisees, Jesus went on to teach His disciples that personal defilement is not something that enters the body from the outside. Rather, people are made unclean by sin that comes from their hearts in rebellion against God. He cited a litany of sins, including murder, adultery, greed, envy, and arrogance. "All these evil things come from inside you," He declared, "and make you unclean" (Mark 7:23 GNT).

THE DAUGHTER OF A GENTILE WOMAN HEALED

With His disciples, Jesus withdrew northward into Gentile territory near the cities of Tyre and Sidon along the coast of the Mediterranean Sea. This was a two-day journey by foot, and it took Him the greatest distance He ever traveled from Jewish territory during His entire public ministry. The purpose of this withdrawal was probably to get some much-needed rest from the demands of the crowds and the harassment of the Pharisees.

A woman in this region had heard about Jesus, and she begged Him to heal her demon-possessed daughter. He ignored her at first, stating that His priority was to minister among the Jewish people. When she persisted with her pleading, He healed her daughter because of her great faith (Matthew 15:21–28). In this encounter Jesus taught His disciples another lesson about God's love and concern for all people.

A HEALING IN THE DECAPOLIS

Leaving the region of Tyre and Sidon, Jesus and His disciples entered another Gentile area known as the Decapolis. Situated northeast of the Sea of Galilee, this territory was a center of Greek culture. The word comes from a Greek term meaning "ten cities."

In the Decapolis, Jesus healed a deaf man with a speech impediment. He put His fingers into the man's ears, then spit on His fingers and touched His tongue. He spoke a single word, *ephphatha*, an Aramaic term meaning "be opened." Instantly the man could hear and speak. This healing amazed the people, and news of Jesus' power spread throughout the territory (Mark 7:31–37).

THE FEEDING OF THE FOUR THOUSAND

While in the Decapolis, Jesus performed another spectacular miracle. He multiplied a few pieces of bread and fish to feed a crowd of four thousand people (Matthew 15:29–38). This event was similar to another feeding miracle that He had performed earlier (see "The Feeding of the Five Thousand," p. 213).

There is one major difference between these two miracles. The crowd of five thousand consisted of Jews in Jewish territory, while the four thousand were a Gentile crowd in non-Jewish territory.

By recording this second feeding miracle, the Gospel of Matthew shows that Jesus broke down the wall of prejudice between Jews and Gentiles. He did not exclude people because of their race or ethnic background. What He did for the Jewish people, He also did for Gentiles.

WATCH OUT FOR THE PHARISEES AND SADDUCEES

PHARISEES AND SADDUCEES

This passage in Matthew's Gospel (see 16:5–12) is one of the rare places where Pharisees and Sadducees are mentioned together as enemies of Jesus. They usually avoided one another, but their opposition to Jesus brought them together on this occasion.

The Sadducees rejected the oral traditions that had grown up around the written Old Testament law, while the Pharisees considered these human traditions just as important as the law itself.

Back in Jewish territory near Lake Galilee, Jesus condemned the Pharisees and Sadducees because they continued to ask Him for a sign to prove His authority. He refused their request because He realized it was futile to give new signs to those who were blind to the signs He had already displayed through His teachings and miracles.

Then Jesus warned His disciples to avoid the influence of these two groups. He compared them to the yeast that caused bread to rise. Like yeast that worked its way into a lump of dough, the legalism and hypocrisy of these two Jewish parties could poison the mind, making people inflexible and unteachable, just like them (Matthew 15:39–16:12). (See sidebar, "Pharisees and Sadducees.")

A TWO-STAGE MIRACLE

Traveling toward Caesarea Philippi north of the Sea of Galilee, Jesus and His disciples came to the village of Bethsaida. Several people who lived here brought a blind man to Jesus for healing. Jesus took him outside the town away from the crowd, perhaps to avoid creating a public spectacle (Mark 8:22–26).

The healing of this blind man is the only recorded miracle of Jesus that occurred in two stages. He touched the man's eyes once, and he was able to see only faint images. But at Jesus' second touch, he could see everything clearly and distinctly.

Only Mark's Gospel records this miracle and the interesting detail about a "progressive" healing. Some interpreters believe Mark recorded this event to symbolize the gradual growth of understanding among the disciples about who Jesus really was.

CONFESSION AND DENIAL AT CAESAREA PHILIPPI

After Jesus and His disciples arrived at Caesarea Philippi, He put His disciples to a test. He asked them who they thought He was—not what He was being called by other people (Matthew 16:13–20). Peter seemed to speak for the other disciples when he declared, "You are the Messiah, the Son of the living God."

The title *Christ* means "anointed one"—a term

that referred to the deliverer whom God had promised to send to His people. Thus, Peter's confession shows that he believed Jesus was the long-looked-for Messiah.

Jesus commended Peter for his insight. He had arrived at this truth not through the power of human reason but by direct revelation from God the Father and by watching the actions of

Jesus Heals a Blind Man in Stages, El Greco (1541–1614)

His Son. Jesus promised to build His church and continue His work through people like Peter who committed themselves to Him as their Savior and Lord.

After this great confession from Peter, Jesus went on to give His disciples some bad news. He predicted that He would be persecuted by His enemies and eventually killed in the city of Jerusalem. But He tempered this bad news with the assurance that He would be raised from the dead on the third day (Matthew 16:21).

This prediction was hard for the disciples to accept. Peter denied that such a thing could happen to the Messiah, whose awesome power

WHO AM I?

No-Stress Bible Reading
Matthew 16:13–28

No-Stress Bible Guide
Pages 216–218
(to "A Glorious Transformation")

Think About It:

- Why were there were so many different opinions about who Jesus was?

- Why do you think Jesus chose this time to tell the disciples about His future death and resurrection?

he and the other disciples had seen with their own eyes. Jesus condemned Peter's disbelief with some of His strongest words in the Gospels: "Get behind me, Satan!" (Matthew 16:23 NRSV).

At the beginning of His ministry, Satan had tried to turn Him aside from Jesus' ministry of redemptive suffering by offering Him an easy way out. Now one of His own disciples was reminding Him that Satan's temptation was still alive and well. Peter's words must have made Jesus realize that His disciples didn't yet fully understand who He was and the mission of redemptive suffering for which He had been sent into the world.

A GLORIOUS TRANSFORMATION

About a week after Peter's confession at Caesarea Philippi, Jesus took three of His disciples—Peter, James, and John—to a mountain to pray. As He was praying, His face took on a strange appearance and His clothes glowed like a bright light. This event is known as His transfiguration or transformation (Luke 9:28–36).

While this was happening, two famous Bible personalities—Moses and Elijah—appeared on the scene with the same bright light around their bodies. Moses represented the Old Testament law, and Elijah represented the prophets of the Old Testament. They signified that Jesus was the fulfillment of the Old Testament law as well as the ultimate prophet whom God was sending among His people.

The scene was made even more awesome when God spoke from a cloud: "This is My beloved Son. Hear Him!" (Luke 9:35 NKJV). This was the third time God had expressed His approval of His Son in an audible voice. The other two occasions were at His baptism (Mark 1:11) and at His triumphal entry into Jerusalem (John 12:28).

Jesus' transfiguration was probably His way of giving His disciples a preview of His future glory. He told them several times that He would be glorified by the Father and received into heaven before returning to earth one day in all His glory (Matthew 25:31). This dramatic demonstration of His glory while He was on earth would help sustain the disciples through the ordeal of His future suffering, crucifixion, and death.

A BOY WITH A STUBBORN DEMON

Coming down from the mountain where His transfiguration had occurred, Jesus found His disciples in a dispute. They had been unable to cast a demon out of a boy. A group of scribes were using this situation to discredit Jesus and His disciples before the crowd that had gathered (Mark 9:14–29).

Jesus immediately stopped the controversy by healing the boy. In Matthew's account of this event, His disciples later asked Him why they had been unable to heal him. Jesus replied that they had failed because of their lack of faith. He had delegated to them as His disciples the power to heal. But they were still hampered by doubt and uncertainty over the source of this power. "If you have faith as small as a mustard seed," He told them, "nothing will be impossible for you" (Matthew 17:20 NIV).

JESUS' SECOND PREDICTION OF HIS DEATH

While people were still expressing their amazement over this boy's healing, Jesus told

His disciples for the second time that He would soon suffer and die. He wanted to make sure they were prepared for what would happen. But again, His disciples could not believe His solemn words (Luke 9:43–45).

THE GREATNESS OF SERVICE

Jesus learned that His disciples had been arguing about which one of them was the greatest. So He called them together and taught them about the true meaning of greatness for citizens of God's kingdom. Whoever wanted to be great, He told them, must be last in earthly terms but number one in service to Him and to others (Mark 9:33–50).

Then He called a little child to His side as an object lesson. A child is a perfect illustration of humility and purity in motives and thought. A citizen of God's kingdom must have the characteristics of a little child—not seeking fame and the praise of others but trying to please God by his actions.

Another interesting metaphor that Jesus used in His teaching on service was that of giving a cup of water in His name to a thirsty traveler.

In the hot, dry climate of Palestine, this was an act of hospitality. Thus, even the smallest act of kindness, if performed in Jesus' name, would be honored by God the Father.

Later on, as Jesus neared the end of His earthly ministry, He repeated this lesson on greatness to His disciples to make sure they got the message. This happened after James and John came to Him with the request that they be given the highest places of honor in His future kingdom.

Jesus taught them patiently about true greatness by contrasting the view of the world with His own. Referring to Himself, He told them, "The Son of Man came not to be served but to serve, and to give his life a ransom for many" (Mark 10:45 NRSV).

Stained glass of Jesus and the little children

A PARABLE ON FORGIVENESS

Peter, one of Jesus' disciples, came to Him with a question about forgiveness. "How many times shall I forgive my brother or sister who sins against me?" he wanted to know. "Up to seven times?" (Matthew 18:21 NIV; see 18:21–35).

Peter knew the popular teaching of the time was that forgiveness for the same offense did not have to be granted after the third time. He probably thought he was being generous by suggesting that forgiveness might be extended to the seventh misdeed.

Jesus' reply, "seventy-seven times" (verse 22 NIV), must have shocked Peter. Jesus said, in effect, that forgiveness had no limits for citizens of the kingdom of God. They should forgive others for their wrongful actions without keeping count.

To drive home His point, Jesus went on to tell a parable about an unforgiving servant. He described a king who wrote off a huge debt that one of his servants owed him. But this man refused to show the same generosity to another servant who owed him money—a pittance compared to the enormous debt he had owed.

When the king heard about what the unforgiving servant had done, he threw him in prison and demanded that he pay back every penny of his debt. The lesson of Jesus' parable is clear: Forgiveness cuts both ways. Those who have been forgiven must extend the same courtesy to others. A harsh, unforgiving spirit cuts people off from God's love and grace.

A CALL FOR COMMITMENT

As Jesus and His disciples walked along, three men called out that they wanted to become His followers. But none of them were willing to make the unconditional commitment that He demanded (Luke 9:57–62).

One would-be follower had probably felt a surge of excitement when he witnessed Jesus' great miracles. But Jesus questioned whether he had the perseverance to stand up to the hardships that following Him demanded.

The other two men were not willing to make following Jesus their first priority. Their family responsibilities prevented them from becoming disciples.

Response to Jesus should not be hedged about with "ifs," "soons," and "maybes." As Jesus put it, "Anyone who starts to plow and then keeps looking back is of no use for the Kingdom of God" (Luke 9:62 GNT).

JESUS AT THE FEAST OF TABERNACLES

A major Jewish holiday known as the Feast of Tabernacles was being observed in Jerusalem. This event celebrated the time during the exodus from Egypt when the Israelites lived in crude shelters in the wilderness.

At first Jesus was hesitant about attending this festival because the religious leaders in Jerusalem were looking for an opportunity to arrest Him on a charge of blasphemy. But He

finally decided to go. The account of this trip to Jerusalem is recorded only in the Gospel of John (John 7:1–53).

On the last day of the festival, priests poured water on the altar in the temple to commemorate God's provision of water for the Israelites during their wilderness-wandering years. Jesus chose this day to declare that He offered life-giving water to all who would receive Him. This was not physical water but spiritual water that would satisfy their thirst for God's love and acceptance.

This claim of Jesus to be God's agent of salvation angered the religious elite of Jerusalem. They tried to arrest Him. But He foiled their attempt, probably because of His popularity with the common people.

Jesus Christ and the Woman Taken in Adultery, Lucas Cranach the Elder (1472–1553)

THE CHARGE AGAINST A SINFUL WOMAN

While Jesus was teaching near the temple, the scribes and Pharisees brought a woman who was accused of adultery. Under the Old Testament law, death by stoning was the prescribed punishment for any person who committed this sin. They asked Jesus what they should do in her case, hoping to trick Him into making a statement that would give them grounds for His arrest (John 8:1–11).

Jesus did not answer their question. Instead, He bent down and began writing in the dirt. Finally, He looked at her accusers. "Let any one of you who is without sin," he challenged them, "be the first to throw a stone at her" (verse 7 NIV).

At this, the woman's accusers walked away. Jesus also refused to condemn her, though this does not mean He approved of her sinful actions. He went on to encourage her to give up her life of sin.

JESUS AS THE LIGHT OF THE WORLD

While in Jerusalem, Jesus got into a long discussion with the Pharisees about who He claimed to be. He told them clearly that He was the Light of the world, a reference to a prediction of the prophet Isaiah in the Old Testament. Isaiah had declared that a great light would dawn upon the world, bringing salvation to those who lived in darkness (Isaiah 9:2). Jesus declared that this prophecy had been fulfilled in Him (John 8:12–59).

The Pharisees were so disturbed by Jesus' claim that they accused Him of being a demon-possessed Samaritan (John 8:48). This was a great insult, since the pure-blooded Jews despised the Samaritans because they had corrupted their bloodline by intermarrying with pagan foreigners. Jesus denied their charge, declaring that He was honoring God through the words He was speaking. He went on to promise eternal life to everyone who placed their faith in Him.

This sent the Pharisees into a rage. They accused Him of claiming to be superior to Abraham, the father of the Jewish people, since Abraham had died long ago. But Jesus pushed His claim one step further. "Before Abraham was, I am," He declared (John 8:58). With these words He identified Himself as the divine Son of God who had existed from eternity.

To the Pharisees, Jesus' words were the ultimate affront to the sanctity of God—claiming to be equal with God Himself. They picked up stones to kill Jesus—the Old Testament form of execution for the sin of blasphemy. But He slipped away and left them seething with anger.

SIGHT FOR A BLIND MAN

Jesus healed a man in Jerusalem who had been blind his entire life. Not surprisingly, this healing set off a long controversy with the Pharisees, who tried to deny the miracle and discredit the healer. They questioned the man and his parents about the miracle, trying to find flaws in his story. They claimed that Jesus was a sinner who could not possibly have performed such a miracle (John 9:1–41).

Finally, the healed man gave the doubting Pharisees a testimony that was hard to deny. "I do not know whether he is a sinner," he declared. "One thing I do know, that though I was blind, now I see" (verse 25 NRSV).

This man's reward for telling the truth was his rejection by the Pharisees. They may have ejected him from the synagogue, an action that would have banned him from attending its services and hearing instructions from the law. When Jesus heard how they had treated this man, He looked him up and gave him the ultimate reward—forgiveness of his sins when he placed his faith in Him.

Jesus pointed out the irony of this situation. A man who was born blind could now see both physically and spiritually. But the Pharisees—who had never had any problem with their physical sight—remained in the dark because of their spiritual blindness.

JESUS AS THE GOOD SHEPHERD

While teaching in Jerusalem, Jesus claimed to have the right credentials for serving as the leader of God's people. He compared Himself to the door through which sheep entered the sheepfold. He also claimed to be the Good Shepherd who watched over God's people, just as a shepherd cared for his sheep (John 10:1–21).

The Pharisees claimed to be the leaders, or shepherds, of God's people. But they were actually false prophets who were leading the people astray. As the true Shepherd, Jesus was God's Son who had been sent by His Father to be the Savior and Redeemer of His people.

THE MISSION OF THE SEVENTY

During His Galilean ministry, Jesus had sent out His twelve disciples on a teaching and healing mission (see "A Mission for the Twelve," chapter 18, p. 210). Now he decided to do the same thing again—this time sending out seventy from His larger group of followers.

The procedures these two groups were to follow—traveling in pairs, what to take with them, where to lodge, etc.—were similar. But each group seems to have been sent out with a distinct purpose.

Jesus charged the Twelve with announcing the nearness of the kingdom of God. But His sending of the Seventy had a broader missionary purpose. These seventy believers pointed to the time in the future when Jesus' followers would be sent out to preach the Gospel to all nations. The number seventy is significant, reflecting the seventy Gentile nations listed in the Old Testament (Genesis 10).

THE SEEING AND THE BLIND

No-Stress Bible Reading
John 9

No-Stress Bible Guide
Pages 218–222
(from "A Glorious Transformation"
to "Jesus as the Good Shepherd")

Think About It:

• Why do you think the Pharisees were so anxious to deny this man's claim that he had been healed by Jesus?

• How does this miracle show that Jesus is "the light of the world" (John 9:5)?

Stained glass of Jesus, the Good Shepherd (St. John the Baptist's Anglican Church in Ashfield, New South Wales)

THE PARABLE OF THE GOOD SAMARITAN

One day Jesus talked with a Jewish official, an expert in the law, about the greatest law in the Old Testament. Both agreed that the commandment to love God and to love one's neighbor was superior to all the others.

This Old Testament expert then asked Jesus, "Who is my neighbor?" (Luke 10:29 NKJV). Jesus responded by telling the parable of the good Samaritan. This is probably His best-known parable in the Gospels (Luke 10:25–37).

Jesus described a Jewish traveler who was robbed by thieves, beaten, and left for dead

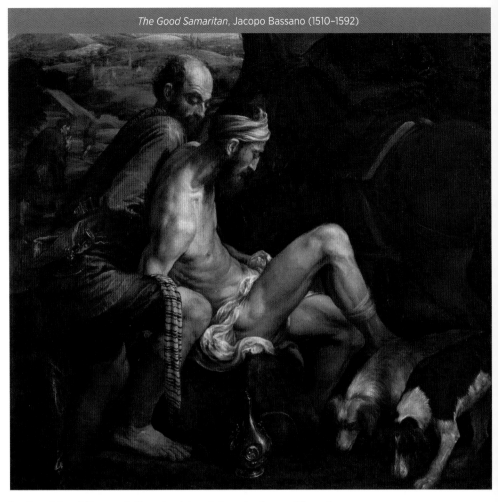

The Good Samaritan, Jacopo Bassano (1510–1592)

by the side of the road. Two Jewish religious authorities—a priest and a Levite—happened by. They ignored the wounded traveler and continued on their way. But a kind Samaritan stopped, treated the man's wounds, and even paid for his treatment and recuperation at a nearby inn.

Jesus knew that most Jews hated Samaritans, yet He made a member of this despised race the hero of His parable. He asked the Jewish expert, "Which of these three do you think was neighbor to him who fell among the thieves?"

(verse 36 NKJV).

The man had to admit that the kind Samaritan was the one who acted with neighborliness toward the Jewish traveler. The message of Jesus' parable was clear: Belonging to the same race, class, neighborhood, political party, or religion does not make neighbors. True neighbors are those people who extend love, mercy, and compassion to others.

MARY AND MARTHA

One day Jesus was visiting in the home of Mary, Martha, and Lazarus in Bethany, a town near Jerusalem. Martha was scurrying around in the kitchen, preparing a meal for their distinguished guest (Luke 10:38–42).

Martha's sister, Mary, was sitting with Jesus, taking in every word He said. Martha was irritated because Mary was not pitching in to help out with the meal. When she expressed her frustration to Jesus, He told her that she had things all turned around. She should quit worrying about the meal and listen to His teachings.

Jesus realized His time on earth was growing short. These two sisters might not have another chance to spend time with Him and hear the message about God's kingdom that He had been sent to deliver.

TEACHINGS ON PRAYER

Jesus spent a lot of time alone in prayer. This impressed the disciples, so they asked Him to teach them how to pray. Jesus responded by teaching them the Model Prayer, often referred to as the Lord's Prayer (Luke 11:1–13). A longer version of this prayer appears in His Sermon on the Mount (Matthew 6:9–13).

The Model Prayer teaches us to call on God as a loving Father; to ask for His provision for our daily needs; to seek His forgiveness for our sins; to ask for help extending forgiveness to others; and to ask for strength to resist the temptations of Satan.

Jesus went on to teach us to be persistent in our prayers by asking, seeking, and knocking to determine His purpose for our lives. Prayers offered in this spirit will be honored and answered by the Lord.

One of Jesus' parables emphasized the importance of persistent prayer. He told about a poor widow who kept coming to a judge to persuade him to hear her case. Finally, the judge rendered a favorable judgment in her behalf—not because he was just and fair but because she wore him down with her persistent pleading. The parable shows that our heavenly Father will answer our prayers if we place them before Him with persistence, expectancy, faith, and trust (Luke 18:1–8).

SO RICH YET SO POOR

While Jesus was teaching the crowd, a man asked Him to talk to his brother about dividing the family inheritance. Apparently this man thought he had not received a fair share of his father's estate.

The man's request reminded Jesus of the problem of greed. He told the crowd a parable about a rich farmer who never seemed to have enough. His crops yielded such a big harvest that he tore down his old barns and built bigger ones to hold the bounty (Luke 12:13–34).

After God called the farmer a fool for his self-centered attitude, the man died unexpectedly without enjoying any of the benefits of his riches. The parable shows how foolish it is to place our confidence in earthly possessions, because they can be taken away at any time.

Jesus went on to encourage His followers to build up spiritual treasures—or God's favor—in heaven rather than physical riches on earth. Doing so will deliver us from fruitless worry. God promises that if we live by the values of His kingdom—righteousness, unselfishness, and faith in the Lord—He will meet our basic physical needs.

BE ON THE WATCH

Jesus had told the disciples on two different occasions that He would be executed and resurrected at some time in the future. But now He jumped even further ahead with a prediction of His return to earth after He had ascended to God the Father (Luke 12:35–59).

He used the analogy of an oil-burning lamp of that time to show His followers that they should always be ready and on the watch for His return. They should have their lamps burning, just as servants had theirs ready to light the way for their master when he returned from a wedding banquet.

A FIG TREE WITH NO FIGS

Jesus told a parable about a fig tree that had yielded no fruit for three years. Finally, its owner ordered it to be cut down. His servant persuaded him to wait one more year to see if the tree would respond to fertilizer and careful cultivation (Luke 13:6–8).

This parable referred to the nation of Israel. The Jewish people had been given multiple opportunities to represent God before the other nations of the world. But they had failed, becoming proud of their heritage and excluding the Gentiles from any hope of salvation.

God was giving the nation of Israel a final chance. If they repented and accepted Jesus—God's special messenger of hope and grace to all the world—they would continue to be favored by the Lord. But it they persisted in their sin and unbelief, they would be cut down from their position as God's chosen people.

A LAMENT OVER JERUSALEM

Jesus was teaching and healing in the region east of the Jordan River. This territory was ruled by Herod Antipas, the Roman despot who had executed John the Baptist. Some Pharisees warned Jesus to leave the area because of Herod's unpredictability. But Jesus replied that He would stay there until His work was completed (Luke 13:31–35).

While in this area, Jesus looked across the Jordan toward Jerusalem and lamented the Holy City's hardness of heart and unbelief. He realized that resentment toward Him among the religious elite of Jerusalem was growing stronger every day. He knew this was the place where He would finally be arrested, condemned, and put to death.

A BANQUET FOR THE POOR

While Jesus was dining at the home of a Pharisee, He noticed that some guests insisted on being seated at the places of highest honor around the table. He reminded them that true humility consists of putting others before oneself. People who do this will be honored by the Lord (Luke 14:7–24).

Then Jesus told the group a parable about a large banquet. Perhaps the fictional banquet was similar to this meal at which He was a guest. The host in the parable invited several of his prominent friends to an elaborate meal. But they all gave weak excuses why they couldn't attend.

Finally, the host sent his servant out into

the streets and alleys of the city and into the countryside to invite the poor and outcasts to come and enjoy the meal. These have-nots represented the kinds of people whom the Pharisees rejected as undeserving sinners. They considered them unworthy of God's favor.

Jesus' parable declared that the outcasts in this situation were actually the Pharisees.

Their self-righteous, know-it-all attitude kept them from accepting Jesus and enjoying the heavenly feast that God had prepared for those who accepted Him. But the poor and afflicted—those who repented and turned in faith to Jesus—were enjoying the benefits of the banquet that the Pharisees had rejected.

RECOVERY OF THE LOST

The Pharisees were criticizing Jesus because He welcomed tax collectors and other sinners to hear His teachings. To the Pharisees, these were "unclean" people who passed on their sin and corruption to everyone who associated with them. In response to this criticism, Jesus told three parables about several lost items that were eventually recovered—a sheep, a coin, and a son (Luke 15:1–32).

In the parable of the lost sheep, Jesus told about a shepherd with one hundred sheep who searched until he found one of the sheep that had strayed from the fold. In the parable of the lost coin, a woman searched her house diligently until she recovered a lost coin.

Both of these people called on their friends and neighbors to rejoice with them when they found what had been lost. In the same way, Jesus pointed out, "there is joy in the presence of the angels of God over one sinner who repents" (verse 10 NKJV). Thus, He served notice to the Pharisees that He was sent to call the lost to repentance and salvation. This task was more important to Him than trying to live up to the expectations of the unrepentant and unteachable Pharisees.

In the parable of the prodigal son, Jesus actually told about two lost sons. The son who left home and wasted his inheritance eventually turned his life around, came back, and was restored and forgiven by his father. But the older

The Return of the Prodigal Son,
Pompeo Batoni (1708–1787)

son of the family wound up lost and trapped by his resentment toward his brother when he returned.

The disgruntled attitude of the second son reflected the mind-set of the Pharisees. In their pride and self-righteousness, they looked down on everyone who did not conform to their strict standards of righteousness. They thought they earned favor with God by keeping every minor detail of the Old Testament law. It was clear that they were just as lost as the three items in these parables of Jesus—and they would remain so until they repented.

A SHREWD MANAGER

Jesus told His disciples a parable about a manager, or steward, who was employed by a rich man to take care of his assets. Through carelessness and negligence, this manager lost a lot of his employer's money. Facing the loss of his job, he made secret deals with his employer's creditors to make sure they would come to his aid after he was fired. His resourcefulness and foresight were commended by his employer (Luke 16:1–12).

The message of this parable is that all followers of Jesus are managers of the blessings of God. We should be wise and creative in taking care of the resources—both physical and spiritual—that God has committed to our care.

A ROLE REVERSAL

In His teachings Jesus often turned things on their head, showing that the truth was the exact opposite of popular thinking. This is particularly true of His parable about Lazarus and the rich man (Luke 16:19–31).

Lazarus, a poor but righteous man, often begged for scraps of food at the gate of a man who had all the luxuries that life could offer. This man was self-centered and had no concern for God or other people. Both he and Lazarus died about the same time and went to separate places in the afterlife—Lazarus to paradise and the rich man to Hades. Now it was the rich man's turn to beg. He pleaded for someone to cool his tongue with a drop of water, while Lazarus was comfortable and content in paradise.

An unbridgeable chasm separated the two, showing that the choices they had made in life had eternal consequences. Jesus was saying that a life devoted to material values and lived only for oneself will separate us from God—in this life as well as the life to come.

"LAZARUS, COME OUT!"

Jesus was ministering some distance away when He learned that Lazarus of Bethany was seriously ill. He was a close friend of Lazarus and his two sisters, Mary and Martha. He had often been a guest in their home. So Jesus' disciples were puzzled when He did not immediately set out for this little town just a stone's throw from Jerusalem (John 11:1–44).

When Jesus arrived in Bethany, He learned that Lazarus had died four days before. Martha met Him with a gentle criticism. If He had come as soon as they sent word about her brother's illness, she told Him, He could have healed Lazarus before he died. Jesus assured her that it was not too late for a miracle. Then He raised Lazarus from the dead with a simple command: "Lazarus, come out!" (verse 43 NIV).

News of this spectacular miracle soon reached the religious leaders in Jerusalem. They called a meeting of the Sanhedrin, the high court that regulated the religious life of the Jewish people. They declared that Jesus had to be stopped because his activities might lead to a disturbance that would bring the Roman army down on their heads. But the real reason for their opposition was jealousy. They considered His claim to be divine as a blasphemy against God and a serious threat to their authority.

The Resurrection of Lazarus, artist unknown (on display at the church Chiesa di San Gaetano and the Chapel of the Crucifixion)

TEN LEPERS HEALED

Jesus was on His way to Jerusalem when ten men with leprosy called to Him from a distance. People with this disease were not allowed to get close to others. Because of their isolation, lepers often gathered into small groups for mutual friendship and support.

After they were healed, nine of the men walked away. Only one approached Jesus to express thanks for his restoration. Jesus commended him for his thoughtfulness and declared that his faith had made him spiritually clean. This was a better gift than a healthy body (Luke 17:11–19).

A LESSON IN HUMILITY AND PRIDE

Jesus told a parable about a tax collector and a Pharisee to emphasize the contrast between humility and pride. Both men prayed to God. The tax collector—who was the very personification of sin to the Pharisees—prayed out of a deep sense of his unworthiness. But the Pharisee reminded God of his spiritual superiority by condemning the sins of others (Luke 18:9–14).

Jesus declared that the tax collector rather than the Pharisee enjoyed God's favor. In a spirit of humility, he recognized his sin, repented of it, and pleaded for God's mercy and grace. This parable teaches that honest confession of our sins is the key to God's acceptance and forgiveness.

A PROFOUND QUESTION

One day a young man who had plenty of money came to Jesus with a serious question: "What shall I do that I may inherit eternal life?" (Mark 10:17; see 10:17–31). Jesus replied by quoting the Ten Commandments, implying that keeping these laws was one key to finding what he was looking for. The man replied that he had known and observed these guidelines since he was a boy.

Jesus sensed this young man's need. Up to now, his religion had not involved any sacrifice from him. If he really wanted to experience eternal life in all its dimensions, he must be willing to give up what he valued most—his earthly riches and financial security. But this he could not bring himself to do.

After the man walked away, Jesus used the encounter to teach His disciples about money and its power. The desire to acquire material possessions can actually keep people from becoming citizens of God's kingdom. "It is easier for a camel to go through the eye of a needle," He told them, "than for a rich man to enter the kingdom of God."

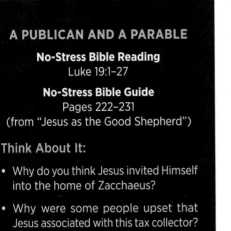

A PUBLICAN AND A PARABLE

No-Stress Bible Reading
Luke 19:1–27

No-Stress Bible Guide
Pages 222–231
(from "Jesus as the Good Shepherd")

Think About It:

- Why do you think Jesus invited Himself into the home of Zacchaeus?

- Why were some people upset that Jesus associated with this tax collector?

- What message did Jesus deliver to His critics in the parable of the pounds?

WORKERS IN THE VINEYARD

Jesus told His disciples a parable about a man who hired several people at different times during the day to work in his vineyard. At the end of the day, he paid each of them the same amount. Some of the workers complained that they had worked a full day yet received the same pay as those who had worked only an hour or two (Matthew 20:1–16).

This parable teaches an important lesson about the kingdom of God. Our acceptance into His kingdom is a result of His love and grace—not our worthiness or the number of days or hours we devote to His service. We should serve God for the sheer joy of doing His will—not because we expect a reward for doing so.

A THIRD DEATH PREDICTION

On His way to Jerusalem to celebrate the Passover festival, Jesus called His disciples aside for a private conversation. He told them plainly for the third time that the time of His betrayal and death was near. This trip to Jerusalem would be His final visit to the Holy City (Mark 10:32–34).

The parallel account in Luke's Gospel records that His disciples "did not understand any of this" (Luke 18:34 NIV). For three years they had

Christ and the Rich Young Ruler, Heinrich Hofmann (1824–1911), currently on display at Riverside Church, New York

seen Jesus' spectacular power with their own eyes and heard His revolutionary teachings with their own ears. They could not believe that He would be put to death like a common criminal.

A STOP IN JERICHO

The last stop on Jesus' final trip to Jerusalem was at Jericho, a city about fifteen miles from the Holy City. Just outside Jericho he healed a blind man named Bartimaeus (Mark 10:46–52).

Inside Jericho was a tax collector named Zacchaeus, who was anxious to see Jesus. He climbed a tree so he could get a good look at this miracle worker as He passed through. Zacchaeus must have been shocked when Jesus stopped, called him down from his perch, and invited Himself into his home (Luke 19:1–10).

This encounter with Jesus changed Zacchaeus's life. He vowed to repay those whom he had cheated and to give half of his possessions to the poor. Best of all, he placed his faith in Jesus and received His assurance of salvation.

After leaving Jericho, Jesus continued His journey toward Jerusalem, where His enemies lay in wait. His suffering and death were just a few days away. The next chapter focuses on the final events of His earthly life and ministry.

Christ in the House of Martha and Mary, Henryk Siemiradzki (1843–1902)

The Gospel of John reports that Jesus arrived in Bethany about two miles east of Jerusalem "six days before the passover" (John 12:1). Here He probably stayed in the home of Lazarus, Mary, and Martha while He waited for the festival to begin.

The events between Jesus' arrival in Bethany and His death and resurrection occurred in just a few days—probably about a week to ten days. But the Gospel writers devoted about one-third of their total content to these few days. It's obvious that they considered His atoning death and glorious resurrection the crowning achievement of His short earthly life and ministry.

MARY ANOINTS JESUS

While Jesus was in the home of Lazarus, Mary poured an expensive perfume on His feet and wiped them with her hair. It was unthinkable for a woman to use her long hair—her crowning glory—to wipe someone's feet, which was the lowliest part of the body. This humble act showed her love for Jesus. But His disciple Judas criticized her, declaring that this perfume could have been sold and the proceeds given to the poor (John 12:1–11).

Jesus had a different interpretation of this lavish display of Mary's love and respect. He considered it an anointing for His burial within just a few days. Bodies of the dead were often treated with precious perfumes and spices before they were buried.

While this act of devotion was taking place inside Lazarus's house, a large crowd gathered outside, hoping to see Jesus and Lazarus. Jesus' raising of Lazarus from the dead just a few days before had caused many people to acclaim Him as a great prophet. This infuriated the chief priests of the Jews, who grew even more determined to have Jesus arrested and executed.

PREPARATION FOR BURIAL

No-Stress Bible Reading
John 12:1–11

No-Stress Bible Guide
Pages 233–236
(to "A Question About Taxes")

Think About It:

- How do you think Jesus knew that the time for His death was getting close?

- Why were the Jewish religious leaders upset at Jesus' growing popularity with the common people?

Mary Magdalene, Jan van Scorel (1495–1552)

The Triumphal Entry of Christ into Jerusalem, artist unknown (Palatine Chapel, Palermo, Italy)

A KING ON A DONKEY

At last the time had arrived for Jesus to reveal Himself to the crowds that had gathered in Jerusalem for the Passover celebration. He chose to do so by making a triumphal entry into the Holy City (John 12:12–19).

The people expected a conquering general who would charge into town on a white horse. Instead, Jesus rode in on the back of a donkey, fulfilling the prediction of the prophet Zechariah: "Behold, your King is coming to you; He is just and having salvation, lowly and riding on a donkey" (Zechariah 9:9 NKJV). This prophecy indicated He was not the military deliverer they expected but

a spiritual servant-king whose mission was to set people free from their bondage to sin.

Some people in the crowd missed the message Jesus was sending. According to the Gospel of Matthew, they placed their robes and tree branches in His path—a gesture of honor for a conquering king—and shouted, "Hosanna to the son of David!" (Matthew 21:9 NIV). They welcomed Jesus as the kind of king they wanted, not the spiritual King from God the Father, whom He intended to be.

A POLLUTED TEMPLE AND A BARREN FIG TREE

When Jesus arrived at the temple in the center of Jerusalem, He witnessed a scene that made Him angry. Some merchants were selling sacrificial animals in the temple's outer courtyard. Others were exchanging foreign coins for the appropriate coins needed to pay the annual temple tax (Matthew 21:12–17).

Jesus overturned the tables of the money changers and chased the merchants who were selling animals from the temple area. He declared that these commercial activities were turning the Lord's "house of prayer" into a "den of thieves" (verse 13).

The next day, Jesus and His disciples were coming back into Jerusalem when He saw a fig tree that contained no figs. He cursed the tree because it had no fruit, declaring that it would never bear figs again.

This tree symbolized the nation of Israel. God had blessed the Jews as His special people. They had the potential to bear fruit for Him but had repeatedly failed to do so. Because of their failure to do God's bidding and their rejection of Jesus, they would suffer the Lord's severe judgment (Matthew 21:18–22).

GREEKS ASK TO SEE JESUS

Jesus' disciples Philip and Andrew informed Him that a group of Greeks wanted to talk to Him. These Greeks were probably God-fearers—Gentiles who were attracted to Judaism because of its moral and ethical standards. They had probably heard about Jesus, and they wanted to hear what He had to say about the Old Testament law and other Jewish teachings.

This request from the Greeks set Jesus off on a long monologue about His approaching death and the mission for which He had been sent into the world (John 12:20–50). In these inquiring Gentiles, He saw a future ingathering of people of all races who would respond to the Gospel and become citizens of the kingdom of God.

At the same time, Jesus realized the price He would pay for this vision to become a reality. He must die to become the Savior of humankind. He had known the cost from the beginning, but events were now pointing to an immediate crisis. Only by choosing to give up His own life could He make possible a rich harvest of believers—including many people from the Gentile world.

While Jesus was reflecting on these truths, a voice confirming Jesus' commitment to the cross was heard from heaven. At the beginning of His ministry (Matthew 3:17), at His transfiguration (Luke 9:35), and now toward the close of His public ministry, He was fortified by words of approval and encouragement from His heavenly Father.

Jesus ended His monologue with a victory speech. His death on the cross would spell defeat for Satan. As He was "lifted up" (John 12:34) on the cross, all kinds of people would be drawn to Him. Gentiles as well as Jews would respond in faith to the message of the Gospel.

A QUESTION ABOUT AUTHORITY

The religious leaders demanded that Jesus tell them by what authority He had cleansed the temple, since they were responsible for its operation. They probably hoped Jesus would make some statement that would give them grounds to arrest Him.

Instead of replying to their question, Jesus asked them a question about John the Baptist. "Where did John's baptism come from?" He wanted to know. "From heaven or from men?" (Matthew 21:25 HCSB; see 21:23–32).

This question put the religious leaders in a quandary. If they acknowledged that John's authority came from God, they were admitting they had resisted the Lord by refusing to accept John's message. If they said John spoke without authority from God, this would offend the common people, who had great admiration for the prophet. The religious leaders did not answer the question, so Jesus refused to reveal His source of authority to them.

Jesus went on to tell these Jewish leaders a parable about two sons. One son refused his father's request to work in the family vineyard but later changed his mind and went to work. The second son agreed to work in the vineyard but never followed through and did as he promised.

The first son represented the outcasts and sinners of that time. They were far from God's kingdom at first, but they believed John the Baptist and repented. The second son symbolized the religious leaders of Israel. They were sworn to do God's work and follow His will. But they refused to believe John, who called them to repentance and pointed them to Jesus as the Messiah.

THE PARABLE OF THE MURDERED SON

Jesus had another parable with an even stronger message for these hypocritical religious leaders. He told them about another vineyard owner who hired tenants to take care of his property. At harvesttime he sent his servants to claim his share of the crop. But the tenants refused to pay what they owed (Luke 20:9–19). Next the vineyard owner sent his own son to collect his share of the harvest. But the wicked tenants killed the son and dumped his body outside the vineyard.

The message of this parable is that the Jewish religious leaders executed Jesus, God's Son, when He was sent to call people to repentance and faith. But God's purpose would not be thwarted. He turned from the nation of Israel to the non-Jewish world that was eager to hear the good news of the Gospel.

Another parable of Jesus that teaches basically the same message is the parable of the wedding banquet (Matthew 22:1–14). A king invited all his friends to a wedding feast for his son. When these people refused to attend, he invited people from off the streets and throughout the countryside to come and enjoy the meal. The invited guests who refused to come to the banquet symbolized the stubborn nation of Israel, and the street people represented the receptive Gentiles.

The reaction of the religious leaders to the parable of the murdered son demonstrated the truth of its message. They became more determined than ever to arrest Jesus. But Jesus' popularity with the people prevented them from doing so. The Jewish officials finally left without arresting Him.

A QUESTION ABOUT TAXES

In an attempt to trap Jesus, the Jewish religious leaders sent a delegation of Pharisees and Herodians to ask Him about paying taxes to the Roman government. Was it right or wrong to do so? A yes answer would alienate Him from His fellow Jews. A no answer would make Him a rebel against Roman authority (Mark 12:13–17). (See sidebar, "Jesus and the Herodians.")

But Jesus was not taken in by their trickery. He gave both a yes and a no answer to their question. "Render to Caesar [the Roman emperor] the things that are Caesar's," He declared, "and to God the things that are God's" (verse 17). With these words, He pointed out the difference between the material and the spiritual realms of life.

The Roman government had the right to require material taxes from its subjects as long as it was the ruling authority in the land. On the other hand, matters of the spirit belonged to God alone, and these should be rendered only to Him. Jesus probably had in mind our worship of and uncompromising devotion to the supreme ruler of the universe. No earthly ruler had the right to demand spiritual loyalty from his subjects.

A QUESTION ABOUT THE RESURRECTION

A group of Sadducees came to Jesus with a trick question about the resurrection. They cited a hypothetical case of a woman who was married to seven brothers, one after the other. They asked Jesus which brother's wife she would be in the afterlife. They didn't believe in a bodily resurrection, and they hoped to make Jesus come across as ridiculous in His response to this question (Luke 20:27–40).

Jesus told these Sadducees they were judging heavenly matters with earthly logic. The afterlife, He pointed out, will bring a totally different way of living and relating to one another. The close family ties we have experienced on earth will be fulfilled by the richer relationships we will enjoy as members of the family of God.

HARSH WORDS FOR THE PHARISEES

Jesus had clashed with the legalistic Pharisees several times during His ministry throughout Palestine. But He waited until His final days in Jerusalem before issuing His severest complaint against them and their dangerous doctrines. He pronounced a series of "woes" against them in some of the harshest words He ever spoke. This indictment appears in a section of Matthew's Gospel known as the "woe chapter" of the New Testament (Matthew 23:1–36).

One of Jesus' most serious charges against the Pharisees was their emphasis on minor rules in the Old Testament law. This increased the burden on the common people, who did not have the time or resources to observe all these petty regulations.

Jesus also criticized the Pharisees for their hypocrisy. They pretended to be more zealous in their commitment to the law than any other group in Israel. But Jesus declared that their zeal was counterfeit, a cover-up for their inner corruption and lack of compassion. "You are like whitewashed tombs, which look fine on the outside," He told them, "but are full of bones and decaying corpses on the inside" (Matthew 23:27 GNT).

Jesus ended His denunciation of the Pharisees by accusing them of murdering the prophets

Woe Unto You, Scribes and Pharisees, James Tissot (1836–1902)

whom God had sent to them throughout the history of Israel. He knew they harbored the same hate against Him and that He was destined to become their next victim.

A POOR WIDOW'S OFFERING

In the temple in Jerusalem, Jesus watched as people dropped their offerings into one of the collection boxes. He was not impressed by some of the large contributions made by the wealthy. But He took notice when a poor widow dropped in her meager offering, consisting of two small coins.

Jesus used her contribution as an object lesson for His disciples. "This poor widow has put in more than all the others," He told them. "All these people gave their gifts out of their wealth; but she out of her poverty put in all she had to live on" (Luke 21:3–4 NIV).

BE READY FOR JESUS' RETURN

Jesus had talked with His disciples several times about His forthcoming death and resurrection. But He had said little about His ascension to heaven and His second coming. Now that His death was near, He told them two parables to prepare them to be on the watch for His second coming at the end of the age.

One of these parables was about five foolish virgins who missed part of a wedding celebration because they didn't have enough oil to keep their lamps burning. He contrasted these foolish women with five wise virgins, who made sure they had enough fuel for the occasion. His message in this parable was clear: Make sure you are ready for My return (Matthew 25:1–13).

He communicated another truth about His return in a second story known as the parable of the talents. A landowner went on a long journey, leaving three of his servants different sums of money—or talents—to manage while he was gone.

Two of these servants multiplied their master's talents through wise investments. But the third servant played it safe and buried his talent, failing to earn any return on the money. His master was not pleased when he returned and learned that this servant had been a poor manager of the talent with which he had been entrusted (Matthew 25:14–30).

This parable teaches that believers should be wise stewards of the gifts we have been given by the Lord while we wait for His return. What we do with what God has entrusted to us determines whether we are judged faithful or unfaithful by the Lord.

Jesus told these two parables within the context of a large section of scripture known as His "eschatological speech" or His "Olivet Discourse." Proclaimed to His disciples on the Mount of Olives just outside Jerusalem, it is one of His longest speeches in the Gospels (see Matthew 24:1–25:46).

In this long speech, Jesus responded to two separate questions from His disciples. He had just declared that Jerusalem's beautiful temple would be destroyed, and they wanted to know when this would happen. They also asked about the signs that would indicate the end of the age. The Olivet Discourse is difficult for interpreters because Jesus intermingled His answers to these two questions.

Most interpreters believe Jesus dealt with the question about the destruction of the temple in Matthew 24:4–25, ending with the phrase, "See, I have told you ahead of time" (verse 25 NIV). This prophecy was fulfilled in AD 70, when the city of Jerusalem and its beautiful temple were destroyed by the Roman army. The remainder of His long speech deals with the end of the age and the second coming of Christ.

Jesus concluded His Olivet Discourse with a vivid picture of the final judgment. At Jesus' return He will separate people into two groups, much as a shepherd would separate his flock into sheep and goats when they bedded down for the night. This great separation of the righteous from the unrighteous pictures salvation not on the basis of good deeds but on the basis of good hearts. Those who have faith in Jesus act out their faith by loving others (Matthew 25:31–46).

The Parable of the Ten Virgins, Phoebe Traquair (1852–1936), Mansfield Traquair Church, Edinburgh

LOOKING AHEAD

No-Stress Bible Reading
Matthew 25

No-Stress Bible Guide
Pages 236–239
(from "A Question About Taxes")

Think About It:

- Why do believers need to be ready for Jesus' return at any time?

- Why do you think some Christians cultivate and grow their spiritual gifts, while others do not?

- Why will the righteous at the final judgment be surprised when Jesus commends them for ministering to Him?

- Do you believe that meeting the needs of others in Jesus' name is just the same as ministry to Him?

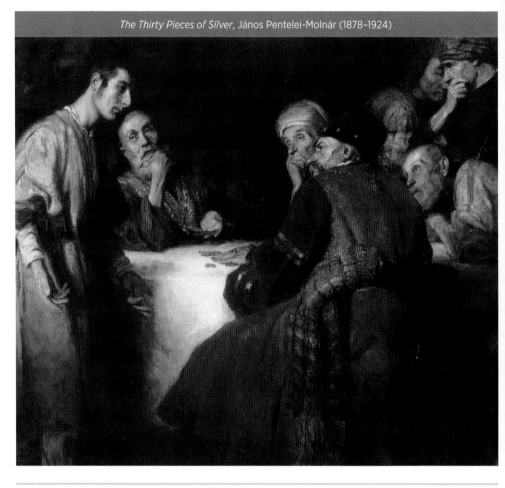
The Thirty Pieces of Silver, János Pentelei-Molnár (1878–1924)

JUDAS MAKES A DEAL

The religious leaders assembled at the palace of the high priest to decide how to deal with Jesus. They decided not to kill Him until after the Passover celebration, since the crowds would not tolerate His being harmed (Matthew 26:1–16).

Into this volatile state of affairs stepped the scheming Judas, one of Jesus' disciples. He realized the Jewish Sanhedrin would arrest Jesus sooner or later, so he saw an opportunity to make some easy money in the situation. He went to the religious authorities and made a deal to lead them to Jesus at an opportune time in return for thirty pieces of silver.

To Judas's credit, he later repented of what he had done when Jesus was arrested. He tried to return the money he had been paid, but the Jewish authorities refused to take it back. In a state of remorse, he committed suicide by hanging himself. His betrayal fee was used to buy a plot of land for use as a cemetery for foreigners (Matthew 27:1–10).

THE LAST SUPPER

Jesus' final meal with His disciples on the night before He was arrested and crucified is known as the Last Supper, the Memorial Supper, or the Lord's Supper. During the Passover festival in Jerusalem, it was customary for the Jewish people to eat a meal to symbolize God's deliverance of His people from Egyptian slavery. Jesus turned this meal into a supper of remembrance to signify His approaching death.

All four Gospels contain an account of this meal. Several significant events occurred during this last meal of Jesus with His disciples.

Washing of His disciples' feet. While His disciples were seated at the table, Jesus took a basin of water and a towel and washed their feet. This hospitality ritual was generally performed by a household servant for visiting guests. Walking in sandals on the primitive roads of Palestine resulted in hot, tired, and dirty feet that were soothed by this thoughtful gesture (John 13:1–17).

Jesus had just explained to His disciples that true greatness in the kingdom of God consists in humble service to others. By washing their feet, He showed them the real meaning of His words. "I have given you an example," He told them, "that you also should do just as I have done for you" (John 13:15 HCSB).

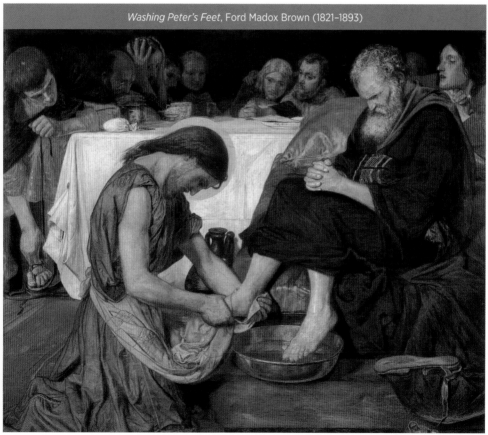

Washing Peter's Feet, Ford Madox Brown (1821–1893)

Identification of His betrayer. The Passover meal was in progress when Jesus made the startling announcement that one of His disciples would betray Him to His enemies. Astonished at this statement, each of the Twelve declared his own loyalty by saying, "Surely, Lord, you don't mean me?" (Matthew 26:22 GNT; see 26:20–25).

Judas showed cold hypocrisy by making the same statement as the others. Jesus left no doubt that He knew about Judas's plot when He told Him directly, "You have said so" (verse 25 NRSV). This bold, matter-of-fact reply shows that Jesus was in control of His fate. He realized that His death was just hours away, but He did not cut and run. He moved deliberately toward the purpose for which He had been sent into the world.

Prediction of His disciples' denial. Jesus also knew that the other disciples would abandon Him after He was arrested and condemned. He told them clearly that this would happen (Mark 14:27–31).

All of them protested that they would remain faithful, but Peter was the most vocal in his objection. "Even if all fall away," he declared, "I will not" (verse 29 NIV). Jesus replied that the rooster that signaled the dawn of the next day would not crow twice before Peter had denied Him three times.

The parallel account in Luke's Gospel adds the interesting detail that Peter's denial would not be the final chapter in this apostle's story. Jesus encouraged him by predicting that he would be restored to usefulness in His service. After this restoration, he should strengthen the other disciples in their faith and commitment to Christ (Luke 22:31–32).

Farewell to His disciples. According to the Gospel of John, Jesus delivered a long farewell speech to His disciples during their last meal together. This is one of His longest speeches in the Gospels. It showed His close friendship with the Twelve and His concern for their well-being in the days after His death, resurrection, and ascension (John 14:1–16:33).

Although Jesus was going away, He promised His disciples they would not be left alone. He would send the Holy Spirit to serve as their counselor and guide. This Spirit—the very presence of God Himself—would continue the work of God's kingdom through the followers of Jesus and the church He had founded.

Jesus also reminded His disciples of the importance of love in their lives. Just as He had loved them, they should love one another. Such love would bring joy to God the Father and Jesus the Son—the ultimate source of love.

Jesus was direct and honest with His disciples about what to expect as His followers. They would be condemned and criticized just as He had been, because "a servant is not greater than his master" (John 15:20 NIV). He wanted them to be prepared for future hardships.

In spite of these troubles, Jesus assured His disciples that they would experience peace and joy if they remained faithful to Him and the truths He had taught them. No, they would not escape the problems of this world. "But take heart!" He declared. "I have overcome the world" (John 16:33 NIV).

Prayer for His disciples. After bidding farewell to His disciples, Jesus prayed for them. This prayer in John 17 is His longest prayer in the Gospels. It is called His "High Priestly Prayer" because He assumed the role of Israel's high priest in praying for Himself, His disciples, and all future believers. Soon He would make the ultimate sacrifice for humankind—His own atoning death on the cross.

While praying for Himself, Jesus spoke of His death as an event through which He would glorify God and in turn be glorified. He looked beyond the cross to its result. In the future the world would see His sacrifice as a revelation of the love of God.

Jesus prayed fervently for His disciples,

who had been with Him for the past three years. He asked God to protect them in His absence. He had guarded them closely while He was with them, and only Judas had fallen away. He entrusted to them the elevation of His mission to the next level—the proclamation of the Gospel to a lost world.

Future generations of believers were included in Jesus' prayer as well. He prayed that they would have a oneness of spirit—a unity similar to the oneness that existed between God the Father and God the Son. The purpose of this harmony was that people might place their faith in Jesus Christ as their Lord and Savior.

JESUS' STRUGGLE IN GETHSEMANE

After finishing their Passover meal together, Jesus and His disciples left Jerusalem and walked across the Kidron Valley to the nearby Mount of Olives. Somewhere on this mountain, He went into a garden called Gethsemane. Jesus may have known the owner of this site. Perhaps he had his permission to use the garden as a place where He could withdraw for prayer and meditation (Matthew 26:36–46).

Jesus' spiritual struggle in this garden gives us a full-blown look at the human side of His God-man nature. He knew the cross was His destiny and thus part of God's plan for the salvation of the world. But He still shuddered at the thought of dying.

In an agonizing prayer, He asked God to save Him from the suffering He faced, if it could be avoided. In this perilous time, He especially needed the support of His three closest friends—Peter, James, and John. But they fell asleep without uttering a word of encouragement. He had to face this dark time alone.

But Jesus conquered His fear and temptation with the words that make Gethsemane one of the most sacred spots on earth. "If this cup [of suffering] cannot be taken away unless I drink it," He prayed to His Father, "your will be done" (Matthew 26:42 NLT).

AGONY IN THE GARDEN

No-Stress Bible Reading
Matthew 26:36–46

No-Stress Bible Guide
Pages 240–245
(to "Off to Pilate")

Think About It:

- How did this temptation differ from the appeals of Satan at the beginning of Jesus' public ministry (see Matthew 4:1–11)?

- Why did Jesus need the support of Peter, James, and John in His hour of struggle?

JESUS' BETRAYAL AND ARREST

Jesus' disciple Judas knew that Jesus often went to Gethsemane to pray. So he fulfilled the bargain he had made with the religious authorities just a few days before. He informed them they could find Him in this private spot apart from the crowds. Judas himself brought a detachment of Roman soldiers and temple guards to make the arrest (John 18:1–12).

In an emotional outburst, Jesus' disciple Peter drew a sword and took a swing at the high priest's servant—a man named Malchus. Malchus dodged the blow and lost only an ear. According to Luke's parallel account of this event, Jesus restored this severed ear (Luke 22:50–51).

Then He told His disciples to stand down and put their weapons away. He went peacefully with his captors, believing this to be the will of His Father.

THE HEARING BEFORE ANNAS

The party that arrested Jesus brought Him before Annas, a corrupt religious leader who was probably an influential member of the Jewish Sanhedrin. Annas had been the high priest of Israel in the past. But in Jesus' time, he had passed this position on to his son-in-law Caiaphas.

Annas must have been the power behind the high priestly office, reaping its benefits without having to shoulder its responsibilities. When he failed to get any helpful information out of Jesus, he sent Him to Caiaphas for further questioning (John 18:12–23).

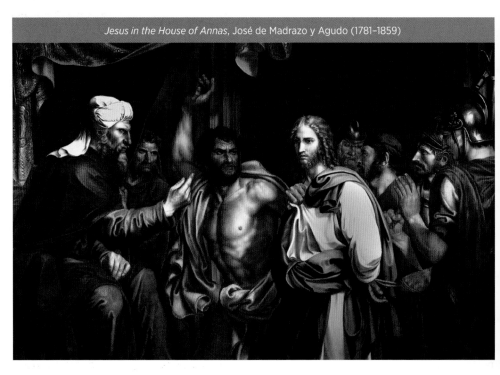

Jesus in the House of Annas, José de Madrazo y Agudo (1781–1859)

CONDEMNED BY THE SANHEDRIN

Caiaphas, as high priest, assembled the entire Jewish Sanhedrin to hear the charges against Jesus. This group, consisting of seventy-one

priests, scribes, and elders, had the authority to bring Jewish citizens to trial for religious offenses as well as other minor crimes (Mark 14:53–65).

The charge against Jesus was blasphemy, or showing disrespect toward God and other sacred elements of the Jewish religion. The Sanhedrin produced two witnesses who claimed they had heard Jesus say He would tear down the temple and raise it again in three days. This was a distortion of His words. When Jesus made this statement, He was referring to His death and resurrection.

The Sanhedrin also questioned Jesus about His claim to be the Messiah. At first He refused to answer. But when the high priest placed Him under oath to tell the truth, Jesus stated plainly that He was the Messiah, the Son of God.

This was all the members of the Sanhedrin wanted to hear. To them, Jesus' statement was the ultimate blasphemy—claiming to be equal with God Himself. Their verdict was that Jesus deserved to die for this crime. But then they faced a dilemma: How could they get rid of this troublemaker for good, when only the Roman courts could carry out the death penalty?

MEANWHILE, OUT IN THE COURTYARD

While Jesus was on trial inside the palace of the high priest, Peter was outside in the courtyard. He had apparently followed Jesus here to see what would happen at His trial. As Peter sat warming himself by a fire, a servant girl of the high priest insisted she recognized him as one of Jesus' disciples. But Peter denied knowing anything about Him—not once but three times (Mark 14:66–72).

As soon as Peter issued his third denial—this time with an oath that he was telling the truth—he heard a rooster crow for the second time. Then he realized that the prediction of Jesus had come true. He was so ashamed of his blatant denial that "he broke down and wept" (verse 72 NIV).

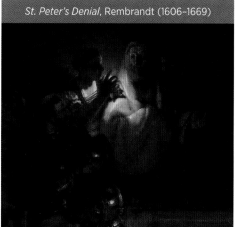

St. Peter's Denial, Rembrandt (1606–1669)

OFF TO PILATE

The Jewish Sanhedrin brought Jesus to Pilate, the Roman governor in Jerusalem, because they were determined that He should die. Only the Roman justice system had the authority to exercise capital punishment.

The Sanhedrin also realized that a strictly religious offense was not sufficient grounds for His execution. So they convinced Pilate that Jesus was an enemy of the state because He claimed to be the king of the Jews—an act of rebellion against Roman authority (John 18:28–38).

Pilate asked Jesus if He considered Himself to be the king of the Jews. Jesus agreed that He was a king but not a political ruler. He reigned over a spiritual realm known as the kingdom of God.

After this interview, Pilate was convinced that Jesus had committed no crime that deserved the death penalty. He tried to get off the hook by asking the Sanhedrin to allow him to release Jesus rather than a notorious Jewish rebel known as Barabbas. As a gesture of goodwill to the Jews, he always set one Jewish prisoner free

Ecce Homo, Antonio Ciseri (1821–1891)

PILATE AND HEROD

Luke's Gospel includes an interesting detail about Jesus' appearance before Pilate that does not appear in any other Gospel. Luke records that Pilate sent Jesus to Herod Antipas, Roman governor of Galilee, when he learned that Jesus was from Galilee. Herod happened to be in Jerusalem that day for the Passover celebration. Pilate apparently wanted to shift responsibility for Jesus' fate from himself to Herod (Luke 23:6–12).

But Herod didn't take the bait. After questioning Jesus and receiving no answers, he insulted Him by dressing Him in an elaborate robe to mock His claim to be a king. Then he sent Him back to Pilate without ruling on His guilt or innocence. Pilate had to take full responsibility for sentencing Jesus to die.

during the annual Passover celebration.

But the Sanhedrin rejected his suggestion. They had worked behind the scenes to generate hostility against Jesus among the Jewish crowds. When Pilate gave the people a choice of freeing either Jesus or this infamous criminal, they chose Barabbas (Matthew 27:21). They shouted to Pilate that they wanted Jesus to be crucified (verse 22).

At this response, Pilate washed his hands of any responsibility for Jesus' death. "I am innocent of this man's blood," he told the crowd. "It is your responsibility!" (Matthew 27:24 NIV). Then he handed Jesus over to a detachment of Roman soldiers for His execution (verses 26–29). (See sidebar, "Pilate and Herod.")

A SAVIOR ON A CROSS

Jesus appeared before Pilate on late Thursday night or early Friday morning. The Roman governor's execution order was carried out immediately. Several significant events associated with His crucifixion occurred during the next twelve hours—a day on the Christian calendar known as Good Friday.

Flogged and mocked by soldiers. Before Jesus was marched away to the execution site, He was beaten, or flogged, by the Roman soldiers who served as Pilate's death squad (Mark 15:15). They used a whip with sharp pieces of metal or bone embedded in the leather strips. This form of torture often led to death from shock or loss of blood.

A crucifixion victim was usually forced to carry his own cross to the execution site. But the soldiers in Jesus' case pressed a passerby named Simon into service to carry His cross (Matthew 27:32). Jesus may have been too weak to do so after His savage beating.

To compound their cruelty, the soldiers also heaped emotional abuse on Jesus. As they led Him away, they insulted Him by dressing Him in a purple robe to mock His claim to be a king. They placed a crown of thorns on His head, spat in His face, struck Him with a staff, and bowed down before Him in mock worship (Mark 15:16–20).

Humiliated by the crowd and religious officials. This mockery of Jesus was echoed by the spectators who gathered around the cross. They taunted Jesus to use His powers to save Himself from such a degrading and dishonorable death (Matthew 27:39–43).

Then the religious officials joined in the abuse. They mocked Jesus by saying that He claimed to have saved others, but He was not able to save His own life. They also taunted Him about His claim to be God's Son. Where was His Father now, they jeered, that He allowed His Son to die in such pain and disgrace?

Their mockery contained more truth than they realized. Jesus could have saved Himself from the cross. But He knew that if He saved Himself, He could not rescue sinners—the purpose for which He had been sent into the world.

Honored by faithful women. While the crowd jeered at and mocked Jesus, several loyal female followers stood near the cross. They are named later in connection with the resurrection of Jesus. These women were probably His mother, Mary; her sister, generally thought to be Salome, the mother of James and John; Mary the wife of Clopas; and Mary Magdalene. Most of Jesus'

PILATE'S PREDICAMENT

No-Stress Bible Reading
John 18:29–40; 19:1–22

No-Stress Bible Guide
Pages 245–246
(from "Off to Pilate"
to "A Savior on a Cross")

Think About It:

- If Pilate thought Jesus was innocent, why did he give in to the cries of the crowd for His crucifixion?

- Why did the religious leaders want Pilate to change the sign he had posted on Jesus' cross?

MOCKED AND HUMILIATED

No-Stress Bible Reading
Matthew 27:35–44; Mark 15:15–20

No-Stress Bible Guide
Pages 246–250 (from "A Savior on a Cross to "Up from the Grave")

Think About It:

- How do you feel when you reflect on the abuse that Jesus endured for you (and all lost sinners) during His trial and crucifixion?

Christ on the Cross between the Two Thieves, Peter Paul Rubens (1577–1640) disciples had fled in fear of the Jewish and Roman authorities when Jesus was arrested and sentenced to die. But these women were His faithful followers to the very end (Luke 23:27).

In His final hour, Jesus commended His mother to the care of the "disciple. . .whom he loved" (John 19:26), generally thought to be the apostle John.

Executed on a false charge. When the soldiers nailed Jesus to the cross, they posted a sign above His head that read, "This is Jesus, the king of the Jews" (Matthew 27:37). It was customary for the Romans to post such a sign for crucifixion victims, declaring the crime for which a criminal was being put to death. This sent a message to the Jewish people that the same thing would happen to them if they dared to disobey the law.

The charge against Jesus was that He claimed to be the king of the Jewish people. This was considered an act of sedition against the Roman government. Only the emperor had the authority to appoint rulers over the nations that Rome controlled. But it was actually a false charge, since Jesus never claimed to be a political king. As the Messiah, He was a spiritual leader who came into the world to bring people into a heavenly kingdom—the kingdom of God.

Crucified between two criminals. Jesus was not the only person who was executed by the Roman authorities on that day. Two criminals were crucified along with Him (Luke 23:39–43). Their reaction to Jesus in their hours of shared suffering reflects how people had responded to the Gospel He had proclaimed during His public ministry.

One criminal insulted Jesus and refused to believe He was God's special messenger. But the other believed and asked Jesus to remember him in the kingdom of God He had come to establish. The first criminal died in his sins, but the second was redeemed and assured of an eternal inheritance in the life to come. Jesus promised him, "Today shalt thou be with me in paradise" (verse 43).

Startling events in Jesus' final hours. Around noon, about three hours before Jesus died, an eerie darkness covered the land. Was this a sign of Satan's attempt to destroy Jesus? Or was God using the dark to hide the suffering of His Son? This strange event could be interpreted either way. But there's no doubt about the effect of this phenomenon: it struck fear into everyone—Roman soldiers as well as Jewish religious leaders—who had anything to do with Jesus' execution (Matthew 27:45–56).

This siege of darkness was followed by several other shocking events at the moment when Jesus died. The earth trembled from an earthquake, and a heavy curtain that hung in the nearby temple was "torn in two from top to bottom" (verse 51 NIV).

This curtain separated the Holy Place from the Most Holy Place in the temple. Only the Jewish high priest was allowed behind this curtain. He could go into the Most Holy Place only once per year—on the Day of Atonement—to offer sacrifices to atone for the sins of the people. The tearing of the curtain at Jesus' death signified that He had paid the price for human sin and that all people now had equal access to God's love and grace.

Only Matthew's Gospel reports that the earthquake at Jesus' death caused the tombs of many believers to break open, and that they came out of their graves (Matthew 27:52). After Jesus' resurrection three days later, these believers went into Jerusalem and "appeared unto many" (verse 53).

This verse is one of the most puzzling in the Bible. Did these believers go back into their graves again after they had been raised, or were they taken into heaven with Jesus when He ascended to the Father? No one knows. Perhaps Matthew intended this verse as an allegory. These people could represent all deceased believers of

Jesus Receives a Jewish Burial, artist unknown (St. Jacob's Church, Bruges, Belgium)

the future who are assured of bodily resurrection at Jesus' second coming (1 Thessalonians 4:14–18).

Burial in Joseph's tomb. After Jesus died, a man named Joseph of Arimathea asked Pilate for permission to claim His body and bury it in his own new tomb. Joseph had been a secret follower of Jesus in the past. But now he stepped from the shadows to declare His loyalty to Jesus. In this act of love and boldness, he was joined by Nicodemus, the Pharisee with whom Jesus had discussed the new birth at the beginning of His public ministry (see Matthew 27:57–60; John 19:39).

UP FROM THE GRAVE

Jesus' body was placed in Joseph's tomb sometime before sundown on Friday, when the Jewish Sabbath began. Joseph and Nicodemus had prepared Jesus' body quickly to avoid conflict with the Sabbath.

The Gospels record several important events in connection with Jesus' resurrection.

Women at the tomb. The same women who had watched Jesus die on the cross hurried to His tomb shortly after sunrise on Sunday morning. They wanted to finish the job of anointing His body with spices that Joseph and Nicodemus had started two days before (Mark 16:1–3).

These women were shocked to learn that the huge stone that sealed the opening of the tomb had been rolled away and that Jesus' body was missing. Inside they found two angels, who asked them, "Why do you look for the living among the dead? He is not here; he has risen!" (Luke 24:5–6 NIV). Then the angels told the women to go and tell the disciples that Jesus had been raised from the dead (Mark 16:6–7).

Peter and John at the tomb. When Peter and the "other disciple" heard the news from the women, they hurried off to the tomb (John 20:3–9). This "other disciple" was probably John, the author of the Gospel of John.

Peter entered the tomb ahead of John. He noticed that the burial cloth that had been wound around Jesus' head was not lying with the burial shroud but was "folded up in a separate place by itself" (verse 7 HCSB). This indicated that something supernatural had happened. Jesus' body had passed miraculously through this cloth, just as it later went through closed doors.

John came into the tomb right behind Peter. In his Gospel, John makes this interesting observation about his reaction to the empty tomb: "He saw, and believed" (John 20:8). Then John recorded this observation as a parenthetical statement: "They [Jesus' disciples] still did not understand the scripture which said that he must rise from death" (John 20:9 GNT).

On the road to Emmaus. A few hours after His resurrection, Jesus appeared to two men as they walked from Jerusalem to Emmaus, a distance of about seven miles. These men were not His disciples; they were part of the larger group of Jesus' followers.

As the three walked along the road together,

ON WITH THE TASK

No-Stress Bible Reading
Matthew 28:16–20; John 20:19–31

No-Stress Bible Guide
Pages 251–253
(from "On the Road to Emmaus")

Think About It:

- Why do you think Thomas doubted that Jesus had been raised from the dead?

- Why did Jesus single out Peter to test his loyalty and commitment?

- How does Jesus empower His church to continue His work in the world?

Jesus did not reveal who He was. But He showed them what the Old Testament scriptures taught about the suffering and glory of the Messiah (Luke 24:13–32).

Jesus breaks bread in Emmaus with two of His followers before disappearing.

When they reached Emmaus, the two travelers invited Jesus to stop and eat with them. As He offered thanks for the meal, they recognized that this talkative stranger was none other than Jesus, the very Messiah He had been telling them about.

Then Jesus disappeared, just as quickly as He had appeared on the Emmaus road. These two followers immediately hurried back to Jerusalem, where they told the disciples that they had seen the Lord. This was just one more proof that Jesus was alive.

Appearance to all the disciples. Finally, Jesus appeared to all His disciples when they were together behind locked doors, probably hiding from the religious leaders and Roman authorities who had put Jesus to death. He materialized suddenly among them, going right through the locked door; it presented no barrier to His resurrection body.

Jesus greeted His disciples with the customary Jewish hello, "Peace be unto you" (John 20:19; see 20:19–31). He went on to assure them that He was sending the Holy Spirit to strengthen them for the task of continuing His work in the world.

One of Jesus' disciples, Thomas, was not present on this occasion. When the other disciples told him they had seen Jesus, he declared, "Unless I see the nail marks in his hands and put my finger where the nails were. . .I will not believe" (verse 25 NIV).

A week later, Jesus appeared to His disciples again when Thomas was present. He invited Thomas to touch his wounds and stop doubting the reality of His resurrection. This convinced "Doubting Thomas" that Jesus was indeed alive. "Because you have seen me, you have believed," He told Thomas; "blessed are those who have not seen and yet have believed" (verse 29 NIV).

These words of Jesus show that believers in later years would base their faith on the testimony of those who had seen the Lord in the flesh—His apostles. Modern believers accept as truth their testimony about Jesus' life and ministry as recorded in the Gospels.

Encounter at the Sea of Galilee. According to the Gospel of John, the final appearance that Jesus made to several of His disciples was at Lake Galilee. Perhaps He chose this location because it was a familiar landmark in the region of Galilee, where He had spent some of His most productive years as a healer and teacher.

Several disciples of Jesus—Peter, Thomas, Nathanael, James, John, and two unnamed disciples—were fishing in the lake when Jesus greeted them from the shore. He enabled them to make a miraculous catch of fish, then called them to the shore, where He prepared a breakfast from some of the fish they had caught (John 21:1–17). This probably reminded them of the time when He multiplied a few pieces of fish and bread to feed a crowd of several thousand hungry people.

After they had satisfied their physical hunger, Jesus turned to Peter to deal with a spiritual matter. He asked the outspoken apostle if he loved Him, deliberately repeating the question twice. This same question asked three times was probably meant to remind Peter of the three times he had denied Jesus.

Peter replied that he did love Jesus, in spite of his three denials. Jesus then assured Peter that he had been forgiven and restored to usefulness as His disciple. He charged the apostle to continue to follow Him and to minister in His name.

Peter's courageous preaching in the early chapters of the book of Acts shows that he made the most of his second chance. He eventually developed into the strong witness and courageous church leader that Jesus knew he could be when He first called him as His disciple.

ON TO THE NEXT STEP

Jesus left no doubt about what His disciples were expected to do after His earthly ministry came to a close. He summed it up in a few words known as His great commission: "Go, therefore, and make disciples of all nations, baptizing them in the name of the Father and of the Son and of the Holy Spirit, teaching them to observe everything I have commanded you. And remember, I am with you always, to the end of the age" (Matthew 28:19-20 HCSB).

This command from Jesus is often referred to as the "marching orders" of the church. His followers were not to be a club of like-minded people idling away their time in trivial pursuits. He expected His church to be a living, moving, aggressive force that spread His message of God's love and grace throughout the entire world.

For Jesus' followers, obeying His orders involved stepping outside their familiar surroundings ("go"), witnessing to total strangers ("all nations"), bringing people into God's kingdom ("make disciples," "baptizing"), and nurturing them into effective followers of the Savior ("teaching them to observe everything I have commanded you" [HCSB]).

In essence, this command of Jesus is a brief summary of His continuing work in the world through the church. The account of how this work was carried out in the early years of the Christian movement appears in the next chapter.

The Ascension of Christ, attributed to Dosso Dossi (1490–1542)

Stained glass of the ascension
of Christ (the German Church,
Stockholm, Sweden)

CHAPTER 21
A Gospel for All the World

This key period of biblical history is recounted in the book of Acts—the only book of history in the New Testament. Acts picks up where the Gospels come to an end—with Jesus' ascension to the Father and His great commission to His followers to take the Gospel into all the world.

Acts records how Jesus' charge to His followers was accomplished. In about forty years (AD 28–68), Christianity spread from Jerusalem to Rome, capital city of the Roman Empire. From a movement that appealed mainly to Jews in an isolated part of the world, it exploded into a universal faith that appealed to people of all ethnic backgrounds.

Acts was written by Luke, a physician and early church leader, as a sequel to the Gospel of Luke. He addressed both books to a mysterious person known as Theophilus (Luke 1:3–4; Acts 1:1). Luke apparently accompanied the apostle Paul on several of his preaching tours. In several travel narratives in the book of Acts, Luke used the personal pronouns *we* and *us*, indicating he was with Paul when these events took place (Acts 16:9–10; 20:5–16; 21:1–18; 27:1–28:16).

The two dominant personalities of the book of Acts are Peter and Paul. Peter, a disciple of Jesus, took the lead in proclaiming the Gospel to people of Jewish background in and around Jerusalem. But Paul moved front and center after his dramatic conversion to Christianity on the road to Damascus. He became the great "apostle to the Gentiles" who founded numerous churches in non-Jewish territory throughout the Roman Empire.

This historical narrative of the expansion of the Gospel into all the world falls naturally into six major sections: (1) preparation for witness, (2) the Gospel in Jerusalem, (3) the Gospel in Judea and Samaria, (4) the Gospel among the Gentiles, (5) Paul's troubles in Jerusalem and Caesarea, and (6) Paul's trip to Rome.

PREPARATION FOR WITNESS (1:1–2:47)

Luke set the stage for the work of the church in the book of Acts by reviewing Jesus' appearance to His disciples after His resurrection. According to Luke, Jesus appeared to them over a period of forty days (see Acts 1:3). During this extended time, He gave His disciples final instructions about the kingdom of God. His lingering presence also strengthened the disciples to continue His work by carrying out His Great Commission: "You will be My witnesses in Jerusalem, in all Judea and Samaria, and to the ends of the earth" (1:8 HCSB).

Finally, Jesus ascended to God the Father in heaven—but not before reminding the disciples of His promise to send the Holy Spirit to empower them for their witnessing task. The apostle Peter stepped forward as the leader of a small body of believers in Jerusalem. He led the group to select a man named Matthias to replace Judas as one of the Twelve (see 1:15–26).

While celebrating the festival of Pentecost in Jerusalem, Jesus' twelve apostles were filled with the Holy Spirit. They uttered words in languages that were different from the ones they normally spoke. This was not gibberish or ecstatic utterances but words that came from actual languages spoken in other parts of the world. These languages were recognized by

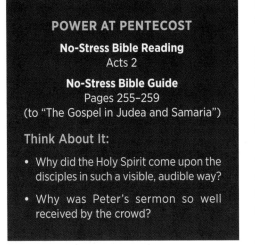

POWER AT PENTECOST

No-Stress Bible Reading
Acts 2

No-Stress Bible Guide
Pages 255–259
(to "The Gospel in Judea and Samaria")

Think About It:

• Why did the Holy Spirit come upon the disciples in such a visible, audible way?

• Why was Peter's sermon so well received by the crowd?

Jews from beyond Israel who had traveled to Jerusalem for the annual Pentecost celebration. Many of them were amazed at this spectacular display (2:1–15).

Peter took advantage of this opportunity to preach the first Gospel sermon recorded in the book of Acts. He assured the crowd that this miracle of speaking in different languages was a fulfillment of the prophecy of Joel. God had promised long ago that He would pour out His Spirit on all people (Joel 2:28–32).

Then Peter turned the people's attention to Jesus, who offered salvation to hopeless sinners. Through these powerful words and the movement of the Holy Spirit, three thousand people repented of their sins, placed their faith in Jesus, and were baptized. This was the first of many powerful sermons recorded in the book of Acts that the Holy Spirit used to bring people to faith in Jesus Christ.

THE GOSPEL IN JERUSALEM (3:1–8:3)

In His Great Commission, Jesus declared that His followers would first witness about Him in Jerusalem. This stage of the church's growth occurred mostly through the ministry of the apostles Peter and John and a deacon named Stephen.

FALLOUT FROM A MIRACLE (3:1–4:31)

One day Peter and John were going into the temple in Jerusalem when they noticed a crippled beggar. He asked them for money, but Peter gave him something better—healing in the name of Jesus. This event drew a curious crowd, and Peter told them about Jesus Christ, who had been rejected and crucified by the Jewish religious authorities.

Members of the Sanhedrin, the Jewish high court, questioned the two apostles about this miracle and the claims they were making about Jesus. But Peter and John stood their ground, insisting that He was the Messiah and the only hope of salvation.

The Sanhedrin finally decided to let these apostles go. The religious authorities warned them to stop speaking about this Jesus, whom they considered a fraud and a troublemaker. To their threats, Peter and John replied, "We cannot keep from speaking about what we have seen and heard" (4:20 NRSV).

After their release by the Sanhedrin, Peter and John met with other believers. In a spirit of unity, they prayed for strength and boldness to continue to witness about Jesus. God honored their prayers by strengthening them again with the Holy Spirit.

INTEGRITY VERSUS DISHONESTY (4:32–5:11)

The fellowship among the early believers in Jerusalem was so strong that they had a keen sense of responsibility for one another. This led them to share everything they had with their brothers and sisters in Christ. The entire Christian community pooled their resources to care for the needy believers in the church. They did this voluntarily, not because they were forced to do so.

The best example of this generous spirit was a believer named Barnabas, also known as Joseph. He sold some land he owned and brought the proceeds to the apostles to place in the common treasury (4:36–37).

But this spirit of generosity was dramatically reversed by a man named Ananias. Like Barnabas, he sold some property that he owned. But he kept some of the proceeds for himself and pretended he had contributed the entire amount for the common good. His wife, Sapphira, also lied about the cover-up. Both paid the ultimate price for their deception when they were struck dead (5:1–11).

This incident bothers many interpreters. They wonder how such a severe punishment could be exacted for a couple of lies. One possible explanation is that the stakes were high for the church during these years when it was gaining a foothold in the pagan world. Was Christianity a fad that would disappear after a few years, or was it a stable, life-changing faith that made a difference in the way people lived?

The deaths of Ananias and Sapphira showed the community that absolute integrity was demanded of all who claimed to be followers of Jesus Christ. The message of this event was not lost on the church or the outside world: "Great fear seized the whole church and all who heard about these events" (5:11 NIV).

"WORTHY OF SUFFERING" (5:12–42)

The church continued to multiply in Jerusalem as people listened to the apostles' teaching and observed their healing miracles. This rapid growth brought on a new round of persecution by the Jewish Sanhedrin. They put the apostles in prison, only to see them appear near the temple after being released by an angel.

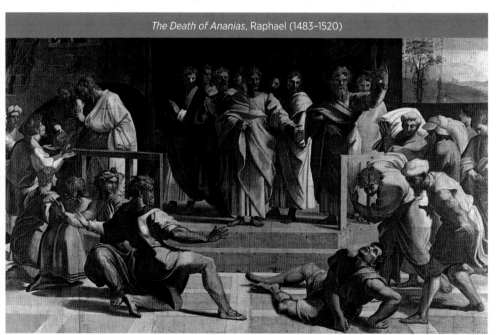
The Death of Ananias, Raphael (1483–1520)

This turn of events sent the members of the Sanhedrin into a rage. They wanted to execute the apostles, but a Pharisee named Gamaliel came to their defense. His reasoning was that their work would come to nothing if they were not speaking for God. And if they were the Lord's agents, nothing the Sanhedrin did could stamp out the message they were preaching. If this Pharisee had known how God would bless the work of these humble servants, he might have been adamantly opposed to what they were doing.

Finally, the Sanhedrin set the apostles free after giving them a beating and warning them not to speak in the name of Jesus anymore. But this only made them more determined to prove themselves "worthy of suffering" (5:41 NIV) for the cause of Christ.

SEVEN SERVANTS CHOSEN (6:1–7)

If not for these seven verses in Acts, one might think that the early church in Jerusalem was a portrait of harmony and unity. But some believers of Greek-speaking background showed otherwise when they came to the apostles with a complaint. It seemed to them that the widows of Grecian or Hellenistic background—those who spoke Greek as their main language—were not receiving their fair share of the food that was being distributed among the needy widows in the fellowship.

ST. STEPHEN'S GATE

One of the eight gates into the Old City of Jerusalem is named "St. Stephen's Gate," to commemorate Stephen's martyrdom for the cause of Christ. According to an ancient tradition, this gate is near the site where Stephen was dragged out of the city and stoned to death.

The apostles acted immediately to solve the problem. They led the church to appoint seven men to supervise the food distribution system to make sure everyone was treated fairly. While these seven servants are not referred to as deacons, they are probably the model for the formal office of deacon that developed in the church in later years.

Only two of these seven servants are mentioned again in the book of Acts. Stephen became the first martyr of the church. Philip witnessed boldly for Christ in the region of Samaria and the coastal section of Palestine.

A MARTYR NAMED STEPHEN (6:8–8:3)

Stephen was not content just to serve on the benevolence committee of the Jerusalem church. He began to perform signs and wonders and to debate with Jewish zealots about the revolutionary changes that Jesus had brought to Judaism. This landed him before the Sanhedrin on the charge that he was committing blasphemy against the law of Moses.

In a long speech—the longest in the book of Acts—Stephen presented his defense against these charges. He reviewed the history of the Jewish people, accusing them of rejecting such gifted leaders as Joseph and Moses. Then he claimed that the religious leaders of the nation had done the same thing with Jesus. He had been sent as a spiritual deliverer for God's people, but they rejected Him and put Him to death. This showed that the Jews were actually the ones who were guilty of blasphemy against God and His will for His people.

Enraged by Stephen's claims, the members of the Sanhedrin stoned him to death. Among the angry crowd was a proud Pharisee named Saul. He did not participate in this mob action against Stephen, but it was obvious that he was consenting to Stephen's death (8:1). (See sidebar, St. Stephen's Gate.")

Stephen's death incited fierce persecution from the Jewish religious leaders against the church in Jerusalem. Many Christians fled the city into the outlying areas of Judea and as far away as the region of Samaria. Saul was one of the ringleaders in these efforts to stamp out the church.

THE GOSPEL IN JUDEA AND SAMARIA (8:4–12:25)

When persecuted believers fled Jerusalem, they carried their faith with them and shared it with others wherever they went. This stage of the church's growth was the next point in Jesus' Great Commission: "You will be My witnesses in. . .all Judea and Samaria" (Acts 1:8 HCSB).

WITNESS IN SAMARIA (8:4–25)

Philip, one of the seven servants selected to distribute food to the needy in Jerusalem, was the first person to proclaim the Gospel in the region of Samaria. This territory was populated by half-breed Jews who had intermarried with foreigners. Full-blooded Jews despised the Samaritans because they had corrupted their bloodline.

Philip harbored no prejudice against the Samaritans, and they responded positively to his preaching. When the church in Jerusalem heard about this, they sent the apostles Peter

Baptism of the Ethiopian Eunuch by Philip, artist unknown (Cathedral of Our Lady, Antwerp, Belgium)

and John to help Philip in his Samaritan ministry. They taught these new believers about the Holy Spirit. They also helped a magician named Simon to understand that God's grace could not be bought but was free to all who accepted Jesus as their Savior and repented of their sins. (See sidebar, "Simon and Simony.")

WITNESS ON THE OPEN ROAD (8:26–40)

Leaving Samaria, Philip obeyed an angel's orders to head down a road that led through the desert toward the Mediterranean Sea. Here on the open road he met an Ethiopian eunuch, a government official in charge of the treasury of the queen of Ethiopia.

This man was probably a God-fearer, a non-Jew who was attracted to the moral principles and monotheism (worship of one God) of the Jewish religion. He was searching for spiritual insight, for he was reading from the book of Isaiah as he was riding along in his chariot.

Philip revealed to this seeker of truth that Isaiah's prophecy had been fulfilled in Jesus Christ. He then led him to Christ and baptized him in a pool of water near the road. As soon as this happened, Philip was snatched away by the Holy Spirit. He continued his ministry in the coastal towns along the Mediterranean Sea.

The Ethiopian went on his way, rejoicing over his new birth and his entry into the kingdom of God. The Gospel was beginning to break down all barriers that the Jews had placed between themselves and the rest of the world. Even a seeker of truth from as far away as Ethiopia had experienced the saving grace of the Lord Jesus Christ.

MIRACLE ON THE DAMASCUS ROAD (9:1–31)

Meanwhile, Saul's silent disapproval of Stephen and the faith he represented soon grew into outright hatred. He asked the Sanhedrin for authority to travel to the city of Damascus and arrest Christians who had fled to that city. Damascus was about 140 miles north of Jerusalem. This journey by foot took about a week.

But God had a surprise in store for this zealous Pharisee. As he approached Damascus, he was struck blind by a bright light from heaven. Jesus spoke to him in an audible voice, assuring him that He had a plan for Saul's life that was radically different from what he was doing. This purpose was revealed to him a few days later after he reached Damascus. Saul was God's "chosen vessel" to preach the Gospel to the Gentile world (verse 15).

This abrupt about-face from persecutor of the church to preacher of the Gospel was so dramatic that other conversions of this type are often referred to as "Damascus Road" experiences. Saul never forgot this life-changing experience with the Lord. He told others about it on two different occasions while bearing his witness for the Lord (Acts 22:1–21; 26:2–23).

After Saul's sight was restored in Damascus, he witnessed for Christ in one of the local Jewish synagogues. Now the persecution he had practiced against the church was turned against him by a group of Jewish zealots. They were determined to kill him. But Saul's new brothers in Christ helped him escape by letting him down in a basket over the city wall.

Soon after leaving Damascus, Saul traveled back to Jerusalem. Here he tried to join the apostles in the Jerusalem church. At first they didn't trust him because of his reputation as an opponent of the Christian movement. Finally, Barnabas overcame their resistance by telling them about Saul's conversion and assuring them of his sincerity.

Saul worked with the apostles in Jerusalem for a while until his life was threatened by radical Jews. These Jews probably considered him a traitor who had turned his back on the Jewish

Conversion on the Way to Damascus,
Caravaggio (1571–1610)

A ROADSIDE CONVERSION

No-Stress Bible Reading
Acts 9:1–30

No-Stress Bible Guide
Pages 259–262
(from "The Gospel in Judea and Samaria" to "Twin Coastal Miracles")

Think About It:

- Why do you think Paul was struck blind for three days?

- Why was Ananias of Damascus hesitant about serving as the Lord's messenger to Paul?

religious system he had once defended. For Saul's own safety, his fellow believers sent him off to Tarsus, his hometown.

TWIN COASTAL MIRACLES (9:32–43)

Soon after Saul left Jerusalem, the apostle Peter visited believers along the coast of the Mediterranean Sea. At a coastal town known as Lydda, he healed a crippled man. Just a few miles away, at Joppa, he brought a godly woman named Dorcas back from the dead. News of this miracle spread throughout the area. Many people believed in Jesus, the agent of healing and wholeness whom Peter represented.

PETER'S REVOLUTIONARY VISION (10:1–11:18)

While ministering along the Mediterranean coast,

Peter lodged at the house of Simon the tanner in Joppa. About thirty miles up the coast, God was setting up a scenario that would change Peter's cherished Jewish beliefs and revolutionize the outreach of the church.

It all started at Caesarea, a coastal city north of Joppa. Cornelius, a Roman centurion, and thus a Gentile, was praying and worshipping God at Caesarea when he had a vision. In this vision God instructed Cornelius to send for the apostle Peter, who would tell him what he should do. Cornelius obeyed and sent three men to Joppa to find Peter at Simon's house.

As Cornelius's servants and one soldier approached the city of Joppa, Peter was praying in the cool outdoor space on top of Simon's house. God chose this very moment to give Peter a vision. The apostle saw a sheet filled with unclean animals that were forbidden as food for the Jews. But God told Peter to kill and eat these animals. When he protested, God commanded, "Do not call anything impure that God has made clean" (10:15 NIV).

Just then, the three servants of Cornelius arrived at Peter's house. After he learned that they wanted him to go to Caesarea to talk with Cornelius, the apostle invited them in to spend the night. The next day he accompanied them to Caesarea and went into Cornelius's house—something the Jewish people would not normally do because they considered such dwellings unclean.

Thanks to Peter's revolutionary vision, he had gotten the message that Gentiles were not unclean outcasts but people made in God's image who were included in the divine plan of salvation. He told Cornelius, "God has shown me that I must not call any person common or unclean" (10:28 HCSB). Then Peter put his words into action by baptizing the Roman centurion and several members of his household upon their profession of faith in Jesus.

The church at Jerusalem heard that these Gentiles at Caesarea had become believers and received the Holy Spirit. They called on Peter to explain his actions. He convinced them that these conversions were genuine and that nothing prevented Gentiles from receiving God's gift of salvation. So the Jerusalem church concluded, "God has given even to the Gentiles the repentance that leads to life" (11:18 NRSV).

From this point on in the book of Acts, the church was no longer restricted to people of Jewish background. It was open to all people, no matter what their race or national origin. Some Jewish fringe groups continued to insist that believers had to submit to certain ceremonial requirements such as circumcision. But the general trend of the church was away from Jewish ritualism. It realized that God's love was wide enough to include everyone.

Once the Christian movement began to act on these principles, nothing could stop its explosive growth.

AN AWESOME WORK AT ANTIOCH (11:19–29)

The city of Antioch in Syria was the first place where large numbers of Gentiles began to profess faith in Christ. Believers from Jerusalem fled to this city following the persecution that broke out when Stephen was executed. From this small beginning, the Antioch church soon began to reach many Gentiles.

When the church at Jerusalem heard about these happenings at Antioch, they sent Barnabas to investigate. He soon concluded that God was doing an awesome work in this Gentile city. So he traveled to Tarsus and enlisted Saul to help evangelize and teach the new converts in this growing church.

Saul had fled Jerusalem several years

A STARTLING VISION AND A GROWING CHURCH

No-Stress Bible Reading
Acts 10; 11:19–26

No-Stress Bible Guide
Pages 262–264
(from "Twin Coastal Miracles" to "The Gospel Among the Gentiles")

Think About It:

- Do you think Peter accepted Gentiles instantly, or was his change a series of gradual steps?

- Why do you think the believers at Jerusalem sent Barnabas to check on the church at Antioch?

before when radical Jews threatened to kill him. Barnabas realized that Saul's background made him an ideal leader for the Antioch congregation. A former Pharisee, he could stand his ground against the Jews who opposed the Christian movement. Saul also supported the concept of an unlimited Gospel and the church's witness to the Gentile world.

PETER AND HEROD AGRIPPA I (12:1–25)

The stage was now set for the aggressive preaching of the Gospel to the Gentiles. But first, the apostle Peter back in Jerusalem had to contend with persecution by the Roman overlord of Judea, Herod Agrippa I. To gain the favor of the Jews, Agrippa had the apostle James put to death, then had Peter thrown into prison.

Through God's miraculous intervention, Peter was released from prison by an angel. Herod paid the ultimate price for his pride and resistance to God. An angel struck him down with a serious illness from which he never recovered.

THE GOSPEL AMONG THE GENTILES (13:1–21:16)

Up to this point in the book of Acts, the church at Jerusalem had taken the lead in the Christian movement. The apostle Peter had stepped forward as the church's main leader. But all this changed, beginning with the thirteenth chapter of Acts and continuing throughout the rest of the book. From now on, the church at Antioch took center stage, and Saul emerged as the church's major leader in his role as the Lord's "apostle to the Gentiles."

This stage of the church's ministry is a

Liberation of St. Peter, Bartolomé Esteban Murillo (1617–1682)

fulfillment of Jesus' challenge to His followers to take the good news of the Gospel "to the ends of the earth" (1:8 NIV).

PAUL'S FIRST MISSIONARY JOURNEY (13:1–14:28)

The Holy Spirit selected Saul and Barnabas, leaders in the Antioch church, for missionary work. The congregation obeyed the Spirit's leading. After praying and fasting, they commissioned the two missionaries to take the Gospel to places where it had not been preached. (See map, "Paul's First Missionary Journey," p. 315.)

Cyprus (13:4–12). Saul and Barnabas stopped first at Cyprus, perhaps because Barnabas was a native of this island in the Mediterranean Sea (4:36). They witnessed to the governor of the region, and he became a believer. Saul rebuked a magician named Bar-Jesus when he tried to hinder their work. From this point on in the narrative, Saul (his Hebrew name) is referred to as Paul (his Greek name). This subtle change probably reflects his identification with the non-Jewish audience to which he was speaking.

Perga (13:13). Leaving Cyprus, Paul and Barnabas stopped at the city of Perga in the province of Pamphylia. A young man named John Mark, who had been accompanying them on the trip, decided to turn back and return to his home in Jerusalem.

Antioch of Pisidia (13:14–50). Paul preached about Jesus in the Jewish synagogue in this city. Unbelieving Jews were skeptical of his Gospel message, but it was well received by Gentiles. On the next Sabbath, a crowd gathered to hear Paul speak again. This time the Jews in the crowd condemned Paul, accused him of blasphemy, and forced the two missionaries to leave town. Paul declared that from then on he would witness mostly to the Gentiles because they were more receptive to the Gospel.

Saint Paul, Bartolomeo Montagna (1450–1523)

Iconium (13:51–14:5). Many Gentiles and Jews of Greek-speaking background turned to the Lord in this city. But Paul and Barnabas were eventually forced to leave Iconium because of strong opposition from the radical Jews.

Lystra (14:6–20). When Paul healed a lame man in Lystra, the superstitious citizens of the town thought he and Barnabas were gods. They were on the verge of bowing down to worship the two missionaries with sacrifices when Paul urged them to "turn from these vanities unto the living God, which made heaven, and earth" (verse 15). Their reception by the unbelieving Jews was totally opposite. They tried to stone Paul, but he was miraculously delivered by the Lord.

After a brief stop at Derbe, about sixty miles from Lystra, Paul and Barnabas retraced their steps, visiting the churches they had established. During these follow-up visits, they appointed elders, or pastors, to lead these new congregations. They had grown to the point where they needed official leadership. This church-planting trip by Paul and Barnabas was more than just a short excursion; it probably lasted about two or three years.

When these two missionaries got back to Antioch, they reported on the results of their work to the entire church. The believers rejoiced at the news that God had "opened the door of faith unto the Gentiles" (14:27).

A CRUCIAL MEETING AT JERUSALEM (15:1-29)

Not all believers in and around Jerusalem were as jubilant as the Christians at Antioch about the reception of uncircumcised Gentiles into the church. A minority group continued to insist that Gentiles had to convert to Judaism and be circumcised—in accordance with the law of Moses—before they could be saved. To deal with this controversial issue, leaders of both points of view met in Jerusalem.

The apostle Peter, followed by Paul and Barnabas, spoke against circumcision as a requirement for Gentile believers. James, the half brother of Jesus and a leader in the Jerusalem church, issued the church's decision on the matter—all persons, Jews and Gentiles alike, are saved through faith alone. Paul and Barnabas delivered this good news to the church at Antioch.

PAUL'S SECOND MISSIONARY JOURNEY (15:36-18:23)

Paul and Barnabas prepared to set out on another mission trip. But they disagreed on whether to take John Mark along. He had left them and returned home during their first journey. Finally,

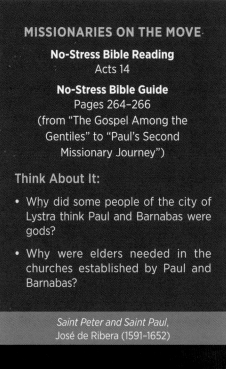

MISSIONARIES ON THE MOVE

No-Stress Bible Reading
Acts 14

No-Stress Bible Guide
Pages 264–266
(from "The Gospel Among the Gentiles" to "Paul's Second Missionary Journey")

Think About It:

- Why did some people of the city of Lystra think Paul and Barnabas were gods?

- Why were elders needed in the churches established by Paul and Barnabas?

Saint Peter and Saint Paul,
José de Ribera (1591–1652)

the two missionaries agreed to go their separate ways. Barnabas took Mark and sailed for the island of Cyprus. Paul traveled north through the provinces of Syria and Cilicia, accompanied by Silas, a believer in the church at Antioch. (See map, "Paul's Second Missionary Journey," p. 316.)

Derbe and Lystra (16:1–3). Paul and Silas encouraged believers in these two cities—places he had visited during his first missionary tour. At Lystra Paul met a young man named Timothy, whom he enlisted as a second partner on this mission trip. In later years Paul wrote two of his pastoral epistles—1 and 2 Timothy—to this young man.

Vision at Troas (16:6–10). After traveling through several provinces, Paul and Silas were persuaded by the Holy Spirit not to enter the regions of Asia and Bithynia. These would have been the next places on the route they were traveling. Instead, they were persuaded through a vision at the city of Troas to enter the province of Macedonia. In this vision a man appealed to Paul, "Cross over to Macedonia and help us!" (verse 9 HCSB).

Philippi (16:11–40). In this city in the province of Macedonia, Paul and Silas met a businesswoman named Lydia. She responded to Paul's Gospel message, and she and her entire household became believers. Then Paul and Silas met and healed a demented slave girl. This act of compassion landed them in jail on charges from her owner. He had been profiting from her disability by selling her services as a fortune-teller.

Locked up in the jail at Philippi, Paul and Silas bore witness for Christ by praying and singing hymns. Even the hardened criminals in the prison listened to these strange believers who were rejoicing in spite of their misfortune. Then God shook the prison with an earthquake, and the two missionaries were miraculously released from their cells. This chaotic situation led to the conversion of the keeper of the prison and the members of his family.

Thessalonica (17:1–9). Unbelieving Jews created an uproar in this city after Paul preached in the local Jewish synagogue. But a few Jews, along with many Gentiles, professed faith in Christ. Some radical Jews were so upset with Paul's preaching that they arrested the owner of the house where Paul and Silas were lodging.

Berea (17:10–14). Paul found an open and eager audience in the city of Berea. The citizens listened eagerly to his message and even compared his words with the Old Testament scriptures "to see if what Paul said was true" (verse 11 NIV). But enraged Jews who had followed Paul, Silas, and Timothy from Thessalonica raised a mob to protest their teachings. Paul left Silas and Timothy to continue evangelistic work in Berea while he moved on to Athens, the cultured city of ancient Greece.

Athens (17:15–34). Paul waited for Silas and Timothy to join him in Athens. He took advantage of this brief visit to preach to the philosophers and intellectuals of this fabled city where Plato and Aristotle had taught several centuries before. He noticed the many temples and shrines devoted to worship of the ancient Greek gods, particularly one altar erected to "the unknown god" (verse 23). He declared that the god who was unknown to them was actually the supreme God of the universe who had sent His Son to call all people to repentance.

Most of these philosophers were skeptical of Paul's message, especially the part about the resurrection of Jesus. But a few were receptive and turned to the Lord.

Corinth (18:1–18). Leaving Athens, Paul traveled to Corinth, where he joined forces with a Christian couple, Priscilla and Aquila. Here they supported themselves for eighteen months while witnessing for Christ and growing a body of believers. Silas and Timothy joined them here, and the church soon grew into an outpost of light in a city noted for its godless way of life.

Ephesus (18:18–22). Leaving Silas and Timothy in charge at Corinth, Paul traveled to the city of Ephesus. Here he ministered for just a short time, but he promised the Ephesian believers that he would return later. Then he returned to Antioch, bringing his second missionary tour to a close.

PAUL'S THIRD MISSIONARY JOURNEY (18:23–21:16)

Paul may have left the church at Antioch on his third missionary journey without any missionary associates. At least, none are mentioned in the biblical record. Perhaps he had left all his former partners in charge of the young churches that now existed throughout the Roman Empire. Besides that, he also planned to visit several places where he had ministered before, including Ephesus. Perhaps traveling partners were not needed as much on these repeat visits.

Galatia and Phrygia (18:23). Paul visited believers in several churches throughout these two provinces. No details are recorded about his visits to any of these churches. But we do know from his later letter to the Galatian churches that he was disappointed in their understanding of the essentials of the Gospel. He reminded them in this letter to resist the teachings of the Judaizers. They were trying to convince the believers of Galatia that salvation for Gentiles was not possible unless they submitted to circumcision and observed Jewish holy days.

Ephesus (19:1–41). Paul had already worked with the believers in this city for a short time.

The Preaching of St Paul at Ephesus, Eustache Le Sueur (1616–1655)

Now he kept his promise that he would return for an extended ministry. He labored at Ephesus for two to three years—longer than he stayed at any other place during his entire ministry. In addition to preaching and teaching here, he performed miraculous healings among the people of the city. Black magic and superstition also yielded to the power of the word of God.

Ephesus, with a population of about three hundred thousand people, was a major city of the Roman Empire. It was a strategic site for the planting of the Gospel. Once a church was established here, it could serve as a witness to the numerous merchants who passed through the city. From Ephesus, the Gospel could spread into the cities and towns in the outlying areas.

The Gospel soon exerted its power in an unexpected way. A riot incited by Ephesian artisans swept through the city. These skilled craftsmen were angry because the silver replicas of a pagan temple that they made for sale to pagan worshippers were losing their appeal.

OFF TO JERUSALEM (20:1–21:16)

After the riot at Ephesus, Paul spent several months checking on the churches he had established roughly between Corinth and Philippi. During this time he decided to conclude his third missionary tour by visiting the church at Jerusalem. He apparently wanted to take an offering he had collected from the Gentile churches to the city where the church had started about three decades before. The believers of Jewish background in Jerusalem were suffering from a severe famine.

On the way to Jerusalem by ship, Paul stopped at several coastal cities. At Troas he brought a young believer named Eutychus back to life after he fell from an upper-story window (20:7–12). At Miletus, south and slightly west of Ephesus, he met with the elders of the Ephesian church to say goodbye. These were close friends

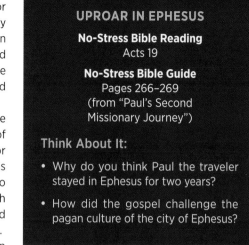

UPROAR IN EPHESUS

No-Stress Bible Reading
Acts 19

No-Stress Bible Guide
Pages 266–269
(from "Paul's Second Missionary Journey")

Think About It:

- Why do you think Paul the traveler stayed in Ephesus for two years?

- How did the gospel challenge the pagan culture of the city of Ephesus?

as well as ministry partners whom he had worked with for two to three years.

Paul realized that Jewish zealots were out to get him and that they were particularly strong and numerous in Jerusalem. It was possible, he told these leaders, that he would never make it back to Ephesus. At these sad words, they all wept as they embraced and kissed him (20:32–38).

After sailing across the Mediterranean Sea, Paul's ship docked at the coastal city of Tyre, about one hundred miles north of Jerusalem. Here he met and encouraged other believers, then traveled south to the city of Caesarea, where he visited in the home of Philip the evangelist. This is the same Philip who had preached to the Samaritans and witnessed to the Ethiopian eunuch about thirty years before.

At Caesarea Paul was warned by a prophet named Agabus that he would be arrested by the radical Jews if he went on to Jerusalem (21:10–14). But Paul disregarded the warning, continued his journey, and finally arrived in the city. His arrival in Jerusalem marks the end of his third missionary journey.

PAUL'S TROUBLES IN JERUSALEM AND CAESAREA (21:17–26:32)

As Paul had been warned, his arrival in Jerusalem did not go smoothly. First he was mobbed by a crowd of Jewish zealots, then imprisoned by the Roman authorities. But even in these less-than-ideal circumstances, he managed to witness to others about the Gospel of Jesus Christ.

TURMOIL IN THE TEMPLE (21:17–22:22)

The believers in Jerusalem rejoiced over the acceptance of the Gospel by the Gentiles under Paul's ministry. But they warned him about the extreme hostility his work had aroused. Many zealous Jews thought he had been encouraging their race to turn away from the law of Moses.

This, of course, was not true. The apostle had taught only that a Gentile did not have to convert to Judaism in order to become a Christian. He had never tried to turn the Jewish people away from following their cherished customs and traditions. To show that he harbored no hostility toward his own people, he agreed to serve as sponsor for several Jewish men who were undergoing purification rituals in the temple.

While in the temple, Paul was grabbed by an angry Jewish mob. They jumped to the conclusion that he had taken a Gentile into an area of the temple reserved only for Jews—and thus polluted the holy sanctuary. Paul might have been beaten to death, if not for a quick-acting detachment of Roman soldiers who rescued him from the crowd (21:30–36).

The apostle asked permission to address the people. He told them that he was a zealous Jew just like them until he was converted in a dramatic encounter with Jesus Christ. The crowd listened quietly to this testimony until he reached the point where he was commissioned to preach the Gospel to the Gentiles. Then they renewed their cry that he deserved to die for his blasphemous actions. "Away with him!" they shouted. "Kill him! He's not fit to live!" (22:22 GNT).

"YOU MUST ALSO TESTIFY IN ROME" (22:23–23:35)

To protect Paul from the mob, the soldiers placed him in one of their own prisons. Here they learned that he was a Roman citizen. This guaranteed that he would be treated with respect and fairness while in Roman custody. The Roman commander in charge of Paul wanted to find out exactly what offense he had committed against the Jewish law. So he took the apostle to face the Sanhedrin, the Jewish high court.

Paul knew how to deal with this group, since he had once been a zealous Pharisee. His declaration that Jesus was raised from the dead caused dissension among the Pharisees and Sadducees on the court. They were unable to agree on what to do in his case. Returned to the Roman prison, Paul had a vision of the risen Lord that assured him his work was not over. "Have courage!" the Lord told the apostle. "For as you have testified about Me in Jerusalem, so you must also testify in Rome" (23:11 HCSB).

But before this could happen, Paul had to suffer other hardships. News of a plot against his life by Jewish zealots motivated the Roman commander at Jerusalem to send the apostle to Caesarea. This coastal city was the seat of the Roman provincial authorities who ruled over Judea. Here Paul languished in prison for two years.

PAUL BEFORE FELIX AND FESTUS (24:1–25:12)

Felix, the Roman governor at Caesarea, allowed the Jewish authorities in Jerusalem to present their case against Paul. But he delayed rendering a judgment in his case, hoping to receive a bribe to set him free. Festus eventually succeeded Felix as governor. Festus asked Paul if he was willing to have his case heard before the Sanhedrin in Jerusalem. The apostle realized he could never receive a fair trial before the Jewish authorities. So he appealed his case to a higher court in Rome—the right of every Roman citizen.

PAUL BEFORE FESTUS AND AGRIPPA (25:13–26:32)

While Paul was waiting to go to court in Rome, Festus discussed his case with Herod Agrippa II, another Roman ruler over the Jewish territories. Agrippa asked for Paul to appear before him so he could hear his story firsthand. The apostle made a passionate speech in his defense before these two Roman officials. He recounted his conversion experience and told how he was called by the Lord to serve as a messenger to the Gentiles.

Paul challenged Agrippa to consider the truth of his message, implying that even an agent of the Roman government was not excluded from God's love and grace. These remarks impressed Agrippa, but he failed to see that the Gospel had any claim on him. He asked Paul, "Do you think that in such a short time you can persuade me to be a Christian?" (26:28 NIV).

Paul's response to this question reveals his great missionary heart that had made him such an effective witness for Christ for more than thirty years. "Short time or long," he told Agrippa, "I pray to God that not only you but all who are listening to me today may become what I am, except for these chains" (26:29 NIV).

Both Festus and Agrippa agreed that Paul was innocent of the charges against him. But since he had appealed his case to Caesar, to Rome he must go.

PAUL THE PRISONER

No-Stress Bible Reading
Acts 21:26–36; 26

No-Stress Bible Guide
Pages 270–271
(to "Paul's Trip to Rome")

Think About It:

- Why did the radical Jews in Jerusalem want to kill Paul?

- Why do you think Paul told Agrippa about his conversion experience?

- How would you rate Paul's testimony for Christ as he stood before this pagan king?

An ancient Roman aqueduct, one of the great building projects that turned Caesarea into an important port city on the Mediterranean Sea in Israel

PAUL'S TRIP TO ROME (27:1–28:31)

The last two chapters of Acts record Paul's final journey on behalf of the Gospel. The details that Luke, the author of Acts, recorded about this trip make the narrative one of the most interesting in the New Testament. Luke must have accompanied the apostle, since the pronouns *we* and *us* appear throughout the account.

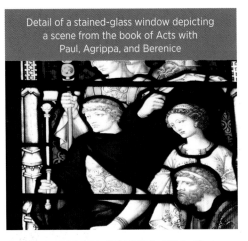

Detail of a stained-glass window depicting a scene from the book of Acts with Paul, Agrippa, and Berenice

FROM CAESAREA TO MYRA (27:1-5)

Under guard by a Roman centurion, Paul set sail from Caesarea for the long voyage to Rome—a distance of about fifteen hundred miles. The ship made a brief stop at Sidon, where the kind centurion allowed the apostle to visit with some of his fellow believers. Next they sailed around the island of Cyprus and veered due west toward the next stop—the city of Myra, now a part of modern Turkey. (See map, "Paul's Voyage to Rome," p. 317.)

FROM MYRA TO DISASTER AT MALTA (27:6-28:10)

At Myra Paul was transferred to a grain ship that was headed to the city of Rome. By this time it was late in the shipping season, and the weather was getting bad. The captain of the ship planned to land at a port known as Phoenix on the island of Crete to wait out the approaching winter storms.

But the heavily loaded vessel never reached Crete. Struck by a severe storm, it drifted off course as it was buffeted by the violent sea. The storm continued for many days. The dire situation of the ship, its crew, and the passengers on board comes through in this observation from Luke, the author of Acts, who was on the ship: "Neither sun nor stars appeared for many days and. . .we finally gave up all hope of being saved" (27:20 NIV).

The one person on board who remained calm was the apostle Paul. During the night an angel appeared to him, assuring Paul that he and all the people on the ship would not be killed. But the ship would run aground on an island (27:21-26). About two weeks later, this prediction was fulfilled when the ship broke apart off the island of Malta and everyone on board managed to make it safely to land.

Paul and the other passengers lived on Malta for three months. He spent this time witnessing and teaching, even healing the father of the island's chief official. This opened the door for a fruitful ministry among the rest of the population.

FROM MALTA TO ROME (28:11-31)

Finally, Paul and the other passengers boarded another ship headed to Rome, making several stops along the way. Once in the city, the apostle took the initiative to meet with a group of Jews. He tried to show them that Jesus was the Messiah, God's messenger who had brought the good news of God's grace to all humankind. But their response was just what he had come to expect during his long ministry of proclaiming the Gospel: "Some were persuaded by what he said, but others did not believe" (28:24 HCSB).

For two years Paul waited for his case to be heard by court officials while he remained under house arrest in Rome. During this time he wrote letters to several churches he had founded, including the congregation in Philippi. In his Philippian letter, he claimed that his imprisonment had actually resulted in the furtherance of the Gospel. He was able to witness to the soldiers who guarded him and the court officials who interviewed him. This news encouraged the believers in Rome to become bolder in bearing their Christian witness to others (Philippians 1:12-14).

So Acts comes to a conclusion by showing that the Gospel is the "power of God to salvation for everyone who believes" (Romans 1:16 NKJV). This powerful message was first proclaimed about forty years before by a small group of believers in Jerusalem. Now it was being preached in the Roman Empire's capital city.

No longer was the Gospel held back by the barriers of nationality, racial prejudice, and the Jewish law. Here, in the very center of the known world, Paul was witnessing for Christ "with all boldness and without hindrance!" (Acts 28:31 NIV).

Even after Paul died, his witness continued through the letters that he wrote to believers and the young churches that had been planted throughout the Roman Empire. The close of Paul's ministry brings us to another important chapter in biblical history and the continuing outreach of the church.

THE GOSPEL IN ROME

No-Stress Bible Reading
Acts 28

No-Stress Bible Guide
Pages 271–273
(from "Paul's Trip to Rome")

Think About It:

- Why did some of the natives on the island of Melita think Paul was a god?

- How did Paul minister to these people during his stay on the island?

- Why do you think Paul quoted from the writings of the prophet Isaiah during his sermon to the Jewish leaders in Rome?

- How did God use Paul's imprisonment to spread the gospel in the pagan city of Rome (see Philippians 1:12–14)?

Saint Paul Shipwrecked on Malta, Laurent de La Hyre (1606–1656)

Ruins of ancient Rome. The famous Colosseum stands in the background.

Because the ministry of the apostle Paul covered such a large area, he used epistles, or letters, to communicate with the churches he founded as well as members of these new congregations. In these epistles he dealt with problems in the churches, instructed new believers in the essentials of the Christian faith, and encouraged local church leaders to remain faithful to their calling. He wrote these letters across a period of about twenty years—from AD 49 until his death in about AD 68.

The great apostle to the Gentiles probably wrote many letters that were lost or destroyed. But thirteen of his epistles did survive and are included in the New Testament. These are generally grouped into three separate categories: (1) early letters, or those he wrote before he was imprisoned in Rome; (2) letters he wrote from prison; and (3) pastoral letters—those that deal with issues of church leadership.

PAUL'S EARLY LETTERS

The earliest of Paul's letters were written during a period of about ten or twelve years—from AD 49 until the time of his imprisonment in Rome in the early AD 60s. These early writings include his three longest epistles—Romans and 1 and 2 Corinthians—as well as three shorter compositions—Galatians and 1 and 2 Thessalonians.

LETTER TO THE ROMANS

Romans is Paul's most important letter, although he wrote it to a church he had never visited. He sent it to believers in Rome, the capital city of the Roman Empire, several years before he arrived in the city as a prisoner.

The central theme of this epistle is the concept of justification by faith. The apostle declared that Gentiles and Jews alike are forgiven of their sins and declared righteous in God's sight not on the basis of human worth or good deeds. Rather, justification comes about through God's gift of grace bestowed on all who accept Jesus Christ by faith.

According to Paul, every person stands in need of God's grace. This was certainly true in the case of Gentiles, or non-Jews, because they worshipped created things rather than God the Creator (Romans 1:25). But the Jewish people were in the same situation, although they claimed to be superior to the Gentiles because they knew God's revealed will through His law. They were condemned by this very law because of their failure to keep it. Thus, Paul pointed out in

---

VICTORY IN JESUS

No-Stress Bible Reading
Romans 8

No-Stress Bible Guide
Pages 275–276
(to "First Letter to the Corinthians")

Think About It:

- How did Paul say the Holy Spirit works in the life of a believer?

- Why do you think Paul was so confident that God's love sustains believers, even in the midst of pain and suffering?

Romans, there was no difference between Jews and Gentiles because "all have sinned, and come short of the glory of God" (3:23).

But the good news is that God reaches out to helpless sinners. He expressed His love and compassion supremely through His Son, who died on behalf of the unrighteous. Several additional themes run like a thread throughout Paul's letter to the Romans.

God demands righteousness (1:17). Because God is righteous, Paul pointed out, He condemns sin and judges sinners. But He has provided a way by which man can fulfill the righteousness that He demands. Faith in God's provision is humankind's only hope.

God is just and fair (2:1–16). God will not judge some people because of their sin and overlook the wrongdoing of others. All who sin can expect to reap the consequences of their actions when God calls them to account. He will judge them in accordance with their deeds, not on the basis of their knowledge or ethnic background.

Abraham, first in faith (4:1–25). Paul went all the way back to Abraham in the Old Testament to show that God has always justified people on the basis of their faith. Before Isaac was born, Abraham had no children of his own, but he had faith in the divine assurance that his descendants would become God's special people. The Lord declared Abraham righteous because of his faith in this hard-to-believe promise.

Jesus, the second Adam (5:12–21). Adam was the first member of a doomed race because of his sin and rebellion in the Garden of Eden. But Jesus is the first member of a saved race—the Second Adam. He offers release from the divine judgment that human sin deserves.

Failure of the law (7:1–25). Keeping God's law is what led to righteousness in Old Testament times. But the law fell short because it failed to change man's sinful nature. The harder people tried to keep the law, the lower their tendency to sin dragged them down.

Victory in Christ (8:1–39). Victory over sin is assured for those who place their faith in Christ. Thinking about this caused the apostle to break out in a song of thanksgiving and praise. Believers can rest assured that they are "more than conquerors" (verse 37) through Christ who loved them and died on their behalf.

Hope for the Jewish people (9:1–11:36). Paul declared that his own people, the Jews, made a mistake by continuing to seek justification through the law rather than accepting Christ. But some had turned to Him as the only way to salvation. This gave the apostle hope for the future of the Jewish people.

Overlook trivial matters (14:1–23). Some of the Roman Christians were threatening the unity of the church by criticizing their fellow believers for eating certain foods. The apostle urged them not to judge one another on such trivial matters. The kingdom of God is not a matter of "eating and drinking," he told them, "but of righteousness and peace and joy in the Holy Spirit" (verse 17 NKJV).

FIRST LETTER TO THE CORINTHIANS

Paul's first epistle to the church at Corinth presents a realistic view of the early church. Just like churches today, this first-century congregation had its problems and shortcomings. It was divided into several different factions, and some members were not living up to the standards of the Gospel. The apostle dealt with these problems head-on in an attempt to make the church a more effective witness for Jesus Christ.

The Corinthian church was a product of Paul's own missionary efforts. He spent about eighteen months in the city in AD 50 through 52. During this time he gathered a large congregation of believers (Acts 18:1–8). Eventually he moved on to other fields of service, leaving this church under the direction of other leaders. About five years later he received word about difficulties in the Corinthian church. He wrote 1 Corinthians to address these problems.

Corinth was a thriving commercial center with numerous temples devoted to worship of false gods. Most of the Corinthian believers had been converted from these pagan forms of religion. They struggled to leave their past behind and commit themselves totally to Christian ethical standards. They also had questions or misunderstandings about some of the doctrines of the faith, including marriage, the Lord's Supper, spiritual gifts, and the afterlife. Paul dealt with all these concerns in this letter.

A cure for strife (1:10–31; 3:1–9). Several factions in the church had pledged their loyalties to different leaders—Apollos, Peter, Paul, or Christ. Paul condemned this lack of unity. The quarreling over human leadership showed a lack of maturity among the Corinthian believers. To Paul, God—not human leaders—was the source of wisdom and spiritual growth.

LOVE'S STAYING POWER

No-Stress Bible Reading
1 Corinthians 13; 2 Corinthians 4

No-Stress Bible Guide
Pages 276–281
(from "First Letter to the Corinthians" to "Paul's Letters from Prison")

Think About It:

- How have you discovered in your own experience that love "endures through every circumstance" (1 Corinthians 13:7 NLT)?

- How do you think Paul's suffering strengthened his effectiveness as a witness to the power of the gospel?

Temple of Apollo, Corinth, Greece

A matter for church discipline (5:1–13). The apostle criticized the church for not dealing with the blatant sexual sin committed by one of its members. He advised the congregation to expel this unrepentant sinner. He declared that the aim of such acts of church discipline was to restore those who had wandered away from the Lord.

How to settle differences (6:1–11). Some believers at Corinth were bringing suits against one another in civil courts to settle their differences. Paul urged them to deal with such problems by working through committees of their fellow believers.

Questions about marriage (7:1–40). Some of the Corinthians had apparently asked the apostle about the nature and meaning of marriage. He replied that marriage is the best option for most people. But singlehood, he admitted, has advantages for those who can control their sexual desires. He declared that all believers should live with happiness and contentment in the lifestyle in which God had placed them.

The Lord's Supper (11:17–34). The Corinthians had turned the Lord's Supper into a feast that excluded some poor believers because they had no food to bring to the common meal. Paul told the church to stop this practice and to make the Lord's Supper an occasion for remembering the sacrificial death of Jesus Christ.

Spiritual gifts (12:1–14:40). Some people in the Corinthian church were elevating the gift of speaking in tongues above all other spiritual gifts. Paul declared that those who had this gift should not consider themselves superior to those who had another less spectacular gift. All spiritual gifts come from God and are given to build up the church, not to build up human pride. In chapter 13 the apostle declared that all spiritual gifts are vain and worthless unless practiced in the spirit of love.

Resurrection of the body (15:1–58). Some Corinthians had questions about the resurrection of believers, particularly the type of body that would be raised. Paul's answer was that it would be a spiritual body, not a body with a physical, earthly form. The exact nature of this risen body was a question that should be left in the hands of God. The important thing was that resurrection would be a reality for all who believed in Jesus, who was raised from the dead as "the firstfruits of those who have fallen asleep" (verse 20 HCSB).

SECOND LETTER TO THE CORINTHIANS

Paul's second letter to the Corinthians was a follow-up to his first Corinthian epistle. Apparently these believers responded positively to some of his advice in the first letter, and he wrote to express his appreciation for their actions.

But at several places in the letter, Paul revealed that all was still not well in the Corinthian church. His credentials as a minister were being questioned by some people in Corinth. Paul defended his calling and ministry, assuring the church that his work among them was motivated by love for Christ and his concern for their welfare.

Second Corinthians is one of the most personal and emotional writings of the apostle Paul. He admitted he suffered from some physical malady that he called his "thorn in the flesh" (12:7). He also cataloged the various sufferings he had endured as a traveling missionary in the cause of Christ (11:16–33). Although he was weak and imperfect, he rejoiced that his shortcomings revealed that "this extraordinary power belongs to God and does not come from us" (4:7 NRSV).

Forgiveness and restoration (2:5–11). In his previous letter, Paul had instructed the church to deal with a man who was living in an immoral sexual relationship. The church had done so, and the man had repented. Now Paul encouraged the church to forgive the man and restore him to full Christian fellowship.

Proof of Paul's authority (3:1–18). Some people in the Corinthian church were apparently questioning Paul's authority as a minister. He replied that he was a genuine minister of the new covenant of grace. The many people whose lives had been changed as a result of his preaching were all the endorsement his ministry required.

Precious treasure in a clay pot (4:1–18). The apostle compared himself as a human minister to a common clay pot. But God had filled this crude vessel with His precious treasure—the glorious Gospel that Paul had been called to preach to the Gentiles.

Ambassadors for Christ (5:1–21). Paul reminded these believers that all Christians, including himself, are "Christ's ambassadors" (verse 20 NIV). Just as an ambassador represents his nation in a foreign land, so Christians are messengers of Christ in an unbelieving world.

Give generously (8:1–9:15). Paul wanted the Corinthian Christians to contribute to an offering he was taking among the churches of the province of Macedonia. This money would be used to help the Christians in Jerusalem, who were suffering from a famine. To motivate the Corinthians to support this effort, Paul cited the example of Christ, who gave His life unselfishly on their behalf.

Strengthened through suffering (11:16–12:10). Paul reminded the church at Corinth about the afflictions he had suffered as a minister of the Gospel—being beaten, shipwrecked, starved, robbed, and betrayed. In addition, he was always burdened for the welfare of the struggling churches under his care. But he admitted that these hardships had actually made him a stronger person and a more committed believer. "I take pleasure in my weaknesses, and in the insults, hardships, persecutions, and troubles that I suffer for Christ," he declared. "For when I am weak, then I am strong" (12:10 NLT).

LETTER TO THE GALATIANS

Paul's epistle to the Galatians was not written to a specific church but to the "*churches* of Galatia" (Galatians 1:2, emphasis added). The apostle visited several cities of this region during his first missionary journey, founding several churches. These cities included Antioch of Pisidia, Iconium, Lystra, and Derbe. He wrote this letter to these young churches several years later.

After the Galatian churches had gotten off to such a good start, the apostle was astonished to learn that they were "turning away so soon from Him who called you in the grace of Christ, to a different gospel" (1:6 NKJV). A group of false teachers known as the Judaizers had won the believers over to the view that faith in the grace of Christ was not sufficient for salvation. They taught that it was also necessary to obey the Jewish law, which involved submitting to circumcision and observing Jewish holy days.

Paul condemned these false teachers and informed the Galatians that they were foolish indeed if they returned to the bondage of the law from which the grace of Christ had set them free (3:1; 5:1).

Credentials as an apostle (1:11–24). The Judaizers among the Galatian churches were claiming that Paul had no authority to preach the Gospel in their territory. In response to this charge, the apostle reviewed the circumstances of his conversion and his call to the ministry.

Confrontation with Peter (2:11–21). Paul described how he confronted the apostle Peter on the matter of accepting Gentiles. Apparently Peter had caved in to the demands of the Judaizers that Gentiles had to be circumcised and observe other rituals of Judaism before they could be saved. Paul insisted that faith in Jesus was the only requirement for acceptance by the Lord.

Sons of Abraham (3:1–4:31). The Judaizers had been insisting on making Gentiles sons of Abraham through the rite of circumcision. Abraham was considered the father of the Jewish nation. Paul insisted that Gentile believers were already sons of Abraham because they shared the faith that Abraham demonstrated.

Fruit of the Spirit (5:16–6:10). The apostle listed some specific examples of behavior that should characterize believers. He called these the fruit of the Spirit, or evidence of the Holy Spirit at work in a person's life—"love, joy, peace, longsuffering, gentleness, goodness, faith, meekness, temperance" (5:22–23).

FIRST LETTER TO THE THESSALONIANS

Thessalonica was the capital city of the Roman province of Macedonia. Paul and his missionary associates preached in this city during his second missionary journey. Opposition from a group of fanatical Jews drove them out of Thessalonica after a short stay, but not before several Gentiles

A Greek icon of the second coming of Christ, spoken of by Paul in his first letter to the Thessalonians

came to faith in Jesus Christ (Acts 17:1–9). These faithful few became the nucleus of the church to which the apostle wrote this letter.

First Thessalonians is probably Paul's earliest letter, written while he was working at Corinth. Paul mentioned Silas and Timothy in the greeting of the letter, which suggests that these two missionary associates worked with Paul to encourage and strengthen this young congregation.

This epistle contains some of the most important teachings in the New Testament on the second coming of Christ. Every chapter contains some reference to this event (see 1:10; 2:19; 3:13; 4:13–18; 5:1–11, 23).

Paul defends his ministry (1:1–10). The apostle's enemies at Thessalonica were trying to discredit him and his ministry. So he recalled the sincerity and honesty with which he had worked among them. He had supported himself with his own labor and had treated them with kindness and compassion.

When Jesus returns (4:13–18). Some of the believers at Thessalonica apparently expected Jesus to return during their lifetime. They wondered what would happen to those believers who had not lived to experience this momentous event. Paul assured them that those who had died would be raised first. "After that," he continued, "we who are still alive and are left will be caught up together with them in the clouds to meet the Lord in the air" (verse 17 NIV).

Readiness for the Second Coming (5:1–11). No one knows exactly when the Lord will return, the apostle told these believers. But they could be assured it would happen when they least expected it. They should make sure they were ready for this great event.

SECOND LETTER TO THE THESSALONIANS

This short letter of only three chapters is closely related to Paul's first letter to the believers at

Thessalonica. It was probably written within a few months of the first letter, while he was ministering among the believers in Corinth. Paul encouraged the believers in this church to remain faithful to the Lord in the midst of the persecution they were experiencing.

The future day of the Lord (2:1–12). False teachers had apparently told the Thessalonian believers that Jesus' second coming had already happened. Paul corrected this view, assuring them that Jesus would not come again until the "son of perdition," or the Antichrist, had appeared (verse 3). (See sidebar, "The Antichrist.")

Get to work (3:6–15). Some of the Thessalonian Christians were apparently waiting idly for the second coming of Christ. Paul criticized such laziness and told these people to get back to work.

PAUL'S LETTERS FROM PRISON

The apostle Paul was imprisoned by the Roman authorities in the city of Rome for about two years in the AD 60s. He was under house arrest for part of this time. This meant he had the freedom to write and mail letters, receive mail, and even preach and teach in a limited way (Acts 28:30–31).

During this time in prison, he wrote five letters, four of which have come to be known as his prison epistles—Ephesians, Philippians, Colossians, and Philemon.

LETTER TO THE EPHESIANS

Paul founded the church at Ephesus and spent two to three years among the believers in this city (Acts 19:1–41)—longer than he stayed at any other place during his entire ministry. He developed a close relationship with the Ephesian believers. The leaders of this church traveled to Miletus to greet him at the end of his third missionary

THE ANTICHRIST

Paul's title for the Antichrist—the "son of perdition"—is the same as the one given to Judas Iscariot, the disciple who betrayed Jesus (John 17:12). As the archenemy of Christ, the Antichrist is the personification of evil itself. His goal is to destroy everything that Christ stands for. But in the last days, he will be defeated by Christ and thrown into a lake of fire (Revelation 19:20).

Antichrist with the devil, detail from the *Deeds of the Antichrist*, Luca Signorelli (c. 1450–1523)

Paul Writing His Epistles, a painting attributed to Valentin de Boulogne (1591–1632)

journey. They sent the apostle away with sadness when they learned that he was determined to return to Jerusalem and face the dangers that awaited him there (Acts 20:17–38).

In this epistle Paul described the exalted Christ, who is Lord of the church, the world, and the entire created order. As the living Lord, through His body—the church—He is completing what He began during His days on earth. Those who belong to Christ, both Jews and Gentiles, are united as one body in His church to serve as agents of reconciliation in a lost world.

Grace, not works (2:1–10). Paul reminded these believers that they had been trapped in their previous existence as hopeless sinners, but God had redeemed them and filled their lives with joy. This rescue from sin came about solely through God's grace, not because they deserved His salvation. "By grace are ye saved through faith," he declared, "and that not of yourselves: it is the gift of God: not of works, lest any man should boast" (verses 8–9).

Oneness in Christ (2:11–3:13). Christ has ushered in a new age when all people—Gentiles as well as Jews—have equal access to God's love and grace. He has broken down the barriers of race, religion, economic status, and social standing that divided people in the past.

Diverse gifts for the church (4:7-16). God has given many different gifts to the people who make up His church. These gifts and talents are not intended for their own edification but for the building up of the body of Christ. Ministry gifts are given particularly to apostles, prophets, evangelists, pastors, and teachers. All these gifts are needed if the church is to function properly and bring glory to God.

Get ready for battle (6:10-20). Paul recognized that living a godly life in a godless world is not an easy task. He urged the Ephesian believers to put on their armor and get ready to take their stand against the forces of evil.

LETTER TO THE PHILIPPIANS

Unlike most of Paul's other letters, Philippians was not written to deal with a church problem. Philippians is best characterized as a "friendship letter." The apostle expressed warm thoughts about the Philippian believers and assured them of his appreciation for their support of his ministry.

The apostle founded the church at Philippi in the early AD 50s, at the beginning of his second missionary journey. A businesswoman named Lydia became one of his first converts in this city. The keeper of the prison from which Paul and Silas were delivered also came to faith in Christ, along with the members of his household (Acts 16:19–34).

Good from bad (1:12-26). Paul wanted the Philippian believers to realize that God had caused something good to come from his Roman imprisonment. It had actually resulted in greater opportunity for the proclamation of the Gospel. The apostle was content with his situation, whether he was executed or released by the Roman authorities. "For to me to live is Christ, and to die is gain," he declared (verse 21).

Christ our example (2:1-11). Christ is the perfect model for all believers. He gave up the

privileges of heaven to be born into the world as a man, to suffer on our behalf, and to bring salvation and eternal life to all who believe.

Shining lights in a dark world (2:12-18). Paul urged the Philippians to continue to "work out your own salvation with fear and trembling" (verse 12). As they applied the Gospel to their own lives while he was away, they would shine like lights in a wicked world.

Stay away from the dogs (3:1-11). The apostle warned these believers to avoid the corrupting influence of the Judaizers, whom he referred to as "dogs" (verse 2), or scavengers. These were Jews who had accepted Christ but insisted that believers must keep the Jewish law. Paul considered them to be dangerous because they had added a human requirement to the Gospel of divine grace.

EPISTLE TO THE COLOSSIANS

Paul wrote this letter to a church he had never visited. Epaphras, one of Paul's missionary associates, may have founded the church in the city of Colossae (Colossians 1:7-8). He brought word to Paul about false teachers who had infiltrated this group of believers. The apostle sent this brief letter to address this problem.

False teachers were adding to the simple Gospel that Paul and others had preached. They claimed it was necessary to observe certain Jewish rituals and to pay homage to angels in their worship. Paul corrected this misunderstanding by showing that Christ is the all-inclusive and all-sufficient Savior. He alone is the basis of our hope for salvation and eternal life.

The centrality of Christ (1:15–23). False teachers were challenging the divinity and supremacy of Christ. Paul rejected their teachings by declaring that Jesus was the divine Son of God, the head of the church, and the One in whom God the Father was fully revealed. Then he issued his greatest statement in all his writings on the supremacy of Christ: "God was pleased to have all His fullness dwell in Him, and through Him to reconcile everything to Himself" (verses 19–20 HCSB).

Work of the church (1:24–29). Christ continues His work of redemption through the church, the body over which He rules as head and master. The apostle expressed his joy to be a minister who labored among the churches as

A second-century mosaic from Dougga, Tunisia, showing slavery in ancient Rome

a representative of the living Christ.

New life in Christ (2:1–23). Paul reminded the Colossian believers of the new life they had experienced by placing their faith in Christ. People who belonged to Christ did not need anything else—neither religious ritual nor special knowledge—to make their salvation complete.

Put off and put on (3:1–4:9). New life in Christ, Paul declared, was maintained by putting off such evil actions as anger, malice, blasphemy, and lying and by putting on such righteous deeds as mercy, kindness, love, and peace.

LETTER TO PHILEMON

Paul's letter to Philemon, consisting of only twenty-five verses, is the shortest of his epistles. Its purpose was to appeal to Philemon, a believer in the church at Colossae, to forgive and welcome back his runaway slave named Onesimus, who had been converted under Paul's ministry in Rome. (See sidebar, "Slavery in Paul's Time.")

Philemon had the legal right as a slave owner to punish and even kill Onesimus for his act of betrayal. But Paul expressed confidence that Philemon would welcome him back as a fellow believer—"a brother beloved" (verse 16) in the Lord.

Paul reminded Philemon that Onesimus was now more than a slave. With his conversion to Christ, he had become a friend and brother to his master. The apostle identified so closely with this slave's redemption that he declared any kindness shown to Onesimus would be the same as showing respect to Paul.

SLAVERY IN PAUL'S TIME

Slavery was a common practice in all cultures when Paul wrote this letter on behalf of a slave. The apostle did not condemn this practice, but he did commend the principle of love to a slave owner. Christian love and brotherhood were two factors that eventually led to the decline of slavery throughout the world.

PAUL'S PASTORAL LETTERS

The three epistles of Paul classified as "pastoral epistles" are 1 and 2 Timothy and Titus. These letters were written to individual church leaders rather than churches. They deal with issues of church leadership, showing the apostle's pastoral concern for effective church organization and administration.

These letters also focus on the qualifications of church leaders. They must be above reproach in their personal behavior and fully committed to God if they are to be effective in the work to which the Lord has called them.

FIRST LETTER TO TIMOTHY

Paul met Timothy in the city of Lystra during his second missionary journey (Acts 16:1–3). Timothy may have been converted under Paul's ministry, since the apostle referred to him in later years as his "beloved son" (1 Corinthians 4:17) and his "son in the faith" (1 Timothy 1:2). Timothy became one of Paul's most dependable missionary partners, accompanying him in his missionary travels (Acts 16:3–4; 19:22).

After establishing a church in the city of Ephesus and ministering there for two to three years, Paul left Timothy in charge and moved on to other locations to preach the Gospel and plant churches. He apparently sent this letter while Timothy was still working with the Ephesian church (1 Timothy 1:3).

Although Timothy was committed to the Lord and loyal to Paul, he was a young and inexperienced church leader. Paul counseled him to do his job and act responsibly in spite of his youth. Paul also advised him to deal forcefully with false teachers who were stirring up trouble in the church.

Myths and idle speech (1:1–7). Paul warned Timothy about the false teachers in the Ephesian church who were concentrating on religious myths and useless genealogies. Their pretense of having great knowledge about such mysterious things was nothing but meaningless talk.

Genuine prayer (2:1–8). Paul reminded Timothy that prayer is one of the most important functions of the church. Prayer should be offered for civil authorities as well as the church's own members.

High standards for church leaders (3:1–13; 5:17–25). Church elders, or pastors, and deacons in the church should be selected with great care. They should be mature, sober, self-disciplined, proven leaders in their families, gentle, peaceable, and not controlled by material desires. Once placed in positions of leadership, they should be treated with respect and honor by the rest of the church.

SOME DOS AND DONTS

No-Stress Bible Reading
2 Timothy 2

No-Stress Bible Guide
Pages 285–287
(from "Paul's Pastoral Letters")

Think About It:

- What virtues did Paul encourage Timothy to cultivate, and what things did he tell him to avoid?

- Do you think this was good advice for a young minister?

SECOND LETTER TO TIMOTHY

Paul wrote this letter to Timothy about two years after he wrote 1 Timothy. This letter might be classified as a prison epistle, since Paul was in prison when he wrote it. But it is generally considered a pastoral epistle because it reflects the apostle's concern for the church and its leaders. He encouraged Timothy to stand firm in his commitment to Christ in the midst of troubling times.

Second Timothy is one of Paul's most personal letters. Locked away in a Roman prison, he expected to be executed at any time. He expressed deep affection for Timothy and looked back with no regrets over his life that had been poured out for Christ.

Safe in God's hands (1:8–18). Paul reflected on his years as a witness for Christ and rejoiced in the assurance of His presence in all of life's circumstances: "I know whom I have believed, and am persuaded that he is able to keep that which I have committed unto him against that day" (verse 12).

Stay the course (2:1–26). Paul charged young Timothy to remain faithful to God as a Christian minister, in spite of the difficulties that serving the church involved. "Join with me in suffering," he declared, "like a good soldier of Christ Jesus" (verse 3 NIV).

Follow the Scripture (3:14–17). A great source of strength in troubling times, Paul declared, was knowledge of the Bible. The apostle urged Timothy to stick to the truths revealed in God's written Word—a reliable and trustworthy guide for all believers.

TITUS

Little is known about the Titus to whom Paul wrote this letter. He is not mentioned at all in the book of Acts. But Paul did mention him several times in his letters. In his second letter to the Corinthians, he described Titus as a reliable and dependable leader (2 Corinthians 7:6; 8:16–17). Titus was a Greek, probably from the Gentile city of Antioch of Syria. The church in Antioch was one of the first to reach Gentiles in significant numbers. Titus apparently accompanied Paul on some of his first missionary efforts when they were sent out by the Antioch church (2 Corinthians 7:13–14; Galatians 2:1–3).

Paul eventually sent Titus to work with the church on the island of Crete in the Mediterranean Sea. This was a tough assignment because the residents of Crete were known for their depraved behavior (1:12). But Paul had confidence that Titus could handle the situation.

Paul instructed Titus to appoint leaders for the Cretan church and to discipline those who were teaching false doctrine. The apostle gave specific instructions for the elderly men of the church; for the elderly women, who were to teach the younger women; for the young men; and for servants. All were to practice holy and righteous living, to do good works, and to be watchful for the Lord's return (2:1–10).

CHAPTER 23
Other New Testament Letters

The last nine books of the New Testament were not written by the apostle Paul. So they are often referred to as the "non-Pauline epistles." But they are also known as the general epistles because they were addressed to broad, general audiences rather than to specific churches or individuals. The only exceptions are the brief letters of 2 and 3 John, which were addressed to individuals.

These nine epistles together make up less than 10 percent of the New Testament, but they are by no means unimportant. Most of them were written during the final years of the first Christian century—from about AD 60 to 90. They give valuable insight into the challenges faced by the church during its formative years.

The book of Revelation is often grouped with the general epistles. But because of its unique content about the end times, it is discussed in chapter 24. What follows here is an overview of the epistles of Hebrews; James; 1 and 2 Peter; 1, 2, and 3 John; and Jude.

LETTER TO THE HEBREWS

Hebrews does not give a single clue about its author. In the early years of the church, many people believed the apostle Paul wrote the book. But this view has been rejected by modern scholarship because Hebrews does not fit the Pauline mold. It does not have a formal greeting or a conclusion—a feature that Paul always used in his letters. Possible authors who have been suggested include several believers mentioned in the book of Acts: Luke, Barnabas, or Apollos. But the bottom line is that no one knows who wrote the epistle to the Hebrews.

The date when this book was written is also a mystery. But it was probably written sometime before AD 70, when the Roman army destroyed the Jewish temple in Jerusalem. The author refers to the temple and its sacrifices several times. It is likely that he would have mentioned this catastrophe if he had written Hebrews after the temple fell.

While the author and date of Hebrews are a mystery, there is no doubt about its purpose. It was written to people from a Jewish background who had become Christians. They were wavering in their commitment and were even considering returning to their old customs and beliefs. The writer of Hebrews urged these weak believers to stand firm in their commitment to Jesus Christ. He was superior in every way to the faith they had practiced in the past.

Superior to angels (1:5–14). Jesus was superior to all previous ways in which God had revealed Himself—particularly to angels, the messengers who often spoke for God in Old Testament times.

Papyrus 46 (containing 2 Corinthians 11:33–12:9), one of the oldest New Testament papyri

Superior to Moses (3:1–6). The Jewish people considered Moses greater than the angels, since he had passed on God's law to His people. But Jesus was greater even than this great servant of the Lord.

Superior to the high priest (4:14–16). The high priest interceded for all the people of Israel on the Day of Atonement. He entered the Most Holy Place in the temple, where he offered a sacrifice to atone for his own sins and the sins of the people. But Jesus is the Great High Priest for all believers because He offered the ultimate sacrifice for sin—Himself. He is able to sympathize with weak human beings because He was "tempted in every way, just as we are—yet he did not sin" (verse 15 NIV).

Superior to the old covenant (8:1–10:18). The old covenant between God and His people required them to offer animal sacrifices and to follow prescribed rituals to atone for their sin. These rituals had to be repeated in an endless cycle because people kept falling into sin. But as the initiator of the new covenant, Jesus offered His own life as a permanent sacrifice for sin.

Other themes that run throughout the book of Hebrews are Christian growth and perseverance. The author encouraged these wavering believers to press on to maturity in their commitment to Christ (5:11–6:12). He cited the example of several Old Testament heroes to encourage them to "run with patience the race that is set before us" (12:1).

LETTER OF JAMES

Some scholars believe James was the first book of the New Testament to be written, perhaps before AD 50. It was written to Christians of Jewish background at a time when the church included only a few Gentile believers.

The recipients of the letter were "twelve tribes scattered among the nations" (1:1 NIV)—Jews who lived in the pagan nations beyond the borders of Palestine. The direct, no-nonsense pronouncements of this epistle are similar to the declarations of the Old Testament prophets.

The James who wrote this epistle was probably the half brother of Jesus, one of four sons born to Mary and Joseph after Jesus was born (Mark 6:3). At first James was skeptical about Jesus and His claim to be the Messiah. But he apparently became a believer after the resurrection and ascension of the Lord. James eventually became a leader in the church at Jerusalem (Acts 15:2–21).

The epistle of James is known for its direct and forthright declarations on the behavior expected of those who follow the Lord. For James the supreme test of religion is how believers act rather than what they profess to believe. Jesus summarized this principle in one brief sentence: "A tree is recognized by its fruit" (Matthew 12:33 NIV).

No unifying theme is evident in James. It consists mainly of short statements on Christian behavior. The writer jumps quickly from one thought to another. These concepts, though briefly stated, are some of the most important teachings in all of scripture.

Faith under fire (1:2–18). James encouraged these Christians of Jewish background who were being persecuted for their faith. Those who persevered would receive the reward that God has promised to all believers—the crown of life.

Centrality of love (1:26–2:9). The test of true love is how we respond to the needs of others. The fulfillment of the royal law of scripture is to "love your neighbor as yourself" (2:8 HCSB). True love always leads to deeds of mercy and kindness.

Rich and poor (2:1–13). The way of the world is to cater to rich people and to discriminate against the poor. But this is not how believers should relate to people. We should treat everyone with respect, regardless of race or social status.

Watch your tongue (3:1–12). The tongue and the words that come from it have the potential to destroy people as well as build them up. Controlling this organ of the body requires self-discipline that comes from God alone.

True wisdom (3:13–4:10). Worldly wisdom brings nothing but conflict and ungodly lust. We should seek the Lord and His wisdom. Doing so will lead us to live righteousness lives and to treat others with respect.

Use time wisely (4:11–17). James warned about the sin of presumption, or making plans with no regard for God and His will. We should make the best use of the limited time we have in this life, since our days are like "a vapor that appears for a little time and then vanishes away" (verse 14 NKJV).

FIRST LETTER OF PETER

This epistle was written by the apostle Peter, the disciple of Jesus who became the leader of the Christian movement during its early days in Jerusalem (Acts 2:14–41). Peter eventually traveled to Rome, capital city of the Roman Empire. From Rome, he addressed his letter to believers who had been scattered abroad to escape persecution by the Roman officials.

Peter cited the example of Jesus as the ultimate sufferer to encourage and motivate these believers. Just as He suffered to purchase salvation for them, they should endure persecution for His sake with a willing and joyful spirit (1 Peter 2:18–25).

This epistle also contains practical instructions for Christian living. All believers should be good citizens; servants should obey their masters; wives should be submissive to their husbands; husbands should love and honor their wives; and all believers should love and respect one another (2:13–17; 3:1–7).

THE BELIEVER'S CROWN

No-Stress Bible Reading
James 1

No-Stress Bible Guide
Pages 289–293

Think About It:

- Do you think a crown is a good symbol of the believer's promise of eternal life? Why or why not?

King David, Paolo Cespedes (1538–1608). James related the imagery of a crown, a symbol of authority and power, to the believer's crown.

One of the best-known passages in 1 Peter describes Jesus as the "living stone" who serves as the foundation for the faith of believers (2:4). Although He was rejected by His own people, God made Him the cornerstone of salvation for the world. People who place their faith in Him become part of His church—a "royal priesthood" and a "holy nation" (2:9 NIV)—that bears witness of Him and His kingdom to others (2:1–17).

SECOND LETTER OF PETER

This brief epistle of only three chapters was also written by the apostle Peter. But unlike in 1 Peter, the author names no audience for this second epistle. It was probably written from Rome just before Peter's martyrdom in that city in about AD 68.

The problem that Peter addressed in this letter was not persecution from without but troubles from within. False teachers were leading people astray with their views of the nature of Christ and His second coming. Peter corrected these false views and advised the leaders of the church to deal firmly with these heretical teachers (2:1–22).

Second Peter contains some of the greatest teachings in the New Testament on the need for growth in the Christian life. After the initial experience of salvation, believers should add to their lives such godly qualities as faith, moral excellence, knowledge, temperance, patience, kindness, and love (1:3–11).

Peter also corrected some misconceptions about Jesus' second coming. Some of these believers apparently thought this event should have happened by now. Peter declared that Jesus' return was a certainty but that it would happen in God's own time. His delay meant that He was biding His time to give more people a chance to respond to His offer of salvation (3:1–10).

FIRST LETTER OF JOHN

The first epistle of John does not name an author, but there seems little doubt that it was written by the apostle John, the disciple of Jesus who also wrote the Gospel of John.

First John is similar to John's Gospel. Both contain numerous contrasts between love and hate, life and death, and darkness and light. The opening verses of the Gospel and 1 John are similar, and the author of 1 John claims that he was personally acquainted with Jesus during His earthly ministry (1 John 1:1–4).

John probably wrote this epistle in about AD 90, shortly after writing his Gospel. A leader in the church at Ephesus, he was in his eighties by this time. During this same general period, he also wrote 2 and 3 John and the book of Revelation.

One reason John wrote his first epistle was to refute false teachers who were denying that Jesus had come to earth in human form. They believed that Jesus was a divine spirit who only seemed to exist in the flesh. But John affirmed that with his own eyes he had seen Jesus walk the earth as a man: "What we have seen and heard we also declare to you" (1:3 HCSB).

Walk in the light (1:5–10). Spiritual fellowship with God is possible for those who walk in the light. This means that believers must be forgiven of their sin and follow the teachings of Jesus Christ. Even believers will occasionally stumble and fall into sin. Rather than denying our wrongdoings, we should confess them and bring them to Jesus for forgiveness.

Avoid false teachers (2:15–29). John warned against teachers who were denying that Jesus had existed in the flesh. He referred to these as "antichrists." To John, their appearance was a sign that the final judgment was at hand.

True righteousness (3:1–10). Because God is righteous, those who abide in Christ, God's Son, will also be righteous. Those who have faith in Him will follow His example of purity and holy living. True children of God will not knowingly or deliberately practice sin.

The supremacy of love (3:11–18). The theme that runs throughout this epistle is love. John declared that love for God and others was Jesus' basic message from the very beginning of His earthly ministry. John applied this principle as a simple test for all believers. God's love for us empowers our lives and motivates us to love others. To John, genuine love is an action as well as an emotion. "Let's not merely say that we love each other," he declared; "let us show the truth by our actions" (3:18 NLT).

SECOND LETTER OF JOHN

Second John is the shortest book in the New Testament, containing only thirteen verses. It was written by the apostle John in about AD 90, when he was more than eighty years old. Identifying himself as "the elder," he wrote to a local church that he characterized as "the elect lady and her children" (verse 1).

John warned this church against false teachers who denied that Jesus had come to earth in the flesh. He also encouraged Christians to obey the commandment of Jesus Christ to love one another—a prominent theme in his Gospel and his first epistle.

THIRD LETTER OF JOHN

This epistle is a brief personal note, written in about AD 90 by John "the elder," to a believer named Gaius. This man was probably a leader in one of the churches of Asia Minor. John commended him for standing for the truth and for showing hospitality to evangelists who traveled from church to church preaching the Gospel.

John had harsh words for a church leader named Diotrephes. He apparently was acting like a dictator over a local church, refusing to receive the apostles and other traveling ministers.

LETTER OF JUDE

The brief epistle of Jude addresses the problem of false teachers within the church. The author probably wrote this letter in about AD 82 to warn church leaders to beware of these heretical teachers and their dangerous doctrines.

This Jude was probably one of the half brothers of Jesus who is mentioned in Matthew's Gospel (Matthew 13:55, usually spelled "Judas"). Jude was skeptical of Jesus and His mission while He was conducting His earthly ministry. But he apparently became a believer after Jesus' resurrection and ascension.

Jude had harsh words for preachers of false doctrine who were leading believers astray. He compared them to brute beasts, clouds without rain, trees that bore no fruit, and falling stars doomed to eternal darkness. He urged believers to stand firm in defense of the doctrines of the Gospel they had been taught by genuine Christian teachers.

Jude's letter closes with one of the most beautiful benedictions in the Bible: "To Him who is able to protect you from stumbling and to make you stand in the presence of His glory, blameless and with great joy, to the only God our Savior, through Jesus Christ our Lord, be glory, majesty, power, and authority before all time, now and forever. Amen" (verses 24–25 HCSB).

John the Evangelist on Patmos,
Titian (c. 1490–1576)

Revelation is generally classified with the general epistles (see chapter 23). But this book is so different from any other in the New Testament that it is best to place it in its own separate category.

The book does have some of the characteristics of a letter, or an epistle. For example, it begins with instructions to the seven churches of Asia Minor. But the rest of Revelation uses symbols and images to portray the end of the present age and the coming of God's future kingdom. These symbols include angels, candlesticks, thrones, seals, trumpets, bowls, winged creatures, and beasts.

This symbolic language is typical of a unique form of biblical writing known as apocalyptic literature. The word comes from the Greek word *apocalypse*, meaning "revelation" or "unveiling." People of Bible times understood what these mysterious symbols were meant to unveil. But their meanings are difficult for people of the modern age to understand. This explains why there are so many different interpretations of the book and its underlying message.

Revelation is the only book of apocalyptic literature in the New Testament. But the Old Testament contains several writings of this type: Daniel (chapters 7–12), Ezekiel (chapters 37–48), and Zechariah (chapters 9–14).

The book of Revelation was probably the last of the New Testament writings, penned in about AD 95 by the apostle John, the last living disciple of Jesus. John was imprisoned at the time by the Roman authorities on the isle of Patmos, a rocky and barren island off the coast of Asia Minor (modern Turkey). He received a series of visions from the Lord that described the events of the final days and the ultimate reign of Christ in the world as King of kings and Lord of lords.

John wrote Revelation during a time of severe suppression of Christianity by the Roman authorities. He used symbolic language to hide the meaning of the book from these enemies of the church. Christian "insiders" got John's meaning, but the persecutors of the Christian movement did not have the "key" that enabled them to understand what he was saying.

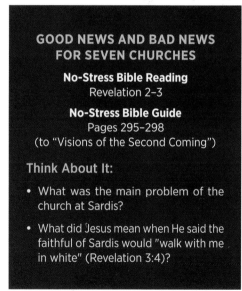

GOOD NEWS AND BAD NEWS FOR SEVEN CHURCHES

No-Stress Bible Reading
Revelation 2–3

No-Stress Bible Guide
Pages 295–298
(to "Visions of the Second Coming")

Think About It:

- What was the main problem of the church at Sardis?

- What did Jesus mean when He said the faithful of Sardis would "walk with me in white" (Revelation 3:4)?

A careful study of Revelation reveals that the book may be divided into several different subjects or themes: (1) Jesus' message to the seven churches, (2) a vision of the omnipotent God, (3) visions of suffering, (4) visions of the Second Coming, (5) visions of the millennium, and (6) visions of the new creation.

Stained glass in the east window at York Minster (York, England) of John's vision of the seven churches of Asia. Designed by John Thornton.

MESSAGE TO THE SEVEN CHURCHES (1:1–3:22)

In a vision, John was told to send a message from Jesus, the Lord of the church, to seven churches, represented by seven candlesticks. Jesus appeared among these candlesticks to assure His presence among these congregations. (See map, "The Churches of Revelation," p. 318.)

These churches were either committing sins or experiencing problems such as growing cold in their commitment to the Lord, undergoing persecution, or worshipping idols. Only the church at Philadelphia received a favorable review. These believers had remained faithful to the Lord in spite of severe persecution. Jesus encouraged this church to "hold on to what you have, so that no one will take your crown" (3:11 NIV).

A VISION OF THE OMNIPOTENT GOD (4:1–5:14)

John had a vision of God seated on His throne in heaven. Surrounding Him were four creatures, probably winged seraphim, who were acknowledging His supremacy as the almighty, omnipotent, and holy Lord of creation. Also gathered around God's throne were twenty-four elders, representing angels who administered God's rule throughout the universe.

God held a book, or scroll, that was sealed with seven wax seals. He handed this scroll to Jesus, who alone had authority from God to remove the seals and open the scrolls. The elders and angels who had bowed before God the Father fell down to worship Jesus the Son. They declared, "The Lamb who was slaughtered is worthy to receive power and riches and wisdom and strength and honor and glory and blessing!" (5:12 HCSB).

VISIONS OF SUFFERING (6:1–19:10)

This is the longest section of the book of Revelation. It describes the visions of John regarding a series of catastrophic events that God would use to judge the earth before the end of the age and the triumphant second coming of Christ.

Seven seals (6:1–8:5). Jesus the Lamb removed the seven wax seals from the scroll

that God gave Him, unleashing a series of divine judgments throughout the world. Seals 1 through 4 showed the horrors of war, including famine, devastation, and death. Seal 5 represented the reward of believers who had been martyred because of their commitment to Christ.

Seal 6 described earth-shaking natural disasters, including earthquakes, meteor showers, and the movement of mountains—perhaps volcanoes. The opening of the seventh seal caused an eerie silence as the earth awaited the coming of the Lord.

Seven trumpets (8:6–11:19). This series of judgments is represented by seven trumpets. Angels blew these trumpets to announce God's judgment against the earth and unbelievers who had rejected Him.

Trumpet 1 brought hail and fire on the earth. The second trumpet resulted in the destruction of sea life and ships. At the sound of trumpet 3, a meteorite poisoned earth's rivers and streams. The next trumpet caused many of the heavenly bodies to grow dark. Trumpet 5 caused widespread misery from swarms of locusts.

With trumpet 6, widespread death occurred, perhaps because of plague and disease. The sounding of the seventh and final trumpet indicated that Christ would soon establish His universal reign over the nations of the earth.

Satan and his allies (12:1–14:20). John was given several disturbing visions about Satan's attempt to usurp God's power and establish his rule over the earth. In one vision, a woman gave birth to a son, who was to rule over all nations. But Satan, represented by a red dragon, tried to kill the child. The archangel Michael and his angels intervened, overcame the dragon, and rescued the child.

In another vision, John saw a beast come out of the sea. He was the Antichrist, the sworn enemy of Christ, who was determined to wipe out the church and all who followed the risen Lord. Then John saw a second beast emerge—this one from the earth. This servant of the first beast used miraculous signs and economic threats to try to turn believers away from loyalty to Christ. This beast wanted people to worship the Antichrist.

The symbol for the second beast was the number 666. Six was the number for evil, so triple sixes showed that this beast was the very personification of evil itself—thoroughly wicked in his nature and purpose.

These visions of evil were tempered somewhat by another vision that came to the apostle John. He saw the Lamb, Jesus Christ, who had returned to earth and was standing with a throng of the redeemed on Mount Zion (14:1–5). John received assurance from several

Four Horsemen of Apocalypse, Viktor Vasnetsov (1848–1926)

angels that doom would come for those people who worshipped the Beast.

Seven bowls (15:1–16:21). John's visions of God's judgment continued when he saw seven bowls of God's wrath poised to be poured out on the earth. Several different calamities struck when the contents of these bowls were poured out—disease, death of sea creatures, deep darkness, storms, earthquakes, and contamination of the earth's water supply.

Fall of Babylon (17:1–19:10). John saw a prostitute named Babylon seated on a scarlet beast. Her name symbolized the forces of evil that opposed God. An angel announced to John, "Fallen is Babylon the Great!" (18:2 NIV). God had brought her down because of her pride, immorality, and idolatry. The elders and seraphim around God's throne offered exuberant thanksgiving for her destruction.

VISIONS OF THE SECOND COMING (19:11–21)

John saw in a glorious vision that Jesus will return to earth in victory as King of kings and Lord of lords. He will be wearing many crowns, symbolizing His universal rule and dominion over all the nations of the earth. In a final battle with the forces of evil, He will defeat the Antichrist and the Beast that worships him. Then He will cast both of them into "the lake of fire that burns with sulfur" (verse 20 HCSB).

The Last Judgment, John Martin (1789–1854)

The Great Day of His Wrath, John Martin (1789–1854)

VISIONS OF THE MILLENNIUM (20:1–15)

The apostle John looked into the future and predicted the events of the final days. Satan will be bound and sealed up in a bottomless pit for a period of one thousand years, or a millennium. Then he will be released to practice his evil and deception among the nations for a time. Finally, he will suffer the same fate as the Antichrist and the Beast when he is cast into the lake of fire.

After these events, according to John's prophecy, the great white throne judgment will occur. The unbelievers of the world—those whose names do not appear in the book of life—will also be sentenced to join Satan, the Antichrist, and the Beast in the fire, where they will spend eternity.

VISIONS OF THE NEW CREATION (21:1–22:21)

In contrast to Satan and his followers, those who belong to Christ will enter a final state of blessedness characterized by a new way of life—a reborn and re-created heaven and earth. John's final vision is of the heavenly Jerusalem, where believers will live for eternity in fellowship with God and His Son.

John concluded Revelation by urging his readers to remain loyal to Jesus Christ—the

"Alpha and Omega, the beginning and the end, the first and the last" (22:13). As the first, He was present with God at the Creation. As the last, He will bring the world to its appointed end in the last days.

So the Bible comes to a close as it began—with an affirmation of the supremacy of the Lord Jesus Christ and His existence with God the Father before time began.

A FLEXIBLE, NO-STRESS PLAN
FOR READING THE ENTIRE BIBLE

Throughout this *No-Stress Bible Guide*, you have been encouraged to read selected Bible passages that relate to the text of the book. If you want to take your understanding of God's Word to the next level, here's a blueprint for reading the entire Bible in a more systematic fashion.

This plan is organized into 365 separate readings, in case you want to read through the Bible in exactly one year. Or, you may want to move through God's Word at your own pace, not following any particular timeline. Either way, each reading should take only twenty to thirty minutes. And you can get started at any time.

Begin with a prayer that these readings will guide your thoughts and actions, as the Bible led the way for the psalmist. "Thy word is a lamp unto my feet," he declared, "and a light unto my path" (Psalm 119:105).

READING 1
Mark 1
Genesis 1
Psalm 1

READING 2
Mark 2
Genesis 2–3
Psalm 2

READING 3
Mark 3
Genesis 4
Psalm 3

READING 4
Mark 4
Genesis 5
Psalm 4

READING 5
Mark 5
Genesis 6
Psalm 5

READING 6
Mark 6
Genesis 7
Psalm 6

READING 7
Mark 7
Genesis 8
Psalm 7
Proverbs 1

READING 8
Mark 8
Genesis 9
Psalm 8

READING 9
Mark 9
Genesis 10–11
Psalm 9

READING 10
Mark 10
Genesis 12
Psalm 10

READING 11
Mark 11
Genesis 13
Psalm 11

READING 12
Mark 12
Genesis 14
Psalm 12

READING 13
Mark 13
Genesis 15
Psalm 13

READING 14
Mark 14
Genesis 16
Psalm 14
Proverbs 2

READING 15
Mark 15
Genesis 17
Psalm 15

READING 16
Mark 16
Genesis 18–19
Psalm 16

READING 17
Romans 1
Genesis 20
Psalm 17

READING 18
Romans 2
Genesis 21
Psalm 18

READING 19
Romans 3
Genesis 22
Psalm 19

READING 20
Romans 4
Genesis 23
Psalm 20

READING 21
Romans 5
Genesis 24
Psalm 21
Proverbs 3

READING 22
Romans 6
Genesis 25
Psalm 22

READING 23
Romans 7
Genesis 26–27
Psalm 23

READING 24
Romans 8
Genesis 28
Psalm 24

READING 25
Romans 9
Genesis 29
Psalm 25

READING 26
Romans 10
Genesis 30
Psalm 26

READING 27
Romans 11
Genesis 31
Psalm 27

READING 28
Romans 12
Genesis 32
Psalm 28
Proverbs 4

READING 29
Romans 13
Genesis 33
Psalm 29

READING 30
Romans 14
Genesis 34–35
Psalm 30

READING 31
Romans 15
Genesis 36
Psalm 31

READING 32
Romans 16
Genesis 37
Psalm 32

READING 33
John 1
Genesis 38
Psalm 33

READING 34
John 2
Genesis 39
Psalm 34

READING 35
John 3
Genesis 40
Psalm 35
Proverbs 5

READING 36
John 4
Genesis 41
Psalm 36

READING 37
John 5
Genesis 42–43
Psalm 37

READING 38
John 6
Genesis 44
Psalm 38

READING 39
John 7
Genesis 45
Psalm 39

READING 40
John 8
Genesis 46
Psalm 40

READING 41
John 9
Genesis 47
Psalm 41

READING 42
John 10
Genesis 48
Psalm 42
Proverbs 6

READING 43
John 11
Genesis 49
Psalm 43

READING 44
John 12
Genesis 50
Psalm 44

READING 45
John 13
Exodus 1
Psalm 45

READING 46
John 14
Exodus 2
Psalm 46

READING 47
John 15
Exodus 3
Psalm 47

READING 48
John 16
Exodus 4
Psalm 48

READING 49
John 17
Exodus 5
Psalm 49
Proverbs 7

READING 50
John 18
Exodus 6
Psalm 50

READING 51
John 19
Exodus 7–8
Psalm 51

READING 52
John 20
Exodus 9
Psalm 52

READING 53
John 21
Exodus 10
Psalm 53

READING 54
Matthew 1
Exodus 11
Psalm 54

READING 55
Matthew 2
Exodus 12
Psalm 55

READING 56
Matthew 3
Exodus 13
Psalm 56
Proverbs 8

READING 57
Matthew 4
Exodus 14
Psalm 57

READING 58
Matthew 5
Exodus 15–16
Psalm 58

READING 59
Matthew 6
Exodus 17
Psalm 59

READING 60
Matthew 7
Exodus 18
Psalm 60

READING 61
Matthew 8
Exodus 19
Psalm 61

READING 62
Matthew 9
Exodus 20
Psalm 62

READING 63
Matthew 10
Exodus 21
Psalm 63
Proverbs 9

READING 64
Matthew 11
Exodus 22
Psalm 64

READING 65
Matthew 12
Exodus 23–24
Psalm 65

READING 66
Matthew 13
Exodus 25
Psalm 66

READING 67
Matthew 14
Exodus 26
Psalm 67

READING 68
Matthew 15
Exodus 27
Psalm 68

READING 69
Matthew 16
Exodus 28
Psalm 69

READING 70
Matthew 17
Exodus 29
Psalm 70
Proverbs 10

READING 71
Matthew 18
Exodus 30
Psalm 71

READING 72
Matthew 19
Exodus 31–32
Psalm 72

READING 73
Matthew 20
Exodus 33
Psalm 73

READING 74
Matthew 21
Exodus 34
Psalm 74

READING 75
Matthew 22
Exodus 35
Psalm 75

READING 76
Matthew 23
Exodus 36
Psalm 76

READING 77
Matthew 24
Exodus 37
Psalm 77
Proverbs 11

READING 78
Matthew 25
Exodus 38
Psalm 78

READING 79
Matthew 26
Exodus 39–40
Psalm 79

READING 80
Matthew 27
Leviticus 1
Psalm 80

READING 81
Matthew 28
Leviticus 2
Psalm 81

READING 82
Luke 1
Leviticus 3
Psalm 82

READING 83
Luke 2
Leviticus 4
Psalm 83

READING 84
Luke 3
Leviticus 5
Psalm 84
Proverbs 12

READING 85
Luke 4
Leviticus 6
Psalm 85

READING 86
Luke 5
Leviticus 7–8
Psalm 86

READING 87
Luke 6
Leviticus 9
Psalm 87

READING 88
Luke 7
Leviticus 10
Psalm 88

READING 89
Luke 8
Leviticus 11
Psalm 89

READING 90
Luke 9
Leviticus 12
Psalm 90

READING 91
Luke 10
Leviticus 13
Psalm 91
Proverbs 13

READING 92
Luke 11
Leviticus 14
Psalm 92

READING 93
Luke 12
Leviticus 15–16
Psalm 93

READING 94
Luke 13
Leviticus 17
Psalm 94

READING 95
Luke 14
Leviticus 18
Psalm 95

READING 96
Luke 15
Leviticus 19
Psalm 96

READING 97
Luke 16
Leviticus 20
Psalm 97

READING 98
Luke 17
Leviticus 21
Psalm 98
Proverbs 14

READING 99
Luke 18
Leviticus 22
Psalm 99

READING 100
Luke 19
Leviticus 23–24
Psalm 100

READING 101
Luke 20
Leviticus 25
Psalm 101

READING 102
Luke 21
Leviticus 26
Psalm 102

READING 103
Luke 22
Leviticus 27
Psalm 103

READING 104
Luke 23
Numbers 1
Psalm 104

READING 105
Luke 24
Numbers 2
Psalm 105
Proverbs 15

READING 106
Acts 1
Numbers 3
Psalm 106

READING 107
Acts 2
Numbers 4–5
Psalm 107

READING 108
Acts 3
Numbers 6
Psalm 108

READING 109
Acts 4
Numbers 7
Psalm 109

READING 110
Acts 5
Numbers 8
Psalm 110

READING 111
Acts 6
Numbers 9
Psalm 111

READING 112
Acts 7
Numbers 10
Psalm 112
Proverbs 16

READING 113
Acts 8
Numbers 11
Psalm 113

READING 114
Acts 9
Numbers 12–13
Psalm 114

READING 115
Acts 10
Numbers 14
Psalm 115

READING 116
Acts 11
Numbers 15
Psalm 116

READING 117
Acts 12
Numbers 16
Psalm 117

READING 118
Acts 13
Numbers 17
Psalm 118

READING 119
Acts 14
Numbers 18
Psalm 119
Proverbs 17

READING 120
Acts 15
Numbers 19
Psalm 120

READING 121
Acts 16
Numbers 20–21
Psalm 121

READING 122
Acts 17
Numbers 22
Psalm 122

READING 123
Acts 18
Numbers 23
Psalm 123

READING 124
Acts 19
Numbers 24
Psalm 124

READING 125
Acts 20
Numbers 25
Psalm 125

READING 126
Acts 21
Numbers 26
Psalm 126
Proverbs 18

READING 127
Acts 22
Numbers 27
Psalm 127

READING 128
Acts 23
Numbers 28–29
Psalm 128

READING 129
Acts 24
Numbers 30
Psalm 129

READING 130
Acts 25
Numbers 31
Psalm 130

READING 131
Acts 26
Numbers 32
Psalm 131

READING 132
Acts 27
Numbers 33
Psalm 132

READING 133
Acts 28
Numbers 34
Psalm 133
Proverbs 19

READING 134
1 Corinthians 1
Numbers 35–36
Psalm 134

READING 135
1 Corinthians 2
Deuteronomy 1
Psalm 135

READING 136
1 Corinthians 3
Deuteronomy 2
Psalm 136

READING 137
1 Corinthians 4
Deuteronomy 3
Psalm 137

READING 138
1 Corinthians 5
Deuteronomy 4
Psalm 138

READING 139
1 Corinthians 6
Deuteronomy 5
Psalm 139

READING 140
1 Corinthians 7
Deuteronomy 6
Psalm 140
Proverbs 20

READING 141
1 Corinthians 8
Deuteronomy 7
Psalm 141

READING 142
1 Corinthians 9
Deuteronomy 8–9
Psalm 142

READING 143
1 Corinthians 10
Deuteronomy 10
Psalm 143

READING 144
1 Corinthians 11
Deuteronomy 11
Psalm 144

READING 145
1 Corinthians 12
Deuteronomy 12
Psalm 145

READING 146
1 Corinthians 13
Deuteronomy 13
Psalm 146

READING 147
1 Corinthians 14
Deuteronomy 14
Psalm 147
Proverbs 21

READING 148
1 Corinthians 15
Deuteronomy 15
Psalm 148

READING 149
1 Corinthians 16
Deuteronomy 16–17
Psalm 149

READING 150
2 Corinthians 1
Deuteronomy 18
Psalm 150

READING 151
2 Corinthians 2
Deuteronomy 19
Job 1

READING 152
2 Corinthians 3
Deuteronomy 20
Job 2

READING 153
2 Corinthians 4
Deuteronomy 21
Job 3

READING 154
2 Corinthians 5
Deuteronomy 22
Job 4
Proverbs 22

READING 155
2 Corinthians 6
Deuteronomy 23
Job 5

READING 156
2 Corinthians 7
Deuteronomy 24–25
Job 6

READING 157
2 Corinthians 8
Deuteronomy 26
Job 7

READING 158
2 Corinthians 9
Deuteronomy 27
Job 8

READING 159
2 Corinthians 10
Deuteronomy 28
Job 9

READING 160
2 Corinthians 11
Deuteronomy 29
Job 10

READING 161
2 Corinthians 12
Deuteronomy 30
Job 11
Proverbs 23

READING 162
2 Corinthians 13
Deuteronomy 31
Job 12

READING 163
Galatians 1
Deuteronomy 32–33
Job 13

READING 164
Galatians 2
Deuteronomy 34
Job 14

READING 165
Galatians 3
Joshua 1
Job 15

READING 166
Galatians 4
Joshua 2
Job 16

READING 167
Galatians 5
Joshua 3
Job 17

READING 168
Galatians 6
Joshua 4
Job 18
Proverbs 24

READING 169
Ephesians 1
Joshua 5
Job 19

READING 170
Ephesians 2
Joshua 6–7
Job 20

READING 171
Ephesians 3
Joshua 8
Job 21

READING 172
Ephesians 4
Joshua 9
Job 22

READING 173
Ephesians 5
Joshua 10
Job 23

READING 174
Ephesians 6
Joshua 11
Job 24

READING 175
Philippians 1
Joshua 12
Job 25
Proverbs 25

READING 176
Philippians 2
Joshua 13
Job 26

READING 177
Philippians 3
Joshua 14–15
Job 27

READING 178
Philippians 4
Joshua 16
Job 28

READING 179
Colossians 1
Joshua 17
Job 29

READING 180
Colossians 2
Joshua 18
Job 30

READING 181
Colossians 3
Joshua 19
Job 31

READING 182
Colossians 4
Joshua 20
Job 32
Proverbs 26

READING 183
1 Thessalonians 1
Joshua 21
Job 33

READING 184
1 Thessalonians 2
Joshua 22–23
Job 34

READING 185
1 Thessalonians 3
Joshua 24
Job 35

READING 186
1 Thessalonians 4
Judges 1
Job 36

READING 187
1 Thessalonians 5
Judges 2
Job 37

READING 188
2 Thessalonians 1
Judges 3
Job 38

READING 189
2 Thessalonians 2
Judges 4
Job 39
Proverbs 27

READING 190
2 Thessalonians 3
Judges 5
Job 40

READING 191
1 Timothy 1
Judges 6–7
Job 41

READING 192
1 Timothy 2
Judges 8
Job 42

READING 193
1 Timothy 3
Judges 9
Ecclesiastes 1

READING 194
1 Timothy 4
Judges 10
Ecclesiastes 2

READING 195
1 Timothy 5
Judges 11
Ecclesiastes 3

READING 196
1 Timothy 6
Judges 12
Ecclesiastes 4
Proverbs 28

READING 197
2 Timothy 1
Judges 13
Ecclesiastes 5

READING 198
2 Timothy 2
Judges 14–15
Ecclesiastes 6

READING 199
2 Timothy 3
Judges 16
Ecclesiastes 7

READING 200
2 Timothy 4
Judges 17
Ecclesiastes 8

READING 201
Titus 1
Judges 18
Ecclesiastes 9

READING 202
Titus 2
Judges 19
Ecclesiastes 10

READING 203
Titus 3
Judges 20
Ecclesiastes 11
Proverbs 29

READING 204
Philemon
Judges 21
Ecclesiastes 12

READING 205
Hebrews 1
Ruth 1–2
Song of Songs 1

READING 206
Hebrews 2
Ruth 3
Song of Songs 2

READING 207
Hebrews 3
Ruth 4
Song of Songs 3

READING 208
Hebrews 4
1 Samuel 1
Song of Songs 4

READING 209
Hebrews 5
1 Samuel 2
Song of Songs 5

READING 210
Hebrews 6
1 Samuel 3
Song of Songs 6–7
Proverbs 30

READING 211
Hebrews 7
1 Samuel 4
Song of Songs 8

READING 212
Hebrews 8
1 Samuel 5–6
Ezra 1

READING 213
Hebrews 9
1 Samuel 7
Ezra 2

READING 214
Hebrews 10
1 Samuel 8
Ezra 3

READING 215
Hebrews 11
1 Samuel 9
Ezra 4

READING 216
Hebrews 12
1 Samuel 10
Ezra 5

READING 217
Hebrews 13
1 Samuel 11
Ezra 6
Proverbs 31

READING 218
James 1
1 Samuel 12
Ezra 7

READING 219
James 2
1 Samuel 13–14
Ezra 8

READING 220
James 3
1 Samuel 15
Ezra 9

READING 221
James 4
1 Samuel 16
Ezra 10

READING 222
James 5
1 Samuel 17
Nehemiah 1

READING 223
1 Peter 1
1 Samuel 18
Nehemiah 2

READING 224
1 Peter 2
1 Samuel 19
Nehemiah 3–4

READING 225
1 Peter 3
1 Samuel 20
Nehemiah 5

READING 226
1 Peter 4
1 Samuel 21–22
Nehemiah 6

READING 227
1 Peter 5
1 Samuel 23
Nehemiah 7

READING 228
2 Peter 1
1 Samuel 24
Nehemiah 8

READING 229
2 Peter 2
1 Samuel 25
Nehemiah 9

READING 230
2 Peter 3
1 Samuel 26
Nehemiah 10

READING 231
1 John 1
1 Samuel 27
Nehemiah 11

READING 232
1 John 2
1 Samuel 28
Nehemiah 12

READING 233
1 John 3
1 Samuel 29–30
Nehemiah 13

READING 234
1 John 4
1 Samuel 31
Isaiah 1

READING 235
1 John 5
2 Samuel 1
Isaiah 2

READING 236
2 John
2 Samuel 2
Isaiah 3

READING 237
3 John
2 Samuel 3
Isaiah 4

READING 238
Jude
2 Samuel 4
Isaiah 5–6

READING 239
Revelation 1
2 Samuel 5
Isaiah 7

READING 240
Revelation 2
2 Samuel 6–7
Isaiah 8–9

READING 241
Revelation 3
2 Samuel 8
Isaiah 10

READING 242
Revelation 4
2 Samuel 9
Isaiah 11

READING 243
Revelation 5
2 Samuel 10
Isaiah 12

READING 244
Revelation 6
2 Samuel 11
Isaiah 13

READING 245
Revelation 7
2 Samuel 12
Isaiah 14–15

READING 246
Revelation 8
2 Samuel 13
Isaiah 16

READING 247
Revelation 9
2 Samuel 14–15
Isaiah 17

READING 248
Revelation 10
2 Samuel 16
Isaiah 18

READING 249
Revelation 11
2 Samuel 17
Isaiah 19

READING 250
Revelation 12
2 Samuel 18
Isaiah 20

READING 251
Revelation 13
2 Samuel 19
Isaiah 21

READING 252
Revelation 14
2 Samuel 20
Isaiah 22–23

READING 253
Revelation 15
2 Samuel 21
Isaiah 24

READING 254
Revelation 16
2 Samuel 22–23
Isaiah 25–26

READING 255
Revelation 17
2 Samuel 24
Isaiah 27

READING 256
Revelation 18
1 Kings 1
Isaiah 28

READING 257
Revelation 19
1 Kings 2
Isaiah 29

READING 258
Revelation 20
1 Kings 3
Isaiah 30

READING 259
Revelation 21
1 Kings 4
Isaiah 31

READING 260
Revelation 22
1 Kings 5
Isaiah 32

READING 261
1 Kings 6–7
Isaiah 33–34

READING 262
1 Kings 8
Isaiah 35
Esther 1

READING 263
1 Kings 9
Isaiah 36
Esther 2

READING 264
1 Kings 10
Isaiah 37
Esther 3

READING 265
1 Kings 11
Isaiah 38
Esther 4

READING 266
1 Kings 12
Isaiah 39
Esther 5

READING 267
1 Kings 13
Isaiah 40
Esther 6

READING 268
1 Kings 14
Isaiah 41–42
Esther 7

READING 269
1 Kings 15
Isaiah 43
Esther 8

READING 270
1 Kings 16
Isaiah 44
Esther 9

READING 271
1 Kings 17
Isaiah 45
Esther 10

READING 272
1 Kings 18
Isaiah 46
Hosea 1

READING 273
1 Kings 19
Isaiah 47–48
Hosea 2

READING 274
1 Kings 20
Isaiah 49
Hosea 3

READING 275
1 Kings 21–22
Isaiah 50–51
Hosea 4

READING 276
2 Kings 1
Isaiah 52
Hosea 5

READING 277
2 Kings 2
Isaiah 53
Hosea 6

READING 278
2 Kings 3
Isaiah 54
Hosea 7

READING 279
2 Kings 4
Isaiah 55
Hosea 8

READING 280
2 Kings 5
Isaiah 56–57
Hosea 9

READING 281
2 Kings 6
Isaiah 58
Hosea 10

READING 282
2 Kings 7–8
Isaiah 59
Hosea 11

READING 283
2 Kings 9
Isaiah 60
Hosea 12

READING 284
2 Kings 10
Isaiah 61
Hosea 13

READING 285
2 Kings 11
Isaiah 62
Hosea 14

READING 286
2 Kings 12
Isaiah 63
Joel 1

READING 287
2 Kings 13
Isaiah 64–65
Joel 2

READING 288
2 Kings 14
Isaiah 66
Joel 3

READING 289
2 Kings 15–16
Jeremiah 1
Amos 1

READING 290
2 Kings 17
Jeremiah 2
Amos 2

READING 291
2 Kings 18
Jeremiah 3
Amos 3

READING 292
2 Kings 19
Jeremiah 4
Amos 4

READING 293
2 Kings 20
Jeremiah 5
Amos 5

READING 294
2 Kings 21–22
Jeremiah 6
Amos 6

READING 295
2 Kings 23
Jeremiah 7
Amos 7

READING 296
2 Kings 24–25
Jeremiah 8
Amos 8

READING 297
1 Chronicles 1
Jeremiah 9
Amos 9

READING 298
1 Chronicles 2
Jeremiah 10
Obadiah

READING 299
1 Chronicles 3
Jeremiah 11
Jonah 1

READING 300
1 Chronicles 4
Jeremiah 12
Jonah 2

READING 301
1 Chronicles 5
Jeremiah 13
Jonah 3

READING 302
1 Chronicles 6
Jeremiah 14
Jonah 4

READING 303
1 Chronicles 7
Jeremiah 15
Haggai 1–2

READING 304
1 Chronicles 8
Jeremiah 16–17
Micah 1

READING 305
1 Chronicles 9
Jeremiah 18
Micah 2

READING 306
1 Chronicles 10
Jeremiah 19
Micah 3

READING 307
1 Chronicles 11
Jeremiah 20
Micah 4

READING 308
1 Chronicles 12
Jeremiah 21–22
Micah 5

READING 309
1 Chronicles 13
Jeremiah 23
Micah 6

READING 310
1 Chronicles 14
Jeremiah 24–25
Micah 7

READING 311
1 Chronicles 15
Jeremiah 26
Nahum 1

READING 312
1 Chronicles 16
Jeremiah 27
Nahum 2

READING 313
1 Chronicles 17
Jeremiah 28
Nahum 3

READING 314
1 Chronicles 18
Jeremiah 29
Habakkuk 1

READING 315
1 Chronicles 19
Jeremiah 30
Habakkuk 2

READING 316
1 Chronicles 20
Jeremiah 31
Habakkuk 3

READING 317
1 Chronicles 21
Jeremiah 32–33
Ezekiel 1

READING 318
1 Chronicles 22
Jeremiah 34
Ezekiel 2

READING 319
1 Chronicles 23
Jeremiah 35
Ezekiel 3

READING 320
1 Chronicles 24
Jeremiah 36
Ezekiel 4

READING 321
1 Chronicles 25
Jeremiah 37
Ezekiel 5

READING 322
1 Chronicles 26
Jeremiah 38
Ezekiel 6

READING 323
1 Chronicles 27
Jeremiah 39
Ezekiel 7

READING 324
1 Chronicles 28
Jeremiah 40–41
Ezekiel 8

READING 325
1 Chronicles 29
Jeremiah 42
Ezekiel 9

READING 326
2 Chronicles 1
Jeremiah 43
Ezekiel 10

READING 327
2 Chronicles 2
Jeremiah 44
Ezekiel 11

READING 328
2 Chronicles 3
Jeremiah 45
Ezekiel 12

READING 329
2 Chronicles 4
Jeremiah 46
Ezekiel 13

READING 330
2 Chronicles 5
Jeremiah 47
Ezekiel 14

READING 331
2 Chronicles 6
Jeremiah 48
Ezekiel 15

READING 332
2 Chronicles 7
Jeremiah 49
Ezekiel 16

READING 333
2 Chronicles 8
Jeremiah 50
Ezekiel 17

READING 334
2 Chronicles 9
Jeremiah 51
Ezekiel 18

READING 335
2 Chronicles 10
Jeremiah 52
Ezekiel 19

READING 336
2 Chronicles 11
Lamentations 1–2
Ezekiel 20

READING 337
2 Chronicles 12
Lamentations 3
Ezekiel 21

READING 338
2 Chronicles 13
Lamentations 4
Ezekiel 22

READING 339
2 Chronicles 14
Lamentations 5
Ezekiel 23

READING 340
2 Chronicles 15
Zephaniah 1
Ezekiel 24

READING 341
2 Chronicles 16
Zephaniah 2
Ezekiel 25

READING 342
2 Chronicles 17
Zephaniah 3
Ezekiel 26

READING 343
2 Chronicles 18
Zechariah 1
Ezekiel 27

READING 344
2 Chronicles 19
Zechariah 2
Ezekiel 28

READING 345
2 Chronicles 20
Zechariah 3
Ezekiel 29

READING 346
2 Chronicles 21
Zechariah 4
Ezekiel 30

READING 347
2 Chronicles 22
Zechariah 5
Ezekiel 31

READING 348
2 Chronicles 23
Zechariah 6
Ezekiel 32

READING 349
2 Chronicles 24
Zechariah 7
Ezekiel 33

READING 350
2 Chronicles 25
Zechariah 8
Ezekiel 34

READING 351
2 Chronicles 26
Zechariah 9
Ezekiel 35

READING 352
2 Chronicles 27
Zechariah 10
Ezekiel 36

READING 353
2 Chronicles 28
Zechariah 11
Ezekiel 37

READING 354
2 Chronicles 29
Zechariah 12
Ezekiel 38

READING 355
2 Chronicles 30
Zechariah 13
Ezekiel 39

READING 356
2 Chronicles 31
Zechariah 14
Ezekiel 40

READING 357
2 Chronicles 32
Daniel 1
Ezekiel 41

READING 358
2 Chronicles 33
Daniel 2
Ezekiel 42

READING 359
2 Chronicles 34
Daniel 3
Ezekiel 43

READING 360
2 Chronicles 35
Daniel 4–5
Ezekiel 44

READING 361
2 Chronicles 36
Daniel 6
Ezekiel 45

READING 362
Malachi 1
Daniel 7–8
Ezekiel 46

READING 363
Malachi 2
Daniel 9
Ezekiel 47

READING 364
Malachi 3
Daniel 10
Ezekiel 48

READING 365
Malachi 4
Daniel 11–12

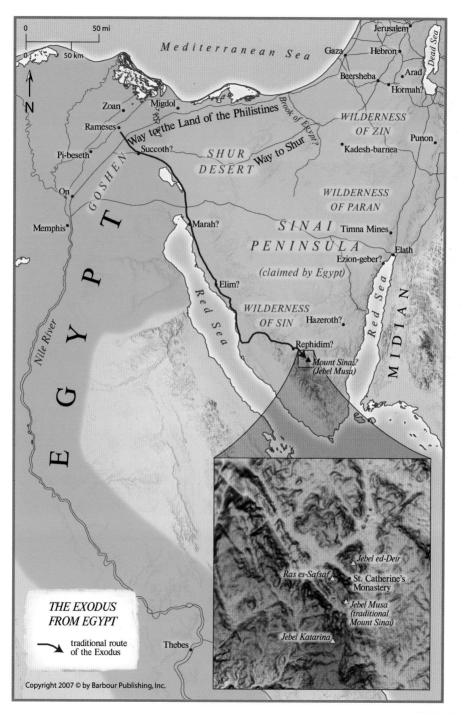

THE EXODUS
FROM EGYPT

→ traditional route
of the Exodus

Copyright 2007 © by Barbour Publishing, Inc.

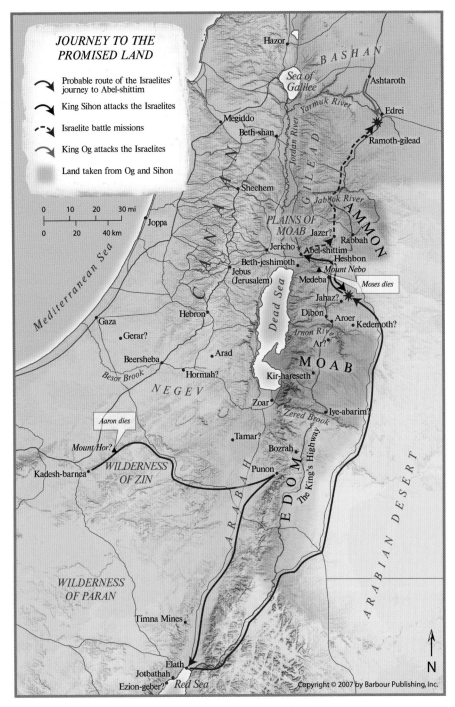

JOURNEY TO THE PROMISED LAND

Probable route of the Israelites' journey to Abel-shittim

King Sihon attacks the Israelites

Israelite battle missions

King Og attacks the Israelites

Land taken from Og and Sihon

0   10   20   30 mi
0   20   40 km

Hazor

BASHAN

Sea of Galilee

Ashtaroth

Yarmuk River

Edrei

Megiddo

Beth-shan

Ramoth-gilead

Jordan River

GILEAD

Shechem

Jabbok River

AMMON

PLAINS OF MOAB

Jazer?

Rabbah

Joppa

Jericho

Abel-shittim

Heshbon

Beth-jeshimoth

Mount Nebo

Jebus (Jerusalem)

Medeba

Moses dies

Mediterranean Sea

Dead Sea

Jahaz?

Dibon

Aroer

Kedemoth?

Hebron

Arnon River

Ar?

Gaza

Gerar?

Arad

M O A B

Beersheba

Hormah?

Kir-hareseth

Besor Brook

N E G E V

Zoar

Zered Brook

Iye-abarim?

Tamar?

Aaron dies

Bozrah

Mount Hor?

Punon

WILDERNESS OF ZIN

E D O M

The King's Highway

A R A B I A N   D E S E R T

Kadesh-barnea

WILDERNESS OF PARAN

A R A B A H

Timna Mines

Elath

Jotbathah

Ezion-geber?

Red Sea

N

Copyright © 2007 by Barbour Publishing, Inc.

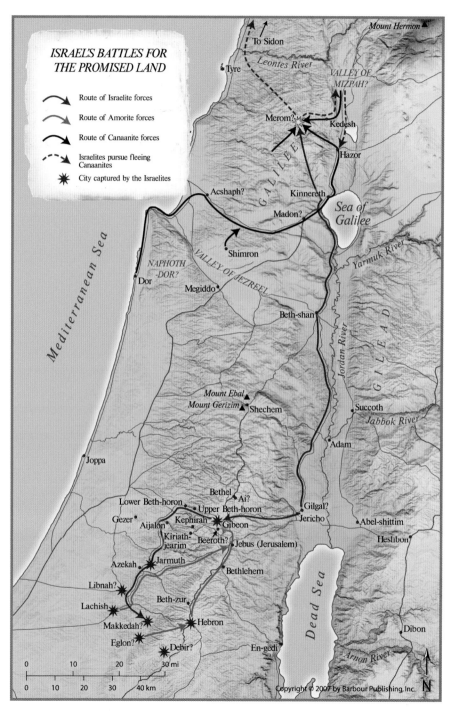

ISRAEL'S BATTLES FOR
THE PROMISED LAND

Route of Israelite forces

Route of Amorite forces

Route of Canaanite forces

Israelites pursue fleeing
Canaanites

City captured by the Israelites

Mount Hermon

To Sidon

Tyre

Leontes River

VALLEY OF
MIZPAH?

Merom?

Kedesh

Hazor

GALILEE

Acshaph?

Kinnereth

Madon?

Sea of
Galilee

Shimron

Yarmuk River

NAPHOTH
-DOR?

VALLEY OF JEZREEL

Dor

Megiddo

Mediterranean Sea

Beth-shan

Jordan River

GILEAD

Mount Ebal

Mount Gerizim

Shechem

Succoth

Jabbok River

Adam

Joppa

Bethel

Ai?

Lower Beth-horon

Upper Beth-horon

Gilgal?

Gezer

Kephirah

Gibeon

Jericho

Abel-shittim

Aijalon

Kiriath-
jearim

Beeroth?

Jebus (Jerusalem)

Heshbon

Azekah

Jarmuth

Bethlehem

Libnah?

Beth-zur

Dead Sea

Lachish

Makkedah?

Hebron

Eglon?

Debir?

En-gedi

Dibon

Arnon River

0   10   20   30 mi

0   10   20   30   40 km

Copyright © 2007 by Barbour Publishing, Inc.

N

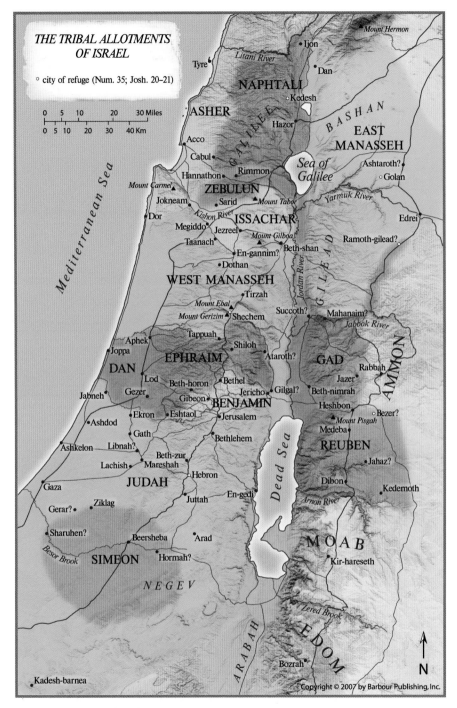

THE TRIBAL ALLOTMENTS
OF ISRAEL

○ city of refuge (Num. 35; Josh. 20–21)

0   5   10   20   30 Miles
0 5 10   20   30   40 Km

Mediterranean Sea

Mount Hermon

Ijon
Tyre
Dan
Litani River

NAPHTALI
Kedesh
ASHER
Hazor
BASHAN
EAST
MANASSEH

Acco
GALILEE
Sea of
Galilee
Ashtaroth?
Cabul
Golan
Hannathon
Rimmon
Mount Carmel
ZEBULUN
Yarmuk River
Jokneam
Sarid
Mount Tabor
Dor
Kishon River
ISSACHAR
Megiddo
Jezreel
Edrei
Taanach
Mount Gilboa
Ramoth-gilead?
En-gannim?
Beth-shan

GILEAD
Jordan River
Dothan
WEST MANASSEH
Tirzah
Succoth?
Mahanaim?
Mount Ebal
Jabbok River
Mount Gerizim
Shechem

Tappuah
Aphek
Shiloh
GAD
AMMON
Joppa
EPHRAIM
Ataroth?
Rabbah
DAN
Lod
Bethel
Jazer
Beth-horon
Jericho
Gilgal?
Beth-nimrah
Jabneh
Gezer
Gibeon
BENJAMIN
Heshbon
Bezer?
Ekron
Eshtaol
Jerusalem
Mount Pisgah
Ashdod
Gath
Medeba
Bethlehem
REUBEN
Ashkelon
Libnah?
Beth-zur
Lachish
Mareshah
Dibon
Jahaz?
Gaza
JUDAH
Hebron
En-gedi
Kedemoth
Gerar?
Ziklag
Juttah
Dead Sea
Arnon River
Sharuhen?
Beersheba
Arad
MOAB
SIMEON
Hormah?
Kir-hareseth

NEGEV

ARABAH
Zered Brook
Besor Brook
EDOM

Bozrah

N

Kadesh-barnea

Copyright © 2007 by Barbour Publishing, Inc.

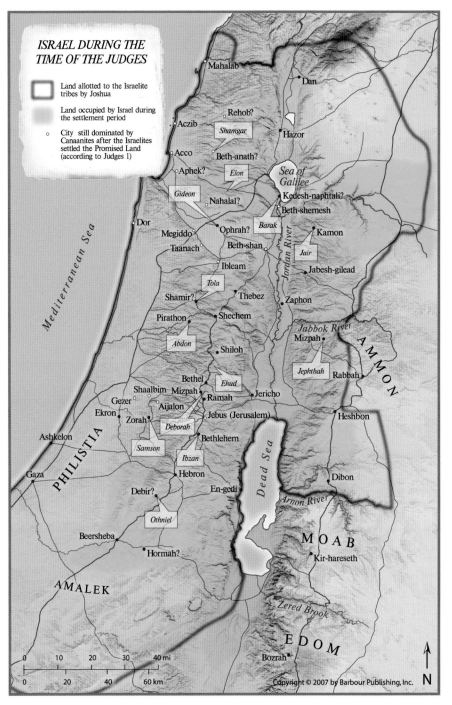

ISRAEL DURING THE TIME OF THE JUDGES

Land allotted to the Israelite tribes by Joshua

Land occupied by Israel during the settlement period

○ City still dominated by Canaanites after the Israelites settled the Promised Land (according to Judges 1)

Mahalab

Dan

Rehob?

Aczib

Shamgar

Hazor

Acco

Beth-anath?

Aphek?

Elon

Sea of Galilee

Gideon

Nahalal?

Kedesh-naphtali?

Beth-shemesh

Dor

Megiddo

Ophrah?

Barak

Kamon

Taanach

Beth-shan

Jair

Ibleam

Jabesh-gilead

Shamir?

Tola

Thebez

Zaphon

Pirathon

Shechem

Jabbok River

Mizpah

AMMON

Abdon

Shiloh

Jephthah

Rabbah

Bethel

Ehud

Shaalbim   Mizpah

Jericho

Gezer

Ramah

Aijalon

Ekron

Zorah

Jebus (Jerusalem)

Heshbon

Ashkelon

Deborah

PHILISTIA

Samson

Bethlehem

Ibzan

Gaza

Hebron

Dead Sea

Dibon

Debir?

En-gedi

Arnon River

Othniel

Mediterranean Sea

Jordan River

Beersheba

MOAB

Hormah?

Kir-hareseth

AMALEK

Zered Brook

EDOM

0   10   20   30   40 mi

0   20   40   60 km

Bozrah

Copyright © 2007 by Barbour Publishing, Inc.

N

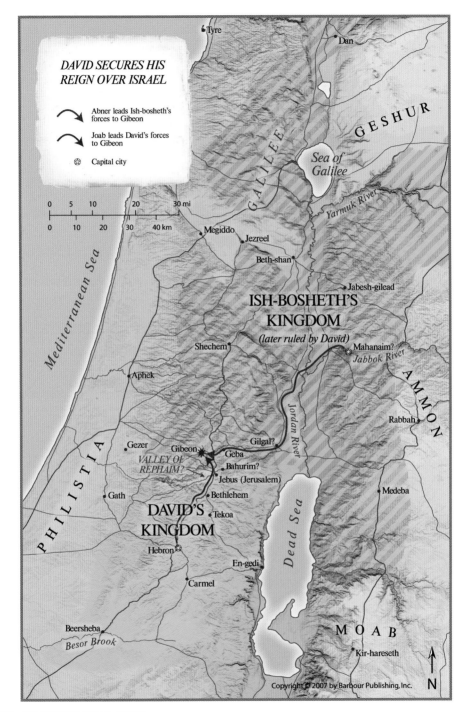

DAVID SECURES HIS
REIGN OVER ISRAEL

↷ Abner leads Ish-bosheth's
   forces to Gibeon

↷ Joab leads David's forces
   to Gibeon

✦ Capital city

0   5   10   20   30 mi
0   10   20   30   40 km

Tyre

Dan

GESHUR

GALILEE

Sea of
Galilee

Yarmuk River

Megiddo

Jezreel

Beth-shan

Jabesh-gilead

ISH-BOSHETH'S
KINGDOM
(later ruled by David)

Shechem

Mahanaim?
Jabbok River

Aphek

AMMON

Jordan River

Rabbah

Gezer

Gilgal?

Gibeon

Geba

VALLEY OF
REPHAIM?

Bahurim?

Jebus (Jerusalem)

Medeba

Gath

Bethlehem

DAVID'S
KINGDOM

Tekoa

Dead Sea

Mediterranean Sea

PHILISTIA

Hebron

En-gedi

Carmel

Beersheba

Besor Brook

MOAB

Kir-hareseth

N

Copyright © 2007 by Barbour Publishing, Inc.

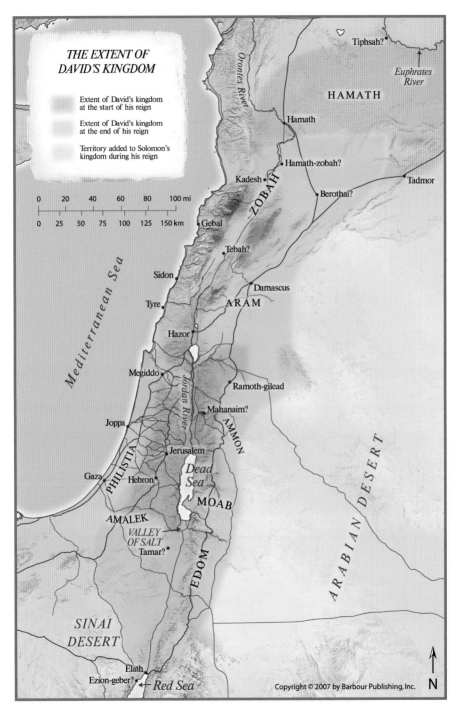

THE EXTENT OF DAVID'S KINGDOM

Extent of David's kingdom at the start of his reign

Extent of David's kingdom at the end of his reign

Territory added to Solomon's kingdom during his reign

0   20   40   60   80   100 mi

0   25   50   75   100   125   150 km

Tiphsah?

Euphrates River

Orontes River

HAMATH

Hamath

Hamath-zobah?

Kadesh

ZOBAH

Berothai?

Tadmor

Gebal

Tebah?

Sidon

Damascus

ARAM

Tyre

Hazor

Mediterranean Sea

Megiddo

Ramoth-gilead

Jordan River

Mahanaim?

Joppa

AMMON

PHILISTIA

Jerusalem

Gaza

Hebron

Dead Sea

MOAB

AMALEK

VALLEY OF SALT

Tamar?

EDOM

ARABIAN DESERT

SINAI DESERT

Elath

Ezion-geber?

Red Sea

Copyright © 2007 by Barbour Publishing, Inc.

N

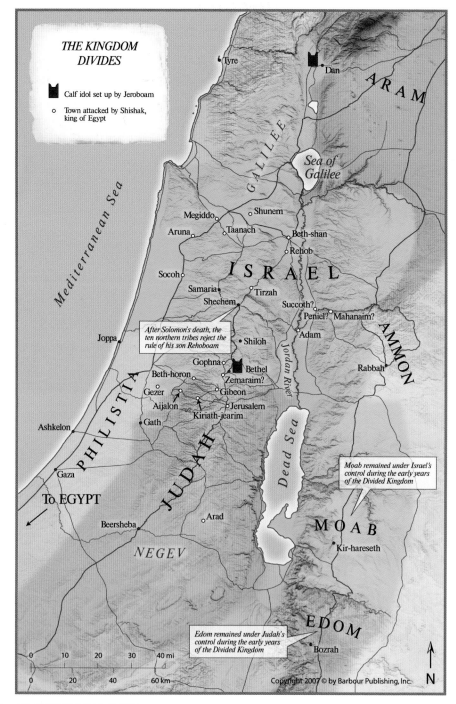

THE KINGDOM DIVIDES

◾ Calf idol set up by Jeroboam

○ Town attacked by Shishak, king of Egypt

Tyre

Dan

A R A M

G A L I L E E

Sea of Galilee

Mediterranean Sea

Megiddo

Shunem

Aruna

Taanach

Beth-shan

Rehob

Socoh

I S R A E L

Samaria

Tirzah

Shechem

Succoth?

Peniel? Mahanaim?

Adam

A M M O N

After Solomon's death, the ten northern tribes reject the rule of his son Rehoboam

Joppa

Shiloh

Jordan River

Gophna

Bethel

Beth-horon

Zemaraim?

Rabbah

Gezer

Gibeon

Aijalon

Jerusalem

Kiriath-jearim

Gath

Ashkelon

P H I L I S T I A

J U D A H

Dead Sea

Moab remained under Israel's control during the early years of the Divided Kingdom

Gaza

To EGYPT

Arad

M O A B

Beersheba

Kir-hareseth

N E G E V

Edom remained under Judah's control during the early years of the Divided Kingdom

E D O M

Bozrah

| 0 | 10 | 20 | 30 | 40 mi |
| 0 | 20 | 40 | 60 km |

Copyright 2007 © by Barbour Publishing, Inc.

N

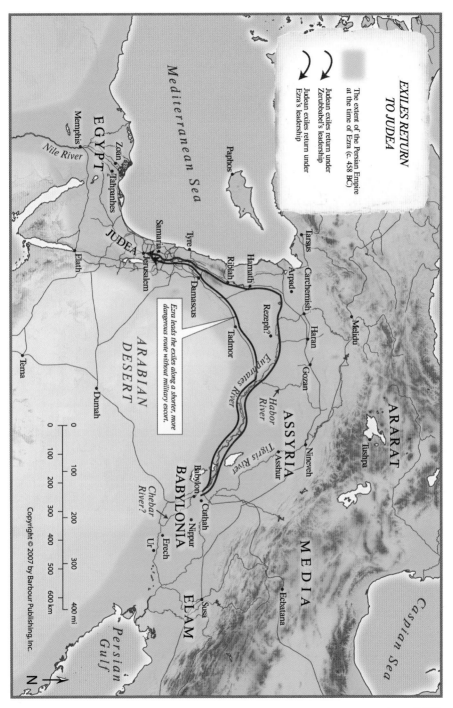

EXILES RETURN
TO JUDEA

The extent of the Persian Empire
at the time of Ezra (c. 458 BC)

Judean exiles return under
Zerubbabel's leadership

Judean exiles return under
Ezra's leadership

Ezra leads the exiles along a shorter, more
dangerous route without military escort.

Copyright © 2007 by Barbour Publishing, Inc.

Mediterranean Sea

Memphis
EGYPT
Nile River
Zoan
Tahpanhes
Elath
Tema

Paphos

JUDEA
Samaria
Jerusalem
Tyre
Riblah
Hamath
Damascus
Tadmor
Rezeph?

ARABIAN
DESERT

Dumah

Tarsus
Arpad
Carchemish
Haran
Gozan

Euphrates River
Habor River

Meldu

ASSYRIA
Nineveh
Asshur

BABYLONIA
Babylon
Chebar River?
Cuthah
Nippur
Ur
Erech

Tigris River

ARARAT
Tushpa

MEDIA

Ecbatana

ELAM
Susa

Caspian Sea

Persian Gulf

N

0   100   200   300   400   500   600 km
0   100   200   300   400 mi

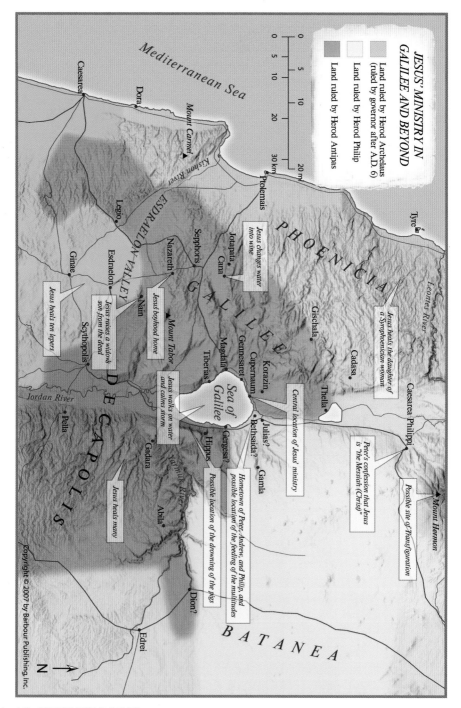

JESUS' MINISTRY IN GALILEE AND BEYOND

Land ruled by Herod Archelaus (ruled by governor after A.D. 6)

Land ruled by Herod Philip

Land ruled by Herod Antipas

0   5   10   20   30 km
0   5   10   20 mi

Mediterranean Sea

Caesarea

Dora

Mount Carmel

Kishon River

Ptolemais

Tyre

PHOENICIA

Leontes River

Legio

ESDRAELON VALLEY

Sepphoris

Jotapata

Cana

Jesus changes water into wine

Jesus heals the daughter of a Syrophoenician woman

Ginae

Esdraelon

Nazareth

Jesus boyhood home

GALILEE

Gischala

Cadasa

Jesus heals ten lepers

Nain

Jesus raises a widow's son from the dead

Mount Tabor

Magdala

Gennesaret

Capernaum

Korazin

Tiberias

Scythopolis

Jesus walks on water and calms storm

Sea of Galilee

Julias?

Bethsaida?

Gamla

Thella

Central location of Jesus' ministry

Caesarea Philippi

Peter's confession that Jesus is "the Messiah (Christ)"

Possible site of Transfiguration

Mount Hermon

Jordan River

DECAPOLIS

Pella

Hippus

Gergesa?

Hometown of Peter, Andrew, and Philip, and possible location of the feeding of the multitudes

Gadara

Possible location of the drowning of the pigs

Yarmuk River

Jesus heals many

Abila

Dion?

Edrei

BATANEA

Copyright © 2007 by Barbour Publishing, Inc.

N →

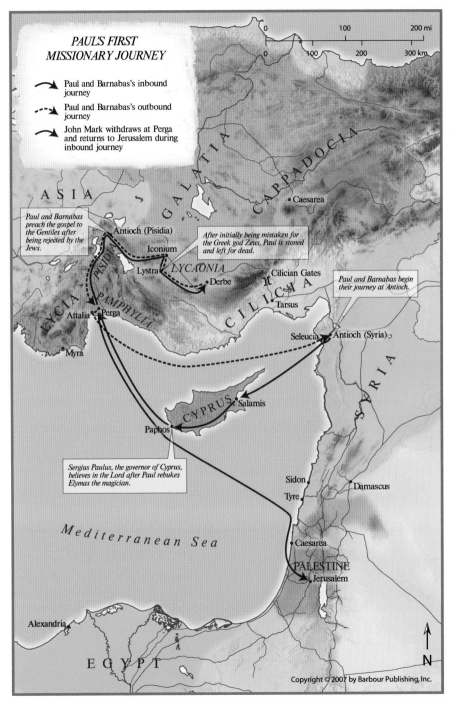

PAUL'S FIRST MISSIONARY JOURNEY

→ Paul and Barnabas's inbound journey

→ Paul and Barnabas's outbound journey

→ John Mark withdraws at Perga and returns to Jerusalem during inbound journey

0   100   200 mi
0   100   200   300 km

A S I A

GALATIA

CAPPADOCIA

• Caesarea

Paul and Barnabas preach the gospel to the Gentiles after being rejected by the Jews.

Antioch (Pisidia)

Iconium

After initially being mistaken for the Greek god Zeus, Paul is stoned and left for dead.

PISIDIA

Lystra

LYCAONIA

• Derbe

Cilician Gates

Paul and Barnabas begin their journey at Antioch.

LYCIA

PAMPHYLIA

Attalia • Perga

Tarsus

C I L I C I A

Myra

Seleucia

Antioch (Syria)

S Y R I A

CYPRUS

Salamis

Paphos

Sergius Paulus, the governor of Cyprus, believes in the Lord after Paul rebukes Elymas the magician.

Sidon

Damascus

Tyre

M e d i t e r r a n e a n   S e a

• Caesarea

PALESTINE

Jerusalem

Alexandria

E G Y P T

N

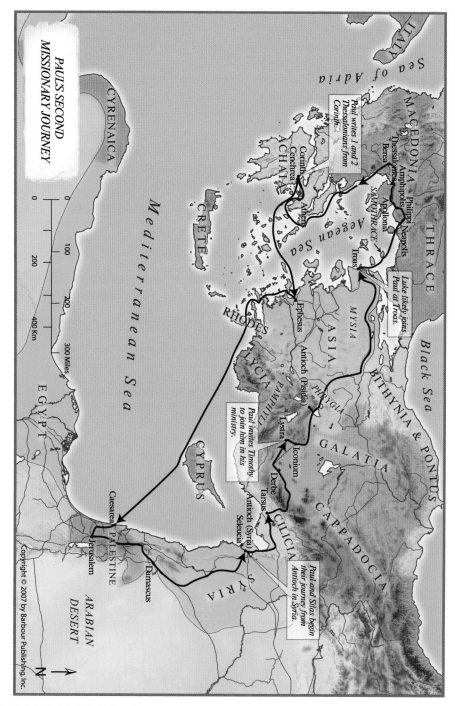

PAUL'S SECOND
MISSIONARY JOURNEY

CYRENAICA

Mediterranean Sea

CRETE

RHODES

EGYPT

CYPRUS

0   100   200   300   400 Km
0   100   200 Miles

Sea of Adria

ITALY

MACEDONIA

THRACE

Black Sea

Philippi
Amphipolis Neapolis
Thessalonica
Berea
Apollonia

Paul writes 1 and 2
Thessalonians from
Corinth.

ACHAIA

Corinth
Cenchrea
Athens

SAMOTHRACE

Aegean Sea

Troas

Luke likely joins
Paul at Troas.

MYSIA

ASIA

PHRYGIA

BITHYNIA & PONTUS

Ephesus

LYCIA

PAMPHYLIA

Antioch (Pisidia)

Lystra

Iconium

GALATIA

CAPPADOCIA

Derbe

Paul invites Timothy
to join him in his
ministry.

Tarsus

CILICIA

Antioch (Syria)
Seleucia

Paul and Silas begin
their journey from
Antioch in Syria.

SYRIA

Caesarea

PALESTINE

Jerusalem

Damascus

ARABIAN
DESERT

N

Copyright © 2007 by Barbour Publishing, Inc.

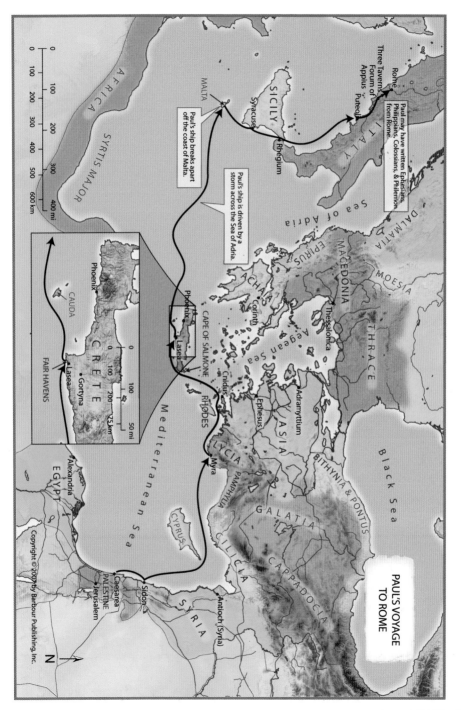

PAUL'S VOYAGE TO ROME

Paul may have written Ephesians, Philippians, Colossians, & Philemon from Rome.

Paul's ship breaks apart off the coast of Malta.

Paul's ship is driven by a storm across the Sea of Adria.

Rome
Three Taverns
Forum of
Appius
Puteoli

SICILY
Syracuse
Rhegium
ITALY

MALTA

Sea of Adria

DALMATIA

EPIRUS
MACEDONIA
MOESIA

ACHAIA
Corinth
Thessalonica

THRACE

Aegean Sea

Phoenix
CAPE OF SALMONE

CRETE

Phoenix
CAUDA
Lasea
FAIR HAVENS
Lasea
Gortyna

Mediterranean Sea

RHODES
Cnidus

Adramyttium
Ephesus
ASIA

BITHYNIA & PONTUS

Black Sea

LYCIA
Myra
PAMPHYLIA

GALATIA

CAPPADOCIA

CYPRUS

CILICIA

Alexandria
EGYPT

Sidon
Caesarea
PALESTINE
Jerusalem
Antioch (Syria)

SYRIA

AFRICA
SYRTIS MAJOR

0 100 200 300 400 500 600 km
0 100 200 300 400 mi

0 100 200 km
75
0 50 mi

Copyright © 2007 by Barbour Publishing, Inc.

N

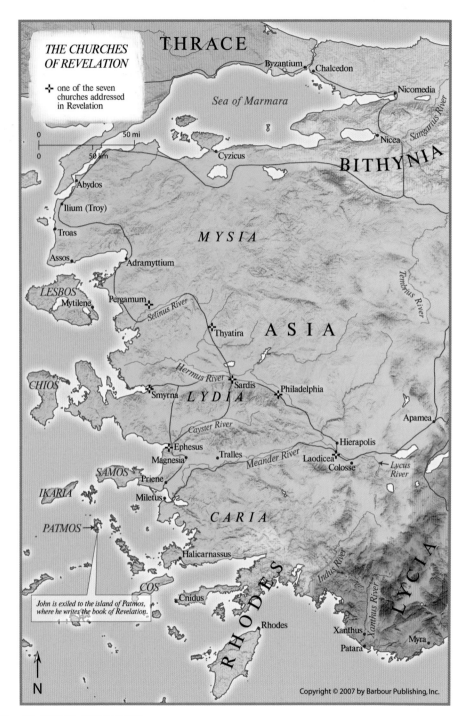

THE CHURCHES OF REVELATION

✛ one of the seven churches addressed in Revelation

THRACE

Byzantium
Chalcedon

Nicomedia

Sea of Marmara

Nicea

BITHYNIA

Cyzicus

Sangarius River

0   50 mi
0   50 km

Abydos

Ilium (Troy)

Troas

Assos

MYSIA

Adramyttium

Tembrius River

LESBOS
Mytilene

Pergamum

Selinus River

Thyatira

ASIA

CHIOS

Hermus River

Smyrna

Sardis

Philadelphia

LYDIA

Apamea

Cayster River

Ephesus

Magnesia

Tralles

Meander River

Hierapolis

Laodicea

Colosse

← Lycus River

SAMOS

Priene

IKARIA

Miletus

CARIA

PATMOS →

Halicarnassus

Indus River

Xanthus River

LYCIA

COS

Cnidus

R H O D E S

John is exiled to the island of Patmos, where he writes the book of Revelation.

Rhodes

Xanthus

Myra

Patara

N

ART CREDITS

Shutterstock: 32, 57, 58, 68, 78, 79, 132, 168, 219, 251, 271, 274, 277

WikiMedia: 8, 10, 11, 12, 14, 17, 18, 21, 22, 24, 27, 30, 35, 36, 39, 40, 42, 44, 46, 49, 50, 54, 60, 62, 63, 65, 70, 73, 75, 77, 80, 82, 85, 86, 88, 89, 91, 92, 94, 97, 100, 104, 106, 110, 113, 114, 116, 120, 123, 125, 133, 134, 141, 146, 147, 149, 152, 157, 158, 162, 166, 171, 174, 177, 182, 184, 187, 188, 192, 194, 196, 198, 199, 202, 205, 211, 212, 214, 217, 221, 224, 227, 231, 232, 233, 234, 238, 239, 240, 241, 244, 245, 246, 253, 257, 259, 261, 262, 264, 265, 266, 268, 272, 273, 280, 281, 282, 288, 294, 297, 298

Andrewrabbott / Wikimedia: 296
Renata Sedmakova / Shutterstock: 47, 191, 229, 248, 250, 260, 291
Permission from zyworld.com / Wikimedia: 121
Osama Shukir Muhammed Amin FRCP(Glasg) / Wikimedia: 128
Gary Dee / Wikimedia: 130
ChameleonsEye / Shutterstock: 140
jorisvo / Shutterstock: 254
Pascal Radigue / Wikimedia: 284
Tamar Hayardeni / Wikimedia: 144
Thomas1313 / Wikimedia: 210
Toby Hudson / Wikimedia: 223
Wellcome Images, CC-4.0 / Wikimedia: 161
Yelkrokoyade / Wikimedia: 207

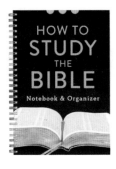
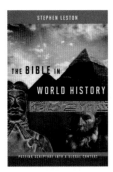